THE MYTHOLOGY OF ALL RACES

Volume VII

ARMENIAN

AFRICAN

PLATE I

Illumination from an Armenian Gospel manuscript in the Library of the Kennedy School of
Missions, Hartford, Connecticut.

THE MYTHOLOGY OF ALL RACES

IN THIRTEEN VOLUMES

CANON JOHN ARNOTT MacCULLOCH, D.D., Editor
GEORGE FOOT MOORE, A.M., D.D., LL.D., Consulting Editor

ARMENIAN

BY

MARDIROS H. ANANIKIAN

B.D., S.T.M., LATE PROFESSOR OF THE HISTORY AND LANGUAGES OF TURKEY, KENNEDY SCHOOL OF MISSIONS, HARTFORD, CONNECTICUT.

AFRICAN

BY

ALICE WERNER

L.L.A., SOMETIME SCHOLAR AND FELLOW NEWNHAM COLLEGE. PROFESSOR OF SWAHILI AND BANTU LANGUAGES, SCHOOL OF ORIENTAL STUDIES, LONDON UNIVERSITY

VOLUME VII

ARCHAEOLOGICAL INSTITUTE OF AMERICA
MARSHALL JONES COMPANY · BOSTON
M DCCCC XXV

CONTENTS

ARMENIAN

AFRICAN

vi CONTENTS

ILLUSTRATIONS

FULL PAGE ILLUSTRATIONS

vii

ILLUSTRATIONS IN THE TEXT

MAP

ARMENIAN MYTHOLOGY

BY

MARDIROS H. ANANIKIAN

B.D., S.T.M.

DEDICATION

THIS LITTLE RECORD OF THE PAST
IS REVERENTLY DEDICATED
TO THE MEMORY OF
THE ARMENIAN HOSTS
WHICH FOUGHT IN THE LAST WAR
FOR FREEDOM
AND OF THE GREAT ARMY OF MARTYRS
WHO WERE ATROCIOUSLY TORTURED TO DEATH
BY THE TURKS

AUTHOR'S PREFACE

THE ancient religion of Armenia was derived from three main sources: National, Iranian, and Asianic. The Asianic element, including the Semitic, does not seem to have extended beyond the objectionable but widely spread rites of a mother goddess. The National element came from Eastern Europe and must have had a common origin with the Iranian. But it, no doubt, represents an earlier stage of development than the Vedas and the Avesta. It is for the well-informed scholar of Indo-European religion to pronounce a judgement as to the value of the material brought together in this study. The lexical, folk-loristic, and literary heritage of the Armenians has much yet to disclose. No one can be more painfully conscious than the author of the defects of this work. He had to combine research with popular and connected exposition, a task far above his ability. The ancient material was not so scanty as broken. So analogy, wherever it could be found within the family, was called upon to restore the natural connections.

Among the numerous writers on Armenian mythology, three names stand high: Mgrdich Emin of Moscow, Prof. Heinrich Gelzer of Jena, and Father Leo Alishan of Venice. Emin laid the foundation of the scientific treatment of Armenian mythology in the middle of the nineteenth century, and his excellent contribution has become indispensable in this field. To Heinrich Gelzer, primarily a scholar of Byzantine history, we owe the latest modern study of the Armenian Pantheon. As for Alishan, he was a poet and an erudite, but had hardly any scientific training. So his *Ancient Faith of Armenia* is a naïve production abounding in more or less inaccessible material of high value and in sometimes suggestive but more often strange speculations.   Manug Abeghian will rightly claim the merit of having given to Armenian folk-lore a systematic form, while A. Aharonian's thesis on the same subject is not devoid of interest.   Unfortunately Stackelberg's article, written in Russian, was accessible to the author only in an Armenian *résumé*.   Sandalgian's *Histoire Documentaire de l'Arménie*, which appeared in 1917 but came to the author's notice only recently, contains important chapters on ancient Armenian religion and mythology.   The part that interprets Urartian inscriptions through ancient Greek and Armenian has not met with general recognition among scholars.   But his treatment of the classic and mediæval material is in substantial accord with this book.   The main divergences have been noted.

Grateful thanks are due to the editors as well as the publishers for their forbearance with the author's idiosyncrasies and limitations. Also a hearty acknowledgement must be made here to my revered teacher and colleague, Prof. Duncan B. Macdonald of the Hartford Theological Seminary, to Prof. Lewis Hodous of the Kennedy School of Missions, and to Dr. John W. Chapman of the Case Memorial Library for many fertile suggestions.   Prof. Macdonald, himself an ardent and able folk-lorist, and Prof. Hodous, a student of Chinese religions, carefully read this work and made many helpful suggestions.

M. H. ANANIKIAN

HARTFORD, CONNECTICUT,
   April 23, 1922.

PUBLISHER'S NOTE

The death of Professor Ananikian occurred while this volume was in preparation.   He did not see the final proofs.

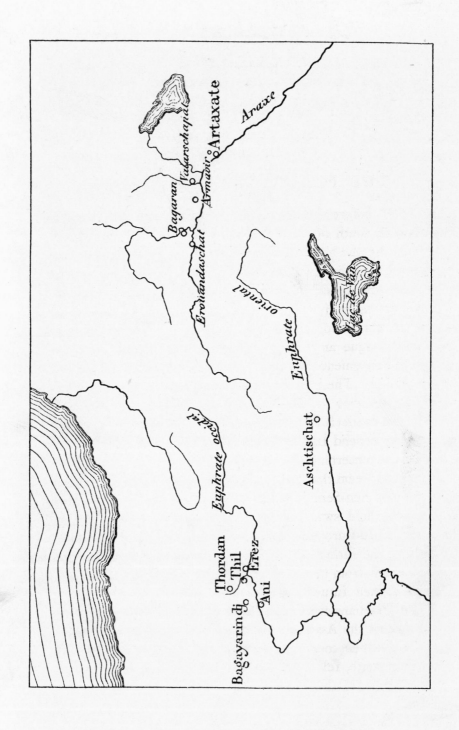

INTRODUCTION
THE POLITICAL BACKGROUND

LONG before the Armenians came to occupy the lofty plateau, south of the Caucasus, now known by their name, it had been the home of peoples about whom we possess only scanty information. It matters little for our present purpose, whether the older inhabitants consisted of different ethnic types, having many national names and languages, or whether they were a homogeneous race, speaking dialects of the same mother tongue and having some common name. For the sake of convenience we shall call them Urartians, as the Assyrians did. The Urartians formed a group of civilized states mostly centreing around the present city of Van. Although they left wonderful constructions and many cuneiform inscriptions, we depend largely on the Assyrian records for our information concerning their political history.

It would seem that the Urartians belonged to the same non-Aryan and non-Semitic stock of peoples as the so-called Hittites who held sway in the Western Asiatic peninsula long before Indo-European tribes such as Phrygians, Mysians, Lydians, and Bithynians came from Thrace, and Scythians and Cimmerians from the north of the Black Sea to claim the peninsula as their future home.

The Urartians were quite warlike and bravely held their own against the Assyrian ambitions until the seventh century B.C., when their country, weakened and disorganized through continual strife, fell an easy prey to the Armenian conquerors (640–600).

The coming of the Armenians into Asia Minor, according to the classical authorities, forms a part of the great exodus from Thrace. By more than one ancient and intelligent writer, they are declared to have been closely related to the Phrygians whom they resembled both in language and costume, and with whom they stood in Xerxes' army, according to Herodotus.[1] Slowly moving along the southern shores of the Black Sea, they seem to have stopped for a while in what was known in antiquity as Armenia Minor, which, roughly speaking, lies southeast of Pontus and just northeast of Cappadocia. Thence they must have once more set out to conquer the promised land, the land of the Urartians, where they established themselves as a military aristocracy in the mountain fastnesses and the fortified cities, driving most of the older inhabitants northward, reducing the remainder to serfdom, taxing them heavily, employing them in their internal and external wars, and gradually but quite effectively imposing upon them their own name, language, religion, and cruder civilization. It is very natural that such a relation should culminate in a certain amount of fusion between the two races. This is what took place, but the slow process became complete only in the middle ages when the Turkish (Seljuk) conquest of the country created a terrible chaos in the social order.

Very soon after the Armenian conquest of Urartu, even before the new lords could organize and consolidate the land into anything like a monarchy, Armenia was conquered by Cyrus (558–529 B.C.), then by Darius (524–485 B.C.). After the meteoric sweep of Alexander the Great through the eastern sky, it passed into Macedonian hands. But in 190 B.C., under Antiochus the Great, two native satraps shook off the Seleucid yoke. One of them was Artaxias, who with the help of the fugitive Hannibal, planned and built Artaxata, on the Araxes, as his capital. Under the dynasty of this king, who became a

legendary hero, the country prospered for a while and attained
with Tigranes the Great (94-54 B.C.) an ephemeral greatness
without precedent until then and without any parallel ever
since.   In 66 A.D. a branch of the Parthian (Arsacid) Dynasty
was established in Armenia under the suzerainty and protection of Rome.   The first king of this house was Tiridates I,
formerly the head of the Magi of his country, who may have
done much in Armenia for the establishment of Zoroastrianism.
It was under Tiridates II, a scion of this royal house, that,
in the beginning of the fourth century of our era, Christianity,
long present in the country, and often persecuted, achieved its
fuller conquest.

ARMENIAN MYTHOLOGY

CHAPTER I

THE RELIGIOUS DEVELOPMENT

THE URARTIANS believed in a supreme being, the god of heaven, whose name was Khaldi. If not the whole, at least a large part of the population called itself Khaldian, a name which survived the final downfall of the Urartian state in a province situated northwest of Armenia where evidently the old inhabitants were driven by the Armenian conquerors. In their ancient non-Aryan pantheon, alongside of Khaldi stood Theispas, a weather-god or thunderer of a very wide repute in Western Asia, and Artinis, the sun-god. These three male deities came to form a triad, under Babylonian influence. From the fact that in one Babylonian triad composed of Sin (the moon), Shamas (the sun) and Ramman (a weather-god), Sin is the lord of the heavens, scholars have concluded that Khaldi may have been also (or become) a moon-god. Whether this be the case or not, the Urartian pantheon contains a secondary moon-god called Shelartish. Besides these no less than forty-six secondary, mostly local, deities are named in an official (sacrificial?) list. The original Khaldian pantheon knew no female deity. Thus it stands in glaring contrast with Asianic (Anatolian) religions in which the mother goddess occupies a supreme position. But in the course of time, Ishtar of Babylon, with her singularly pervasive and migratory character, found her way into Urartu, under the name of Sharis.[1]

One may safely assume that at least in the later stage of its political existence, long before the arrival of the Armenians

on the scene, Urartu had made some acquaintance with the
Indo-Iranians and their Aryan manners and beliefs. For
the Medes had begun their national career long before 935
B.C., and a little later the Scythians had established themselves
in Manna, an Eastern dependency of Urartu.[2]

As an undeniable evidence of such influences we may point
to the fact that in Manna, Khaldi had become identified with
Bag-Mashtu (Bag-Mazda) a sky-god and probably an older
form of the Iranian Ahura Mazda.

It is in the midst of such a religion and civilization that the
Armenians came to live. Their respect for it is attested by the
fact that the ancient Urartian capital, Thuspa (the present
Van), was spared, and that another (later) capital, Armavira
in the North, became a sacred city for them, where according
to the national legend even royal princes engaged in the art of
divination through the rustling leaves of the sacred poplar
(Armen. *Saus*). On the other hand the vestiges of Armenian
paganism conclusively show that the newcomers lent to the
Urartians infinitely more than they borrowed from them.

The Thracians and Phrygians, with whom the Armenians
were related, had in later times a crude but mystic faith and
a simple pantheon.

Ramsay, in his article on the Phrygians [3] assumes that the
chief deity whom the Thracian influx brought into Asia-
Minor was male, and as the native religion was gradually
adopted by the conquerors, this god associated himself with,
and usurped certain functions of, the Asianic goddess. At all
events the Phrygians, who had a sky-god called Bagos Papaios,
must have had also an earth-goddess *Semele* (Persian Zamin)
who no doubt became identified with some phase of the native
goddess (Kybele, Ma, etc.). The confusion of the earth-
goddess with the moon seems to have been a common phenomenon in the nearer East. Dionysos or Sabazios represented the
principle of fertility of nature, without any marked reference

to the human race. He was a god of moisture and vegetation. The corn that sustains life, and the wine and beer that gladden the heart, were his gifts. These things sprang from the bosom of mother earth, through his mysterious influence, for the earth and he were lovers.

Further the Thracians and Phrygians at the winter solstice, held wild orgies (Bacchanalia), when naked women, wrought into frenzy by music and dance, and driven by priests, wandered in bands through fields and forests, shouting the name of the deity or a part of it (like Saboi), and by every barbarous means endeavouring to awaken the dead god into reproductive activity.[4] He was imagined as passing rapidly through the stages of childhood, adolescence and youth. And as he was held to be incarnate in a bull, a buck, a man, or even in an infant, the festival reached its climax in the devouring of warm and bloody flesh just torn from a live bull, goat, or a priest. Sabazios under the name of *Zagreus* was thus being cut to pieces and consumed by his devotees. In this sacramental meal, the god no doubt became incarnate in his votaries and blessed the land with fertility.[5]

We have no clear traces of such repulsive rites in what has been handed down to us from the old religion of the Armenians in spite of their proverbial piety. Whatever they have preserved seems to belong to another stratum of the Phrygo-Thracian faith.[6]

A careful examination of this ancient material shows among the earliest Armenians a religious and mythological development parallel to that observed among other Indo-European peoples, especially the Satem branch of the race.

Their language contains an important fund of Indo-European religious words such as *Tiu* (Dyaûs = Zeus = Tiwaz), " day-light," and *Di-kh* (pl. of *Di*, i.e. Deiva = Deus, etc.), " the gods." When the ancient Armenians shouted, " Ti (or Tir), forward," they must have meant this ancient Dyaûs

Pitar who was also a war-god, and not *Tiur*, their much later very learned but peaceful scribe of the gods. Even the name of *Varuna* appears among them in the form of *Vran* (a cognate of οὐρανός) and in the sense of "tent," "covering." It is not impossible that *astwads*, their other word for "God," which in Christian times supplanted the heathen *Di-kh*, "Gods," was originally an epithet of the father of the gods and men, just like the *Istwo* of Teutonic mythology, of which it may well be a cognate.[7]

The Perkunas of the Lithuanians and the Teutonic Fjörgynn, one as a god of heaven and of weather, and the other as a goddess of the earth, are still preserved in the Armenian words *erkin*, "heaven," and *erkir* (*erkinr?*) "earth."[8] The word and goddess, *iörd*, *erd*, "earth," seems to survive in the Armenian *ard*, "land," "field."

Another ancient Armenian word for Mother-earth is probably to be found in *armat*, which now means "root." But in its adjectival form *armti-kh*, "cereals," it betrays a more original meaning which may shed some light upon the much disputed Vedic *aramati* and Avestic *armaiti*. The word *holm*, "wind," may have originally meant "sky," as cognate of *Himmel*. The Vedic and Avestic *vata* (Teut. *Votan?*) is represented in Armenian by *aud*, "air," "weather," "wind," while Vayu himself seems to be represented by more than one mythological name. Even the Vedic *Aryaman* and the Teutonic *Irmin* may probably be recognized in the name of Armenak, the better-known eponymous hero of the Armenians, who thus becomes identical with the ancient *Dyaûs-Tiwaz*. To these may be added others whom we shall meet later. And in the Vahagn myths we see how, as in India and Teutonic lands, a violent storm-god has supplanted the grander figure of the heaven-god.

The oak (which in Europe was sacred to the sky-god) and water played an important part in the Armenian rites of the sacred fire. The sacred fire was, as in Europe, often extinguished in water. This religion was quite agricultural. In view of the general agreement of the Slavic and old Armenian data on this point, one may well ask whether the Thraco-Phrygian mysteries just described were not a localized development of the lightning worship so characteristic of the Slavic family to which the Thraco-Phrygians and the Armenians probably belonged.[9] In fact, according to Tomaschek[10] the lightning-god had a very prominent place in the Thracian religion.

Lightning worship, more or less confused with the worship of a storm-god, was widely spread through Indo-European cults, and it is attested in the Thracian family not only by the name of Hyagnis, a Phrygian satyr (see chapter on Vahagn) and Sbel Thiòurdos, but also by the title of " Bull " that belonged to Dionysos and by such Greek myths as make him wield the lightning for a short time in the place of Zeus.[11]

Soon after their coming into Urartu the Armenians fell under very strong Iranian influences, both in their social and their religious life. Now began that incessant flow of Iranian words into their language, a fact which tempted the philologists of a former generation to consider Armenian a branch of Iranian. When Xenophon met the Armenians on his famous retreat, Persian was understood by them, and they were sacrificing horses to the sun (or, perhaps to Mithra). But we find in the remnants of Armenian paganism no religious literature and no systematic theology, or cult of a purely Zoroastrian type. It would seem that the reformed faith of Iran penetrated Armenia very slowly and as a formless mass of popular beliefs which sometimes entered into *mésalliances* in their new home.[12] In fact the names of the Zoroastrian gods and spirits found in Armenia bear a post-classic and pre-Sassanian stamp.

Finally the contact with Syria and with Hellenistic culture

in Macedonian times and especially under Tigranes the Great
(95–54 B.C.), brought into the religion of the country a new
element.   Statues of Syrian and Greek gods and goddesses
were acquired in some way or other and set up in Armenian
temples.   Thus a small group of Semitic deities came into the
Armenian pantheon, and interesting comparisons were established between the Armenian deities and the Olympians.
Evidently under the influence of the Greek West and the
Syrian South, the Armenians of the upper classes found the
number of their gods inadequate and set themselves to create a
pantheon of an impressive size.   It was a time of conciliations,
identifications, one might say of vandalistic syncretism that
was tending to make of Armenian religion an outlandish
motley.   Their only excuse was that all their neighbours
were following a similar course.   It is, therefore, no wonder
that the Sassanians during their short possession of Armenia
in the middle of the third century seriously undertook to
convert the land to the purer worship of the sacred fire.   However, all was not lost in those days of syncretism and confusion.   Most of the ancient traits can be easily recovered,
while the tenacious conservatism of the common people saved
a great amount of old and almost unadulterated material.
This is, in short, both the historical development and the background of Armenian mythology.   We should expect to find
in it Urartian, Semitic, Armenian, Iranian, and Greek elements.   But as a matter of fact the Urartian faith seems to
have merged in the Armenian, while the Greek could only
touch the surface of things, and the Semitic did not reach very
far in its invasion.   Therefore Armenian paganism, as it has
come down to us, is mainly a conglomerate of native and Iranian elements.

CHAPTER II

CHIEF DEITIES

STRABO, the celebrated Greek traveller of the first century of our era, in his notice of the Anahit worship at Erez (or Eriza), says that " both the Medes and the Armenians honour all things sacred to the Persians, but above everything Armenians honour Anahit."

An official (or priestly) reorganization of the national pantheon must have been attempted about the beginning of the Christian era. Agathangelos tells us plainly that King Khosrau, on his return from successful incursions into Sassanian lands, " commanded to seek the *seven* great altars of Armenia, and honoured (with all sorts of sacrifices and ritual pomp) the sanctuaries of his ancestors, the Arsacids." These sanctuaries were the principal temples of the seven chief deities whose names are: Aramazd, Anahit, Tiur, Mihr, Baal-Shamin (pronounced by the Armenians *Barshamina*), Nane, and Astλik. It is possible that these gods and goddesses were all patrons (genii) of the seven planets.[1] If so, then Aramazd was probably the lord of Jupiter, Tiur corresponded to Mercury, Baal-Shamin or Mihr to the sun, Astλik to Venus, now called *Arusyak*, " the little bride." The moon may have been adjudged to Anahit or Nane.[2] To these seven state deities, was soon added the worship of the very popular Vahagn, as the *eighth*, but he was in reality a native rival of Baal-Shamin and Mihr. We may add that there was a widely spread worship of the sun, moon, and stars as such, and perhaps a certain recognition of Spentaramet and Zatik.

Armenia enjoyed also its full share of nature worship expressed in veneration for mountains, rivers, springs, trees, etc.

Of the main deities Aramazd was the most powerful and Anahit the most popular; with Vahagn they formed a triad. This pre-eminence of the three gods forced the rest of the pantheon into the less enviable position of secondary deities.

We know very little of the cultus of ancient Armenia, but we may perhaps say in general that it was not as much of a mixture as the pantheon.

We have two Armenian words for "temple," Mehyan, probably derived from Mithra-Mihr, and Tajar, which also meant a dining-hall. The plural of *Bagin*, "altar," also meant "temple" or "temples." Temples contained large treasures, and exercised hospitality towards all comers.

Agathangelos [3] describes the sacrifices of Chosroës after his return from victorious incursions in these words:

' He commanded to seek the seven great altars of Armenia, and he honoured the sanctuaries of his ancestors, the Arsacids, with white bullocks, white rams, white horses and mules, with gold and silver ornaments and gold embroidered and fringed silken coverings, with golden wreaths, silver sacrificial basins, desirable vases set with precious stones, splendid garments, and beautiful ornaments. Also he gave a fifth of his booty and great presents to the priests.'

In Bayazid (the ancient Bagravand) an old Armenian relief was found with an altar upon which a strange animal stands, and on each side a man clothed in a long tunic. One is beardless, and carries a heavy club. The other has a beard. Their head-gear, Phrygian in character, differs in detail. Both have their hands raised in the attitude of worship. [4]

Probably the word for sacrifice was *spand* (Lithu. *sventa*, Persian *spenta* "holy," Gr. σπένδω "to pour a libation"); the place of sacrifice was called *Spandaran*, "the place of holy things"; and the priestly family that exercised supervision over the sacrificial rites was known as the *Spandunis*. They held

PLATE II

Relief found in Bayarid. A priestess (?) and a priest with the Phrygian hood, in the act of worship and of offering a lamb as a sacrifice. The tail of the animal indicates a variety now extinct. The figure of the deity seems to have disappeared. From *Alishan's Ancient Faith of Armenia.*

a high rank among the Armenian nobility.[5] Even to-day *Spandanotz* means "a slaughterhouse" and *Spananel*, "to slay." No other Armenian word has come down to us in the sense of "priest," seeing that *Kurm* is of Syriac or Asianic origin. Besides the Spandunis there were also the Vahunis attached to the temples of Vahagn, probably as priests. The Vahunis also were among the noble families.

The priesthood was held in such high esteem that Armenian kings often set up one or more of their sons as priests in celebrated temples. The burial place for priests of importance seems to have been Bagavan ("the town of the gods"). Whatever learning the country could boast was mainly in the possession of the sacerdotal classes.

CHAPTER III

IRANIAN DEITIES

I. ARAMAZD

WHOEVER was the chief deity of the Armenians when they conquered Urartu, in later times that important position was occupied by Aramazd. Aramazd is an Armenian corruption of the Auramazda of the old Persian inscriptions. His once widely spread cult is one of our strongest proofs that at least a crude and imperfect form of Zoroastrianism existed in Armenia. Yet this Armenian deity is by no means an exact duplicate of his Persian namesake. He possesses some attributes that remind us of an older sky-god.

Unlike the Ahura-Mazda of Zoroaster, he was supreme, without being exclusive. There were other gods beside him, come from everywhere and anywhere, of whom he was the father.[1] Anahit, Nane and Mihr were regarded as his children in a peculiar sense.[2] Although some fathers of the Greek Church in the fourth century were willing to consider Armenian paganism as a remarkable approach to Christian monotheism, it must be confessed that this was rather glory reflected from Zoroastrianism, and that the supremacy of Aramazd seems never to have risen in Armenia to a monotheism that could degrade other gods and goddesses into mere angels (Ameshas and Yazatas). Aramazd is represented as the creator of heaven and earth by Agathangelos in the same manner as by Xerxes who says in one of his inscriptions: "Auramazda is a great god, greater than all gods, who has created this heaven and this earth." The Armenian Aramazd was called "great"[3] and he must have been supreme in wisdom (Arm.

imastun, a cognate of *mazdao*) but he was most often characterised as *ari*, " manly," " brave," which is a good Armenian reminiscence of " Arya." [4]

He seems to have been of a benign and peaceloving disposition, like his people, for whom wisdom usually conveys the idea of an inoffensive goodness. As far as we know he never figures as a warlike god, nor is his antagonism against the principle of evil as marked as that of the Avestic Ahura-Mazda. Nevertheless he no doubt stood and fought for the right (Armen. *ardar*, " righteous," Iran., *arda*, Sansk. *rita*).

Aramazd was above all the giver of prosperity and more especially of " abundance and fatness " in the land. Herein his ancient character of a sky-god comes into prominence. *Amenaber*, " bringer of all (good) things," was a beloved title of his.[5] He made the fields fertile and the gardens and the vineyards fruitful, no doubt through rain. The idea of an Earth goddess had become dim in the Armenian mind. But it is extremely possible that in this connection, something like the Thracian or Phrygian belief in Dionysos lingered among the people in connection with Aramazd, for, besides his avowed interest in the fertility of the country, his name was sometimes used to translate that of the Greek Dionysos.[6] Yet even the Persian Ahura-mazda had something to do with the plants (Ys. xliv. 4), and as Prof. Jackson says, he was a " generous" spirit.

It was in virtue of his being the source of all abundance that Aramazd presided at the *Navasard* (New Year's) festivals. These, according to the later (eleventh century) calendar, came towards the end of the summer and, beginning with the eleventh of August (Julian calendar), lasted six days, but originally the Armenian Navasard was, like its Persian prototype, celebrated in the early spring.[7] In spite of the fact that al-Biruni, according to the later Persian (Semitic?) view, makes this a festival commemorating the creation of the world, one may be reasonably sure that both in Armenia and in Persia, it was an agricultural celebration connected with commemoration of the dead (see also chapter on Shahapet) and aiming at the increase of the rain and the harvests. In fact al-Biruni [8] informs us that in Navasard the Persians sowed "around a plate seven kinds of grain in seven columns and from their growth they drew conclusions regarding the corn of that year." [9] Also they poured water upon themselves and others, a custom which still prevails among Armenians at the spring sowing and at the festival of the Transfiguration in June.[10] This was originally an act of sympathetic magic to insure rain. Navasard's connection with Fravarti (Armen. *Hrotik*), the month consecrated to the ancestral souls in Persia and perhaps also in Armenia, is very significant, for these souls are in the old Aryan religion specially interested in the fertility of the land.

The later (Christian) Navasard in August found the second crop of wheat on the threshing floor or safely garnered, the trees laden with mellowing fruit and the vintage in progress.[11] In many localities the Navasard took the character of a *fête champêtre* celebrated near the sanctuaries, to which the country people flocked with their sacrifices and gifts, their rude music and rustic dances. But it was also observed in the towns and great cities where the more famous temples of Aramazd attracted great throngs of pilgrims. A special mention of this festival is made by Moses (II, 66) in connection with Bagavan, the town of the gods. Gregory Magistros (eleventh century) says that King Artaxias (190 B.C.) on his death-bed, longing for the smoke streaming upward from the chimneys and floating over the villages and towns on the New Year's morning, sighed:

" O! would that I might see the smoke of the chimneys,
   And the morning of the New Year's day,
   The running of the oxen and the coursing of the deer!
   (Then) we blew the horn and beat the drum as it beseemeth
      Kings."

This fragment recalls the broken sentence with which al-Biruni's chapter on the Nauroz (Navasard) begins: "And he divided the cup among his companions and said, 'O that we had Nauroz every day!'"[12]

On these joyful days, Aramazd, the supremely generous and hospitable lord of Armenia, became more generous and hospitable.[13] No doubt the flesh of sacrifices offered to him was freely distributed among the poor, and the wayworn traveller always found a ready welcome at the table of the rejoicing pilgrims. The temples themselves must have been amply provided with rooms for the entertainment of strangers. It was really Aramazd-Dionysos that entertained them with his gifts of corn and wine.

Through the introduction of the Julian calendar the Armenians lost their Navasard celebrations. But they still preserve the memory of them, by consuming and distributing large quantities of dry fruit on the first of January, just as the Persians celebrated Nauroz, by distributing sugar.[14]

No information has reached us about the birth or parentage of the Armenian Aramazd. His name appears sometimes as Ormizd in its adjectival form. But we do not hear that he was in any way connected with the later Magian speculation about Auramazda, which (perhaps under Hellenistic influences) made him a son of the limitless time (Zervana Akarana) and a twin brother of Ahriman. Moreover, Aramazd was a bachelor god. No jealous Hera stood at his side as his wedded wife, to vex him with endless persecutions. Not even Spenta-Armaiti (the genius of the earth), or archangels, and angels, some of whom figure both as daughters and consorts of Ahuramazda in the extant Avesta (Ys. 454 etc.), appear in such an intimate connection with this Armenian chief deity. Once only in a martyrological writing of the middle ages Anahit is called his wife.[15] Yet this view finds no support in ancient authorities, though it is perfectly possible on a priori grounds.

Our uncertainty in this matter leaves us no alternative but to speculate vaguely as to how Aramazd brought about the existence of gods who are affiliated to him. Did he beget or create them? Here the chain of the myth is broken or left unfinished.

Aramazd must have had many sanctuaries in the country, for Armenian paganism was not the templeless religion which Magian Zoroastrianism attempted to become. The most highly honored of these was in Ani, a fortified and sacred city (perhaps the capital of the early Armenians) in the district of Daranali, near the present Erzinjan. It contained the tombs and mausolea of the Armenian kings,[16] who, as Gelzer suggests, slept under the peaceful shadow of the deity. Here stood in later times a Greek statue of Zeus, brought from the West with other famous images.[17] It was served by a large number of priests, some of whom were of royal descent.[18] This sanctuary and famous statue were destroyed by Gregory the Illuminator during his campaign against the pagan temples.

Another temple or altar of Aramazd was found in Bagavan (town of the gods) in the district of Bagrevand,[19] and still another on Mount Palat or Pashat along with the temple of Astλik. Moses of Khoren incidentally remarks[20] that there are four kinds of Aramazd, one of which is *Kund* ("bald")[21] *Aramazd*. These could not have been four distinct deities, but rather four local conceptions of the same deity, represented by characteristic statues.[22]

II. ANAHIT

After Aramazd, Anahit was the most important deity of Armenia. In the pantheon she stood immediately next to the father of the gods, but in the heart of the people she was supreme. She was " the glory," " the great queen or lady," " the one born of gold," " the golden-mother."

Anahit is the Ardvi Sura Anahita of the Avesta, whose name, if at all Iranian, would mean "moist, mighty, undefiled," a puzzling but not altogether unbefitting appellation for the *yazata* of the earth-born springs and rivers. But there is a marked and well-justified tendency to consider the Persian Anahita herself an importation from Babylonia. She is thought to be Ishtar under the name of Anatu or the Elamite "Nahunta." If so, then whatever her popular character may have been, she could not find a place in the Avesta without being divested of her objectionable traits or predilections. And this is really what happened. But even in the Avestic portraiture of her it is easy to distinguish the original. This Zoroastrian golden goddess of the springs and rivers with the high, pomegranate-like breasts had a special relation to the fecundity of the human race. She was interested in child-birth and nurture, like Ishtar, under whose protection children were placed with incantation and solemn rites. Persian maids prayed to her for brave and robust husbands. Wherever she went with the Persian armies and culture in Western Asia, Armenia, Pontus, Cappadocia, Phrygia, etc., her sovereignty over springs and rivers was disregarded and she was at once identified with some goddess of love and motherhood, usually with Ma or the Mater Magna. It would, therefore, be very reasonable to suppose that there was a popular Anahita in Persia itself, who was nothing less than Ishtar as we know her. This is further confirmed by the fact that to this day the planet Venus is called Nahid by the Persians.[23]

The Armenian Anahit is also Asianic in character. She does not seem to be stepping out of the pages of the Avesta as a pure and idealized figure, but rather she came there from the heart of the common people of Persia, or Parthia, and must have found some native goddess whose attributes and ancient sanctuaries she assimilated. She has hardly anything to do with springs and rivers. She is simply a woman, the fair daughter of Aramazd, a sister of the Persian Mihr and of the cosmopolitan Nane. As in the Anahit Yashts of the Avesta, so also in Armenia, " golden " is her fairest epithet. She was often called " born in gold " or "the golden mother " probably because usually her statue was of solid gold.

In the light of what has just been said we are not surprised to find that this goddess exhibited two distinct types of womanhood in Armenia, according to our extant sources. Most of the early Christian writers, specially Agathangelos, who would have eagerly seized upon anything derogatory to her good name, report nothing about her depraved tastes or unchaste rites.

If not as a bit of subtle sarcasm, then at least as an echo of the old pagan language, King Tiridates is made to call her " the mother of all sobriety," i.e. orderliness, as over against a lewd and ribald mode of life.[24] The whole expression may also be taken as meaning "the sober, chaste mother." No suggestion of impure rites is to be found in Agathangelos or Moses in connection with her cultus.

On the other hand no less an authority than the geographer Strabo (63 B.C.–25A.D.) reports that the great sanctuary of Anahit at Erez (or Eriza), in Akilisene (a district called also Anahitian [25] owing to the widely spread fame of this temple) was the centre of an obscene form of worship. Here there were hierodules of both sexes, and what is more, here daughters of the noble families gave themselves up to prostitution for a considerable time, before they were married. Nor was this an obstacle to their being afterwards sought in marriage.[26]

Strabo is not alone in representing Anahit in this particularly sad light. She was identified with the Ephesian Artemis by the Armenians themselves. Faustus of Byzantium, writing in the fifth century, says of the imperfectly Christianized Armenians of the preceding century, that they continued " in secret

PLATE III

Bronze Head of Anahit, a Greek work (probably Aphrodite) found at Satala, worshipped by the Armenians, now in the British Museum.

the worship of the old deities in the form of fornication." [27]
The reference is most probably to the rites of the more popular Anahit rather than her southern rival, Astλik, whom the
learned identified with Aphrodite, and about whose worship
no unchastity is mentioned. Mediæval authors of Armenia
also assert similar things about Anahit. Vanakan Vardapet
says, " Astarte is the shame of the Sidonians, which the Chal-
deans (Syrians or Mesopotamians) called Kaukabhta, the
Greeks, Aphrodite, and the Armenians, Anahit." [28]

In a letter to Sahag Ardsruni, ascribed to Moses of Khoren,[29]
we read that in the district of Antzevatz there was a famous
Stone of the Blacksmiths. Here stood a statue of Anahit and
here the blacksmiths (no doubt invisible ones) made a dread-
ful din with their hammers and anvils. The devils (i.e.
idols) dispensed out of a melting pot bundles of false medicine which served the fulfilling of evil desires, " like the
bundle of St. Cyprian intended for the destruction of the Virgin Justina." [30] This place was changed later into a sanctuary
of the Holy Virgin and a convent for nuns, called *Hogeatz
vank*.

There can be no doubt, therefore, that the Armenian Anahit
admitted of the orgiastic worship that in the ancient orient
characterized the gods and especially the goddesses of fertility.
No doubt these obscene practices were supposed to secure her
favor. On the other hand it is quite possible that she played
in married life the well-known rôle of a mother of sobriety
like Hera or rather Ishtar,[31] the veiled bride and protector of
wedlock, jealously watching over the love and faith plighted
between husband and wife, and blessing their union. We may
therefore interpret in this sense the above mentioned description of this goddess, which Agathangelos [32] puts in the mouth
of King Tiridates: " The great lady (or queen) Anahit, who is
the glory and *life-giver* of our nation, whom all kings honour,
especially the King of the Greeks (sic!), who is the mother of

all *sobriety*, and a *benefactress* (through many favours, but especially through the granting of children) of all mankind; through whom Armenia lives and maintains her life." Although clear-cut distinctions and schematic arrangements are not safe in such instances, one may say in general that Aramazd once created nature and man, but he now (speaking from the standpoint of a speculative Armenian pagan of the first century) sustains life by giving in abundance the corn and the wine. Anahit, who also may have some interest in the growth of vegetation, gives more especially young ones to animals and children to man, whom she maternally tends in their early age as well as in their strong manhood. Aramazd is the god of the fertility of the earth, Anahit the goddess of the fecundity of the nation.

However, as she was deeply human, the birth and care of children could not be her sole concern. As a merciful and mighty mother she was sought in cases of severe illness and perhaps in other kinds of distress. Agathangelos mentions the *care* with which she tends the people. In Moses [33] we find that King Artaxias, in his last sickness, sent a nobleman to Erez to propitiate the tender-hearted goddess. But unlike Ishtar and the Persian Anahita, the Armenian Anahit shows no war-like propensities, nor is her name associated with death.

Like Aramazd, she had many temples in Armenia, but the most noted ones were those of Erez, Artaxata, Ashtishat, and Armavir.[34] There was also in Sophene a mountain called the Throne of Anahit,[35] and a statue of Anahit at the stone of the Blacksmiths. The temple at Erez was undoubtedly the richest sanctuary in the country and a favorite centre of pilgrimage. It was taken and razed to the ground by Gregory the Illuminator.[36] It was for the safety of its treasures that the natives feared when Lucullus entered the Anahitian province.[37]

Anahit had two annual festivals, one of which was held, according to Alishan, on the 15th of Navasard, very soon after the New Year's celebration. Also the nineteenth day of every month was consecrated to her. A regular pilgrimage to her temple required the sacrifice of a heifer, a visit to the river Lykos near-by, and a feast, after which the statue of the goddess was crowned with wreaths.[38] Lucullus saw herds of heifers of the goddess,[39] with her mark, which was a torch, wander up and down grazing on the meadows near the Euphrates, without being disturbed by anyone. The Anahit of the countries west of Armenia bore a crescent on her head.

We have already seen that the statues representing Anahit in the main sanctuaries, namely in Erez, Ashtishat, and probably also in Artaxata, were solid gold. According to Pliny [40] who describes the one at Erez, this was an unprecedented thing in antiquity. Not under Lucullus, but under Antonius did the Roman soldiers plunder this famous statue. A Bononian veteran who was once entertaining Augustus in a sumptuous style, declared that the Emperor was dining off the leg of the goddess and that he had been the first assailant of the famous statue, a sacrilege which he had committed with impunity in spite of the rumours to the contrary.[41] This statue may have been identical with the (Ephesian) Artemis which, according to Moses,[42] was brought to Erez from the west.

III. TIUR (TIR)

Outside of Artaxata, the ancient capital of Armenia (on the Araxes), and close upon the road to Valarshapat (the winter capital), was the best known temple of Tiur. The place was called Erazamuyn (Greek 'ονειρομούσος), which probably means "interpreter of dreams." [43] Tiur had also another temple in the sacred city of Armavir.[44]

He was no less a personage than the scribe of Aramazd, which may mean that in the lofty abode of the gods, he kept record of the good and evil deeds of men for a future day of reckoning, or what is more probable on comparative grounds, he had charge of writing down the decrees (*hraman*, Pers. *firman*) that were issued by Aramazd concerning the events of each human life.[45] These decrees were no doubt recorded not only on heavenly tablets but also on the forehead of every child of man that was born. The latter were commonly called the " writ on the forehead " [46] which, according to present folk-lore, human eyes can descry but no one is able to decipher.

Besides these general and pre-natal decrees, the Armenians seem to have believed in an *annual* rendering of decrees, resembling the assembly of the Babylonian gods on the world-mountain during the Zagmuk (New Year) festival. They located this event on a spring night. As a witness of this we have only a universally observed practice.

In Christian Armenia that night came to be associated with Ascension Day. The people are surely reiterating an ancient tradition when they tell us that at an unknown and mystic hour of the night which precedes Ascension silence envelops all nature. Heaven comes nearer. All the springs and streams cease to flow. Then the flowers and shrubs, the hills and stones, begin to salute and address one another, and each one declares its specific virtue. The King Serpent who lives in his own tail learns that night the language of the flowers. If anyone is aware of that hour, he can change everything into gold by dipping it into water and expressing his wish in the name of God. Some report also that the springs and rivers flow with gold, which can be secured only at the right moment. On Ascension Day the people try to find out what kind of luck is awaiting them during the year, by means of books that tell fortune, or objects deposited on the previous day in a basin of water along with herbs and flowers. A veil covers these things which have been exposed to the gaze of the stars during the mystic night, and a young virgin draws them out one by one while verses divining the future are being recited.[47]

Whether Tiur originally concerned himself with all these things or not, he was the scribe of Aramazd. Being learned and skilful, he patronized and imparted both learning and skill. His temple, called the archive [48] of the scribe of Aramazd, was also a temple of learning and skill, i.e. not only a special sanctuary where one might pray for these things and make vows, but also a school where they were to be taught. Whatever else this vaunted learning and skill included, it must have had a special reference to the art of divination. It was a kind of Delphic oracle. This is indirectly attested by the fact that Tiur, who had nothing to do with light, was identified with Apollo in Hellenic times,[49] as well as by the great fame for interpretation of dreams which Tiur's temple enjoyed. Here it was that the people and the grandees of the nation came to seek guidance in their undertakings and to submit their dreams for interpretation. The interpretation of dreams had long become a systematic science, which was handed down by a clan of priests or soothsayers to their pupils. Tiur must have also been the patron of such arts as writing and eloquence, for on the margin of some old Armenian MSS. of the book of Acts (chap. xiv, v. 12), the name of Hermes, for whom Paul was once mistaken because of his eloquence, was explained as " the god Tiur."

Besides all these it is more than probable that Tiur was the god who conducted the souls of the dead into the nether world. The very common Armenian imprecation, " May the writer carry him! " [50] or " The writer for him! " as well as Tiur's close resemblance to the Babylonian Nabu in many other respects, goes far to confirm this view.

In spite of his being identified with Apollo and Hermes, Tiur stands closer to the Babylonian Nabu [51] than to either of these Greek deities. In fact, Hermes himself must have developed on the pattern of Nabu. The latter was a god of learning and of wisdom, and taught the art of writing. He knew — and so he could impart — the meaning of oracles and incantations. He inspired (and probably interpreted) dreams. In Babylonia Nabu was identified with the planet Mercury.

But the name of Tiur is a proof that the Babylonian Nabu did not come directly from the South. By what devious way did he then penetrate Armenia?

The answer is simple. In spite of the puzzling silence of the Avesta on this point, Iran knew a god by the name of Tīr. One of the Persian months, as the old Cappadocian and Armenian calendars attest, was consecrated to this deity (perhaps also the thirteenth day of each month). We find among the Iranians as well as among the Armenians, a host of theophorous names composed with "Tir" such as Tiribazes, Tiridates, Tiran, Tirikes, Tirotz, Tirith, etc., bearing unimpeachable witness to the god's popularity. Tīro-naKathwa is found even in the Avesta [52] as the name of a holy man. It is from Iran that Tīr migrated in the wake of the Persian armies and civilization to Armenia, Cappadocia, and Scythia, where we find also Tīr's name as Teiro on Indo-Scythian coins of the first century of our era.[53]

We have very good reasons to maintain that the description of the Armenian Tiur fits also the Iranian Tīr, and that they both were identical with Nabu. As Nabu in Babylonia, so also Tīr in Iran was the genius presiding over the planet Mercury and bore the title of *Dabir*, "writer." [54]

But a more direct testimony can be cited bearing on the original identity of the Persian Tīr with Nabu. The Neo-Babylonian king Nebuchadnezzar was greatly devoted to Nabu, his patron god. He built at the mouth of the Euphrates a city which he dedicated to him and called by a name containing the deity's name, as a component part. This name was rendered in Greek by Berossus (or Abydenus?) as Τερήδων and Διρίδωτις, "given to Mercury." The latter form, says Rawlinson, occurs as early as the time of Alexander.[55] The arrow-like writing-wedge was the commonest symbol of Nabu, and could easily give rise to the Persian designation.[56] That the arrow seems to have been the underlying idea of the Persian conception of Nabu is better attested by the fact that both Herodotus and Armenian history know the older form of Tiran, Tigranes, as a common name. Tigranes is, no doubt, derived from *Tigriš*, old Persian for " arrow."

IV. MIHR (MITHRA)

Our knowledge of the Armenian Mihr is unfortunately very fragmentary. He was unquestionably Iranian. Although popular at one time, he seems to have lost some ground when we meet with him. His name Mihr (Parthian or Sassanian for Mithra) shows that he was a late comer. Nevertheless he was called the son of Aramazd, and was therefore a brother of Anahit and Nane. In the popular Zoroastrianism of Persia, especially in Sassanian times, we find that the sun (Mihr) and moon were children of Ormazd, the first from his own mother, or even from a human wife, and the moon, from his own sister.[57] Originally Mihr may have formed in Armenia a triad with Aramazd and Anahit like that of Artaxerxes Mnemon's inscriptions. If so he soon had to yield that place to the national god Vahagn.

The Armenian Mithra presents a puzzle. If he was a genius of light and air, a god of war and contracts, a creature of Aramazd equal in might to his creator, as we find him to be in the Avesta, no trace of such attributes is left. But for the Armenians he was the genius or god of fire, and that is why he was identified with Hephaistos in syncretistic times.[58] This strange development is perhaps further confirmed by the curious fact that until this day, the main fire festival of the Armenians comes in February, the month that once corresponded to the Mehekan (dedicated to Mihr) of the Armenian calendar. But it must not be overlooked that all over the Indo-European world February was one of the months in which the New Fires were kindled.

The connection of Mihr with fire in Armenia may be explained as the result of an early identification with the native Vahagn, who, as we shall see, was a sun, lightning, and fire-god. This conjecture acquires more plausibility when we remember that Mihr did not make much headway in Armenia and that finally Vahagn occupied in the triad the place which, by right and tradition, belonged to Mihr.

Of Mithraic mysteries in Armenia we hear nothing. There were many theophorous names compounded with his name, such as Mihran, Mihrdat. The Armenian word "*Mehyan*," "temple," seems also to be derived from his name.

We know that at the Mithrakana festivals when it was the privilege of the Great King of Persia to become drunk (with haoma?), a thousand horses were sent to him by his Armenian vassal. We find in the region of Sassun (ancient Tarauntis) a legendary hero, called Meher, who gathers around himself a good many folk-tales and becomes involved even in eschatological legends. He still lives with his horse as a captive in a cave called Zympzymps which can be entered in the Ascension night. There he turns the wheel of fortune, and thence he will appear at the end of the world.

The most important temple dedicated to Mihr was in the village of Bagayarij (the town of the gods) in Derjan, Upper Armenia, where great treasures were kept. This sanctuary also was despoiled and destroyed by Gregory the Illuminator. It is reported that in that locality Mihr required human sacrifices, and about these Agathangelos also darkly hints.[59] This is, however, very difficult to explain, for in Armenia offerings of men appear only in connection with dragon (i.e. devil) worship. On the basis of the association of Mihr with eschatological events, we may conjecture that the Armenian Mihr had gradually developed two aspects, one being that which we have described above, and the other having some mysterious relation to the under-world powers.[60]

V. SPANTARAMET

The Amesha Spenta, Spenta Armaiti (holy genius of the earth) and the keeper of vineyards, was also known to the translators of the Armenian Bible who used her name in 2 Macc. vi. 7, to render the name of Dionysos.

However, it would seem that she did not hold a place in the Armenian pantheon, and was known only as a Persian goddess. We hear of no worship of Spantaramet among the Armenians and her name does not occur in any passage on Armenian religion. It is very strange, indeed, that the translators should have used the name of an Iranian goddess to render that of a Greek god. Yet the point of contact is clear. Among the Persians Spenta Armaiti was popularly known also as the keeper of vineyards, and Dionysos was the god of the vine. But, whether it is because of the evident dissimilarity of sex or because the Armenians were not sufficiently familiar with Spantaramet, the translators soon (2 Macc. xiv. 33; 3 Macc. ii. 29) discard her name and use for Dionysos "Ormzdakan god," i.e. Aramazd, whose peculiar interest in vegetation we have already noticed. Spenta Armaiti was better known to the ancient religion of Armenia as Santaramet, the goddess of the under-world.

The worship of the earth is known to Eznik [61] as a magian and heathen practice, but he does not directly connect it with the Armenians, although there can be little doubt that they once had an earth-goddess, called Erkir (Perkunas) or Armat, in their pantheon.

CHAPTER IV

SEMITIC DEITIES

SEMITIC deities were introduced into the Armenian pantheon comparatively late, notwithstanding the fact that the Armenians had always been in commercial intercourse with their southern neighbours. It was Tigranes the Great (94–54 B.C.) who brought these gods and goddesses back from his conquests along with their costly statues.[1] It is not easy to say how much of politics can be seen in this procedure. As a semi-barbarian, who had acquired a taste for western things, he surely was pleased with the æsthetic show and splendor of the more highly civilized Syrian empire of the Seleucids and its religion. He must have seen also some underlying identity between the Syrian deities and their Armenian brothers. However, in Armenia itself no real fusion took place between the native and foreign gods. The extant records show that out of all the Syrian gods and goddesses who migrated north, only Astλik (Astarte-Aphrodite) obtained a wide popularity. On the contrary, the others became little more than local deities, and that not without at first having encountered fierce opposition. The early stage of things is clearly reflected in the relation of Ba'al Shamin to Vahagn and in the manner in which he figures in the hero stories of Armenia as one who is discomfited or slain in battle. It is becoming more and more certain that almost all of these Semitic gods were brought from Phoenicia. But they hardly can have come in organized, coherent groups like Ba'al Shamin — Astλik as Jensen thinks in his fantastic *Hittiter und Armenier.*

I. BA'AL SHAMIN (Armen. Barshamina)

In the village of Thortan, where patriarchs descended from Gregory the Illuminator were buried, later stood the " brilliantly white " statue of the Syrian god Ba'al Shamin, the lord of heaven. This statue was made of ivory, crystal, and silver.[2] It was a current tradition that Tigranes the Great had captured it during his victorious campaign in Syria. No doubt the costly material was expressive of the character and story of the deity whom it endeavored to portray. In the legendary history of Armenia, where euhemerism rules supreme, Ba'al Shamin appears as a giant whom the Syrians deified on account of his valorous deeds, but who had been vanquished by Aram and slain by his soldiers.[3] In reality Ba'al Shamin was originally a supreme god of the heavens, who gave good and evil, life and death, rain and sunshine, but who had already merged his identity in that of the Syrian sun-god, when he came to Armenia. In his adoptive home he ever remained a more or less unpopular rival of Vahagn, a native sun and fire god.

The one genuine Armenian myth about him that has survived is that Vahagn stole straw from him in a cold winter night. The Milky Way was formed from the straw that dropped along as the heavenly thief hurried away.[4] This may be a distinctly Armenian but fragmentary version of the Prometheus legend, and the straw may well have something to do with the birth of fire. (See chapter on Vahagn.) Needless to say that the myth which was current even in Christian Armenia was not meant as a compliment to the foreign deity. It was an Armenian god playing a trick on a Syrian intruder. If Astλik was the wife of Ba'al Shamin, Vahagn won another victory over him, by winning her love.

II. NANE (HANEA?)

Nane is undoubtedly the Nana of ancient Babylonia, originally a Sumerian goddess. In Erech (Uruk), a city of South Babylonia, she was the goddess of the evening star and mistress of heaven. In fact, she was simply the Ishtar of Erech, the heroine of the famous Gilgamesh epic, a goddess of the life and activity of nature, of sensual love, of war and of death. Her statue had been in olden times captured by the Elamites, and its return to Erech was celebrated as a great triumph. Her worship in later times had spread broadcast west and north. She was found in Phrygia and even as far as Southern Greece. According to the *First Book of the Maccabees* (Chap. vi, v. 2) her temple at Elam contained golden statues and great treasures.

She may have come to Armenia long before Tigranes enriched the pantheon with Syrian and Phoenician gods. It is difficult to explain how she came to be called the daughter of Aramazd, unless she had once occupied an important position.

We hear nothing about orgiastic rites at her Armenian temple in Thil (the Θαλίνα of Ptolemy). On the contrary, in Hellenizing times she was identified with Athene,[5] which perhaps means that she had gradually come to be recognised as a wise, austere and war-like goddess.

III. ASTΛIK

Among all the Semitic deities which found their way into the Armenian pantheon, none attained the importance that was acquired by AstΛik, especially in Tarauntis. In spite of the presence of Anahit and Nana—two goddesses of her own type and therefore in rivalry with her—she knew how to hold her own and even to win the national god Vahagn as her lover.

For her temple at Ashtisat (where Anahit and Vahagn also had famous sanctuaries) was known as "Vahagn's chamber," and in it stood their statues side by side. However it is now impossible to reconstruct the myth that was at the basis of all this. It may be that we have here the intimate relation of a Syrian Ba'al to Astarte. It may also be that the myth is purely Greek and reflects the adventures of Ares with Aphrodite, for Astλik was called Aphrodite by Hellenizing Armenians.[6] Hoffman recognized in the Armenian name Astλik (which means " little star ") a translation of the Syrian Kaukabhta, a late designation of Ashtart (Ishtar) both as a goddess and as the planet Venus. The latter is no more called Astλik by the Armenians, but *Arusyak*, "the little bride," which is an old title of Ishtar, " the veiled bride," and shows that the Armenians not only identified the planet Venus with their goddess Astλik, but were familiar with one of her most important titles.

In view of their essential identity it was natural that some confusion should arise between Astλik and Anahit. So Vanagan Vartabed says: "Astarte is the shame of the Sidonians, whom the Syrians called Kaukabhta, the Greeks Aphrodite, and the Armenians Anahit." Either this mediæval author meant to say Astλik instead of Anahit, or for him Astλik's name was not associated with sacred prostitution in Armenia.

The custom of flying doves at the Rose-Sunday of the Armenians in Shirag (see Chapter VIII) suggests a possible relation of Astλik to this festival, the true character of which will be discussed later.

Her memory is still alive in Sassoun (ancient Tarauntis), where young men endeavor to catch a glimpse of the goddess at sunrise when she is bathing in the river. But Astλik, who knows their presence, modestly wraps herself up with the morning mist. Her main temple was at Ashtishat, but she had also other sanctuaries, among which was that at Mount Palat or Pashat.

IV. ZATIK

The Armenian translation of the Bible calls the Jewish passover " the festival of Zatik," while the Armenian church has from time immemorial applied that name to Easter. Zatik, in the sense of Passover or Easter, is unknown to the Greeks and Syrians. Here occurs, no doubt, an old word for an old deity or an old festival. But what does it mean? The Iberians have a deity called " Zaden," by whom fishermen used to swear, but about whom we know nothing definite except that this deity is feminine and her name probably under-lies that of Sathenik, the Albanian queen of King Artaxias (190 B.C.). We may perhaps infer from this queen's reputed devotion to Astλik that Zaden was a northern representative of Ishtar. But Zatik's form and associations remind us of the Palestinian Sedeq = Phoenician Σγδγκ. It is becoming clearer and clearer that once in Canaan there was such a chief deity whose name occurs in *Melchi-sedeq,* " Sedeq is my King," *Adoni-Sedeq,* " Sedeq is my Lord," or, according to a later view, " Sedeq is King," " Sedeq is Lord." Farther East, the Babylonian Shamash has two sons called respectively Kettu (which, like Sedeq, means " righteousness ") and Misharu (" rectitude "). These two deities are mentioned also in the Sanchoniatho fragments of Philo Byblios under the names of Sydyk and Misor, as culture-heroes who have discovered the use of salt. Phoenician inscriptions have *Sedeqyathan,* " Sedeq gave," as a personal name, as well as combinations of Sedeq with Ramman and Melek. Fr. Jeremias thinks that Sydyk and Misor were respectively the spring and autumn sun in sun-worship and the waxing and waning moon in moon worship.

As twins they were represented by Ashera at the door of Phoenician temples. According to the above mentioned San-

choniatho fragments, Sydyk was in Phoenicia the father
of the seven Kabirs (great gods) and of Eshmun (Asklepios)
called the Eighth. In conformity with this in Persian
and Greek times Sedeq was recognized among the Syrians
as the angel (genius) of the planet Jupiter, an indication
that he once was a chief deity. This god may have had also
some relation to the Syrian hero-god Sandacos mentioned
by Apollodorus of Athens,[7] while on the other hand Sandakos may be identified also with the Sanda of Tarsus. At all
events Sandakos went to Cilicia and founded (i.e. he was the
god of) the city of Celenderis and became through two generations of heroes the father of Adonis. Zatik, as well as Sedeq,
was probably a vegetation god, like Adonis, whose resurrection began at the winter solstice and was complete in the
spring. The spring festival of such a god would furnish a
suitable name both for the Jewish passover and the Christian
Easter. The spring celebrations of the death and resurrection
of Adonis were often adopted and identified by the Christian
churches with the Death and Resurrection of Christ. However, no trace of a regular worship of Zatik is found among
the Armenians in historical times, although their Easter celebrations contain a dramatic bewailing, burial, and resurrection
of Christ.

Unsatisfactory as this explanation is, it would seem to come
nearer the truth than Sandalgian's (supported by Tiryakian
and others) identification of Zatik with the Persian root *zad*,
"to strike," from which is probably derived the Armenian
word *zenum*, " to slaughter."

CHAPTER V

VAHAGN "THE EIGHTH" GOD

A NATIONAL DEITY

IN the extant records Vahagn presents himself under the
double aspect of a national hero and a god of war or
courage.[1] A thorough study, however, will show that he was
not only a deity but the most national of all the Armenian gods.
It is probable that Vahagn was intentionally overlooked when
the Armenian pantheon was reorganized according to a stereo-
typed scheme of seven main "worships." For his official
cult is called "the eighth," which probably means that it
was an after-thought. Yet once he was recognized, he soon
found himself at the very side of Aramazd and Anahit,
with whom he formed a triad[2] on the pattern of that of
Auramazda, Anahita, and Mithra of the later Persian inscriptions. Moreover, he became a favorite of the Armenian
kings who brought sacrifices to his main temple at Ashtishat.[3]

How did all this take place? We may venture to suggest
that when Zoroastrian ideas of a popular type were pervading
Armenia and a Zoroastrian or perhaps Magian pantheon of a
fragmentary character was superseding the gods of the country
or reducing them to national heroes, Vahagn shared the fate
of the latter class. Yet there was so much vitality in his worship, that Mithra himself could not obtain a firm foothold in
the land, in the face of the great popularity enjoyed by
this native rival.

Moses of Khoren reports an ancient song about Vahagn's
birth, which will give us the surest clue to his nature and origin.
It reads as follows:

The heavens and the earth travailed,
There travailed also the purple sea,
The travail held
The red reed [4] (stalk) in the sea.
Through the hollow of the reed (stalk) a smoke rose,
Through the hollow of the reed (stalk) a flame rose
And out of the flame ran forth a youth.
He had hair of fire,
He had a beard of flame,
And his eyes were suns.

Other parts of this song, now lost, said that Vahagn had fought and conquered dragons. Vishapaχaλ, "dragon-reaper," was his best known title. He was also invoked, at least in royal edicts, as a god of courage. It is mostly in this capacity that he became a favorite deity with the Armenian kings, and in later syncretistic times, was identified with Herakles. Besides these attributes Vahagn claimed another. He was a sun-god. A mediæval writer says that the sun was worshipped by the ancients under the name of Vahagn,[5] and his rivalry with Ba'al Shamin and probably also with Mihr, two other sun-gods of a foreign origin, amply confirms this explicit testimony.

These several and apparently unconnected reports about Vahagn, put together, evoke the striking figure of a god which can be paralleled only by the Vedic Agni, the fire-god who forms the fundamental and original unity underlying the triad: — Indra, the lightning, Agni, the universal and sacrificial fire, and Surya, the sun. Besides the fact that Vahagn's name may very well be a compound of Vah and Agni, no better commentary on the birth, nature and functions of Vahagn may be found than the Vedic songs on these three deities.

From the above quoted fragment which was sung to the accompaniment of the lyre by the bards of Goλthn [6] long after the Christianization of Armenia, we gather that Vahagn's birth had a universal significance.　He was a son of heaven, earth, and sea, but more especially of *the sea*.　This wonderful youth may be the sun rising out of the sea, but more probably he is the fire-god surging out of the heavenly sea in the form of the lightning, because the travail can be nothing else than the raging storm.　However, this matters little, for in Aryan religion, the sun is the heavenly fire and only another aspect of Agni.　It is very significant that Armenians said both of the setting sun and of the torch that went out, that " they were going to their mother," i.e. they returned to the common essence from which they were born.　Once we recognize the unity of all fire in heaven, in the skies, and on earth, as the Vedas do, we need no more consider the universal travail at Vahagn's birth as a poetic fancy of the old Armenian bards.　Here we are on old Aryan ground.　At least in the Rgveda the fire claims as complex a parenthood as Vahagn.　It is the child of heaven, earth, and water.[7]　Even the description of the external appearance of the Vedic Agni (and of Indra himself) · agrees with that of Vahagn.　Agni is always youthful, like Vahagn, with a continual fresh birth.　Agni (as well as Indra) has tawny hair and beard like Vahagn, who has " hair of fire and beard of flame."　Surya, the sun, is Agni's eye.　Vahagn's eyes are suns.

However, the key to the situation is the "reed " or "stalk."　It is a very important word in Indo-European mythology in connection with fire in its three forms, sun, lightning, and earthly fire.　It is the specially sacred fuel which gives birth to the sacred fire.　The Greek culture-hero Prometheus brought down the fire stolen from the gods (or the sun) in a fennel stalk.　Indra, the lightning-god of the Vedas, after killing Vrtra was seized with fear and hid himself for a while in the stalk of a lotus flower in a lake.　Once Agni hid himself in the water and in plants, where the gods finally discovered him.　The sage Atharvan [8] of the Vedas extracted Agni from the lotus flower, i.e. from the lotus stalk. Many dragon-killers, who usually have some relation to the fire, sun, or lightning, are born out of an enchanted flower.[9] We must regard it as a very interesting and significant echo of the same hoary myth that Zarathustra's soul was sent down in the stalk of a haoma-plant. Such a righteous soul was no doubt conceived as a fiery substance derived from above.

It is not more than reasonable to see one original and primitive myth at the root of all these stories, the myth of the miraculous birth of the one universal fire stolen from the sun or produced by the fire-drill in the clouds whence it comes down to the earth (see Chapter VII).

Further, the dragon-slaying of ancient mythology is usually the work of fire in one or another of its three aspects. The Egyptian sun-god (evidently a compound being) kills the dragon through his fire-spitting serpents. The *Atar* of the Avesta (who gives both heat and light) fights with Aži Dahaka. The Greek Herakles, manifestly a sun-god, strangles serpents in his early childhood. Agni, as well as Indra and Surya, is a Vrtra-slayer. Nothing scares away the Macedonian dragon so successfully as the name of the thunderbolt, and it is well known how the evil spirits of superstition and folk-lore, which are closely allied with dragons, as we shall see, are always afraid of fire-brands and of fire in general. Macdonell says that Agni is very prominent as a goblin-slayer, even more so than Indra.

Finally, Vahagn's attributes of courage and victory are not strangers to the Vedic Agni and Indra.[10] Both of them are gods of war and victory, no doubt mostly in virtue of their meteorological character. The war-like nature of weather-gods is a commonplace of universal mythology. Even the Avestic Verethraghna inherits this distinctive quality from his original Indo-European self, when his name was only a title of Indra or Vayu.

We purposely delayed the mention of one point in our general description of Vahagn. Modern Armenian folk-lore knows a storm god called *Dsovean* (sea-born), who with an angry storm goddess, *Dsovinar* (she who was born of the sea), rules supreme in the storm and often appears to human eyes.[11] In view of the fact that we do not know any other sea-born deity in Armenian mythology, who else could this strange figure of folk-lore be but Vahagn, still killing his dragons in the sky with his fiery sword or arrow and sending down the fertilizing rain? His title " sea-born," which must have been retained from an ancient usage and is in perfect keeping with the extant Vahagn song, strongly recalls the Vedic *Apam napat* " water child," who is supreme in the seas, dispensing water to mankind, but also identical with Agni clad with the lightning in the clouds.[12] Dsovinar may very well be a reminiscence of the mermaids who accompanied the " water-child," or even some female goddess like Indrani, the wife of Indra.

From these considerations it becomes very plain that Vahagn is a fire and lightning god, born out of the stalk [13] in the heavenly (?) sea, with the special mission among other beneficent missions, to slay dragons. His title of dragon-reaper is a distant but unmistakable echo of a pre-Vedic Vrtrahan.

In fact, the Armenian myth about him is an independent tradition from the original home of the Indo-Iranians, and confirms the old age of many a Vedic myth concerning Agni, which modern scholars tend to regard as the fancies of later poets.[14] And is it not a striking coincidence that the only surviving fragment about Vahagn should be a birth-song, a topic which, according to Macdonell, has, along with the sacrificial functions of Agni, a paramount place in the minds of the Vedic singers of Agni? [15]

CHAPTER VI

NATURE WORSHIP AND NATURE MYTHS

I. SUN, MOON, AND STARS

MOSES of Chorene makes repeated allusions to the worship of the sun and moon in Armenia. In oaths the name of the sun was almost invariably invoked,[1] and there were also altars and images of the sun and moon.[2] Of what type these images were, and how far they were influenced by Syrian or Magian sun-worship, we cannot tell. We shall presently see the mediæval conceptions of the forms of the sun and moon. Modern Armenians imagine the sun to be like the wheel of a water-mill.[3] Agathangelos, in the alleged letter of Diocletian to Tiridates, unconsciously bears witness to the Armenian veneration for the sun, moon and stars.[4] But the oldest witness is Xenophon, who notes that the Armenians sacrificed horses to the sun,[5] perhaps with some reference to his need of them in his daily course through the skies. The eighth month of the Armenian year and, what is more significant, the first day of every month, were consecrated to the sun and bore its name, while the twenty-fourth day in the Armenian month was consecrated to the moon. The Armenians, like the Persians and most of the sun-worshipping peoples of the East, prayed toward the rising sun, a custom which the early church adopted, so that to this day the Armenian churches are built and the Armenian dead are buried toward the east, the west being the abode of evil spirits. As to the moon, Ohannes Mantaguni in the Fifth Century bears witness to the belief that the moon prospers or mars the plants,[6] and Anania of Shirak says in his *Demonstrations*,[7] " The first fathers called her the nurse of the plants," a quite widely spread idea which has its parallel, both in the west and in the short Mah-yasht of the Avesta, particularly in the statement that vegetation grows best in the time of the waxing moon.[8] At certain of its phases the moon caused diseases, especially epilepsy, which was called the moon-disease, and Eznik tries to combat this superstition with the explanation that it is caused by demons whose activity is connected with the phases of the moon![9] The modern Armenians are still very much afraid of the baleful influence of the moon upon children and try to ward it off by magical ceremonies in the presence of the moon.[10]

As among many other peoples, the eclipse of the sun and moon was thought to be caused by dragons which endeavor to swallow these luminaries. But the "evil star" of the Western Armenians is a plain survival of the superstitions current among the Persians, who held that these phenomena were caused by two dark bodies, offspring of the primæval ox, revolving below the sun and moon, and occasionally passing between them and the earth.[11] When the moon was at an eclipse, the sorcerers said that it resembled a demon (?). It was, moreover, a popular belief that a sorcerer could bind the sun and moon in their course, or deprive them of their light. He could bring the sun or moon down from heaven by witchcraft and although it was larger than many countries (worlds?) put together, the sorcerers could set the moon in a threshing floor, and although without breasts, they could milk it like a cow.[12] This latter point betrays some reminiscence of a primæval cow in its relation to the moon and perhaps shows that this luminary was regarded by the Armenians also as a goddess of fertility. Needless to add that the eclipses and the appearance of comets foreboded evil. Their chronologies are full of notices of such astronomical phenomena that presaged great national and universal disasters. Along with all these practices, there was a special type of divination by the moon.

Both sun and moon worship have left deep traces in the popular beliefs of the present Armenians.[13]

A few ancient stellar myths have survived, in a fragmentary condition. Orion, Sirius, and other stars were perhaps involved in myths concerning the national hero, Hayk, as they bear his name.

We have seen that Vahagn's stealing straw from Ba'al Shamin and forming the Milky Way, has an unmistakable reference to his character. The Milky Way [14] itself was anciently known as " the Straw-thief's Way," and the myth is current among the Bulgarians, who may have inherited it from the ancient Thracians.

Some of the other extant sun-myths have to do with the great luminary's travel beyond the western horizon. The setting sun has always been spoken of among the Armenians and among Slavs as the sun that is going to his mother. According to Frazer " Stesichorus also described the sun embarking in a golden goblet that he might cross the ocean in the darkness of night and come to his mother, his wedded wife and children dear." The sun may, therefore, have been imagined as a young person, who, in his resplendent procession through the skies, is on his way to a re-incarnation. The people probably believed in a daily occurrence of death and birth, which the sun, as the heavenly fire, has in common with the fire, and which was most probably a return into a heavenly stalk or tree and reappearance from it. This heavenly stalk or tree itself must therefore have been the mother of the sun, as well as of the fire, and in relation to the sun was known to the Letts and even to the ancient Egyptians. The Armenians have forgotten the original identity of the mother of the sun and have produced other divergent accounts of which Abeghian has given us several.[15] They often think the dawn or the evening twilight to be the mother of the sun. She is a brilliant woman with eyes shining like the beams of the sun and with a golden garment, who bestows beauty upon the maidens at sunset. Now she is imagined as a good woman helping those whom the sun punished, now as a bad woman cursing and changing men into stone. The mother of the sun is usually supposed to reside in the palace of the sun, which is either in the east at the end of the world or in a sea, like the Lake of Van. In the absence of a sea, there is at least a basin near the mother. Like the Letto-Lithuanians, who thought that Perkuna Tete, the mother of the thunder and lightning, bathes the sun, and refreshes him at the end of the day, the Armenians also associate this mother closely with the bath which the sun takes at the close of his daily journey. The palace itself is gorgeously described. It is situated in a far-off place where there are no men, no birds, no trees, and no turf, and where the great silence is disturbed only by the murmur of springs welling up in the middle of each one of the twelve courts, which are built of blue marble and spanned over by arches. In the middle court, over the spring, there is a pavilion where the mother of the sun waits for him, sitting on the edge of a pearl bed among lights. When he returns he bathes in the spring, is taken up, laid in bed and nursed by his mother.

Further, that the sun crosses a vast sea to reach the east was also known to the Armenians. Eznik is trying to prove that this is a myth but that the sun passes underneath the earth all the same. The sea is, of course, the primæval ocean upon which the earth was founded. It is on this journey that the sun shines on the Armenian world of the dead as he did on the Babylonian Aralu and on the Egyptian and Greek Hades. The following extract from an Armenian collection of folklore unites the sun's relation to Hades and to the subterranean ocean: "And at sun-set the sun is the *portion* of the dead. It enters the sea and, passing under the earth, emerges in the morning at the other side." [16]

Mediæval writers [17] speak about the horses of the sun,

an idea which is no more foreign to the Persians than to the Greeks. One counts four of them, and calls them Enik, Menik, Benik, and Senik, which sound like artificial or magic names, but evidently picture the sun on his quadriga. Another, mingling the scientific ideas of his time with mythical images, says: " The sun is a compound of fire, salt, and iron, light blended with lightning, fire that has been shaped — or with a slight emendation — fire drawn by horses. There are in it twelve windows with double shutters, eleven of which look upward, and one to the earth. Wouldst thou know the shape of the sun? It is that of a man deprived of reason and speech standing between two horses. If its eye (or its real essence) were not in a dish, the world would blaze up before it like a mass of wool." The reader will readily recognize in " the windows of the sun " a far-off echo of early Greek philosophy.

Ordinarily in present-day myths the sun is thought to be a young man and the moon a young girl. But, on the other hand, the Germanic idea of a feminine sun and masculine moon is not foreign to Armenian thought. They are brother and sister, but sometimes also passionate lovers who are engaged in a weary search for each other through the trackless fields of the heavens. In such cases it is the youthful moon who is pining away for the sun-maid. Bashfulness is very characteristic of the two luminaries, as fair maids. So the sun hurls fiery needles at the bold eyes which presume to gaze upon her face, and the moon covers hers with a sevenfold veil of clouds.[18] These very transparent and poetic myths, however, have little in them that might be called ancient.

The ancient Armenians, like the Latins, possessed two different names for the moon. One of these was *Lusin*, an unmistakable cognate of *Luna* (originally *Lucna* or *Lucina*), and the other *Ami(n)s*, which now like the Latin *mens*, signifies " month." No doubt *Lusin* designated the moon as a female goddess, while *Amins* corresponded to the Phrygian *mên* or *Lunus*.

The same mediaeval and quasi-scientific author who gives the above semi-mythological description of the sun, portrays the moon in the following manner: " The moon was made out of five parts, three of which are light, the fourth is fire, and the fifth, motion . . . which is a compound. It is cloud-like, light-like (luminous) dense air, with twelve windows, six of which look heavenward and six earthward. What are the forms of the moon? In it are two sea-buffaloes (?). The light enters into the mouth of the one and is waning in the mouth of the other. For the light of the moon comes from the sun! " [19] Here again the sea-buffaloes may be a dim and confused reminiscence of a " primæval cow " which was associated with the moon and, no doubt, suggested by the peculiar form of the crescent. Let us add also that the Armenians spoke of the monthly *rebirth* of the moon, although myths concerning it are lacking.

Fragments of Babylonian star-lore found their way into Armenia probably through Median Magi. We have noticed the planetary basis of the pantheon. In later times, however, some of the planets came into a bad repute.[20] Anania of Shirak (seventh century) reports that heathen (?) held Jupiter and Venus to be beneficent, Saturn and Mars were malicious, but Mercury was indifferent.

Stars and planets and especially the signs of the Zodiac were bound up with human destiny upon which they exercised a decisive influence. According to Eznik [21] the Armenians believed that these heavenly objects caused births and deaths. Good and ill luck were dependent upon the entrance of certain stars into certain signs of the Zodiac. So they said: " When Saturn is in the ascendant, a king dies; when Leo (the lion) is ascendant, a king is born. When the Taurus is ascendant, a powerful and good person is born. With Aries, a rich person is born, ' just as the ram has a thick fleece.' With the Scorpion, a wicked and sinful person comes to the world. Whoever is born when Hayk (Mars?) is in the ascendant dies by iron, i.e., the sword." Much of this star lore is still current among the Mohammedans in a more complete form.

Eznik alludes again and again to the popular belief that stars, constellations, and Zodiacal signs which bear names of animals like Sirius (dog), Arcturus (bear), were originally animals of those names that have been lifted up into the heavens.

Something of the Armenian belief in the influence that Zodiacal signs could exercise on the weather and crops is preserved by al-Bīrūnī [22] where we read: " I heard a number of Armenian learned men relate that on the morning of the *Fox-day* there appears on the highest mountain, between the Interior and the Exterior country, a white ram (Aries?) which is not seen at any other time of the year except about this time of this Day. Now the inhabitants of that country infer that the year will be prosperous if the ram bleats; that it will be sterile if it does not bleat."

FIG. 1. RELIEF

Found in the neighborhood of Ezzinjan

CHAPTER VII

NATURE WORSHIP AND NATURE MYTHS

II. FIRE

THE worship of fire was possessed by Armenians as a venerable heirloom long before they came into contact with Zoroastrianism. It was so deeply rooted that the Christian authors do not hesitate to call the heathen Armenians ash-worshippers, a name which they apply also to the Persians with less truth. We have seen that the old word " Agni " was known to the Armenians in the name of Vahagn and that their ideas of the fire-god were closely akin to those of the Rgveda. Fire was, for them, the substance of the sun and of the lightning. Fire gave heat and also light. Like the sun, the light-giving fire had a " mother," most probably the water-born and water-fed stalk or tree out of which fire was obtained by friction or otherwise.[1] To this mother the fire returned when extinguished. Even today to put out a candle or a fire is not a simple matter, but requires some care and respect. Fire must not be desecrated by the presence of a dead body, by human breath, by spitting into it, or burning in it such unclean things as hair and parings of the finger nail. An impure fire must be rejected and a purer one kindled in its place, usually from a flint. All this may be Zoroastrian but it is in perfect accord with the older native views.

The people swear by the hearth-fire just as also by the sun. Fire was and still is the most potent means of driving the evil spirits away. The Eastern Armenian who will bathe in the night scares away the malignant occupants of the lake or pool

by casting a fire-brand into it, and the man who is harassed by
an obstinate demon has no more powerful means of getting rid
of him than to strike fire out of a flint. Through the sparks
that the latter apparently contains, it has become, along with
iron,[2] an important weapon against the powers of darkness.
Not only evil spirits but also diseases, often ascribed to demoniac influences, can not endure the sight of fire, but must flee
before this mighty deity. In Armenian there are two words
for fire. One is *hur*,[3] a cognate of the Greek πῦρ, and the
other *krak*, probably derived, like the other Armenian word
jrag, "candle," "light," from the Persian *čiraġ* (also *čirah*,
čaraġ). *Hur* was more common in ancient Armenian, but we
find also *krak* as far back as the Armenian literature reaches.
While Vahagn is unmistakably a male deity, we find that the
fire as a deity was female, like Hestia or Vesta. This was also
true of the Scythian fire-god whom Herodotus calls Hestia.
On the contrary the Vedic *Agni* and the Avestic *Ātar* were
masculine.

The worship of fire took among the Armenians a two-fold
aspect. There was first the hearth-worship. This seems to
have been closely associated with ancestor spirits,[4] which naturally flocked around the center and symbol of the home-life.
It is the lips of this earthen and sunken fireplace which the
young bride reverently kisses with the groom, as she enters
her new home for the first time. And it is around it that they
piously circle three times. A brand from this fire will
be taken when any member of the family goes forth to found
a new home. Abeghian, from whose excellent work on the
popular beliefs of the Armenians we have culled some of this
material, says that certain villages have also their communal
hearth, that of the founder of the village, etc., which receives
something like general reverence, and often, in cases of marriage and baptism, is a substitute for a church when there is
none at hand. Ethnologists who hold that the development

of the family is later than that of the community would naturally regard the communal fire as prior in order and importance.

A very marked remnant of hearth and ancestor worship is found in special ceremonies like cleaning the house thoroughly and burning candles and incense, which takes place everywhere on Saturdays.

The second aspect of fire-worship in Armenia is the public one. It is true that the Persian Atrushans (fire-temples or enclosures) found little favor in both heathen and Christian Armenia, and that fire, as such, does not seem to have attained a place in the rank of the main deities. Nevertheless, there was a public fire-worship, whether originally attached to a communal hearth or not. It went back sometimes to a Persian *frobag* or *farnbag* (Arm. *hurbak*) fire, and in fact we have several references to a Persian or Persianized fire-altar in Bagavan, the town of the gods.[5] Moreover, there can be little doubt that Armenians joined the Persians in paying worship to the famous seven fire-springs of Baku in their old province of Phaitakaran. But usually the Armenian worship of the fire possessed a native character.

The following testimonies seem to describe some phases of this widely spread and deeply rooted national cult.

In the hagiography called the " Coming of the Rhipsimean Virgins "[6] wrongly ascribed to Moses of Chorene, we read that on the top of Mount Palat (?) there was a house of Aramazd and Astλik (Venus), and on a lower peak, to the southeast, there was " a house of fire, of insatiable fire, the god of incessant combustion." At the foot of the mountain, moreover, there was a mighty spring. The place was called Buth. " They burnt the Sister Fire and the Brother Spring."

Elsewhere we read, in like manner: " Because they called the fire sister, and the spring brother, they did not throw the ashes away, but they wiped them with the tears of the brother."[7]

Lazare of Pharpe, a writer of the fifth century,[8] speaking
of an onslaught of the Christian Armenians on the sacred fire,
which the Persians were endeavoring to introduce into Armenia, says: " They took the fire and carried it into the water
as into the bosom of her brother, according to the saying of
the false teachers of the Persians." The latter part of his
statement, however, is mistaken. So far as we know, the Persians did not cast the sacred fire into the water, but allowed
the ashes to be heaped in the fire enclosure. When the floating
island (sea-monster) upon which Keresaspa had unwittingly
kindled a fire, sank and the fire fell into the water, this was
accounted to him a great sin. The above was rather a purely
Armenian rite. It would seem that it was a part of the Armenian worship of the Sister Fire to extinguish her in the
bosom of her loving brother, the water, a rite which certainly
hides some nature myth, like the relation of the lightning
to the rain, or like the birth of the fire out of the stalk in the
heavenly sea. Whatever the real meaning of this procedure
was, the ashes of the sacred fire imparted to the water with
which they were " wiped " healing virtue. Even now in Armenia, for example, in Agn and Diarbekir the sick are given
this potent medicine to drink which consists of the flaky ashes
of oak-fire mixed with water. W. Caland reports the same
custom of the ancient Letts in his article on the Pre-Christian
Death and Burial Rites of the Baltic People.[9] As the oak in
the European world is the tree sacred to the god of the
heavens and the storm, we may easily perceive what underlies
the ancient custom.

But it is not clear whether the Armenians (like many Western nations) had several fire-festivals in the year. We have,
however, the survival of an indubitable fire-festival — which
originally aimed at influencing the activity of the rain-god —
in the annual bonfire kindled everywhere by Armenians at
Candlemas, or the Purification of the Blessed Virgin, on the

13th of February, in the courts of the churches. The fuel often consists of stalks, straw, and thistles, which are kindled from a candle of the altar.[10] The bonfire is usually repeated on the streets, in the house-yards, or on the flat roofs. The people divine the future crops through the direction of the flames and smoke. They leap over it (as a lustration?) and circle around it. Sometimes also they have music and a dance. The ashes are often carried to the fields to promote their fertility. It is perhaps not entirely without significance that this festival falls within the month of Mehekan (consecrated to Mihr), as the Armenian Mithra had distinctly become a fire-god.[11] Another fire-festival, rather locally observed, will be mentioned in the next chapter.

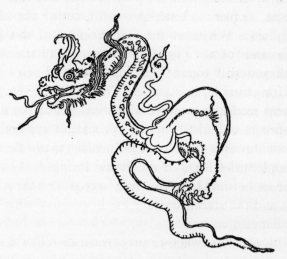

FIG. 2. DRAGON-LIKE FIGURE

CHAPTER VIII

NATURE WORSHIP AND NATURE MYTHS

III. WATER

IF FIRE were a female principle, water was masculine, and as we have noticed, they were somehow very closely associated as sister and brother in the Armenian fire-worship. It is possible that this kinship was suggested by the trees and luxuriant verdure growing on the banks of rivers and lakes. As we know, reeds grew even in the heavenly sea.

Many rivers and springs were sacred, and endowed with beneficent virtues. According to Tacitus,[1] the Armenians offered horses as a sacrifice to the Euphrates, and divined by its waves and foam. The sources of the Euphrates and Tigris received and still receive worship.[2] Sacred cities were built around the river Araxes and its tributaries. Even now there are many sacred springs with healing power, usually called " the springs of light," and the people always feel a certain veneration towards water in motion, which they fear to pollute. The people still drink of these ancient springs and burn candles and incense before them, for they have placed them under the patronage of Christian saints.

The Transfiguration Sunday, which comes in June, was connected by the Armenian Church with an old water festival. At this time people drench each other with water and the ecclesiastical procession throws rose water at the congregation during the Transfiguration Day rites. On this day the churches are richly decorated with roses and the popular name of the Festival is *Vartavar*, " Burning with Roses." [3]

It is also reported that in various parts of Armenia, the *Vartavar* is preceded by a night of bonfires. Therefore it can be nothing else than the water festival which seems to have once gone hand in hand with the midsummer (St. John's, St. Peter's, etc.) fires in Europe, at which roses played a very conspicuous part.[4] It is barely possible that the Armenian name of this festival, " Burning with Roses," preserves some allusion to the original but now missing fire, and even that flowers were burnt in it or at least cast across the fire as in Europe. In Europe the midsummer water festival was observed also with bathings and visits to sacred springs. In parts of Germany straw wheels set on fire were quenched in the river; and in Marseilles, the people drenched each other with water. There can be little doubt that the water was used in these various ways not only as a means of purification from guilt and disease, but also and principally as a rain-charm. Frazer, who, in his *Golden Bough*, has heaped together an enormous mass of material on the various elements and aspects of these festivals, has thereby complicated the task of working out a unified and self-consistent interpretation.

The custom of throwing water at each other is reported by al-Bīrūnī[5] of the Persians, in connection with their New-Year's festival. As the Persian new year came in the spring, there can be little doubt that the festival aimed at the increase of the rain by sympathetic magic.[6] In fact, even now in certain places of Armenia the tillers returning from their first day of labour in the fields are sprinkled with water by those who lie in wait for them on the way. So it may be safely assumed that in Armenia also in ancient times the Navasard brought with it the first water-festival of the year. In certain places like the region of Shirak, flying doves form a part of the Vartavar celebrations. Whether this has some reference to an old Astλik (Ishtar) festival, is difficult to say. It is quite possible that as in Europe, so also in ancient Armenia, love-making and other more objectionable rites, formed an important feature of these mid-summer celebrations.

The great centre of the Armenian Navasard and of the water festival (Vartavar) was Bagavan, probably because both had the same character. The fact that Bagavan was also a centre of fire-worship emphasizes once more the close association of these two elements which we have already pointed out.

CHAPTER IX

NATURE WORSHIP AND NATURE MYTHS

IV. TREES, PLANTS, AND MOUNTAINS

WE HAVE old testimony to tree and plant worship in Armenia. There were first the poplars (*sausi*) of Armenia, by which a legendary *saus* (whose name and existence were probably derived from the venerated tree itself) divined. Then we have the words *Haurut, Maurut,* as names of flowers (*Hyacinthus racemosus Dodonei*). These, however, seem to be an echo of the Iranian Haurvatat and Ameretat ("health" and "immortality"), two Amesha-Spentas who were also the genii of plants and water. The oak and other trees are still held to be sacred, especially those near a spring, and upon these one may see hanging pieces of clothing from persons who wish to be cured of some disease. This practice is often explained as a substitution of a part for the whole, and it is very common also among the Semites in general and the Mohammedans in particular.[1]

Many mountains were sacred, while others, perhaps sacred by themselves in very ancient times, became the sites of famous temples. The towering Massis (Ararat) was called *Azat* (Yazata?), "venerable." It was a seat of dragons and fairies, but the main reason of its sacredness must be sought in its imposing grandeur, its volcanic character, or even its association with some deity like Marsyas-Masses, by the Phrygo-Armenians.[2] This Phrygian god Marsyas-Masses was famous for his skill with the flute but especially for his widely known interest in rivers. He was the son of Hyagnis, probably a lightning god, and like the Norwegian Agne *was hung* from a tree by Apollo, who skinned him alive (Apuleius). In fact Marsyas was no more than a tribal variety of Hyagnis, and Hyagnis can be nothing else but the Phrygian form of Vahagn.

Mount Npat (Νιφάτης of Strabo), the source of the mighty Tigris, must have enjoyed some veneration as a deity, because the 26th day of each Armenian month was dedicated to it. It has been maintained that Npat was considered by Zoroastrians the seat of Apam-Napat, an important Indo-Iranian water deity.

Mt. Pashat or Palat was the seat of an Aramazd and Astλik temple and a centre of fire-worship. Another unidentified mountain in Sophene was called the Throne of Anahit.

One may safely assume that the Armenians thought in an animistic way, and saw in these natural objects of worship some god or spirit who in Christian times easily assumed the name and character of a saint.

CHAPTER X

HEROES

THE loss of the ancient songs of Armenia is especially regrettable at this point, because they concerned themselves mostly with the purely national gods and heroes. The first native writers of Armenian history, having no access to the ancient Assyrian, Greek, and Latin authors, drew upon this native source for their material. Yet the old legends were modified or toned down in accordance with euhemeristic views and accommodated to Biblical stories and Greek chronicles, especially that of Eusebius of Caesarea. It is quite possible that the change had already begun in pagan times, when Iranian and Semitic gods made their conquest of Armenia.

I. HAYK

There can be little doubt that the epic songs mentioned Hayk first of all. Hayk was a handsome giant with finely proportioned limbs, curly hair, bright smiling eyes, and a strong arm, who was ready to strike down all ambition, divine or human, which raised its haughty head and dreamt of absolute dominion. The bow and the triangular arrow were his inseparable companions. Hayk was a true lover of independence. He it was, who, like Moses of old, led his people from the post-diluvian tyranny of Bel (Nimrod) in the plain of Shinar to the cold but free mountains of Armenia, where he subjugated the native population.[1] Bel at first plied him with messages of fair promise if he would return. But the hero met them with a proud and defiant answer. Soon after, as was expected, Cadmus, the grandson of Hayk, brought tidings of an invasion of Armenia by the innumerable forces of Bel. Hayk marched south with his small but brave army to meet the tyrant on the shores of the sea (of Van) " whose briny waters teem with tiny fish." [2] Here began the battle. Hayk arranged his warriors in a triangle on a plateau among mountains in the presence of the great multitude of invaders. The first shock was so terrible and costly in men that Bel, confused and frightened, began to withdraw. But Hayk's unerring triangular arrow, piercing his breast, issued forth from his back. The overthrow of their chief was a signal for the mighty Babylonian forces to disperse.

Hayk is the eponymous hero of the Armenians according to their national name, Hay, used among themselves. From the same name they have called their country *Hayastan* or the Kingdom (Ashkharh = Iran. Khshathra) of the Hays. Adjectives derived from *Hayk* describe both gigantic strength and great beauty. Gregory of Narek calls even the beauty of the Holy Virgin, Hayk-like! The word Hayk itself was often used in the sense of a " giant."

Some have tried to give an astronomical interpretation to this legend. Pointing out the fact that Hayk is also the Armenian name for the constellation Orion, they have maintained that the triangular arrangement of Hayk's army reflects the triangle which the star Adaher in Orion forms with the two dogstars. However, any attempt to establish a parallelism between the Giant Orion and Hayk as we know him, is doomed to failure, for beyond a few minor or general points of resemblance, the two heroes have nothing in common. Hayk seems to have been also the older Armenian name of the Zodiacal sign Libra, and of the planet Mars,[3] while the cycle of Sirius was for the Armenians the cycle of Hayk.

The best explanation of Hayk's name and history seems to lie in the probable identity of Hayk (Hayik, " little Hay,"

just as Armenak means " little Armenius ") with the Phrygian sky-god Hyas whom the Greeks called ὕης. Both the
Greeks and the Assyrians⁴ know him as an independent
Thraco-Phrygian deity. The Assyrians call him the god
of Moschi.⁵ In a period when everything Thracian and Phrygian was being assimilated by Dionysos or was sinking into
insignificance before his triumphant march through the
Thraco-Phrygian world, Hyas, from a tribal deity, became
an epithet of this god of vegetation and of wine. For us
Hyas is no one else but the Vayu of the Vedas and the
Avesta. So in the legend of Hayk we probably have the
story of the battle between an Indo-European weather-god
and the Mesopotamian Bel. It is very much more natural
to derive a national name like *Hay* from a national deity's
name, according to the well-known analogies of Assur and
Khaldi, than to interpret it as *pati*, " chief." ⁶

II. ARMENAK

According to Moses of Chorene, Armenak is the name of
the son of Hayk. He chose for his abode the mountain Ara-
gads (now Alagez) and the adjacent country.

He is undoubtedly another eponymous hero of the Armenian race. Armenius, father of Er, mentioned by Plato
in his *Republic*,⁷ can be no other than this Armenak who,
according to Moses of Chorene and the so-called Sebeos-frag-
ments, is the great-grandfather of Ara (Er). The final
syllable is a diminutive, just as is the " k " in Hayk. Popular legend, which occupied itself a good deal with Hayk,
seems to have neglected Armenak almost completely. It is
quite possible that Armenak is the same as the Teutonic Irmin and the Vedic Aryaman, therefore originally a title of the
sky-god. The many exploits ascribed to Aram, the father of
Ara, may indeed, belong by right to Armenak.⁸

III. SHARA

Shara is said to be the son of Armais. As he was uncommonly voracious his father gave him the rich land of Shirak to prey upon. He was also far-famed for his numerous progeny. The old Armenian proverb used to say to gluttons: " If thou hast the throat (appetite) of Shara, we have not the granaries of Shirak." One may suspect that an ogre is hiding behind this ancient figure. At all events his name must have some affinity with the Arabic word *Sharah,* which means gluttony.[9]

IV. ARAM

Aram, a son of Harma, seems to be a duplicate of Armenak, although many scholars have identified him with Arame, a later king of Urartu, and with Aram, an eponymous hero of the Aramaic region. The Armenian national tradition makes him a conqueror of Barsham "whom the Syrians deified on account of his exploits," of a certain Nychar Mades (Nychar the Median), and of Paiapis Chalia, a Titan who ruled from the Pontus Euxinus to the Ocean (Mediterranean). Through this last victory Aram became the ruler of Pontus and Cappadocia upon which he imposed the Armenian language.

In this somewhat meagre and confused tale we have probably an Armenian god Aram or Armenius in war against the Syrian god Ba'al Shamin, some Median god or hero called Nychar,[10] and a western Titan called Paiapis Chaλia, who no doubt represents in a corrupt form the Urartian deity Khaldi with the Phrygian (?) title of Papaios. The legend about the Pontic war probably originated in the desire to explain how Armenians came to be found in Lesser Armenia, or it may be a distant and distorted echo of the Phrygo-Armenian struggles against the Hittite kingdoms of Asia Minor.

V. ARA, THE BEAUTIFUL

With Ara we are unmistakably on mythological ground.
Unfortunately this interesting hero has, like Hayk and
Aram, greatly suffered at the hands of our ancient Hellenizers. The present form of the myth, a quasi-classical version of the original, is as follows: When Ninus, King of
Assyria, died or fled to Crete from his wicked and volup-
tuous queen Semiramis, the latter having heard of the manly
beauty of Ara, proposed to marry him or to hold him for a
while as her lover. But Ara scornfully rejected her advances for the sake of his beloved wife Nvard. Incensed by
this unexpected rebuff, the impetuous Semiramis came
against Ara with a large force, not so much to punish him
for his obstinacy as to capture him alive. Ara's army was
routed and he fell dead during the bloody encounter. At
the end of the day, his lifeless body having been found
among the slain, Semiramis removed it to an upper
room of his palace hoping that her gods (the dog-spirits
called *Aralezes*) would restore him to life by licking his
wounds. Although, according to the rationalizing Moses of
Chorene, Ara did not rise from the dead, the circumstances
which he mentions leave no doubt that the original myth
made him come back to life and continue his rule over
the Armenians in peace. For, according to this author,[11]
when Ara's body began to decay, Semiramis dressed up
one of her lovers as Ara and pretended that the gods had
. fulfilled her wishes. She also erected a statue to the gods in
thankfulness for this favor and pacified Armenian minds by
persuading them that Ara was alive.

Another version of the Ara story is to be found at the
end of Plato's *Republic*,[12] where he tells us that a certain
Pamphylian hero called Er, son of Armenius, " happening on
a time to die in battle, when the dead were on the tenth day

carried off, already corrupted, was taken up sound; and being carried home as he was about to be laid on the funeral pile, he revived, and being revived, he told what he saw of the other state." The long eschatological dissertation which follows is probably Thracian or Phrygian, as these peoples were especially noted for their speculations about the future life.

The Pamphylian Er's parentage, as well as the Armenian version of the same story, taken together, make it highly probable that we have here an Armenian (or Phrygian), rather than Pamphylian,[13] myth, although by some queer chance it may have reached Greece from a Pamphylian source. Semiramis may be a popular or learned addition to the myth. But it is quite reasonable to assume that the original story represented the battle as caused by a disappointed woman or goddess. An essential element, preserved by Plato, is the report about life beyond the grave. The Armenian version reminds us strongly of that part of the Gilgamesh epic in which Ishtar appears in the forest of Cedars guarded by Khumbaba to allure Gilgamesh, a hero or demi-god, with attributes of a sun-god, into the rôle of Tammuz. We know how Gilgamesh refused her advances. Eabani, the companion of Gilgamesh, seems to be a first (primæval) *man* who was turning his rugged face towards civilization through the love of a woman. He takes part in the wanderings of Gilgamesh, and fights with him against Ishtar and the heavenly bull sent by Anu to avenge the insulted goddess. Apparently wounded in this struggle Eabani dies. Thereupon Gilgamesh wanders to the world of the dead in search of the plant of life. On his return *he meets with Eabani who has come back from the region of the dead to inform him of the condition of the departed and of the care with which the dead must be buried in order to make life in Aralu (Hades) bearable.*[14]

Possibly the original Ara story goes back to this Babylonian epic but fuses Gilgamesh and Eabani into one hero.

Sayce suggests that Ara may be the Eri of the Vannic inscriptions and the latter may have been a sun-god.[15]

VI. TIGRANES, THE DRAGON–FIGHTER

This story also must be interpreted mythologically, although it is connected with two historical characters. It is a dragon legend which does not contain the slightest fraction of historical fact, but was manifestly adapted to the story of Astyages in the first book of Herodotus. For the sake of brevity we shall not analyse it in detail, as its chief elements will be brought out in the chapter on dragons. The rationalizing zeal of the later Armenian authors has evidently made use of the fact that *Aždahak*, "dragon," was also the name of a famous Median king in the times of Cyrus the Great.[16]

The legend was as follows: Tigranes (from *Tigrish*, "arrow," the old Iranian name of the Babylonian Nabu), King of Armenia, was a friend of Cyrus the Great. His immediate neighbor on the east, Aždahak of Media, was in great fear of both these young rulers. One night in a dream, he saw himself in a strange land near a lofty ice-clad mountain (the Massis). A tall, fair-eyed, red-cheeked woman, clothed in purple and wrapped in an azure veil was sitting on the summit of the higher peak, caught with the pains of travail. Suddenly she gave birth to three full-grown sons, one of whom, bridling a lion, rode westward. The second sat on a zebra and rode northward. But the third one, bridling a dragon, marched against Aždahak of Media and made an onslaught on the idols to which the old king (the dreamer himself) was offering sacrifice and incense. There ensued between the Armenian knight and Astyages a bloody fight with spears, which ended in the overthrow of Aždahak. In the morning, warned by his Magi of a grave and imminent danger from Tigranes, Aždahak decides to marry Tigranuhi, the sister of Tigranes, in

order to use her as an instrument in the destruction of her
brother. His plan succeeds up to the point of disclosing his
intentions to Tigranuhi. Alarmed by these she immediately
puts her brother on his guard. Thereupon the indomitable
Tigranes brings about an encounter with Aždahak in which he
plunges his triangular spear-head into the tyrant's bosom
pulling out with it a part of his lungs.[17] Tigranuhi had already
managed to come to her brother even before the battle.
After this signal victory, Tigranes compels Aždahak's family
to move to Armenia and settle around Massis. These
are the children of the dragon, says the inveterate ration-
alizer, about whom the old songs tell fanciful stories, and
Anush, the mother of dragons, is no one but the first queen
of Aždahak.[18]

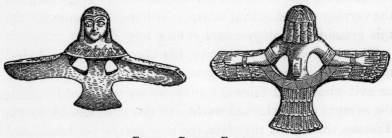

FIG. 3. BRONZE FIGURES

Found in Van usually explained as Semiramis in the form of a dove and
possibly representing the Goddess Sharis, the Urartion Ishtar.

CHAPTER XI

THE WORLD OF SPIRITS AND MONSTERS

THE ARMENIAN world of spirits and monsters teems with elements both native and foreign. Most of the names are of Persian origin, although we do not know how much of this lore came directly from Iran. For we may safely assert that the majority of these uncanny beings bear a general Indo-European, one might even say, universal character. So any attempt to explain them locally, as dim memories of ancient monsters or of conquered and exterminated races will in the long run prove futile. One marked feature of this vital and ever-living branch of mythology is the world-wide uniformity of the fundamental elements. Names, places, forms, combinations may come and go, but the beliefs which underlie the varying versions of the stories remain rigidly constant. On this ground mythology and folklore join hands.

The chief actors in this lower, but very deeply rooted stratum of religion and mythology are serpents and dragons, good or evil ghosts and fairies, among whom we should include the nymphs of the classical world, the elves and kobolds of the Teutons, the *vilas* of the Slavs, the *jinn* and *devs* of Islam, etc.[1]

At this undeveloped stage of comparative folklore it would be rash to posit a common origin for all these multitudinous beings. Yet they show, in their feats and characteristics, many noteworthy interrelations and similarities all over the world.

Leaving aside the difficult question whether serpent-worship precedes and underlies all other religion and mythology, we have cumulative evidence, both ancient and modern, of a world-wide belief that the serpent stands in the closest rela-

PLATE IV

Illuminations from an Armenian Gospel manuscript in the Library of the Kennedy School of Missions, Hartford, Connecticut.

tion to the ghost. The genii, the ancestral spirits, usually appear in the form of a serpent. As serpents they reside in and protect, their old homes. Both the serpent and the ancestral ghost have an interest in the fecundity of the family and the fertility of the fields. They possess superior wisdom, healing power, and dispose of wealth, etc. They do good to those whom they love, harm to those whom they hate. Then these serpents and dragons frequently appear as the physical manifestation of other spirits than ghosts, and so we have a large class of serpent-fairies in all ages and in many parts of the world, like the serpent mother of the Scythian race,[2] and like Melusine, the serpent-wife of Count Raymond of Poitiers (Lusignan). Further, the ghosts, especially the evil ones, have a great affinity with demons. Like demons they harass men with sickness and other disasters. In fact, in the minds of many people, they pass over entirely into the ranks of the demons.

Keeping, then, in mind the fact that, as far back and as far out as our knowledge can reach, the peoples of the world have established sharp distinctions between these various creatures of superstitious imagination, let us run over some of the feats and traits which are ascribed to all or most of them. This will serve as an appropriate introduction to the ancient Armenian material.

They all haunt houses as protectors or persecutors; live in ruins, not because these are ruins, but because they are ancient *sites;* have a liking for difficult haunts like mountains, caves, ravines, forests, stony places; live and roam freely in bodies of water, such as springs, wells, rivers, lakes, seas; possess subterranean palaces, realms and gardens, and dispose of hidden treasures; although they usually externalize themselves as serpents, they have a marked liking for the human shape, in which they often appear. They exhibit human habits, needs, appetites, passions, and organizations. Thus they are born, grow, and die (at least by a violent death). They are hungry and thirsty and have a universal weakness for milk; they often steal grain and go a-hunting. They love and hate, marry and give in marriage. In this, they often prefer the fair sons and daughters of men (especially noble-born ladies), with whom they come to live or whom they carry off to their subterranean abodes. The result of these unions is often — not always — a weird, remarkable, sometimes also very wicked, progeny. They steal human children, leaving change-lings in their stead. They usually (but not always) appear about midnight and disappear before the dawn, which is heralded by cockcrow. They cause insanity by entering the human body. Flint, iron, fire, and lightning, and sometimes also water,[3] are very repugnant to them. They hold the key to magical lore, and in all things have a superior knowledge, usually combined with a very strange credulity. They may claim worship and often sacrifices, animal as well as human.

Although these beings may be classified as corporeal and incorporeal, and even one species may, at least in certain countries, have a corporeal as well as incorporeal variety, it is safe to assert that their corporeality itself is usually of a subtle, airy kind and that the psychical aspect of their being is by far the predominating one. This is true even of the serpent and the dragon. Finally, in one way or another, all of these mysterious or monstrous beings have affinities with chthonic powers.

Largely owing to such common traits running through almost the whole of the material, it is difficult to subject the Armenian data to a clean-cut classification.

I. SHAHAPET OF LOCALITIES

The Shahapet (Iranian *Khshathrapati*, Zd. *Shoithrapaiti*, lord of the field or of the land) is nothing else than the very widely known serpent-ghost (genius) of places, such as fields, woods, mountains, houses, and, especially, graveyards. It appears both as man and as serpent. In connection with houses, the Armenian Shahapet was probably some ancestral ghost which appeared usually as a serpent. Its character was always good except when angered. According to the Armenian translation of John Chrysostom, even the vinestocks and the olive-trees had Shahapets. In Agathangelos Christ Himself was called the Shahapet of graveyards,[4] evidently to contradict or correct a strong belief in the serpent-keeper of the resting place of the dead. We know that, in Hellenistic countries, grave-stones once bore the image of serpents. We have no classical testimony to the Shahapet of homesteads, but modern Armenian folklore, and especially the corrupt forms Shvaz and Shvod, show that the old Shahapet of Armenia was both a keeper of the fields and a keeper of the house. The Shvaz watches over the agricultural products and labours, and appears to men once a year in the spring. The Shvod is a guardian of the house. Even today people scare naughty little children with his name. But the identity of these two is established by a household ceremony which is of far-off kinship to the Roman *paternalia*, itself an old festival of the dead or of ghosts, which was celebrated from February 13 to 21. In this connection Miss Harrison has some remarks " on the reason for the placating of ghosts when the activities of agriculture were about to begin and the powers of the underground world were needed to stimulate fertility." [5] But the Armenians did not placate them with humble worship and offerings: they rather forced them to go to the fields and take part in the agricultural labours. This ancient ceremony in its present form may be described as follows: [6] On the last day of February the Armenian peasants, armed with sticks, bags, old clothes, etc., strike the walls of the houses and barns saying: " Out with the Shvod and in with March! " On the previous night a dish of water was placed on the threshold, because, as we have seen, water is supposed to help the departure of the spirits, an idea also underlying the use of water by the Slavic peoples in their burial rites. Therefore, as soon as the dish is overturned, they close the doors tightly and make the sign of the cross. Evidently, this very old and quaint rite aims at driving the household spirits to the fields, and the pouring out of the water is regarded as a sign of their departure. According to the description in the Pshrank, the Shvods, who are loath to part with their winter comforts, have been seen crying and asking, " What have we done to be driven away in this fashion? " Also they take away clean garments with them and return them soon in a soiled condition, no doubt as a sign of their hard labours in the fields.

The house-serpent brings good luck to the house, and sometimes also gold. So it must be treated very kindly and respectfully. If it departs in anger, there will be in that house endless trouble and privation. Sometimes they appear in the middle of the night as strangers seeking hospitality and it pays to be kind and considerate to them, as otherwise they may depart in anger, leaving behind nothing but sorrow and misfortune.

As there are communal hearths, so there are also district serpents. The serpent-guardian of a district discriminates carefully between strangers and the inhabitants of the district, hurting the former but leaving the latter in peace.[7]

As the Armenian ghost differs little from other ghosts in its manner of acting, we shall refer the reader for a fuller description to the minute account of it given in Abeghian's *Armenischer Volksglaube* (chapters 2 and 6).

II. DRAGONS

The close kinship of the dragon with the serpent has always been recognized. Not only have they usually been thought to be somewhat alike in shape, but they have also many mythical traits in common, such as the dragon's blood, the serpent's or the dragon's stone,[8] the serpent's or the dragon's egg, both of the latter being talismans of great value with which we meet all over the world and in all times. They are corporeal beings, but they have a certain amount of the ghostly and the demoniac in them. Both can be wicked, but in folklore and mythology they are seldom as thoroughly so as in theology. Of the two, the dragon is the more monstrous and demoniac in character, especially associated in the people's minds [9] with evil spirits. He could enter the human body and possess it, causing the victim to whistle. But even he had redeeming qualities, on account of which his name could be adopted by kings and his emblem could wave over armies. In the popular belief of Iran the dragon can not have been such a hopeless reprobate as he appears in the Avestan Aži Dahaka.

Mount Massis, wrongly called Ararat by Europeans, was the main home of the Armenian dragon. The volcanic character of this lofty peak, with its earthquakes, its black smoke and lurid flames in time of eruption, may have suggested its association with that dread monster. But the mountain was sacred independently of dragons, and it was called Azat (i.e., *Yazata* (?), "venerable").

The Armenian for dragon is Vishap, a word of Persian origin meaning "with poisonous saliva." It was an adjective that once qualified Aži Dahaka, but attained an independent existence even in Iran. In the Armenian myths one may plausibly distinguish "the chief dragon" and the dragons, although these would be bound together by family ties; for the dragon breeds and multiplies its kind. The old songs told many a wonderful and mysterious tale about the dragon and the brood or children of the dragon that lived around the Massis. Most of these stories have a close affinity with western fairy tales. Some wicked dragon had carried away a fair princess called Tigranuhi, seemingly with her own consent. Her brother, King Tigranes, a legendary character, slew the dragon with his spear in a single combat and delivered the abducted maiden.[10]

Queen Sathenik, the Albanian wife of King Artaxias, fair and fickle as she was, had been bewitched into a love affair with a certain Argavan who was a chief in the tribe of the dragons. Argavan induced Artaxias himself to partake of a banquet given in his honour in " the palace of the dragons," where he attempted some treacherous deed against his royal guest. The nature of the plot is not stated, but the King must have escaped with his life for he kept his faithless queen and died a natural death.[11]

The dragon (or the children of the dragons) used to steal children and put in their stead a little evil spirit of their own brood, who was always wicked of character. An outstanding victim of this inveterate habit — common to the dragons and Devs of Armenia and their European cousins, the fairies [12] — was Artavasd, son of the above mentioned Artaxias, the friend of Hannibal in exile and the builder of Artaxata. History tells us that Artavasd, during his short life, was perfectly true to the type of his uncanny ancestry, and when he suddenly disappeared by falling down a precipice of the venerable Massis, it was reported that spirits of the mountain or the dragons themselves had caught him up and carried him off.

More important than all these tales, Vahagn, the Armenian god of fire (lightning), won the title of " dragon-reaper " by fighting against dragons like Indra of old. Although the details of these encounters have not come down to us, the dragons in them must have been allied to Vrtra, the spirit of drought.

The epic songs mentioned also Anush, as the wife of the dragon and the mother of the children of the dragon. She lived in the famous ravine in the higher peak of the Massis.

The records as they stand, permit us to conjecture that besides the dragon as such, there was also a race of dragonmen, born of the intermarriage of the dragon with human

wives. But we cannot be very certain of this, although there
would be nothing strange in it, as the history of human beliefs
teems with the " serpent fathers " of remarkable men, and
the character of the Iranian Aži Dahaka himself easily lends
itself to these things. The children of the dragon also,
whether mixed beings or not, dwelt around the Massis and
were regarded as uncanny people with a strong bent towards,
and much skill in, witchcraft.[13]

However it may be about the children of the dragon, it is
incontestable that the dragons themselves were a very real
terror for the ancient Armenians. We are told that they lived
in a wide ravine left by an earthquake on the side of the higher
peak of the Massis. According to Moses, Eznik, and Vahram
Vardapet,[14] they had houses and palaces on high mountains, in
one of which, situated on the Massis, King Artaxias had enjoyed the dangerous banquet we have mentioned.

These dragons were both corporeal and personal beings
with a good supply of keen intelligence and magical power.
They boasted a gigantic size and a terrible voice (Eλishe).
But the people were neither clear nor unanimous about
their real shape. They were usually imagined as great serpents and as sea-monsters, and such enormous beasts of the
land or sea were called dragons, perhaps figuratively. We find
no allusion to their wings, but Eznik says that the Lord pulls
the dragon up " through so-called oxen " in order to save men
from his poisonous breath.[15] The dragons appeared in any
form they chose, but preferably as men and as serpents, like
the jinn of the Arabs. They played antics to obtain their live-
lihood. They loved to suck the milk of the finest cows.[16]
With their beasts of burden or in the guise of mules and
camels they were wont to carry away the best products of the
soil. So the keepers of the threshing floor, after the harvest,
often shouted, " Hold fast! Hold fast! " (*Kal! Kal!*)
probably to induce them to leave the grain by treating them as

guarding genii.[17]   But they carefully avoided saying " Take!
Take! " (*Ar! Ar!*).

The dragons also went hunting just as did the Kaches with
whom we shall presently meet. They were sometimes seen
running in pursuit of the game (Vahram Vardapet) and they
laid traps or nets in the fields for birds. All these things point
to the belief that their fashion of living was like that of men
in a primitive stage of development, a trait which we find also
in western and especially Celtic fairies.

It would seem that the dragons as well as their incorporeal
cousins the Kaches claimed and kept under custody those mor-
tals who had originally belonged to their stock. Thus Artavasd was bound and held captive in a cave of the Massis for
fear that he might break loose and dominate or destroy the
world.[18] Alexander the Great, whose parentage from a serpent or dragon-father was a favorite theme of the eastern
story-mongers, was, according to the mediæval Armenians,
confined by the dragons in a bottle and kept in their mountain
palace at Rome. King Erwand also, whose name, according
to Alishan, means serpent, was held captive by the dragons
in rivers and mist. He must have been a changeling, or rather
born of a serpent-father. For he was a worshipper of Devs
and, according to Moses, the son of a royal princess from an
unknown father. He was proverbially ugly and wicked and
possessed an evil eye under the gaze of which rocks crumbled
to pieces.[19]

Like most peoples of the world, Armenians have always
associated violent meteorological phenomena with the dragon.
This association was very strong in their mind. In a curious
passage in which Eλishe (fifth century) compares the wrath
of Yezdigerd I to a storm, the dragon is in the very centre
of the picture. We need not doubt that this dragon was
related to the foregoing, although ancient testimony on this
subject leaves much to be desired. Eznik's account of the

ascension of the dragon "through so-called oxen" into the
sky, is in perfect accord with the mediæval Armenian accounts
of the "pulling up of the dragon." This process was always
accompanied by thunder, lightning, and heavy showers. Vanakan Vardapet says: "They assert that the Vishap (the dragon)
is being pulled up. The winds blow from different directions
and meet each other. This is a whirlwind. If they do not
overcome each other, they whirl round each other and go
upward. The fools who see this, imagine it to be *the dragon*
or something else." [20]   Another mediæval author says: "The
whirlwind is a wind that goes upward. Wherever there are
abysses or crevasses in the earth, the wind has entered the veins
of the earth and then having found an opening, rushes up
together in a condensed cloud with a great tumult, uprooting
the pine-trees, snatching away rocks and lifting them up noisily
to drop them down again. This is what they call pulling up
the dragon." [21]

Whether the dragon was merely a personification of the
whirlwind, the water spout, and the storm cloud is a hard
question which we are not ready to meet with an affirmative
answer, like Abeghian [22] who follows in this an older school.
Such a simple explanation tries to cover too many diverse phenomena at once and forgets the fundamental fact that the
untutored mind of man sees many spirits at work in nature,
but rarely, if ever, personifies Nature itself. To him those
spirits are very real, numerous, somewhat impersonal and ver-
satile, playing antics now on the earth, now in the skies, and
now under the ground. In the case of the dragon causing
storms, to the Armenian mind the storm seems to be a secondary concomitant of the lifting up of the dragon which threat-
ens to destroy the earth. [23]   Yet, that the original, or at least
the most outstanding dragon-fight was one between the thunder
or lightning-god and the dragon that withholds the waters is
an important point which must not be lost sight of. [24]

We must not forget to mention the worship that the dragon enjoyed. Eznik says that Satan, making the dragon appear appallingly large, constrained men to worship him. This worship was no doubt similar in character to the veneration paid to evil spirits in many lands and perhaps not entirely distinguished from serpent-worship. According to the same writer, at least in Sassanian times even Zrvantists (magians?) indulged in a triennial worship of the devil on the ground that he is evil by will not by nature, and that he may do good or even be converted.[25] But there was nothing regular or prescribed about this act, which was simply dictated by fear. As the black hen and the black cock[26] make their appearance often in general as well as Armenian folk-lore as an acceptable sacrifice to evil spirits, we may reasonably suppose that they had some rôle in the marks of veneration paid to the dragon in ancient times. But we have also more definite testimony in early martyrological writing (*History of St. Hripsimeans*) about dragon worship. The author, after speaking of the cult of fire and water (above quoted) adds: " And two dragons, devilish and black, had fixed their dwelling in the cave of the rock, to which young virgins and innocent youths were sacrificed. The devils, gladdened by these sacrifices and altars, by the sacred fire and spring, produced a wonderful sight with flashes, shakings and leapings. And the deep valley (below) was full of venomous snakes and scorpions."

Finally the myth about the dragon's blood was also known to the Armenians. The so-called " treaty " between Constantine and Tiridates, which is an old but spurious document, says that Constantine presented his Armenian ally with a spear which had been dipped in the dragon's blood. King Arshag, son of Valarshag, also had a spear dipped in the blood of " reptiles " with which he could pierce thick stones.[27] Such arms were supposed to inflict incurable wounds.

III. KACHES

The Kaches form a natural link between the Armenian dragon and the Armenian Devs of the present day. In fact they are probably identical with the popular (not theological) Devs. They are nothing more or less than the European fairies, kobolds, etc. Their name means " the brave ones," which is an old euphemism (like the present day Armenian expression " our betters," or like the Scots " gude folk ") used of the spirit world and designed to placate powerful, irresponsible beings of whose intentions one could never be sure. From the following statements of their habits and feats one may clearly see how the people connected or confused them with the dragons. Our sources are the ancient and mediaeval writers. Unlike the dragon the Kaches were apparently incorporeal beings, spirits, good in themselves, according to the learned David the Philosopher, but often used by God to execute penalties. Like the Devs, they lingered preferably in stony places with which they were usually associated and Mount Massis was one of their favorite haunts. Yet they could be found almost everywhere. The country was full of localities bearing their name and betraying their presence, like the Stone of the Kaches, the Town of the Kaches, the Village of the Kaches, the Field of the Kaches (*Katchavar*, "*where the Kaches coursed*"), etc.[28]

Like the dragons, they had palaces on high sites. According to an old song it was these spirits who carried the wicked Artavazd up the Massis, where he still remains an impatient prisoner. They hold also Alexander the Great in Rome, and King Erwand in rivers and darkness, i.e., mists.[29] They waged wars, which is a frequent feature of serpent and fairy communities, and they went hunting.[30] They stole the grain from the threshing floor and the wine from the wine press. They often found pleasure in beating, dragging, torturing men, just as their brothers and sisters in the West used to pinch their victims black and blue. Men were driven out of their wits through their baleful influence. Votaries of the magical art in mediæval Armenia were wont, somewhat like Faust and his numerous tribe, to gallop off, astride of big earthen jars,[31] to far-off places, and walking on water, they arrived in foreign countries where they laid tables before the gluttonous Kaches and received instructions from them. Last of all, the mediæval Kaches (and probably also their ancestors) were very musical. The people often heard their singing, although we do not know whether their performance was so enthralling as that ascribed to the fairies in the West and to the Greek sirens. However, their modern representatives seem to prefer human music to their own. According to Djvanshir, a historian of the Iberians of Transcaucasia, the wicked Armenian King Erwand built a temple to the Kaches at Dsung, near Akhalka-λak in Iberia (Georgia).

IV. JAVERZAHARSES (NYMPHS)

These are not mentioned in the older writers, so it is not quite clear whether they are a later importation from other countries or not. They probably are female Kaches, and folk-lore knows the latter as their husbands. Alishan, without quoting any authority, says that they wandered in prairies, among pines, and on the banks of rivers. They were invisible beings, endowed with a certain unacquired and imperishable knowledge. They could neither learn anything new nor forget what they knew. They had rational minds which were incapable of development. They loved weddings, singing, tambourines, and rejoicings, so much so, that some of the later ecclesiastical writers confused them as a kind of evil spirits against whose power of temptation divine help must be invoked. In spite of their name (" *perpetual* brides ") they were held to be mortal.[32]   The common people believed that these spirits were especially interested in the welfare, toilette, marriage, and childbirth of maidens.   There are those who have supposed that Moses of Chorene was thinking of these charming spirits when he wrote the following cryptic words: " The rivers having quietly gathered on their borders along the knees (?) of the mountains and the fringes of the fields, the youths wandered as though at the side of maidens."

V. TORCH (OR TORX)

Torch is in name and character related to the Duergar (Zwerge, dwarfs) of Northern Europe and to the Telchins of Greece or rather of Rhodes.[33]   This family of strange names belongs evidently to the Indo-European language, and designated a class of demons of gigantic or dwarfish size, which were believed to possess great skill in all manner of arts and crafts.   They were especially famous as blacksmiths.   In antiquity several mythical works were ascribed to the Greek Telchins, such as the scythe of Cronos and the trident of Poseidon.   They were mischievous, spiteful genii who from time immemorial became somewhat confused with the Cyclops.   The Telchins were called children of the sea and were found only in a *small* number.

The Torch, who can hardly be said to be a later importation from Greece, and probably belongs to a genuine Phrygo-Armenian myth, resembles both the Telchins and the Cyclops. In fact he is a kind of Armenian Polyphemos. He was said to be of the race of Pascham (?) and boasted an ugly face, a gigantic and coarse frame, a flat nose, and deep-sunk and cruel eyes. His home was sought in the west of Armenia most probably in the neighbourhood of the Black Sea. The old epic songs could not extol enough his great physical power and his daring. The feats ascribed to him were more wonderful than those of Samson, Herakles, or even Rustem Sakjik (of Segistān), whose strength was equal to that of one hundred and twenty elephants.[34]

With his bare hands the Armenian Torch could crush a solid piece of hard granite. He could smooth it down into a slab and engrave upon it pictures of eagles and other objects with his finger-nails. He was, therefore, known as a great artisan and even artist.

Once he met with his foes, on the shores of the Black Sea, when he was sore angered by something which they had evidently done to him. At his appearance they took to the sea and succeeded in laying eight leagues between themselves and the terrible giant. But he, nothing daunted by this distance, began to hurl rocks as large as hills at them. Several of the ships were engulfed in the abyss made by these crude projectiles and others were driven off many leagues by the mighty waves the rocks had started rolling.[35]

VI. THE DEVS

Ahriman, the chief of the Devs, was known in Armenia only as a Zoroastrian figure. The Armenians themselves probably called their ruler of the powers of evil, *Char, " the evil one."* Just as Zoroastrianism recognized *zemeka,* " winter," as an arch demon, so the Armenians regarded snow, ice, hail, storms, lightning, darkness, dragons and other beasts, as the creatures of the *Char* or the Devs.[36] Although they knew little of a rigid dualism in the moral world or of a constant warfare between the powers of light and the powers of darkness, they had, besides all the spirits that we have described and others with whom we have not yet met, a very large number of Devs. These are called also *ais* (a cognate of the Sanscrit *asu* and Teutonic *as* or *aes*), which Eznik explains as " breath." Therefore a good part of the Devs were pictured as beings of " air." They had, like the Mohammedan angels, a subtile body. They were male and female, and lived in marital relations not only with each other, but often also with human beings.[37] They were born and perhaps died. Nor did they live in a state of irresponsible anarchy, but they were, so to speak, organized under the absolute rule of a monarch. In dreams they often assumed the form of wild beasts [38] in order to frighten men. But they appeared also in waking hours both as human beings and as serpents.[39]

Stony places, no doubt also ruins, were their favorite haunts, and from such the most daring men would shrink. Once when an Armenian noble was challenging a Persian viceroy of royal blood to ride forward on a stony ground, the Prince retorted: " Go thou forward, seeing that the Devs alone can course in stony places." [40]

Yet according to a later magical text, there can be nothing in which a Dev may not reside and work. Swoons and insanity, yawning and stretching, sneezing, and itching around the throat or ear or on the tongue, were unmistakable signs of their detested presence. But men were not entirely helpless against the Devs. Whoever would frequently cut the air or strike suspicious spots with a stick or sword, or even keep these terrible weapons near him while sleeping, could feel quite secure from their endless molestations.[41] Of course, we must distinguish between the popular Dev, who is a comparatively foolish and often harmless giant, and the theological Dev, who is a pernicious and ever harmful spirit laying snares on the path of man. To the latter belonged, no doubt, the Družes (the Avestic Drujes), perfidious, lying, and lewd female spirits. Their Avestic mode of self-propagation, by tempting men in their dreams,[42] is not entirely unknown to the Armenians. They probably formed a class by themselves like the Pariks [43] (Zoroastrian *Pairikas*, enchantresses), who also were pernicious female spirits, although the common people did not quite know whether they were Devs or monsters.[44] These, too, were mostly to be sought and found in ruins.[45]

VII. ALS

The most gruesome tribe of this demoniac world was that of the Als. It came to the Armenians either through the Syrians or through the Persians, who also believe in them and hold them to be demons of child-birth.[46] Al is the Babylonian *Alu*, one of the four general names for evil spirits. But the Armenian and Persian Al corresponds somewhat to the Jewish Lilith and Greek Lamia.

Probably the Als were known to the ancient Armenians, but it is a noteworthy fact that we do not hear about them until mediæval times. They appear as half-animal and half-human beings, shaggy and bristly. They are male and female and have a " mother." [47] They were often called beasts, nevertheless they were usually mentioned with Devs and Kaches. According to Gregory of Datev [48] they lived in watery, damp and sandy places, but they did not despise corners in houses and stables. A prayer against the Als describes them as impure spirits with fiery eyes, holding a pair of iron scissors in their hands, wandering or sitting in sandy places. Another unnamed author describes an Al as a man sitting on the sand. He has snake-like hair, finger-nails of brass, teeth of iron and the tusk of a boar. They have a king living in abysses, whom they serve, and who is chained and sprinkled up to the neck with (molten?) lead and shrieks continually.

The Als were formerly disease-demons who somehow came to restrict their baleful activities to unborn children and their mothers. They attack the latter in child-birth, scorching her ears, pulling out her liver and strangling her along with the unborn babe. They also steal unborn children of seven months, at which time these are supposed in the East to be fully

PLATE V

Thepta, a variety of Al. From *Alishan's Ancient Faith of Armenia*.

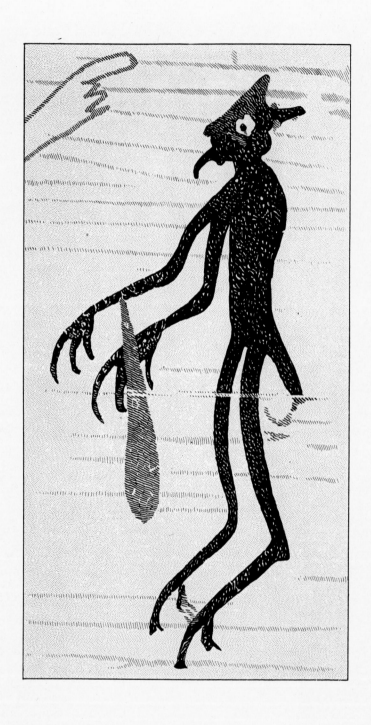

formed and mature, in order to take them "deaf and dumb" (as a tribute?) to their dread king.[49]   In other passages they are said to blight and blind the unborn child, to suck its brain and blood, to eat its flesh, and to cause miscarriage, as well as to prevent the flow of the mother's milk.   In all countries women in child-bed are thought to be greatly exposed to the influence and activity of evil spirits.   Therefore, in Armenia, they are surrounded during travail with iron weapons and instruments with which the air of their room and the waters of some neighbouring brook (where these spirits are supposed to reside) are frequently beaten.[50]   If, after giving birth to the child, the mother faints, this is construed as a sign of the Al's presence. In such cases the people sometimes resort to an extreme means of saving the mother, which consists in exposing the child on a flat roof as a peace-offering to the evil spirits.[51]   Identical or at least very closely connected with the Al is Thepla, who by sitting upon a woman in child-bed causes the child to become black and faint and to die.[52]

VIII. NHANGS

These monster spirits, at least in Armenian mythology, stand close to the dragons.   The word means in Persian, "crocodile," and the language has usually held to this matter-of-fact sense, although in the Persian folk-tale of Hātim Tāī, the Nhang appears in the semi-mythical character of a sea-monster, which is extremely large and which is afraid of the crab.   The Armenian translators of the Bible use the word in the sense of "crocodile" and "hippopotamus."   However, the Nhangs of Armenian mythology, which has confused an unfamiliar river monster with mythical beings, were personal[53] and incorporeal.   They were evil spirits which had fixed their abode in certain places and assiduously applied themselves to working harm.   They sometimes appeared as women (mermaids?) in the rivers. At other times they became seals (*phok*) and, catching the swimmer by the feet, dragged him to the bottom of the stream, where, perhaps, they had dwellings like the fairies.[54] In a geography (still in MS.) ascribed to Moses, the Nhangs are said to have been observed in the river Araçani (Murad Chay?) and in the Euphrates. After using an animal called *charchasham* for their lust, vampire-like they sucked its blood and left it dead. The same author reports that, according to some, the Nhang was a beast, and according to others, a Dev. John Chrysostom (in the Armenian translations) describes the daughter of Herodias as more bloodthirsty than "the Nhangs of the sea."[55]

IX. ARLEZ (ALSO ARALEZ, JARALEZ)

Ancient Armenians believed that when a brave man fell in battle or by the hand of a treacherous foe, spirits called "Arlez" descended to restore him to life by licking his wounds. In the Ara myth, these spirits are called the gods of Semiramis; also in a true and realistic story of the fourth century about the murder of Mushegh Mamigonian, the commander of the Armenian king's forces.[56] "His family could not believe in his death . . . others expected him to rise; so they sewed the head upon the body and they placed him upon a tower, saying, 'Because he was a brave man, the Arlez will descend and raise him.'" Presumably their name is Armenian, and means "lappers of brave men," or "lappers of *Ara*,"[57] or even "ever-lappers." They were invisible spirits, but they were derived from dogs.[58] No one ever saw them. Evidently the dogs from which they were supposed to have descended were ordinary dogs, with blood and flesh, for Eznik wonders how beings of a higher spiritual order could be related to bodily creatures. The Arlez were imagined to exist in animal form as dogs.[59]

X. OTHER SPIRITS AND CHIMERAS

The Armenians believed also in the existence of chimeras by the name of *Hambaris* or *Hambarus*, *Jushkapariks* (Vushkapariks), Pais, and sea-bulls, all of which are manifestly of Persian provenience. Yet the nature and habits of these beings are hidden in confusion and mystery.

The Hambarus are born and die. They appear to men assuming perhaps different forms like the Devs and Pasviks. They are probably feminine beings with a body, living on land and particularly, in desert places or ruins. Von Stackelberg thinks that the word *Hambaruna* means in Persian, " house-spirits." This is possibly justified by the shorter form, *Anbar*, which may convey the sense of the falling of a house or wall; so the original Hambaru may be interpreted as a ghostly inhabitant of a deserted place. The word may also mean " beautiful " or even " a hyena." An old Armenian dictionary defines it as *Chartho*λ (?) if it lives on land, and as " crocodile," if it lives in water. But the oldest authorities, like the Armenian version of the Bible and Eznik, consider the Hambarus as mythological beings. Threatening Babylon with utter destruction Isaiah (Armenian version, xiii. 21–22) says, " There shall the wild beasts rest and their houses shall be filled with shrieks. There shall the Hambarus take their abode and the Devs shall dance there. The Jushkapariks shall dwell therein and the porcupines shall give birth to their little ones in their palaces." Hambaru here and elsewhere is used to render the σειρήν (siren) of the Septuagint.[60]

Another chimerical being was the Jushkaparik or Vushkaparik, the Ass-Pairika, an indubitably Persian conception about which the Persian sources leave us in the lurch. Its name would indicate a half-demoniac and half-animal being, or a Pairika (a female Dev with amorous propensities) that appeared in the form of an ass and lived in ruins. However

Eznik and the ancient translators of the Bible use the word through a hardly justifiable approximation to translate Ὀνοκένταυρος, the ass-bull of the Septuagint (Isaiah xiii. 22, xxxiv. 11, 14). According to Vahram Vardapet (quoted by Alishan) the Jushkaparik was imagined, in the middle ages, as a being that was half-man and half-ass, with a mouth of brass. Thus it came nearer the conception of a centaur, which word it served to translate in Moses of Khoren's history. Sometimes also to make the confusion more confounded, it is found in the sense of a siren and as a synonym of Hambaru.

We are completely in the dark in regard to the *Pais* which boasted human parenthood (presumably human mothers). There were those in Eznik's time who asserted that they had seen the Pais with their own eyes. The old Armenians spoke also of the Man-Pai.[61] The Pais seem to be a variety of the Pariks.

The case is not so hopeless with the sea-bull, a chimerical monster which propagated its kind through the cow, somewhat after the manner of the sea-horses of Sinbad the Sailor's first voyage. Men asserted that in their village the sea-bull assaulted cows and that they often heard his roaring. We can well imagine that immediately after birth, the brood of the monster betook themselves to the water, like the sea-colts of the Arabian Nights' story which we have just mentioned.[62] But this sea-bull may also recall the one which Poseidon sent to Minos for a sacrifice and which was by the wise king unwisely diverted from its original purpose and conveyed to his herds, or the one which, on the request of Theseus, Poseidon sent to destroy Theseus' innocent son, Hippolytus.

Another such chimeric monster, but surely not the last of the long list, was the elephant-goat (*phlachal*).[63]

CHAPTER XII

COSMOGONY, DEATH, AND ESCHATOLOGY

NOTHING certain of the old Armenian cosmogony has survived and we may well doubt they had any, seeing that a definite cosmogony is not an integral part of Indo-European mythology. The early Christian writers, as Agathangelos and Eznik, often explain how God established the earth on " nothing," which they call the Syrian view. They maintain this against those who, according to the more general Semitic (Biblical etc.) view, teach that the earth was founded on a watery abyss. Only in modern Armenian folklore do we hear about the primæval ox or bull upon whose horns the world was set and which causes earthquakes by shaking his head whenever he feels any irritation.[1] Agathangelos conceives the heavens as a solid cube hanging on nothing, and the earth " compactly formed and provided with a thick bottom, standing on nothing." For all the Armenian authors the earth stands firm and is practically the whole of the world. The star-spangled heaven upon which transparent spheres were sometimes supposed to be revolving, was of little consequence.

Whether the early Armenians had a distinct cosmogony or not we find that in the Zoroastrian stage of their religion, they held the world and all that is therein to be the work of Aramazd, who, by Agathangelos, is plainly called the creator of heaven and earth. The invisible world for them was thickly populated with occult powers, gods, angels (*Hreshtak*, from the Persian *firishtak*, " messenger "), spirits, demons and demoniac monsters of many kinds. Human life, its events and end, were predestined either by divine decrees (*Hraman*,

Pers. *Farman*) which were unchangeable and unerring, or through their mysterious connection with stars, constellations, and the zodiacal signs. We do not know positively, but it is very likely, that the stars were thought to be the *fravashi* (double, the external soul or self) of human beings. In modern folklore whenever a shooting star drops, a human being dies. In a word, the old Armenians were thorough-going fatalists. This view of life was so deeply rooted, and proved so pernicious in its effects, that the early Christian writers strenuously endeavored to destroy it by arguments both theological and practical.

Man was composed of a body (*marmin*) and a soul (*hogi* or *shunch*, "breath," ψυχή). *Uru*, the Iranian *urva*, may have originally been used also in the sense of soul, but it finally came to mean a phantom or a ghostly appearance. Ghosts were called *urvakan*, i.e., ghostly creatures. That these spirits received a certain kind of worship is undeniably attested by the old word *urvapast*, "ghost-worshippers," applied by Agathangelos to the heathen Armenians. The linguistic evidence shows that originally the soul was nothing more than "breath," although this conception was gradually modified into something more personal and substantial. It was never called a "shade," but in Christian times it was closely associated with light, a view which has a Zoroastrian tinge. Death was the separation or rather extraction of the soul — a more or less subtle material, from the body, through the mouth. This has always been conceived as a painful process, perhaps owing to the belief that the soul is spread through the whole body. The "soul-taking" angel and the "writer"[2] are nowadays the principal actors in this last and greatest tragedy of human life. After death the soul remains in the neighbourhood of the corpse until burial has taken place. The lifeless body usually inspires awe and fear. It is quickly washed and shrouded, and before and after this, candles and incense burn in the death-room, perhaps not so much to show the way to the disembodied and confused soul (Abeghian) as to protect the dead against evil influences. They may also be a remnant of ancestor-worship, as the Saturday afternoon candles and incense are.   Death in a home necessitates the renewal of the fire, as the presence of the dead body pollutes the old one.   In ancient times the weeping over the dead had a particularly violent character.   All the kinsmen hastened to gather around the deceased man.   The dirge-mothers, a class of hired women, raised the dirge and sang his praises.   The nearest relatives wept bitterly, tore their hair, cut their faces and arms, bared and beat their chests, shrieked and reproached the departed friend for the distress that he had caused by his decease.   It is very probable that they cut also their long flowing hair as a sign of mourning, just as the monks, who, technically speaking, are spiritual mourners ($abe\lambda a$, from the Syriac $abh\bar{\imath}l\bar{a}$), did, at the very beginning of their taking the ecclesiastical orders.   The dead were carried to their graves upon a bier.   We have no mention whatever of cremation among the Armenians.   On the open grave of kings and other grandees a large number of servants and women committed suicide, as happened at the death of Artaxias, to the great displeasure of his ungrateful son, Artavasd.   The fortified city of Ani in Daranaλi contained the mausoleums of the Armenian kings.   These were once opened by the Scythians, who either expected to find great treasures in them or intended by this barbarous method to force a battle with the retreating natives.[3]

The hankering of the spirits for their ancient home and their " wander-lust " are well known to the Armenians.   The many prayers and wishes for the " rest " of the departed soul, as well as the multitudinous funeral meals and food-offerings to the dead, show the great anxiety with which they endeavored to keep the soul in the grave.   The gravestones were often made in the form of horses and lambs, which perhaps symbolized the customary sacrifices for the dead, and even now they often have holes upon them to receive food and drink offerings. Even the rice-soup in which the *pitaras* (ancestral souls) of the ancient Indians (Hindus) delighted is recalled by the present of rice which in some localities friends bring to the bereaved house on the day following the burial.

Like the Letts, Thracians, Greeks, and many other peoples, the Armenians also passed from a wild sorrow to a wilder joy in their funeral rites. This is proved by the boisterous revels of ancient times around the open grave, when men and women, facing each other, danced and clapped hands, to a music which was produced by horns, harps, and a violin.[4] There was and is still a regular funeral feast in many places.[5]

It is very difficult to give a clear and consistent description of the Armenian beliefs in regard to life after death. There can be no doubt that they believed in immortality. But originally, just as in Greece and other lands, no attempt was made to harmonize divergent and even contradictory views, and contact with Zoroastrianism introduced new elements of confusion. The ordinary Armenian word for grave is *gerezman*, which is nothing else but the Avestic *garo-nmana*, " house of praise," i.e., the heavenly paradise as the place of eternal light, and as the happy abode of Ahura Mazda.[6] The use of this important word by the Armenians for the grave may be simply a euphemism, but it may also be expressive of an older belief in happiness enjoyed or torture suffered by the soul in the grave, very much like the foretaste of paradise or hell which is allotted to the Mohammedan dead, according to their deserts. If this be the case, the departed soul's main residence is the grave itself in the neighbourhood of the body. This body itself is greatly exposed to the attack of evil spirits.

There are also marked traces of a belief in a Hades. The Iranian Spenta Armaiti (later Spentaramet), " the genius of the earth," occurs in Armenian in the corrupt form of Santara-

met and only in the sense of Hades or Hell. The Santaramet-
akans are the dwellers in Santaramet, i.e. the evil spirits. Even
the Avesta betrays its knowledge of some such older and popular usage when it speaks of the " darkness of Spenta Armaiti." [7] The earth contained Hades, and the spirit of the
earth is naturally the ruler of it. Nor is this a singular phenomenon, for the earth goddesses and the vegetation gods in
Western Asia and in the Graeco-Roman world have this indispensable relation to the underworld. Demeter the Black of
Arcadia, or her daughter and duplicate, Persephone, forms the
reverse side of Demeter, the beautiful and generous. Sabazios
(Dionysos) in the Thracian world was also an underworld ruler
(as Zalmoxis?). The Armenian language possesses also the
word *ouydn* as the name of the ruler of Hades. This is
clearly Aidonœus, or Hades. But it is difficult to ascertain
whether it is an Armenized form or a cognate of these Greek
names.

Another word which the Armenian Old Testament constantly uses in the sense of Hades is *Džokh,* from the Persian
Duzakh, used for Hell. However, as the Christian expression
gayank, " station," came into use for the place where, according
to the ancient Fathers of the church, the souls gather and wait
in a semi-conscious condition for the day of judgment, both
Santaramet and Džokh became designations of Hell, if indeed
this had not already happened in heathen times.

There is some uncertainty in regard to the location of Hades.
It may be sought inside the earth at the bottom of or, perhaps,
below the grave. But, on the other hand, a saying of Eznik
about the wicked who have turned their faces towards the West,
although directly alluding to the location of the Christian Hell
and devils, may very well be understood also of the pagan
Hades. For we know that Hell is a further development of
Hades, and that the Babylonians, the Greeks, and the Egyptians all sought Hades, sometimes in the earth, but more usu-

ally in the West. For all of them the setting sun shone upon the world of the dead. And we have already seen how a bit of modern Armenian folklore calls the setting sun, " the portion of the dead." [8] The life led in the grave or in Hades, however sad and shadowy, was held to be very much like the present. The dead needed food, servants, etc., as the food offerings as well as the compulsory or voluntary suicides at the graves of kings clearly show.

The Armenian accounts of the end of the world are based directly upon the Persian. First of all, the people knew and told a popular Persian story about Aždahak Byrasp (Aždahak with the 10,000 horses). According to this version Aždahak Byrasp was the ancestor of the first ruler of the Persians. He was a communist and a lover of publicity. For him nothing belonged to any one in particular and everything must be done in public. So he began his career with a perfidious but ostentatious goodness. Later he gave himself to astrology and he was taught magic by a familiar (?) evil spirit, who kissed his shoulders, thus producing dragons on them, or changing Aždahak himself into a dragon. Now Aždahak developed an inordinate appetite for human flesh and for spreading the lie. Finally Hruden (Thraetona, Feridun) conquered and bound him with chains of brass. While he was conducting him to Mount Damāvand, Hruden fell asleep and allowed Aždahak to drag him up the mountain. When he awoke he led Aždahak into a cave before which he stood as a barrier preventing the monster from coming out to destroy the world. [9]

But both among the Armenians and among their northern neighbours, there arose local versions of this Zoroastrian myth, in which the traditional Aždahak yielded his place to native heroes of wickedness and the traditional mountain was changed into Massis and Alburz. In old Armenia the dreaded monster was Artavazd, the changeling son of King Artaxias. At the burial of his father, when a multitude of servants and wives and concubines committed suicide (or were slain?) on the grave, the ungrateful and unfeeling son complained and said: " Lo!   Thou hast gone and taken the whole Kingdom with thee.   Shall I now rule over ruins? "   Angered by this reproach, Artaxias made answer from the grave and said:

> When thou goest a-hunting
> Up the venerable Massis
> May the Kaches seize thee
> And take thee up the venerable Massis.
> There mayst thou abide and never see the light.

In fact, shortly after his accession to the throne, when he went out to hunt wild boars and wild asses, he became dizzy and falling with his horse down a precipice, disappeared. The people told about him that he was chained in a cave of Massis with iron fetters which were constantly gnawed at by two dogs. When they are broken he will come out to rule over the world or to destroy it.   But the noise of the blacksmith's hammer on the anvil strengthens those chains; therefore, even in Christian times, on Sundays and festival days, the blacksmiths struck their hammers on the anvil a few times, hoping thereby to prevent Artavazd from unexpectedly breaking loose upon the world.   *31326*

It is also worth noting that the story about the serpents standing upon the shoulders of Aždahak and teaching him divination was told in Greek Mythology, of the blind Melampos and possibly of Cassandra and her clairvoyant sister, while the Armenians of the fourth century of our era asserted it of the wicked King Pap, whose fame for magic had reached even the Greek world.

Any story about a catastrophic end of the world may reasonably be followed by the description of a last judgment and of a new heaven and a new earth.   But unfortunately the old records completely break down on this point.   The old Armenian knows the Persian word *ristaxez*, " resurrection," as a proper name (*Aristakes*). Modern Armenian folk-lore has a vivid picture of the *činvat*-bridge which it calls the hair-bridge.[10] There is the word " kingdom " for the heavenly paradise which is called also *drakht* (from the Persian *dirakht*, " tree "). The picture lacked neither fire nor Devs for the torments of the evil doers, while Santaramet and Džokh, once meaning Hades, had also acquired the meaning of Hell. But out of these broken and uncertain hints we cannot produce a connected picture of the Armenian conception of the events which would take place when the world came to an end. Christian eschatology, thanks to its great resemblance to the Zoroastrian, must have absorbed the native stories on this subject. However, as a branch of the Thracian race, the Armenians must have had a strong belief in immortality and brought with them a clear and elaborate account of the future world such as we find in Plato's myth of Er.[11]

AFRICAN MYTHOLOGY

BY

ALICE WERNER

Sometime Scholar and Fellow of Newnham College, Cambridge
Professor of Swahili and Bantu Languages, University of London

To E. T. C. W.

PEKING

Go, little Book, and pass to Kambalu
Greet him who dwells beside the Peaceful Gate,
Hard by the sheep-mart, in the ancient town.
May Peace be his, and happy springs renew
Earth's beauty, marred by foolish strife and hate: —
On his fair garth sweet dews glide gently down.

He loves the ancient lore of Chou and Han
And eke the science of the farthest West;
High thought he broods on ever — yet maybe
He will not grudge an idle hour, to scan
These childlike dreams — these gropings for the Best
Of simple men beyond the Indian sea.

AUTHOR'S PREFACE

THERE may perhaps be an impression in the minds of most readers that Africa, with its practically unwritten languages and comparatively undeveloped religious ideas, can have little or nothing which can properly be described as mythology, or at any rate that the existing material is too scanty to justify a volume on the subject.

I must confess that, until I actually undertook the work, I had no conception of the enormous amount of material that is in fact available — a great deal of it in German periodicals not always readily accessible. The limitations of time, space, and human faculties have prevented my making full use of these materials: I can only hope to supply clues which other investigators may follow up if I cannot do so. I intend, however, should I live long enough, to work out in detail some of the subjects here presented in a very imperfect sketch — for instance, the distribution of the Chameleon-myth in Africa; the "Exchanges" story (fresh material having come to hand since I wrote the article in the *African Monthly*, 1911); the Swallower-myth as exemplified in Kholumolumo of the Basuto and its various African modifications; and several others.

I have not attempted to state any theories or to work out comparisons with any folklore outside Africa, though here and there obvious parallels have suggested themselves. Any approaches to theorising — such as the occasional protests I have felt compelled to make against the assumption that similarity necessarily implies borrowing — must be regarded as merely tentative.

Since completing the chapter on the "Origin of Death," I have found among my papers a Duruma Chameleon-story (kindly supplied to me in MS., with interlinear translations into Swahili, by Mr. A. C. Hollis), which is so interesting that I may perhaps be excused for inserting it here. The Duruma are one of the so-called "Nyika" tribes living inland from Mombasa, neighboured on the east by the Rabai and on the southwest (more or less) by the Digo: they have not been very fully studied up to the present. The legend is as follows:

When man was first made, the Chameleon and the Lizard (*dzonzoko* or *gae* — called in the Swahili translation *mjusika-firi*) were asked their views about his ultimate fate. The Chameleon answered: " I should like all the people to live and not to die," while the dzonzoko said: " I wish all people to die." The matter was settled by the two running a race, a stool (*chiti*) being set up as the goal; the one who reached it first was to have his desire granted. As might be expected, the Lizard won, and ever since, the Chameleon walks slowly and softly, grieving because he could not save men from death.

The mention of the stool is curious, because it affords a point of contact with a Chameleon-story of a widely different type, current both in East and West Africa, but hitherto, so far as I am aware, not much noticed by folklorists. It seems to be an independent form of the idea contained in the well-known Hare and Tortoise race. Pre-eminence among the animals is to be decided by a race to a stool (the chief's seat of honour): the Dog thinks he has won, but the Chameleon gets in first by clinging to his tail and leaping in front of him at the last moment. Of course this folklore tale has, so far as one can see, nothing to do with the older myth.

The author desires to express her most cordial thanks to all who have contributed to the embellishment of this volume: in the first place to Miss Alice Woodward for her beautiful drawings; then to Messrs. E. Torday, P. Amaury Talbot, and F. W. H. Migeod, for the use of original photographs; and to the Clarendon Press for permitting the reproduction of plates from *Bushman Paintings* copied by Miss M. H. Tongue.

ALICE WERNER

School of Oriental Studies
London, January 23, 1922

INTRODUCTION

TO TREAT the mythology of a whole continent is a task not to be lightly undertaken. In the case of Africa, however, there are certain features which make the enterprise less formidable than it would be if directed elsewhere. The uniformity of Africa has become a commonplace with some writers; and, indeed, when we compare its almost unbroken coast-line and huge, undifferentiated tracts of plain or table-land, with Europe and Asia, we cannot picture it as divided into countries occupied by separate nations. This feeling is intensified, if we confine our view to Africa south of the Sahara, as we shall practically have to do for the purposes of this book, which omits from consideration both Egypt and (except for incidental references) the Islamised culture of the Barbary States. Broadly speaking, the whole of this area (which we might describe as a triangle surmounted by the irregular band extending from Cape Verde to Cape Guardafui) is occupied by the black race, and as, to the casual European, all black faces are as much alike as the faces of a flock of sheep, it is a natural inference that their characters are the same. The shepherd, of course, knows better; so does the white man who has lived long enough among " black " people (comparatively few are black in the literal sense) to discriminate between the individual and the type.[1] But, in any case, the inhabitants, even of the limited Africa we are taking for our province, are not all of one kind. We have not only the black Africans, but the tall, light-complexioned Galla, Somali, and Fula, with their Hamitic speech, the Hottentots, whose Hamitic affinities, suspected by Moffat, have been strikingly demonstrated in recent years, the little yellow Bushmen, who are probably responsible for the non-Hamitic elements in the Hottentots, and others. Moreover, there is a very distinct cleavage of speech — though not, perhaps, of race, among the black Africans themselves: between the monosyllabic, uninflected languages of the Gold Coast and the upper Nile, and the symmetrically-developed grammatical structure of the Bantu tongues. And, even taking the Bantu by themselves, we may expect to find great local differences. As the late Heli Chatelain remarked, speaking of a writer who has not greatly advanced the cause of research:

" The material on which he worked consisted of but a few volumes on South African tribes, and he often fell into the common error of predicating of the whole race, the Bantu, and even of all Africans, what he had found to hold true in several South African tribes. To this habit of unwarranted generalisation must be attributed, very largely, the distressing inaccuracy and the contradictory statements with which books and articles on Africa are replete." [2]

At the same time, a study of African folk-lore extending over many years has gradually produced the conviction that both sections of the African race, the Bantu-speaking and the Sudanic, have many ideas, customs and beliefs in common. Some of these may be due to independent development,[3] others to recent borrowing, but there is a great deal which, I feel certain, can only be accounted for by some original community of thought and practice. This will appear, over and over again, in connection with various stories which we shall have to discuss. But this is not all. We shall find that both Negro and Bantu have some elements in common with Galla, Masai, and other Hamitic or quasi-Hamitic peoples (I here leave out of account matter demonstrably introduced by Arabs or Europeans at a more recent date); and some very interesting problems of diffusion are connected with tales originating, perhaps, in the Mediterranean basin and carried to the extreme south of the continent by the nomad herdsmen whom Van Riebeek found in possession at the Cape of Good Hope. The Hausa, whose linguistic and racial affinities have long been a puzzle, have evidently been influenced from both sides — the black aboriginal tribes from whom they are in great part descended, and the pastoral Hamitic immigrants.

Here let me remark in passing that I use the word " aboriginal " in a purely relative sense and without intending to express any opinion on this point. Neither shall I attempt to deal with the vexed question of race. What really constitutes " race " is by no means clear to me, nor, I imagine, can the experts agree on a definition. Whether there is any real distinction of race between Bantu-speaking and other (Sudanic) Negroes,[4] I very much doubt, and, in any case, the problem lies outside our present scope.

As suggesting a common fund of primitive ideas in widely separated parts of the continent, let us take the case of the Zulu word *inkata* and the thing denoted by it. The word is also found in Nyanja as *nkata*, in Swahili *khata* (with aspirated *k*), in Chwana as *khare* (*kχare*), in Herero as *ongata*, and in similar or cognate forms elsewhere. Its original meaning seems to be a " coil " or " twist "; but it generally stands for the twisted pad of grass or leaves used by people who carry heavy loads on the head. But the Zulu *inkata* has another and more recondite meaning. The *inkata yezwe* (" coil of the country ") or *inkata yomuzi* (" coil of the clan ") is both " a symbol of unity and federation of the people "[5] and an actual talisman to ensure the same, together with the personal safety of the chief. It is a large twist or cushion of grass, impregnated with powerful " medicines " and made with special ceremonies by professional " doctors " (*izinnyanga*), on which the chief, at his installation, has to stand. At other times it is kept, carefully hidden from view, in the hut of the chief wife. I do not know whether the *inkata*

PLATE VII

A Somali, member of a typically Hamitic tribe,
who inhabit the " Eastern Horn of Africa." After
a photograph by Dr. Aders.

has everywhere the same ritual significance: I strongly suspect that, where such is not recorded, it has either become obsolete or escaped the notice of inquirers, as — belonging to the most intimate and sacred customs of the people — it would be quite likely to do. But, in Uganda, *enkata* means, not only the porter's head-pad, but the topmost of the grass rings forming the framework of the house and supporting the thatch. This " was of equal importance with the foundation of a brick house," [6] and, in building the house of the King's first wife — the Kadulubare — had to be put in position with special cere- monies. Now, we find that, on the Gold Coast, where the head-pad is called *ekar* in Tŵi, it has some ritual connection with the succession to the chieftainship, while it (or something representing it) figures in some curious magical ceremonies of the Ibibio (Calabar), described by the late Mrs. Amaury Talbot.[7]

Some other facts, interesting in this connection, will come in more fittingly when considering the numerous animal-stories of the " Uncle Remus " type, which are found in these areas.

Whether one studies Africa geographically, ethnologically, or psychologically, one feels the absence of definite frontiers more and more acutely as one goes on. We can recognize Abyssinia or Basutoland as a separate country, just like Switzer- land or Denmark; but such cases are infrequent, and this ap- plies even more strongly to thought, belief and custom, than to physical configuration. Hence I have been forced to give up as hopeless the geographical or " regional " treatment of the subject, and shall attempt, instead, to trace a few main groups and ideas through the different strata of which the African population is made up.

It will make clearer what I have been trying to say, if we picture these strata, not as regular, superimposed beds of hard stone, but as composed of different coloured sands, spread in successive layers, some of each penetrating those below and the lighter particles of the lower beds working up into the higher at every jar or disturbance. And here we come back to our starting-point. With all the diversity to be found in Africa, on which, as we have seen, it is necessary to insist, there is some indefinable quality inherent in the whole of it, as though the continent imparted its own colour and flavor to whatever enters it from the outside. The white man who has grown up among the Zulus very quickly feels at home with Yaos or Giryama, though he may know nothing of their language; and there is always a certain community of feeling between " old Africans," in whatever part of the continent their experiences may have lain.

Without wasting time in speculation on the past, we may now briefly survey the state of things as known at present. In the main, the area we have mapped out, from the Cape of Good Hope to Lake Victoria, and thence eastward to the Tana River and westward to the Cameroons, is occupied by Bantu-speaking tribes. North of these, the peoples of " Negro," " Sudanic," or " Nigritian " speech extend in an irregular band from Cape Verde to the confines of Abyssinia, even to some extent penetrating the latter. The " Eastern Horn," which ends in Cape Guardafui, is inhabited by the Hamitic Somali, while their kinsmen the Galla, and other tribes, probably more or less allied to them (Samburu, Rendile, Turkana, Nandi), spread out to the north, west, and south, their fringes touching on the areas of Bantu and Negro tribes — Pokomo, Kikuyu, Kavirondo, and others.

But these areas are not completely uniform. In South Africa we have two non-Bantu elements, though both are now almost negligible except within a very limited area. The Bushmen, who would seem to have been the oldest inhabitants, are now practically confined to the Kalahari Desert and the adjacent regions, though a few (who have quite lost all memory of their own language and traditions) are to be found scattered

about the Cape Province and Orange Free State. If they are
the Troglodytes alluded to by Herodotus, whose speech was
" like the squeaking of bats," they must either have at one time
overspread the greater part of the continent, or migrated
southward from the Sahara within historic times. The
wretched Troglodytes were hunted with chariots by the Gara-
mantes, and I remember being told of a Natal farmer (by one
of his own relatives) that he used to talk cheerfully of having
shot a Bushman or two before breakfast. Here is at least one
additional point of resemblance.

The treatment of the South African Bushmen by the colonists is one of the most disgraceful pages in Colonial history.
Particulars may be found in G. W. Stow's *Native Races of
South Africa* — it is no part of our plan to give them here;
but there is another point of which we must not lose sight.
To speak of " extermination " in connection with the Bushmen,
though only too true as regards a limited area of South Africa,
is somewhat misleading when we come to survey a larger extent of the continent. In the earlier stages of the Bantu migra-
tion into South Africa, the relations between the Bushmen and
the newcomers appear to have been friendly, and intermarriage frequently took place. There is reason to think that some
Bechwana tribes — e.g. the Leghoya, are largely of Bushman
descent; and the same probably applies to large sections of the
Anyanja, in the districts west of the Shire. The importance of
this point will appear when we have to come back to it in the
chapter on Creation-Legends.

Whether the Bushmen have anything beyond their small
stature and their mode of life, in common with the Pygmies
of the Congo basin and other small races known or reported
to exist in various parts of Africa, remains, at least, doubtful;
but anatomists, I believe, hold that their physical evolution has
proceeded on entirely different lines. Both, in any case, are
interesting, not only as living representatives of a prehistoric

age, but because, like a similar early population of Europe, of whom the Lapps may be a surviving remnant, they have given rise, as we shall see, to a great deal of mythology.

We have already referred to the people whom we are accustomed to call "Hottentots" — their own name for themselves, when speaking of the whole people and not of any particular tribe (e.g. Nama, Kora), appears to be Khoi-Khoin — "men," *par excellence*. Many Hottentot tribes have disappeared, not by actual dying out, but through losing their language and corporate identity and becoming merged in the mixed "coloured"[8] population, who speak only "Cape Dutch" and a corresponding form of English. The Colonial records show that, in the 17th century, they were a numerous and flourishing people; and the researches of Meinhof and others prove that their speech belongs to the Hamitic stock, though it has assimilated the Bushman clicks and perhaps other peculiarities.

In Struck's language-map,[9] the green Bantu ground is diversified, in the Eastern Equatorial region, by a large irregular yellow patch. This denotes the Masai, a nomad, pastoral people, lighter-coloured than the average Bantu, though darker than the pure Galla or Somali. At one time they were spread over seven or eight degrees of latitude — say from Mount Elgon in the north nearly to the Usambara hills in the south; but they have now, in the East African Protectorate, been confined to a reservation. The most probable theory of their language is, that it is Hamitic by origin (which would account for its possessing gender-inflection), but has been strongly influenced by contact with Bantu and Sudanic idioms (*angenegert* is Meinhof's expression). The contact between their legends and those of the Hottentots is one of the most interesting facts which have come to light in recent years.

Besides these, we have to do, in East Africa, with some curious "helot" tribes — not exactly outcasts, though that designation might apply to some of them, but vassals or dependents of stronger tribes who seem both to dread and to despise them. Such are the Dorobo among the Masai, the Wasanye among the Galla, the Midgan and Yibir in Somaliland. These are commonly hunters and have, in some ways, much in common with the South African Bushmen, though their physique differs widely from that of the latter, as we now know them. Their origin is still a matter of debate; but they are most probably connected with certain "outcast" tribes still existing in Abyssinia. The Wasanye and Dorobo formerly had languages of their own, which a few old men still know, but the former now speak Galla and the latter Masai. The Wasanye and the Yibir and some, at any rate, of the rest, have an uncanny reputation as sorcerers, and some of these helot tribes, e.g. the Tumal and the Il-kunono,[10] are blacksmiths. We cannot help being reminded of our own Gypsies and tinkers. The latter are — or were till recently — distinct by race as well as by occupation, and long preserved a language of their own, ascertained to be a prehistoric dialect of Celtic.

Lastly, for we take no account of modern intruders, such as Arabs and Europeans, we have, in Abyssinia, a Semitic people who entered Africa at some unknown period — early as compared with the Arabs, but late, if we look back on the millenniums of ancient Egyptian history. They share with the Copts of Egypt the distinction of being the only Christians in Africa whose existence is not due to European missions established since the sixteenth century.

As this book deals with mythology and not with comparative religion, it would be out of place to discuss at length the distribution and possible origin of the "High God" idea, which undoubtedly occurs in Africa and has been the subject of much heated controversy. I need only refer to the works of the late Andrew Lang, Pater Schmidt, Sir J. G. Frazer and others. Here it is enough to say that, in various parts, we do come across the more or less vague notion of a Supreme Being who is, so far as one can see, neither a personified Nature-Power nor a glorified ancestral ghost. Such may be Nyankupong of the Gold Coast tribes, Nzambi of the Congo and adjacent regions, Leza, Chiuta and Mulungu in Nyasaland, Ngai of the Masai, and Wak of the Galla. But some of these are very difficult to discriminate from the sun, or the sky, or the first ancestor of the tribe; and experience seems to show that different notions are entertained by different individuals among the same people, or that the higher conception may have developed out of the lower. We shall see in the next chapter that it is by no means clear whether the Galla think of Wak as a Personal God or as the sky; that the name Mulungu is sometimes used for the spirits of the dead; and that while some Zulus spoke of Unkulunkulu in terms which suggest a vague Theism, others distinctly said that he was the first man, though no cult was paid him as an *idhlozi* (ancestral spirit), because he had lived so long ago that none could directly trace their descent from him.

Bruno Gutmann, who has written some very interesting books on the Wachaga of Kilimanjaro, and clearly knows them well, insists that their deity, Ruwa, is not identical with the sun (*i-ruwa*), though called by the same name. But many of the customs and legends recorded by him certainly imply some connection.

While, therefore, it seems desirable to devote a chapter apiece to " High Gods," " Ancestral Ghosts," and " Nature-Spirits," we cannot undertake to keep these three classes of beings as separate as strict logic would require.

The High God is not always — perhaps we might say, not often — thought of as a Creator in our sense. Even when he is spoken of as making man, the inanimate world seems to be taken for granted as already in existence; sometimes all animals are felt to need accounting for, sometimes only the domestic

PLATE VIII

Types of the Wasanye "helot" hunting tribe, Malindi District, Kenya Colony. After a photograph by Prof. A. Werner.

ones — cattle, sheep and goats. But the Deity does not always make man, who is sometimes described as appearing on the earth quite independently of him — in fact, one legend introduces him as inquiring where these new creatures have come from. (This same story, from Nyasaland, speaks of the animals, in contradistinction from man, as " Mulungu's people," apparently implying that he made them.) Very often, the progenitors of the human race issue, by a kind of spontaneous generation, from a reed-bed, a tree, a rock, or a hole in the ground.

The numerous myths which attempt to account for the origin of Death are frequently — but not always — connected with a High God. We also sometimes find Death personified under various names — e.g. in Angola as Kalunga, which elsewhere is one of the names for God. The Baganda call Death Walumbe, and make him a son of Heaven (Gulu). The interesting legend of his admission into this world will be told in our third chapter.

But it is the Ancestral Ghosts, the *amadhlozi* of the Zulus, who may be called the central factor in Bantu religion. The same thing is largely true of the non-Bantu populations, and the ghost-cult probably coexists with and underlies the more highly developed religions, with comparatively elaborate mythologies, which we find, e.g., on the Gold Coast, and which, on a superficial view, would seem to deal mainly with nature-spirits. But here, again, it is extraordinarily difficult to draw the line. A nature-god may easily have started as the spirit of a dead man, like those " old gods of the land " who were worshipped by the Yaos along with their own ancestors and came to be looked on as the *genii loci* of particular hills, but were really former chiefs of the Anyanja who had been buried on those hill-tops. Similarly, in Uganda, Roscoe says: " The principal gods appear to have been at one time human beings, noted for their skill and bravery, who were afterwards deified by the people." In the case of such men, as of the Nyasaland chiefs just mentioned, the worship would extend beyond their own immediate relatives, to the whole clan or tribe, and this would in time help to obscure their original status. But the principle is the same. Without committing ourselves unreservedly to the Spencerian view that all religions have their roots in the feelings — whether of awe, dread, or affection — aroused by the ghosts of the dead, we can at least be certain that many religious and mythological conceptions can be traced to this origin.

The habitation of the ghosts is supposed to be underground, in a region sometimes conceived of as a replica of the upper world. This is called, in many Bantu languages, *Ku-zimu*, which has the same root as one of the commonest among the many different names applied to the ghosts.[11] Earthquakes are often said to be caused by the movements of these subterranean hosts. We shall see that stories of people who have penetrated into this mysterious country and returned — or failed to return — are not uncommon. Among these are numerous variants of the tale called, in Grimm's collection, " Frau Holle," which originally referred to the land of the Dead, though most European versions have lost sight of the fact.

Only the most recent ghosts are individualised, so to speak; it is quite natural that all earlier than the grandfather, or, at most, the great-grandfather, should fade into a vague collectivity: perhaps this is one reason why, in most typical Bantu languages, the word for " ghost " is not a personal noun. Some Yaos have explained " Mulungu " as the sum of all the spirits, " a spirit formed by adding all the departed spirits together " — another illustration of the way in which different conceptions overlap and tend to melt into one another. But this rule is not without exceptions, for we come across heroes or demi-gods — and some beings who have to be classed with

them, though they can scarcely lay claim to either appellation
— who may possibly be personified nature-powers, but are more
probably men known or imagined to have lived a long time ago.
Whether they actually existed or not, matters little to our
present purpose; but it is in many cases demonstrable that they
are conceived of as human beings whose eminent services to
their fellows or conspicuous qualities of whatever kind lifted
them, after death, out of the common ruck of ghosts. Such
are Haitsi-aibeb of the Hottentots, Hubeane of the Bechwana,
Mrile of the Wachaga, Sudika-bambi in Angola — perhaps
we might also count Kintu of Uganda. Closely connected with
this part of our subject is the world-wide myth of the Hero-
Deliverer, who rescues mankind (or as much of it as was
known to the original narrators) from the stomach of a monster
which has swallowed it.[12] Several very interesting forms of
this are current in Africa. In some of them, the people's
ingratitude leads them to plan the hero's death; and the cleverness with which their various expedients are baffled forms a
link with another group of tales, exhibiting the Hero as
Trickster. To this group belong the adventures of Hubeane.

We have seen that some gods are personified nature-powers:
the sky, the sun, also rain, lightning, and thunder. Other
things, too, without precisely ranking as gods, are recognized
as personalities and sometimes have rites performed in their
honor — the moon, certain stars, the rainbow. Then there are
mountain-spirits (some of these, however, as we saw just now,
were originally ancestral ghosts), river-spirits, tree-spirits, and
a number of queer, uncanny beings who cannot be classed
under these or any similar headings, but are called by Meinhof " haunting-demons " (*Spukdämonen*).[13] These haunt
lonely places — the deep shade of the forests, or the sun-
baked steppe-country with its weird clumps of thorny bush.
There is a considerable variety of these, and the traveller may
often hear minutely circumstantial, sometimes even first-hand,

accounts of them. But we shall find, as we go on, ample proof, if any were needed, that the mythopœic faculty is still emphatically a living thing in Africa.

Partly connected with these last are the " Little People " — Abatwa, Itowi, Maithoachiana, etc. — really the Bushmen or Pygmy aborigines whom the immigrant Bantu found in occupation of the country and thought so uncanny, with their strange speech, their poisoned arrows, and their proficiency in arts unknown to the more civilized newcomers, that they easily credited them with preter-human powers, while they at the same time detested and despised them.[14] Hence, while we shall have plenty to say about the myths and traditions of the real Bushmen, we shall also have to consider them in the light of purely fabulous beings. Among such demons and monsters the Izimu (Irimu) has such a conspicuous position in Bantu folk-lore that it has seemed advisable to devote a chapter to him.

We have already mentioned the animal-stories which form so large a part of African folk-lore. These, no doubt, sprang from totemism — or rather, they originated in that stage of human life and thought which produced totemism. This, where it exists in Africa, has mostly passed into a state of survival: among the clearest cases seem to be those of the Bechuana, the Nandi, the Baganda, and the Twi (Gold Coast). But besides the general fact of these tales being products of the totemistic attitude of mind, we have a number of particular instances which plainly involve the theory of the totem. Thus there is a well-known legend of the Gold Coast[15] relating how a Chama man married a woman who was really a transformed *bonito*, and their descendants to this day abstain from eating that fish. There is another point of interest about the story: the husband (like Undine's) ultimately loses his wife through the infringement of a tabu. This or some similar catastrophe occurs in a great many tales, both Bantu and Sudanic, and may, in some cases, be connected with totemism.

The animals figuring most prominently in African folk-lore are the Hare, the Tortoise, the Spider, the little Dorcatherium antelope, the Jackal, the Chameleon, the Elephant, the Lion and the Hyena, with many others which are either less frequently met with or play less conspicuous parts.

Transformations of men into animals and *vice versa* are common incidents in folklore and are believed in as actual occurrences at the present day. Were-hyenas, were-leopards and similar creatures lead us on to the subject of Witchcraft, without which no survey of African mythology would be complete.

Finally, while I have tried to confine myself to what is genuinely African, and therefore to rule out, as far as possible, all European and Arab importations, there are some recent products of the myth-making instinct, indirectly, if not directly, due to outside influence, which deserve attention as interesting phenomena in themselves. I must say I do not know what to make of the very curious story from the Tana Valley which I give in the last chapter: I let it stand as communicated to me. Others, while coloured by Moslem ideas, are yet, in their way, genuine products of the soil. Worth notice too, is the very ancient infiltration of Arab, Persian, or Indian ideas, which have become grafted on to and intertwined with the elements of indigenous folklore, and appear in the most unexpected places. This might be laid hold of as an argument by those — if any still exist — who think that all tales must have been diffused from one common centre; but in my view the process has been largely helped on by antecedent coincidences. Thus we find a Jâtaka story at Zanzibar in which the Hare plays a part not found in the original, and almost certainly added after its introduction into Africa. Then Abu Nawâs, the jester of Bagdad, has become immensely popular all down the East Coast of Africa, where his adventures are related, not only in Swahili, but even in Ronga at Delagoa

Bay. But as you go south, you find that his real personality becomes obscured, and " banawasi " is used as a common noun, meaning a clever trickster, or even as a synonym for the Hare, with whom he is apt to get mixed up.

Having thus sketched out our programme, we may return to our starting-point and enter on the consideration of African High Gods.

AFRICAN MYTHOLOGY

CHAPTER I

HIGH GODS AND HEAVEN

IT HAS been denied that such a conception as that of a "High God" exists in Africa, except where introduced by missionaries. The late Major Ellis,[1] finding the name Nyankopong in use on the Gold Coast and supposed to denote such a being, came to the conclusion that he was "really a god borrowed from Europeans and only thinly disguised." Mr. R. S. Rattray,[2] on the other hand, is "absolutely convinced" that this is not the case, one of his reasons being that the name occurs in sayings "known to the *old* Ashanti men and women, and strange or unknown among the *young* and civilized community." The names (O)nyame, (O)nyankopong and several others "are used by the Ashantis to designate some power generally considered non-anthropomorphic, which has its abode in the sky (which by metonymy is sometimes called after it)."

The High God is often, if not always, believed to live in the sky,— a point to which we shall come back later. But it is often difficult to make out whether the people conceive of him as distinct from the actual sky, and in the case of the Galla who told me the legend about Wak (to be given in Chapter III), I found it quite impossible.

The story told about Nyankopong which, Mr. Rattray says, is "universally known among the older people," is very curious, because it seems to suggest that, in an older stage of thought, Nyankopong may have been the actual sky. Moreover, I cannot help thinking (though Mr. Rattray does not notice this) that in its original form this myth was an attempt to explain how Heaven and Earth came to be separated, they having been at first (as the Polynesians also believe) in close contact. There are traces of this myth elsewhere, as in the belief of the Giryama [3] that all things proceeded from the marriage of Heaven and Earth, or in the Herero legend recorded by Irle,[4] which we shall refer to again in the next chapter. But here Heaven is said to have been close to the Earth after a great flood — it is not stated whether this had always been so or was a consequence of the deluge, nor is it clear whether they were actually in contact and needing to be separated; the great anxiety of the Ovakuru (ancestral spirits) seems to have been lest men should climb into Heaven. This may possibly — though Irle thinks the flood story is a genuine native one — be an echo of missionary teaching. Otherwise, the conception in its crude form does not appear to be common in Africa, but Mr. Dennett thinks the idea of the Heaven-Father and the Earth-Mother underlies the ancient religion of the Congo people.[5]

This is the Ashanti myth above referred to, literally translated by Mr. Rattray: [6] "Long, long ago, Onyankopong lived on earth, or at least was very near to us. Now there was a certain old woman who used to pound her *fufu* (mashed yams, etc.), and the pestle used constantly to knock up against Onyankopong (who was not then high up in the sky). So Onyankopong said to the old woman, 'Why do you always do so to me? Because of what you are doing, I am going to take myself away up into the sky.' And of a truth he did so. . . . But now, since people could no longer approach near to Onyankopong, that old woman told her children to search for all the mortars they could find and bring them, and pile one on top of another, till they reached to where Onyankopong was. And so her children did so and piled up many mortars, one on top of another, till there remained but one to

PLATE IX

1. The Baobab at Kurawa, the sacred tree of the Galla.
2. Galla huts at Kurawa.
After photographs by Prof. A. Werner.

reach to Onyankopong. Now, since they could not get the one required anywhere, their grandmother — that is, the old woman — told her children saying: ' Take one out from the bottom and put it on top to make them reach.' So her children removed a single one, and all rolled and fell to the ground, causing the death of many people."

This incident, of the High God retreating into the sky after sojourning for a time on earth, recurs in many different parts of Africa. Sometimes, but not always, the reason given is the wickedness of mankind. The Bushongo of the Kasai country [7] have a High God, Bumba, who, after completing the creation, prescribing tabus to mankind, and appointing rulers over them, retired to Heaven, and thenceforth only communicated his will, from time to time, in dreams and visions.

It is by no means always the case that the High God is also the Creator; we shall return to Bumba in the following chapter.

The name Jambi is used by some divisions of the same people, and various forms of this name are widely distributed through the south-western part of Africa. The Herero speak of Ndyambi Karunga [8] as distinct from the ancestral ghosts,— " he is in heaven above and not in the graves." Nzambi is, in Angola,[9] " the name of one great, invisible God, who made all things and controls all things. . . . Tradition says men have offended him, and he has withdrawn his affection from them." Among the Lower Congo people, Nzambi Mpungu means " what we should call the Creator," [10] but Nzambi-si is the Earth-Mother. Nzambi Mpungu is described in Fiote mythology as " a human being — a naked man." But this, in Mr. Dennett's opinion, is an idea of late growth, suggested by the crucifixes and religious pictures imported by Romanist missionaries.[11]

Mulungu is a name which, in several easily-recognisable cognate forms, can be traced from the Tana to Mozambique.

From the Yaos (to whom, perhaps, it originally belonged), it has spread eastward to the Anyanja and other tribes, wholly or partly superseding the names of Mpambe, Chiuta, and Leza. Leza (Reza, Rezha, etc.) belongs to a group of tribes in the centre of the continent — the Luba, Bemba, Subiya, Ila, and several others. Leza is sometimes identified with the lightning or the rain; but Mr. E. W. Smith [12] says of the Baila: " it is not plain that they regard rain and God as one and the same. . . . Leza is closely identified with nature, but, as Lubumba, the Creator, he is above nature, and, as Chilenga, he is regarded as the grand institutor of custom."

The Anyanja call the rainbow *Uta wa Leza*, " the Bow of Leza."

Mulungu is a name with several perplexing connotations. The Rev. Duff Macdonald [13] and Dr. Hetherwick [14] have both discussed the subject at some length. Certainly, as used by some natives, it seems to express the idea of a High God dwelling in the heavens. I have myself heard a native woman say of the thunder, *Mulungu anena* — " Mulungu is speaking "; and on two occasions, persons who had recently died were said to have " gone to Mulungu." In Nyasaland I never heard any expressions indicating that Mulungu might be the actual sky; but I did once hear it said that the offerings made to the manes of a deceased chief were " for Mulungu."

I find, however, that the Giryama have the word, and with them its primary meaning seems to be the sky, though it is also used in the sense of " God."

It does not seem possible that Mulungu can be, as Bleek [15] thought, the same word as the Zulu Unkulunkulu: the latter is admittedly derived from the root *kulu*, which I cannot by any process of sound-shifting, get out of Mulungu, even with the help of the Mulungulu from Inhambane [16] on which Bleek relied. I fail to find any later authority for this word, which is presumably meant to be Chopi — the nearest one gets to it in any recent books is Nungungulu. On the other hand, Mulungu is clearly the same as the Zulu *umlungu*, which, whatever may have been its original sense, now means " a white man," and no doubt indicates that the first Europeans were taken for supernatural beings. It may be worth noticing that the languages which use the word in this sense do not possess " Mulungu " as a divine name. This is the case with the Baronga of Delagoa Bay, who, however, believe that certain small apparitions called *Balungwana* (plural diminutive of *Mulungu*) sometimes descend from the sky during thunderstorms.[17] These same people use the word *Tilo*, " heaven," to mean, not merely the visible sky but "a spiritual principle which plays a considerable part in the religious conceptions of the tribe." [18] Heaven is thought of as a place: one woman said to M. Junod: " Before you came to teach us that there is an All-Good Being, a Father in Heaven, we already knew there was a Heaven, but we did not know there was any one in it." [19] Another convert, however, said: " Our fathers all believed that life existed in Heaven." But, adds M. Junod:[20] " *Tilo* is something more than a place. It is a power which acts and manifests itself in various ways. It is sometimes called *hosi* (' chief ' or ' lord ') . . . but is generally regarded as something entirely impersonal." They say: " It is Heaven which kills and makes alive." It is associated with cosmic phenomena, especially such as are more or less abnormal and unexpected, such as storms and lightning; with the birth of twins, which is held to be something out of the course of nature; and with convulsions in infants — I suppose because these seizures are sudden and unaccountable. The complaint is hence called *tilo*, and, curiously enough, the Swahili call it " the bird," believing it to be caused by an owl, that universal bird of ill-omen. The idea of the sky as a place accessible to human beings enters into many folk-tales, and we shall recur to it later on.

We have mentioned the name of Unkulunkulu as used by
the Zulus. It sometimes appears to denote a Spiritual Power
and, like Mulungu, has been adopted by native Christians as
the word for " God."   Some natives, however, have quite
distinctly stated that Unkulunkulu was the first man, though
not reckoned as one of the *amadhlozi*, because he died so long
ago that no one now living can trace his descent from him.
We find that many " First Ancestors " are in a similar position
and, conversely, that many " High Gods," if one comes to examine them at close quarters, are really the progenitors of the
human race (at any rate that part of it to which the narrators
belong — these myths do not often concern themselves with
anything more), or at least of their royal line.   The ghost of
a great chief, who is not the direct ancestor of the whole tribe
and who is associated, through his grave, with some prominent
landmark of the country, is a step nearer to godship than that
of a common man.

The Bapedi and Bavenda of North Transvaal have a " god,"
Ribimbi, who was also the first man, and his son Khudjana is
said to have made the world; while the same probably applies
to Nwali or Nyali of the Banyai.[21]   Some tribes in East Africa
give the name of their divinity as *Were*,[22] and it seems to me
by no means improbable that here we have a point of contact
with Vere, the Pokomo ancestor whose story will be related in
the next chapter.

As to Unkulunkulu, we find Bishop Callaway's [23] native
informants saying that " he came out first, he is the *uhlanga* [24]
from which all men broke off. . . . The old men say . . .
he made the first men, the ancients of long ago. . . . What
I have heard is this, that men sprang from Unkulunkulu, as
if he made them because he existed before them."

He is distinguished from " the King which is above "
(*inkosi e pezulu*), who would seem to be identical with the
Thonga *Tilo;* for, of the latter, " we say, he is above, Unku-

lunkulu is beneath; the things which are beneath were made by him." This fits in with the idea that the abode of the dead is under the earth. It is unnecessary to pursue this subject further, as it belongs rather to the domain of Comparative Religion than to that of Mythology; and the principal myth connected with Unkulunkulu — that of the Chameleon — will find a more appropriate place in the chapter on the " Origin of Death."

Imana of the Warundi [25] is similarly envisaged as the Supreme Being, the ancestor of the race and the Chief of the Ancestral Spirits (*umukuru y'imizimu*).

The difficulty, not to say impossibility, of laying down hard and fast definitions, is illustrated in the case of Mukasa, said to hold the highest rank among the gods of Uganda,[26] though he is neither the Creator nor the First Man. He has a father and grandfather among the gods, but neither of these is Katonda, the Creator, nor Gulu, " Heaven," who figures so conspicuously in the story of Kintu, the First Man, as we shall see in our next chapter. In fact, we hear curiously little about Katonda, and Gulu, though said to " command the elements," has nothing like the importance of Mukasa — at any rate in the officially recognised religion.[27] Dr. Roscoe thinks it " certain that he was a human being who, because of his benevolence, came to be regarded as a god." We do not learn whether any Baganda at the present day trace their descent from him. His legend represents him as appearing in a fully peopled world, whereas Kintu found it uninhabited, so that we should have to suppose him long posterior to the latter, if logical consistency went for anything in mythology. Mukasa had temples over all Uganda, and these, with the exception of the principal temple, on Bubembe Island, contained a canoe-paddle as his " sacred emblem." " No one knows for certain what was there; some say it was a large meteoric stone turned first to the east and then to the west according to the phases of the moon." Neither of these objects is alluded to in the story told of Mukasa, nor can I find any explanation of their meaning in connection with him.

Mukasa is said to have been the son of Musisi,[28] the god who causes earthquakes, though elsewhere his father is called Wanema. His mother, presumably a mortal, belonged to the Lung-fish clan: her name was Nambubi. Before the birth of Mukasa, she refused all food but ripe plantains of a special kind; how this affected the child is not very clear, since we are told that, when he was weaned he would eat nothing but the heart and liver of animals, and drank their blood. At a very tender age, he disappeared from his home and was found by the people of Bubembe sitting under a large tree on their island. They built him a house and appointed a man named Semagumba — whose descendants or representatives were down to our own day the priests of the Bubembe temple — to look after him. Some say that, after living there for fourteen generations, he died and was buried in the forest; others that he disappeared as he had come. The most noteworthy fact about his cult is that, unlike many other gods of the Baganda, he did not require human sacrifices.

Whether or not the High God is consciously identified with the material Heaven, we constantly find him conceived as dwelling there. This material sky, of course, is a solid vault, above which is a country much like this familiar earth of ours. The Thonga [29] call the point where heaven touches the earth " *bugimamusi* . . . viz., the place where women can lean their pestles (which elsewhere must be propped against a wall or tree) against the vault." Sometimes it is called " The place where women pound mealies kneeling . . . they cannot stand erect, or their pestles would strike against the sky." Men have frequently attempted to scale this vault without success, as we saw in the legend of Onyankopong: it seems as if all collective efforts had been foredoomed to failure; but individuals have occasionally been more fortunate. The idea seems a very natural one in the childhood of the world: the sky, which seems so near and yet is so inaccessible, even if we travel to the farthest limit of our horizon where it seems to touch the earth, would be one of the first things to draw the questioning mind of man beyond his immediate surroundings. The early school of mythologists, coming upon such tales, might have inferred either a " Primitive Revelation " — or rather, tradition — or an infiltration of European influence which would have introduced echoes of the Tower of Babel story, perhaps even of the classical Giant legends. There is, after all, a connection, though not precisely of the kind early mythologists supposed: all these tales alike have their roots in a Primitive Revelation — a universal instinct of the human heart.

There is a remarkable group of tales describing the adventures of human beings who (like Jack of the Bean-Stalk) have made their way into the sky; but before going on to examine these we must note the fact that, in a number of instances, the High God who now dwells in the sky is said to have retired thither after a more or less prolonged sojourn on earth. This may have been the case with Mukasa, though we are not expressly told that he disappeared to heaven, nor do we know the reason for his disappearance.

The Mbundu people, says Chatelain,[30] " believe in one great, invisible God, who made all things and controls all things. But they confess they know very little about His character. Tradition says men have offended Him, and He has withdrawn His affection from them." True, this does not speak of an actual withdrawal from earth to heaven, but probably some older tradition of the kind underlies the statement.

The Bushongo [31] say that Bumba, the Creator, whom they also call Chembe (= Jambi = Nzambi = Nyambe), after completing his work, prescribed tabus (I think it would not be too much to say, " assigned their totems ") to men, appointed three chiefs over them (from the first and greatest of whom the Bushongo Paramount Chief traces his descent), and then rose into the air and disappeared. Thenceforward he only communicated with men by revealing himself in dreams, and no real worship is paid to him. It may be noted that some tribes have a much more abstract and immaterial conception of him than others, who regard him as a " magnified " and (to some extent) " non-natural man."

Here no blame is assigned to any one for Bumba's disappearance. It is otherwise on the Zambezi,[32] where the Baluyi say that Nyambe once lived on earth, but afterwards ascended into the sky " for fear of men." No explanation, however, is given of this statement, and it does not seem to be borne out by another account, which is as follows: " When Nyambe lived on earth, people said that he had fallen from the sky. When he returned thither, he climbed up by means of a spider's thread. When he was up on high, he said: ' Worship me.' Men, seeing him act like this (offended by what they considered his pride), said: ' Let us kill Nyambe.' He escaped into heaven. . . . They planted long poles in the earth and fixed others on top of them. . . . When they had climbed to a great height, the posts fell, and the men who had climbed up on them were killed."

The Basubiya,[33] however, who call their High God Leza, while they say he went up to heaven by a spider's thread, give no reason for his so doing, unless we are to connect a previous remark, that " men were very much afraid of him," with his action. Some tried to follow him up by the same route, but the thread broke and they came down. So they put out the spider's eyes — an ætiological myth to account for the supposed fact that he has none at the present day. Then they set up a scaffolding with the same result as in the case of the Baluyi. It would almost seem as if their purpose, like that of the

PLATE X.

Some Bantu Types

1. A woman of the Basuto.

2. Zulu Girls.

PLATE X

Ashantis, had been to bring Leza back, for the narrator goes on to say: " They had formerly lived with Leza under a great tree, and here they performed their worship (after his departure?); they used to bring thither great numbers of goats and sheep so that Leza might have food. . . . One day, Leza met a man under this tree and said to him, ' Where do you come from? ' The man answered, ' I am bringing four goats.' Leza said to him, ' Go back to the village and say, " Leza says: when you see a great cloud of dust, you will know that it is Leza." ' One day they saw a column of dust which was followed by a great hurricane. The people gathered in the place of assembly. Leza arrived and stood under a tree, and they heard him say, ' You must pay honour to my house (as representing me?). As for me, you will never see me again — I am going away now.' "

Still, when people see shooting stars, they utter cries and say that it is their chief, Leza, who is coming to see how his children on earth are getting on. If this refers to human beings, we have a hint of the " All-Father "; and, in fact, the Wankonde [34] (at the north end of Lake Nyasa) address their Supreme God, Mbamba or Kiara, as " Father." Mbamba is of human form, " white and shining," and he, too, lives " above the sky." Some kind of worship is paid to Leza by the Basubiya, but M. Jacottet thinks this — or most of it — is really directed to the ancestors, while Leza (or Nyambe) most probably represents the sun. The Baluyi expressly assert this of Nyambe,[35] and they are in the habit of saluting the rising sun with shouts of, " Mangwe! Mangwe! our king! " But the same people may think of him sometimes as the one, sometimes as the other; and it is not difficult to believe that the " All-Father " idea might have grown out of either — or both — of these notions.

The Yao myth of Mulungu [36] is in many ways very suggestive. " At first there were not people, but God and beasts."

Later on, the beasts are repeatedly called "Mulungu's people," as though some special relation existed between them and him; yet he is not said to have made them. The Chameleon, who seems to have been in the habit of setting fish-traps — like the local population to-day — one morning found a man and woman in one of these. He took them to Mulungu who "was staying down here before he went away to heaven," and who was as much perplexed by the strange creatures as he, but advised him to " place them there, they will grow," and " man then grew, both the male and female." All the beasts and birds were called together to look at them, but they too had nothing to say. The next day the new beings were seen making fire by drilling with a stick; they then killed a buffalo which they cooked and ate. " And they kept eating all the beasts in this way," and finally set the Bush on fire as well. " Again Mulungu came, saying, ' Chameleon, I told you that you introduced puzzling beings on the earth here. See now, my people are finished. Now, how shall I act? ' They actually saw the bush at their verandah burning with fire," and had to run for it. " The Chameleon ran for a tree. Mulungu was on the ground, and he said ' I cannot climb a tree! ' Then Mulungu set off and went to call the Spider. The Spider went on high and returned again, and said, ' I have gone on high nicely. You, now, Mulungu, go on high.' Mulungu then went with the Spider on high. And he said, ' When they die, let them come on high here.' "

That is, as the narrator explains, men are to go and be slaves to God "because they ate his people here below." In other words, Mulungu was driven from the earth because of man's cruelty to the animals.

One cannot help thinking — though of course the cases are in no way parallel — of the account given to Mr. Orpen [37] by Qing of the Bushman god Cagn: " Cagn made all things and we pray to him. At first he was very good and nice, *but he got spoilt through fighting so many things. . . .* We do not know where he is, but the elands know. Have you not hunted and heard his cry when the elands suddenly run to his call? " And the prayer to him is, " O Cagn, O Cagn, are we not your children? Do you not see our hunger? Give us food! " There is something very beautiful about this, and it is not surprising that it should have inspired one of Andrew Lang's finest sonnets.

It seems pretty well established that Cagn (| kággen in Dr. Bleek's orthography) was originally the Mantis and therefore possibly a totem-god, but *cela n'empêche pas,* as we shall so often have occasion to notice. There is nothing to prevent the higher conception growing out of the lower.

The Spider's agency is noteworthy because, wherever he appears in Bantu folklore (except in some Duala tales), it is in this capacity of intermediary between heaven and earth — a very different character from the crafty and malignant Anansi of the Gold Coast. In a Congo story he brings down the heavenly fire, with the help of the Tortoise, the Woodpecker, the Rat and the Sand-fly: all have a share in carrying out the enterprise, but it is the Spider who takes them up to the sky.[38]

The idea of a rope by which one could climb up to heaven, whether originally suggested or not by the spider swinging his thread, is found in a very old Zulu saying quoted by Callaway:[39] " Who can plait a rope for ascending, that he may go to heaven? "

This seems to imply that the thing is utterly impossible, yet we find King Senzangakona (Tshaka's father) credited with this very feat in an *isibongo,* which tells how he escaped in this way from the (presumably hostile) " spirits of the house of Mageba."

An old Thonga chant [40] expresses the same hopeless longing: " Ah! if I had but a rope! I would go up to the heavens and be at rest! "

Thonga warriors used to shout to their enemies before a battle: " Get ready your ropes and climb up to heaven! " meaning, of course, " there is no other way by which you can escape us." In a story given by Junod under the title " La Route du Ciel," [41] a young girl who fears her mother's anger is described as " going away and climbing a rope to get to heaven," as if this were the most natural proceeding in the world.

The same object is sometimes attained by climbing a tree. In the Zulu tale of " The Girl and the Cannibals," [42] a brother and sister, escaping from these *amazimu*, climbed a tree and " saw a very beautiful country. They found a very beautiful house there; that house was green, and the floor was burnished. . . . But the earth they saw was at a great distance below them; they were no longer able to go down to it, for they feared the cannibals, thinking they saw them going about on the earth and seeking for food." They found cattle and, it would seem, everything else that they wanted; they slaughtered an ox, ate the meat and made the hide into a rope, with which they drew up one of the cannibals — either fearing he might obstruct their return to earth, or simply for the sake of revenge, and " did him in " in the most callous fashion. They subsequently returned home by means of the rope.

The Wakonyingo — dwarfs or elves supposed to live on the top of Kilimanjaro — are said by the Wachaga to have ladders by which they can reach the sky from the summit. [43]

Mrile, a hero of the same country, having a grievance against his family, sat down on his stool and sang incantations, and the stool rose into heaven with him. There he found a world much like the one he had left. He went on and came to some people who were hoeing. He greeted them, and asked them the way to the kraal of the Moon. [44] They told him to go on till he found some people cutting wood, and ask again. He did so and the wood-cutters directed him how to reach

some men digging an irrigation-trench. These again sent him
on to some people who were weeding, and these to a place
where they were gathering in the crops. (One version says
that all these in turn asked him to help them, which he oblig-
ingly did.) The reapers told him to go on till he came to a
place where the road divided. " If you take the lower road,
you will come to people sitting at a meal." He went on and
was hospitably welcomed by them, but found that the food
offered him was raw. So he took out his fire-sticks and showed
them how to make fire and cook their food. They were so
delighted that they presented him with large numbers of
cattle and goats, and he returned home in triumph. It is a
remarkable point, to which I know no parallel elsewhere, that
the Heaven-dwellers should be unacquainted with the use of
fire, though in Polynesia this is told of the people of the underworld.[45]

The same people have a very curious legend of a Heaven-
tree. A girl named Kichalundu went out to cut grass and was
swallowed up in a bog. Her companions heard her voice
growing fainter and fainter, as she sank through the three successive realms of the Dead — we shall come back to these in
a later chapter — till at last all was silent. By and by, a tree
sprang up on this spot, and kept growing till it reached the sky.
The herd-boys used to drive their cattle into its shade and play
about in the branches. One day, two of them climbed higher
than the rest, quite out of sight. Their companions called to
them to come back but they refused, saying, " We are going up
to the sky — to Wuhuu, the world above! "— and they were
never seen again. People say that they went on beyond the
Wahuu (the Heaven-clan) to the Waranjui, who live above
the sky. Perhaps the human dwellers on " middle earth "
are the first of the series to which these two orders of beings
belong — the three corresponding to the three orders of ghosts
recognised by the Wachaga.

Two other remarkable traditions [46] of heaven-dwellers belong to the same district. A man and woman — said to be the ancestors of the existing Molama clan — came down from the sky and alighted on a certain hill. They said they had been sent down by Ruwa and were found to have tails, which they were afterwards induced to cut off. The other story concerns a being called Mrule (he appears to be quite distinct from Mrile or Nrile), who also came down from heaven and went first to the Masai, afterwards to the Wachaga in the Shira district. He had only one leg, so suggesting the half-men we shall discuss later on, and the people, being frightened by his strange appearance, refused to take him in or give him food. So he returned to heaven, and they regretted their unkindness too late. [47]

We have referred to a Ronga tale about the " Road to Heaven," [48] which is of interest in this connection. It is one of a very wide-spread group of stories, most of which, however, have their scenes laid in the underground regions of the dead and not in the country above the sky. They exhibit an unmistakable relationship to the European tales of which we may take Grimm's " Frau Holle " as the type, but the idea is so likely to occur spontaneously anywhere, that there seems no need to resort to any hypothesis of diffusion, or, at any rate, of introduction from Europe. Fülleborn [49] mentions a tale of this type from the Konde country, which he characterises as " psychologisch recht unverständlich "— probably because the version before him was corrupt, or imperfect in its details. Junod's " La Route du Ciel," is evidently very far from being a primitive version; in fact, the reason for one of the most important incidents has been entirely lost sight of. It will therefore be better to begin with the variant given by Duff Macdonald under the title " The Three Women," [50] which itself is not perfectly clear throughout, and elucidate its difficult points by comparison with others.

"There were three Women with their children, and they went to the water. When they had reached it, one of them was cheated by her companions, who said, 'Throw your child into the water, we have thrown our children into the water.' But they had hidden their children under a tree."

There seems no point in this beyond a senseless and heartless practical joke, but a Chaga tale,[51] which begins quite differently, probably suggests the right version of the incident. A chief's son fetching home his bride puts her into a large honey-barrel and carries her over the hills on his back. On the way she hears the lowing of her father's cattle and asks him to let her out, so that she may take a last look at them. While she is gone, a certain bird called *kirindovo* gets into the honey-barrel in her place, and the bridegroom, being unable to see behind him, thinks the girl has returned and fastens down the lid. The story, however, does not proceed on the usual lines of the "False Bride" incident, for the real bride is reinstated without difficulty, and the *kirindovo* (metamorphosed or not, for we have the usual vagueness about such matters) is relegated to the position of a secondary wife. When the head-wife has a child, the jealous *kirindovo* fabricates a pretended one out of a banana-stalk and throws it into a pool, telling the mother that by so doing she will get it back stronger and more beautiful. The motive for inducing the mother to drown her child is here quite clear.

"So their companion threw her child into the water and a crocodile swallowed it. Then her companions began to laugh at her and said, 'We were only cheating you!'" The mother then "climbed a tree and said 'I want to go on high,' and the tree grew much and reached upwards." She does not here say that she wants to find the dwelling-place of Mulungu, but this appears later. She meets some leopards who ask her where she is going, and she tells them, "I want my child; my companions cheated me and said 'Throw your child into the

water.'" The leopards directed her on to certain creatures
called *nsenzi* (which Dr. Macdonald takes to be birds), and
they to the Mazomba (Masomba? — large fishes), who said,
"What do you want, my girl?" "The girl said, 'I want to
know the way.' The Mazomba said, 'Where to?' The girl
said, 'The way to Mulungu.' The Mazomba said, 'Well, be
strong in your heart.' The girl said, 'Yes, Masters, I understand.'"

The woman is not asked to render any services to those she
meets, but it is evident from what follows, that her civil answers to the leopards and the other creatures are counted to
her for righteousness. When she reaches "the village of Mulungu" and tells her story, Mulungu calls the crocodile and
restores her child. "The girl received the child and went
down" — we are not told how — "to her mother." Her
companions, when they heard what had happened, at once
threw their babies into the water and climbed the tree. They
gave impertinent answers to the leopards, *nsenzi*, and Mazomba and even abused them.

"Then they came to Mulungu. He said, 'What do you
want?' The girls said, 'We have thrown our children into
the water.' But Mulungu said, 'What was the reason of
that?' The girls hid the matter and said, 'Nothing.' But
Mulungu said, 'It is false. You cheated your companion, saying "Throw your child into the water," and now you tell me
a lie.' Then Mulungu took a bottle of lightning and said,
'Your children are in here.' They took the bottle, which made
a report like a gun, and the girls both died."

In "La Route du Ciel," the opening, as we have seen, is
quite different: it is a young girl, afraid of being scolded for
breaking her water-jar, who climbs a rope to take refuge in the
sky. Nothing is said about a baby, actual or prospective, and
the girl's announcement, on reaching "the village of Heaven"
—"I have come to look for a child," is consequently somewhat

PLATE XI

" The Woman who found the Way to Mulungu "

perplexing. It becomes quite intelligible, however, on comparison with the Yao variant, which undoubtedly represents the
older form. We might suppose the beginning to have been
altered in order to point a moral for the benefit of wilful and
ill-behaved daughters, but the world-wide recurrence of the
motive is against this, and the probability is that two different
tales have — perhaps purposely — here been combined into
one. The final catastrophe is very much alike in both. What
makes this view more probable is that the usual story of the
half-sisters, of whom the ill-treated one is kind and helpful
and gets rewarded, while the spoilt and petted one acts in the
opposite way and comes to grief, is always, more or less consciously, connected, not with the sky above, but with the realm
of the dead beneath. The girl in the original " Frau Holle "
story falls into the well; the wife in the Chaga tale (where the
combination of incidents is reversed) throws herself into the
pool where her baby has been drowned, and both come to what
is really, if not avowedly, the country of the ghosts. And the
recollection of this persists, even when the exact nature of the
journey has been forgotten. In the Sierra Leone variant,[52] the
stepmother sends the child to the " Devil," to get the rice-
stick washed, and the mysterious city where the Hausa place
the " Menders of Men," [53] seems to point in the same direction.
In the other Hausa variant,[54] " How the Ill-treated Maiden
became Rich," the girls do not apparently leave the world of
the living; but their goal, the River Bagajun, is presided over
by a witch, and, on their way to it, they pass rivers of sour
milk and honey. This may be some distorted recollection of
a Hindu myth refracted through Islam, or may possibly belong
to an older indigenous stratum of thought.

In the chapter on " The Little People " I shall quote a
Chaga story [55] which belongs to the same type as these, but
substitutes the top of Kilimanjaro for the sky, and the Wakonyingo dwarfs for the Heaven-people. A remarkable point

is that, as the latter seem, in the Chaga view, to be unacquainted with the use of fire, the hero in this case instructs the Wakonyingo in protective magic. It is curious to compare this with the Pokomo tradition which represents the tribal ancestor as getting the knowledge of fire from a member of the aboriginal race, the Wasanye. Some other tales of the kind will be more suitably discussed in connection with Ancestral Ghosts and the Abode of the Dead.

CHAPTER II

MYTHS OF ORIGINS

THIS title seems preferable to that of " Creation Myths,"
for of the creation, as we understand it, we hear singularly little in Bantu legend. The earth, in most cases, seems to
be taken for granted, as if it had existed from the beginning;
and though, occasionally, we may hear of men being actually
made, they more often just " appear," sometimes coming down
from the sky, sometimes up out of the earth, sometimes without any attempt at explanation whence they came. Junod says:
" I believe that the origin of man preoccupies the Bantu mind
more than the origin of the world as a whole." [1] So much is
this the case that one almost feels inclined to wonder whether,
when we find little more than the bald statement that Katonda,
or Mulungu, or Nyambe made the earth, the sun, etc., this
may not be merely the improvised answer to the question of
some European pressing for information on a subject which
had never previously occurred to his listeners. Duff Macdonald says: [2] " The existence of the world itself is accepted as a
fact not to be explained. But there are legends that explain the
introduction of the sun, moon, and stars, clouds and rain, as also
how mountains and rivers appeared on the scene." The Yao
divinity Mtanga (by some said to be the same as Mulungu) is
described as pressing up the surface of the earth into mountain
ridges and excavating rivers, and " putting the country right." [3]
It existed already and only needed shaping; moreover, the
scene of Mtanga's activities seems to be confined to the Yao
country — the original mountain home of the tribe. Probably,
when they had started on their migrations and reached the

Chilwa plain, they felt the need of accounting for the difference.

The Bushongo [4] have something more like a genuine creation legend, of a very peculiar kind. I have not met with its parallel elsewhere in Africa. Bumba, the Creator, who is described as a gigantic white being in human form, existed alone in the beginning, in a universe where there was nothing but water. Some touches in this narrative, apart from the supreme act of creation, are surprisingly suggestive of Genesis I, and but for the fact that the Bushongo were entirely untouched by missionary influence, and that Mr. Torday was to an unusual degree independent of interpreters, one might feel somewhat suspicious. As it is, one may perhaps draw the moral that, without accepting the conclusions which have been or might be based on them, we need not be too incredulous as to the genuineness of Merker's Masai traditions.

Bumba, say the Bushongo, one day felt severe internal pains and, as a consequence, " vomited up the sun, moon, and stars," thus giving light to the world. As the sun's rays dried up the water, sandbanks began to appear above its surface, but there was no life anywhere. Bumba then, in the same manner, produced eight living creatures which, in their turn, gave rise, with some exceptions, to all the rest. These were, the leopard, the crested eagle, the crocodile, a small fish (the parent of all other fish), the tortoise, the lightning (a beast like a black leopard), the white heron, a beetle, and the goat. He then produced men. Whether these included the three sons who now appear on the scene is not stated. The animals undertook to people the world, but it is not quite clear on what principle they did so; the goat produced all horned beasts, the beetle all insects, the crocodile all serpents and the iguana, the white heron all birds except the kite. Then Bumba's sons took a hand. One produced white ants, which, apparently, are not counted as insects, and died in the effort; the second a plant, from which all vegetable life has sprung; and the third tried to bring forth new creatures, but the only result was the kite. Why the kite should thus be set apart from all other birds is not explained.

The Bushongo, according to their own tradition, came from the far north, probably from the region of Lake Chad, and within historical times. This might account for the exceptional character of much in the above legend. It is true that the name of Bumba (who is not only Creator but First Ancestor, whose direct descendants, the reigning chiefs, have preserved every link in their genealogy) is found among other tribes, such as the Baila. But the name is Bantu, and the Bushongo brought with them from the north a strange archaic, non-Bantu language which has nearly, if not quite gone out of use.

Coming now to the conception of origin from trees or plants, we may link together the legends of the Herero, Zulus, and other tribes south of the Zambezi. I have not definitely traced it much farther north, unless we can count the belief of the Bangongo in the Kasai country [5] that the Batwa pygmies came out of trees, and a vague account [6] which I was, unfortunately, never able to check or get further light on, of some sacred tree from which the Wasanye in East Africa deduce their origin.

The Zulus say: " It is said that we men came out of a bed of reeds, where we had our origin." [7] Some content themselves with this general statement, others say that it was Unkulunkulu who " had his origin in a valley where there was a reed-bed (*umhlanga*) here on the earth, and men sprang from Unkulunkulu by generation. All things as well as Unkulunkulu sprang from a bed of reeds — everything, both animals and corn, everything coming into being with Unkulunkulu."

Elsewhere, the word used is *uhlanga*,[8] a single reed (as distinguished from *umhlanga*, a reed-bed). Callaway and

Colenso [9] both thought that these words are not to be taken in their literal meaning, but as referring to some " Primal Source of Being." Yet the former admits that the native who gave the account " clearly understood by it a reed," [10] while adding that " one cannot avoid believing that he did not understand the import of the tradition." But comparison with the traditions of other tribes suggests that this, or something like it, was really the primitive belief, and that *uhlanga* came to mean " source " or " origin " because it was thought that mankind had sprung from a reed. The Basuto certainly thought so, and used to commemorate the belief by sticking a reed (or bunch of reeds) into the thatch of a hut where a child had been born. [11] The Thonga vary between the reed (*lihlanga*) and the reed-bed (*nhlanga*): in the first version " one man and one woman suddenly came out from one reed, which exploded, and there they were! " In the second, " men of different tribes emerged from a marsh of reeds, each tribe already having its peculiar costume, implements, and customs." [12]

The Herero believe in a sacred tree from which their earliest ancestors sprang. It is called *Omumborombonga* and has been identified by botanists as *Combretum primigenum*. The actual tree which produced the human race is supposed to be still in existence, in the " Kaoko veld," west of the Ndonga country and south of the Kunene River. Beiderbecke [13] speaks almost as if he had seen it. " There is nothing particular in the tree, unless it may be its looking old and antediluvian. The Ovaherero, in passing it, bow themselves reverently, holding in the hand a bunch of green twigs which they stick into it, or otherwise throw down at the foot. They also enter into a conversation with the tree, giving the answers themselves in a somewhat altered voice." This presumably refers to the original tree: a note added by another hand tells that the Herero honoured all trees of the same species, saluting them

PLATE XII

The Footprints of the First Man in Ruanda.
(See Appendix, page 375.) After a photograph by
Captain Philipps.

with the words: *Tate Mukuru, uzera!* " Father Mukuru, thou
art holy," or perhaps rather " tabu." " Formerly the Ovaherero had such a reverence for the tree that they would not
even sit down in its shade."

But it should be noted that only the Herero themselves and
their cattle sprang from the sacred *Omumborombonga*. The
" Hill-Damara," a previous population supposed to be Bantu
by race, though speaking a Hottentot dialect, came out of a
rock, together with goats, sheep and baboons. Perhaps a
double racial tradition explains the divergent accounts given
by the Basuto;[14] the one most generally accepted is that men
sprang from a reed-bed, but some say that they issued (together with the animals) from a cave. The Anyanja believe
that the first men came out of a hole in the ground at a place
called Kapirimtiya, where their footprints and those of the
animals are still to be seen impressed on the rock. This is
said to be on a hill, or, according to some, an island in a lake,
somewhere west of Lake Nyasa. A correspondent of *Life and
Work* (the Blantyre Mission Magazine) [15] was shown the alleged site of this event in the Wemba country, " a conglomerate rock, showing what the natives call footprints of a man, a
child, a zebra, a horse, and a dog." The horse, if not the result of a misunderstanding, must be a comparatively recent
addition. The legend may indicate that here or hereabouts was
a centre of dispersion for the Nyanja, Wemba, and perhaps
some other tribes; also it looks as if it had been inherited from
that older stratum of the population which, as we have seen,
was most probably absorbed. The Hill-Damara, who likewise
came out of a rock, may represent the mingling of the advance
guard of the Bantu immigrants with some Bushman tribe.
We know this to have happened in the case of the Leghoya [16] and some other Bechwana clans, and in the absence of
direct proof I should think it probable that these clans were
precisely those who did not hold the theory of the reed origin.

Stow, however, says that in all Bantu myths of the origin of man — whether deriving him from the split reed or the fissure of a rock — the Bushmen are disregarded or taken for granted as existing already. Some of these " traditions state that when their forefathers migrated to the south, they found the land without inhabitants, so that only the wild game and the Bushmen were living in it — evidently classing . . . them together as wild animals." [17]

This reminds us of the Masai,[18] who say that " when God came to prepare the world, he found there a Dorobo, an elephant and a serpent." The Dorobo are a hunting tribe, who must have occupied the country before the Masai, and are now more or less in the position of vassals or serfs to them. The fact that not only the Dorobo but the elephant and the serpent are put on a different level from the rest of creation is highly curious. We are not told what kind of serpent this was, but it is clear that he was not, at any rate, intentionally harmful. The three lived together for some time and the Dorobo, by what means we do not learn, became possessed of a cow. After a time the Dorobo picked a quarrel with the serpent, whose breath, he said, affected him with a most unpleasant irritation of the skin. The poor serpent apologised very humbly, saying: " Oh, my father, I do not blow my bad breath over you on purpose "; but the Dorobo, though he said nothing at the time, waited his opportunity and killed the serpent with a club. The elephant, missing him, asked where the " thin one " was. The Dorobo denied all knowledge of him; but the elephant, who had no doubt come to her own conclusions as to his character, was not deceived. By and by, the elephant produced a calf. The rains were now over, and all the pools had dried up, except in one place, where the Dorobo took his cow every day to drink. The elephant, too, used to come to this pool and, after drinking, lie down in the water, stirring up the bottom, so that the Dorobo, when he came, was much annoyed to find the water very muddy. He appears to have said nothing, but bided his time, till one day he made an arrow and shot the elephant. The young elephant, finding itself thus orphaned, said: " The Dorobo is bad. I will not stop with him any longer. He first of all killed the snake, and now he has killed mother. I will go away and not live with him again." So the young elephant went to another country, where he met a Masai, and, in answer to his questions, told him what had happened. The Masai seems to have been impressed by the Dorobo's qualities, for he said: " Let us go there; I should like to see him." They went and found the Dorobo's hut and saw that God had overturned it, so that the open door faced the sky. This part of the story calls for cross-examination, as, on the face of it, one would suppose this state of things to be a mark of displeasure at the Dorobo's previous conduct, but, if so, it hardly seems consistent with what follows. For we hear, without comment or explanation, that Ngai called the Dorobo and said to him: " I wish you to come to-morrow morning, for I have something to tell you." The Masai overheard this and played the trick which Jacob played on Esau by being on the spot first. But it is somewhat disconcerting to find that, when " he went and said to God ' I have come,' " Ngai does not appear to have noticed the difference, but went on giving him the instructions intended for the Dorobo. He was to build a large cattle-kraal and then go out into the forest till he found a lean calf, which he was to bring home and slaughter, afterwards burning the meat. Then he was to go into his hut — the Dorobo's hut of course, though we do not hear whether it had been restored to its normal position — and not be startled or cry out, whatever he might hear. He did as he was told and waited in the hut till he heard a sound like thunder. Ngai let down a strip of hide from the sky, and down this cattle began to descend into the kraal. They kept on coming till the kraal was full and the animals were so crowded

that they began to break down the hut. The Masai could
not keep back an exclamation of astonishment, and came out
to find that the lariat had been cut and no more cattle were
coming down. Ngai asked him if he had enough, for he
should certainly get no more, as he would have done, had he
been able to hold his tongue.

This is the story told to account for the fact that the Masai
have cattle and the Dorobo have none. " Nowadays," says the
narrator, " if cattle are seen in the possession of Bantu tribes,
it is presumed that they have been stolen or found, and the
Masai say, ' These are our animals, let us go and take them, for
God in olden days gave us all the cattle upon earth.' "

Another version of this myth says nothing of the Dorobo's
previous misdoings, and only relates how the Masai cheated
him out of the cattle, very much as shown above. But there is
one significant addition at the end, which *may* involve a reference to the earlier part of the story: " After this the Dorobo
shot away the cord by which the cattle had descended, *and God
moved and went far off*."

Are we to take this as implying — what perhaps was no
longer clear to the narrator himself — that the Dorobo's
treatment of his fellow-creatures had made the earth impossible as a residence for Ngai? If so, we are reminded of what
the Yaos say about Mulungu. It is true we are not told that
Ngai lived on the earth, but he seems at any rate to have occupied a near and comparatively accessible part of heaven.

This differs considerably from the legend mentioned by
Irle,[19] explaining how the Herero got the cattle which the
Nama spend their lives — or did, not so very long ago — in
" lifting " from them. It appears that some of the first human
beings quarrelled over the skin of the first ox slaughtered for
food. The colour of their descendants was determined by the
distribution of the meat: the ancestors of the Hereros ate the
liver, so their children were black; the Nama are red because

their fathers took the lungs and the blood. The Nandi legend of origins is very similar to the Masai one, but there are some interesting points of difference. In general, we find that when the Masai and Nandi possess different versions of the same story, the latter seem to have the more primitive form. In this case, too, God found the earth tenanted by the Dorobo and the elephant,[20] but the third in the partnership was the Thunder, not the serpent. The Thunder distrusted the Dorobo almost from the beginning, because, when lying down, he could turn over without getting up, which neither the elephant nor, it appears, the Thunder, was able to do. The elephant only laughed at the Thunder's warning, and the latter retreated into the sky, where he has remained ever since. The Dorobo then remarked: " The person I was afraid of has fled; I do not mind the elephant," and at once proceeded to shoot him with a poisoned arrow. The unfortunate elephant, too late, called upon the Thunder to help him and take him up, but received the unfeeling answer: " Die by yourself," with the addition of, " I told you so," or words to that effect. So he was hit by a second arrow, and died, and the Dorobo " became great in all the countries."

One wonders whether these stories reflect some dim notion that the elephant belongs to the older world; that he was not merely existing on the earth before man appeared there, but that he is the survivor of an extinct order. It is possible, too, that others of the earlier vertebrates — giant saurians and cetaceans — may have lingered on in Africa after the coming of man, and that some memory of them survives in the figures made by the Anyanja and Yaos for their *unyago* ceremonies,[21] and in the reports, persistent, but difficult to substantiate, of monstrous fish believed to inhabit the depths of the Great Lakes.

Other tribes believe that the first man, or the first pair, descended from the sky, like the Peruvian Manco Capac and

Mama Oella. The Galla say that the ancestor of their oldest clan — the Uta Laficho — did so, and some, at least, of the other clans, perhaps all those who are not known to have branched off from older stocks within human memory.

It seems also to be held by some of the Baganda that Kintu, the first man, descended from heaven.[22] But this is clearly inconsistent with his story as generally related,[23] which shows that the denizens of Heaven knew no more about him than Mulungu knew of the two strange creatures found in the Chameleon's fish-trap. It is merely said that Kintu and his cow "came into this country" (*mu nsi muno*), whence or how is not explained, and found it vacant — there was nothing to eat. Kintu lived for some time on the products of the cow, till one day he saw several persons coming down from the sky. These were the sons of Heaven (Gulu) and their sister Nambi, who said to her brothers: "Look at this man, where has he come from?" Kintu, on being questioned, said: "Neither do I know where I come from." In the course of a short conversation, he impressed Nambi so favourably that she said to her brothers: *Kintu murungi mmwagala, mmufumbirwe* — "Kintu is good, I like him — let me marry him." They, not unnaturally, demurred, asking whether she were sure that he was really a human being; whereto she replied: "I know he is a man — an animal does not build a house," from which we may infer that Kintu had done so, though the fact has not been previously mentioned. She then turned to him and, with admirable directness, said: "Kintu, I love you. Well, then, let me go home and tell my father that I have seen a man out in the jungle whom I should like to marry." The sons of Heaven were by no means satisfied and told their father privately that Kintu did not eat ordinary food and was certainly a suspicious character. Gulu suggested that his sons should steal Kintu's cow, "and then we shall see whether he dies or not." They did so, and Kintu subsisted precariously for a time on the bark of trees. Nambi, growing anxious about her lover, came down to look after him and brought him back with her to heaven. There he saw "many people and many cattle and banana-trees and fowls and sheep and goats, and much of everything that is eaten." (In short, the Platonic ideas or patterns of things which did not yet exist on earth, were all there in the heavens.) Gulu, when informed of Kintu's arrival, determined to put him to the test. It is not quite clear whether he wished to find out if Kintu could really eat human — or celestial — food, or whether he wished to choke off an unwelcome connection by imposing impossible conditions. He ordered his slaves to make a house without a door and interned Kintu therein, together with ten thousand bundles [24] of mashed plantains (*emere*), the carcases of a thousand bullocks, and a thousand gourds of banana-beer (*omwenge*). If he failed to consume these viands, said Gulu, "he is not really Kintu; he is lying, and we will kill him." The message actually given to Kintu, however, was less *intransigeant* than this. "Guest Kintu, Gulu says, 'Take our guest the *emere* and the meat and the beer; if he cannot eat them, he is not Kintu and he shall not have the cow he has come to fetch, and I will not give him my daughter.'"

Kintu thanked his host politely, but on being left alone was ready to despair, when, behold, he saw that the earth had opened in the middle of the house. He threw in the superfluous food and the pit immediately closed up. In the same way he accomplished two other tasks set him — or rather they were accomplished for him, he could not tell how. There is nowhere any hint who or what is this friendly Power which takes his part against Gulu and is evidently stronger than the latter. Another remarkable point is the statement that Kintu prayed (*yegairira*) in his difficulties, though it is not said to whom. Having passed these three tests, he was next told that he should have his cow, if he could pick her out from the herds which Gulu ordered to be driven up — some twenty thousand beasts. Again Kintu was appalled by the magnitude of the task, when he heard a hornet buzzing at his ear. The hornet said: "Watch me when I fly up — the cow on whose horn I shall settle is yours." The hornet remained quiet, and Kintu said: "Take away these cattle, my cow is not among them." A second herd was driven up, and still the hornet gave no sign, but when the third instalment arrived, it flew off and settled on one of the cows. "That is my cow," said Kintu, going up to it and striking it with his stick. The hornet then flew off to a fine heifer. "That is a calf of my cow," said Kintu; and in the same way he claimed another calf. (This indicates that he must have been living on bark for a considerable period.) Gulu laughed and said: "Kintu is a wonder! No one can take him in! And what he says is true. Well, let them call my daughter Nambi." So he gave her to Kintu in marriage and sent them down to live on the earth, giving them also a fowl, a banana-tree, and the principal seeds and roots now cultivated by the Baganda.[25] He also warned them most particularly not to turn back, once they had started, even if they should find that they had forgotten anything. But, as this warning has to do with the entrance of death into the world, the way in which it was neglected, and the disastrous consequences which followed, it will be better related in the next chapter. The couple came down to earth " here at Magonga,"[26] set up housekeeping and began to cultivate. Nambi planted the banana-tree, which produced numerous other trees, and in course of time they had three children.

This Kintu, of course, is an entirely mythical figure, though we have reason to suppose that the Kintu from whom the Kings of Uganda trace their descent (every link in the pedigree is preserved) was a historical character, who invaded Uganda, coming from the north. In fact, as Roscoe points out, the

PLATE XIII

The Cattle-Troughs of Luganzu. (See Appendix, page 375.) After a photograph by Captain Philipps.

traditions of some clans do not fit in with the legend as given above. Some say that Nambi was not the daughter of Heaven but a woman of the Lung-fish clan, who therefore was already living in the country at the time of Kintu's invasion; and there are still in existence alleged relics of chiefs who were there before Kintu. In the version of the story given by Stanley,[27] he is represented as an ordinary human immigrant, coming from the north with his wife, and bringing with him the principal domestic animals and plants. He disappeared from the earth after many years, disgusted by the wickedness of his descendants, and his successors sought for him in vain. He revealed himself to the twenty-second king, Mawanda, bidding him come to the meeting-place accompanied by no one but his mother. One of Mawanda's councillors, unknown to the king, followed him into the forest. Kintu asked Mawanda why he had disobeyed his orders, and the latter, when he discovered the councillor, killed him. Kintu then disappeared and has never been seen since, but whether on account of the minister's disobedience or the king's deed of violence, does not seem clear. But we may perhaps see in the story a rationalised version of the legend which represents the Creator as leaving the earth, as in the cases of Mulungu and Bumba.

Another case of an ancestor who appears in an uninhabited country, without any indication of his having descended from heaven, is Vere, from whom the Buu tribe of the Pokomo trace their descent. He is sometimes spoken of as a preternatural being " without father or mother." Other narrators content themselves with saying that no one knows where he came from or who his parents were. He wandered about alone in the forests of the Tana Valley, feeding on wild fruits and raw fish, for he had no knowledge of fire and no means of making it. After two years, he met with one Mitsotsozini, who showed him how to make fire by means of two sticks and cook his food. The remarkable part of this story is that Mitsotsozini belonged to the hunter tribe of the Wasanye, who are generally considered less advanced in the arts of life than the Bantu. It may also indicate that the Wasanye — like the Dorobo, with whom, in fact, they have a good deal in common — are supposed to have been there from the beginning of things. As, moreover, some of the Buu clans trace their descent from Mitsotsozini, as well as from Vere, we may infer that intermarriage took place at an early period between the Pokomo and the Wasanye, and a good many facts connected with the former tribe render this extremely probable.[28]

Before concluding this chapter, I should like to refer to a very curious myth of the Nandi, interesting, not only in itself, but because of its points of contact with the traditions of races in the far South-west. Among the Masai folk-tales collected by Hollis is one called " The Old Man and his Knee." [29] It relates how an old man, living alone, was troubled with a swelling in his knee which he took for an abscess; but, at the end of six months, as it did not burst, he cut it open and out came two children, a girl and a boy. The rest of the story proceeds very much on the lines of the Sesuto " Tselane " and other tales of cannibals, though without the usual happy ending. This, as it stands, is not a myth of origins, but an ordinary fairy-tale. The Nandi, however, have what is evidently the more primitive form of it.[30] "Amongst the Moi clan there is a tradition that the first Dorobo "— again we find the Dorobo looked on as the earliest men — " gave birth to a boy and a girl. His leg swelled up one day . . . at length it burst, and a boy issued from the inner side of the calf, while a girl issued from the outer side. These two in course of time had children, who were the ancestors of all the people on earth."

The same idea crops up among the Wakuluwe (between Lakes Nyasa and Tanganyika) who hold that the first human pair came down from heaven, but did not produce offspring in the ordinary way. Ngulwe (the local equivalent of Mulungu) caused a child, known as Kanga Masala, to come out of the woman's knee.[31]

What lies behind this notion it is difficult to see; but it seems to reappear, distorted and half-forgotten, in Hottentot mythology. A good deal of controversy has raged round Tsūi || Goab (or Tsuni || Goam), the "Supreme Being of the Hottentots." [32] This name was long ago interpreted as "Wounded Knee," with the added explanation that the deity (according to some, a famous warrior of old times) [33] had got his knee injured in a fight in which he overcame the evil being || Gaunab. Hahn,[34] who was anxious to prove that the Khoi-khoi (Hottentots) had a relatively high conception of a God, rejected this interpretation in 1881 (though he had previously advocated it) and leaned to the view that Tsuni || Goam means "The Red Dawn," thus placing this being in the category of Sky-gods. Krönlein,[35] one of the best authorities on the Hottentot language, translates the name as "He who is entreated with difficulty" (*der mühsam zu Bittende*), which, though different enough from Hahn's rendering, could be cited in support of a similar view. But a more recent writer, Dr. L. Schultze,[36] shows that Krönlein's interpretation is inadmissible on linguistic grounds, and declares, on the ground of his own independent inquiries, for Hahn's (earlier) derivation, viz., that *tsū || goab* is equivalent to "wounded knee," and is the designation of a hero who had his knee wounded in battle. Dr. Schultze does not mention the view advocated in Hahn's later work.

This, of course, is a very different matter from the Nandi myth as related by Hollis, but we have already seen how the latter has been transformed by the Masai, who no longer seem to recognise it as part of their "Genesis." The Hottentots, while (as has been demonstrated by recent research into their language and customs) remotely connected with the Masai and other Hamitic and semi-Hamitic tribes of the North-east, have been so long separated from their congeners that they might easily have forgotten the original meaning of the Wounded Knee. Especially would this be the case where later generations find the story strange and perplexing, if not repellent, whereas the battle with || Gaunab readily commends itself to the intelligence.

The identity of Tsūi || Goab presents some difficulties. It is impossible to keep him quite distinct from Haitsi-aibeb (about whom we shall have something to say in a later chapter, and to whom some of Tsūi || Goab's adventures are expressly attributed) and || Gurikhoisib, the First Ancestor — the solitary dweller in the wilderness, who reminds us of Vere. Hahn further identifies him with the thunder-cloud and the thunder: this is a question not to be decided here, but it may be interesting to give the story of Tsūi || Goab, as related to Hahn by an old Nama, probably born not much later than 1770, as " he had big grown-up children . . . in 1811." [37]

" Tsūi || Goab was a great, powerful chief of the Khoikhoi; in fact, he was the first Khoikhoib, from whom all the Khoikhoi tribes took their origin. But Tsūi || Goab was not his original name. This Tsūi || Goab went to war with another chief, || Gaunab, because the latter always killed great numbers of Tsūi || Goab's people. In this fight, however, Tsūi || Goab was repeatedly overpowered by || Gaunab, but in every battle the former grew stronger, and at last he was so strong and big that he easily destroyed || Gaunab by giving him one blow behind the ear. While || Gaunab was expiring, he gave his enemy a blow on the knee. Since that day the conqueror of || Gaunab received the name Tsūi || Goab, ' sore knee' or ' wounded knee.' Henceforth he could not walk properly because he was lame. He could do wonderful things, which no other man could do, because he was very wise. He could tell what would happen in future times. He died several times and several times he rose again. And whenever he came back to us, there were great feastings and rejoicings. Milk was brought from every kraal, and fat cows and fat ewes were slaughtered. Tsũi ‖ Goab gave every man plenty of cattle and sheep, because he was very rich. He gives rain, he makes the clouds, he lives in the clouds, and he makes our cows and sheep fruitful."

These repeated deaths and resurrections are a prominent feature, as we shall see, in the legend of Haitsi-aibeb, who also overcame an evil being named ‡ Gama ‡ Goub (according to Hahn " almost identical with ‖ Gaunab ") by hitting him with a stone behind the ear.

These definitely evil powers are not common in African mythology, at least in that of the Bantu, who usually conceive of spirits as good or bad — perhaps one should rather say friendly or hostile — according to circumstances. Where they exist, as here, they are perhaps due to Hamitic influence. The apparent exceptions — Mbasi of the Wankonde,[38] and Mwawa of the Wakuluwe [39] — need to be carefully studied.

CHAPTER III

MYTHS OF THE ORIGIN OF DEATH

IN ALL parts of Bantu Africa we find the Chameleon associated with the entry of death into the world. Or, at any rate, the well-known legend, to be related presently, has been found in so many different parts of the area occupied by these tribes, that we may confidently expect to find it in others, where it has not yet come to light.

The Zulu version of the story, as related by Callaway,[1] is so well known, that I prefer to give, as a fairly typical specimen, one quite independently recorded from Nyasaland:[2] " God sent the Chameleon (*nadzikambe*) and the *msalulu* (a kind of lizard) and said: ' You, Chameleon, when you come to men, tell them, " When you die you will come back," ' and to the *msalulu* also he gave a message, saying: ' Say, " When men die they will pass away completely." ' Then, after the Chameleon had gone ahead, the Lizard followed after him and went along the road and found the Chameleon walking along delicately, going backwards and forwards." Any one who has watched this creature, the almost affected daintiness of its movements, and the caution with which it always plants one foot firmly before lifting the next, will recognise the justice of the description. " And he, the Msalulu, passed on very swiftly till he came to people, and he said: ' When men die, they shall pass away completely.' And after a time the Chameleon arrived, coming in uselessly behind him, and said: ' When men die they will return.' But the people said, ' We have already heard the Msalulu's message — " When we die there will be an end to us," and now he says, " When we die we shall come back,"— what non-sense! ' So people, when they see the Chameleon, put tobacco into his mouth that he may die, because, say they, ' You lingered on the road instead of hurrying on with your message and arriving first.' For after all, it is better to come back than to be dead altogether."

The Chameleon seems everywhere to be considered an unlucky animal, and this special form of retribution by nicotine-poisoning is reported from the Konde country,[3] and from Delagoa Bay,[4] as well as from Nyasaland. One writer, however,[5] says that, in Likoma, the tobacco — whatever its effect — is intended as a reward, not a punishment, the idea being that at any rate the purpose was a good one, though the Chameleon failed, perhaps through natural incapacity, to carry it out. His name, in this particular part of Nyasaland, is Gulumpambe, probably connected with Mpambe, one of the local names for " God." (The name used in the Shire Highlands is *nadzikambe*, of which I can offer no satisfactory explanation; that given in Scott's Dictionary is scarcely admissible.)

The Giryama (British East Africa, to the north of Mombasa) tell the story in much the same way,[6] with one rather important exception, to be considered presently. It is to be noted that in neither of these versions, nor in any other that I have been able to examine, is there any question of the second messenger being sent off to countermand the announcement made by the first, in consequence of the wickedness of mankind which had become manifest after the departure of the Chameleon. This is sometimes stated by European writers, but I can find no hint of it in Callaway's original Zulu texts.

In general, the versions of this story conform to one or other of two types. In one, the Creator despatches both messengers; in the other he sends only the Chameleon, though the blue-headed Gecko, or some other species of lizard, but in one case the Hare, starts on his own account, arrives before the Chameleon and delivers the wrong message, apparently from sheer love of mischief. This is the case in the Giryama version just referred to, whereas in the Nyanja one,[7] Mulungu sends both, though no reason is given. But in some cases it appears as if he had intended the matter to be decided by the first arrival. The Subiya[8] say that Leza sent off the Chameleon with the message as already stated; then, after giving him a good start (in fact, waiting till he had got half-way), he despatched the Lizard with instructions to say nothing if the Chameleon had already arrived; but if he had not yet come in, he was to say, " Men shall die and not live again."

The Luyi story is somewhat different.[9] When Nyambe and his wife Nasilele lived on earth, they had a dog, which died. Nyambe was deeply grieved and wanted to recall him to life, but Nasilele, who did not like the dog, said, " For my part, I don't want him back, he is a thief! " Nyambe insisted: " As for me, I am fond of my dog,"— but the wife was obdurate and the corpse was thrown out. Soon afterwards, Nasilele's mother died, and this time it was the wife who pleaded for the recall of the dead, and the husband who refused. Nasilele's mother died " for good," and it would appear (though this is not expressly stated) that she therefore wanted to destroy the whole human race. The account goes on: " They sent the Chameleon and the Hare, with messages of opposite import: the Hare arrived first, and therefore men have to die without hope of return."

The Subiya[10] tell the first part of this story without any reference to Leza; it is simply " the first man " and his wife who quarrel over the dog. But there is every reason to think that Leza and the First Ancestor are identical. The Subiya legend, moreover, contains an additional episode not found in the Luyi version, at least as related to Jacottet. The man

PLATE XIV

Type of Zanzibar Swahili.
After a photograph by Dr. Aders.

repents and agrees to restore his wife's mother to life. He has her carried into her house and treats her with "medicines" (herbs), giving his wife strict orders to keep the door shut. She begins to revive, and all goes well, till he has to go into the forest to seek some fresh herbs; in his absence his wife opens the door and finds her mother alive, but "immediately her heart came out" (of her body) "and she died again." This time the husband refused to do anything more and no one since then has recovered after dying.

Kropf [11] gives a remarkable variant current among the Amaxosa of the Eastern Cape Province. This is clearer and more coherent than many others, but we cannot be certain that this proves it to be the earlier: it might be the result of later reflection after the primitive story had been partly forgotten. At first, people did not die, and the earth became so overcrowded that its inhabitants could scarcely breathe. An assembly was held to discuss what should be done, and some said: "The only thing that can save us is, that people should die, so that we can get air." Others approved this, and at last it was decided that two messengers should be sent to lay the question before the Creator, the Chameleon and the Lizard being chosen for the purpose. The former was to say: "The great ones of the earth have resolved that people are not to die!" while the Lizard was to say: "We want them to die." Here the question seems to be one of dying or not dying, and not of reviving after death. The Chameleon was given a certain start, in order to make the race a fair one; but, as in the other versions, he lingered, zigzagging along the path and stopping to catch flies by the way (some say, to eat the berries of a certain shrub which is pointed out), and finally went to sleep; when, of course, the Lizard overtook and passed him.

The rest of the story need not be repeated, but we may note that the reception of the Chameleon's message seems to have more point when coming from the authority whose voice has decided the matter in dispute. " Since that time," says Kropf or his informant, " death has reigned on earth. Both animals are hated, the Chameleon is poisoned with tobacco-juice wherever found, and the Lizard has to run for his life, for the Bushman eats every one he catches."

The *intulwa* (or *intulo*), by the bye, is considered by the Zulus as unlucky as the Chameleon, and one entering a hut is an exceedingly bad omen. I remember a pathetic touch in a letter written for Okamsweli, mother of the late Chief Dinuzulu, when her son was in exile at St. Helena, in which was mentioned, among other incidents, that one of these lizards had come into her hut, " but she was not afraid and was ' strengthening her heart ' against the evil influence." Both creatures are perfectly harmless, though the lizard especially is often believed to be poisonous in countries where there is, so far as one knows, no other superstition connected with it.

One does not know whether to conclude that the myth gave rise to the belief in the reptile's poisonous properties, or *vice versa;* among the Bantu, at any rate, I am inclined to think that the former may be the case, and the poison theory a rationalising afterthought. It is interesting, in this connection, to note one or two bits of Swahili folklore with regard to lizards. The little striped lizards, so common in houses, and so useful in ridding them of flies, etc., are called *mjusi kafiri*,[12] " the infidel lizard," and Moslems say it is the duty of every believer to kill them — by biting off their heads, some say, but for this I will not vouch. I have heard two reasons given — one being that when a certain King had ordered the Prophet to be burnt alive (I think this must be some confusion with the legend of Abraham and Nimrod), the *mjusi-kafiri* sat by and endeavoured to blow up the flames with its breath. Others say, that when the Prophet and his two companions were hidden in the cave, whereas the Spider wove a web across the entrance, and the Dove laid two eggs on the threshold to deceive the pursuers, the Lizard tried to betray him by nodding his head in the direction of the cave. Whether these stories are current outside Africa I do not know. Possibly some ancient aboriginal beliefs have been adapted to Moslem tradition. The entry under *Kinyonge* in Krapf's Swahili dictionary seems to indicate that the legend was at one time known here. A larger and beautifully coloured lizard, sky-blue with a golden head, called *Kande* at Lamu, is sometimes seen running up and down the stems of coconut palms. Its habit when at rest, of nodding its head up and down has suggested to the popular mind that it is engaged in counting all who come within its ken, as a result of which, they will die. Women, when they see it, call out: *Kande, Kande, usiniwange!* — " do not count me! " This may have some connection with a forgotten legend of the kind current, as we have seen, among the inland tribes (Giryama, Kamba, etc.). In West Africa, we find the legend among the Duala [13] and the Bakwiri of Kamerun — the latter combining it with another very ancient myth which we must notice in detail later. They also associate the Chameleon with the Salamander instead of the usual Lizard. In Bamum, as also in Abeokuta and Benin, the Chameleon is frequently represented in wood-carving and metal-work, but its exact place in the mythology of these tribes has yet to be determined. It is remarkable that, while the legend of the origin of Death is told on the Gold Coast with the Sheep and the Goat [14] as messengers, there are Twi and Ewe proverbs which indicate that these are of recent introduction and that the Chameleon had his place in the older form of the myth.

The dread which this creature seems to inspire — and indeed, its appearance and its ways, not to mention its changes of colour, make it uncanny enough to suggest any amount of superstition — is well illustrated by Struck. [15] He relates that two boys of the Bulu tribe, whom he had the opportunity of questioning at Hamburg, were very communicative about all the animals known to them in the Zoological Gardens till they caught sight of the Chameleon in the Reptile House. Both immediately fell silent and made a wide circuit to avoid it; the only information they could be induced to give was that, " God had sent it."

Meinhof, some years ago,[16] suggested that the Chameleon figures in this myth because it comes into the category of " soul-animals " (*Seelentiere*),[17] i.e., those thought of as embodiments of departed spirits. Such, for various reasons, are snakes, lizards, birds, fish and others. Animals seen in the neighbourhood of graves, especially such as burrow in the earth and might seem to come out of the grave itself, would easily come to be looked on in such a light. It is true that the Chameleon does not burrow in the earth, and is usually found on trees or bushes, but Wundt thinks that creeping things in general may have become soul-vehicles by an extension of the idea originally associated with the maggots actually found feeding on corpses. In a later work, however,[18] Meinhof has adopted another explanation, thinking that the real reason is given in a Duala tale which describes the Chameleon as " always trembling, as if just about to die — yet it does not die," at the time, and therefore it is presumed that it never will. The Chameleon, moreover, says Meinhof, is the messenger of the Moon, and its changes of colour afford an obvious reason for their connection.

But, unfortunately for the theory, the Chameleon, so far as I am aware, is nowhere said to be the messenger of the Moon. The Moon, with one or two insignificant exceptions, does not come into the Bantu legend at all, and the Hottentot and Bushman myths concerned with it make no mention of the Chameleon, the most usual messenger being the Hare. I think the two groups of tales must be originally distinct; the features they have in common are quite likely to have arisen independently.

The Chaga of Kilimanjaro have both a Moon story and a Chameleon story, but they are not in any way connected, and neither is quite of the usual type. This Bantu tribe has been much in contact with non-Bantu people, such as the Masai; and, while much of their folk-lore is characteristically Bantu, it certainly contains some Masai elements.

The Hottentot myth has been variously reported. Bleek [19] gives four versions, the first differing in an important point from the other three. The part played by the Hare is interesting, as bearing on the very different conceptions of that animal found in Bantu and Hamitic folklore respectively.

This version, translated from an original Nama text taken down by Krönlein, says that the Moon sent a messenger — politely described by Bleek as " an Insect," though more plainly specified in the original [20]— to tell men: " As I die and dying live, so shall ye also die and dying live." The " Insect " was slow, as might be expected (*vide* the first chapter of Sir A. Shipley's *Minor Horrors of War*), and had not gone very far before he was overtaken by the Hare, who asked his errand. On being informed of it, the Hare offered to carry it, being so much swifter, and the messenger consented. The Hare — it is not stated whether out of wanton mischief or stupidity — reversed the terms of the message, and the angry Moon, on his return, hit him with a piece of wood so that his lip is split to this day. One version adds that the Hare, in retaliation, scratched the Moon's face, so that the marks are still visible. But the most important variation is the omission of the Insect — in all three versions the Hare is the original messenger sent, who, whether wilfully or not, falsifies the message. This is also the case in the form of the story obtained from the Nama, at a much later date, by Dr. Schultze, which also supplies the missing explanation, exculpating the Hare at the expense of his intellect. " And the Hare delivered his message, saying: ' As my grandfather the Moon does, so ye also shall pass away and appear again. That is my message.' But when he spoke so, the boys shouted: ' What are you talking about? ' Then the Hare (grew confused and) said: ' As I do — this is my message — so ye also shall die with staring eyes ' " — alluding to the appearance of a dead man whose eyes have not been closed. " Then he went home and came to the Moon; and the Moon asked him (about his errand), but he was silent, well knowing that he had told a lie. So the Moon (hit him and) cut his mouth open."

I was inclined to set down the Moon-myth as characteristically Hamitic, as the Chameleon-myth is characteristically Bantu; but I have not come across the former among either Masai, Somali, or Galla, while, on the other hand, the Bushmen [21] have the legend which I shall presently relate. The Bushmen, however, say nothing about the Hare being sent with a message to mankind; while this is a prominent feature in the Galla and Nandi stories. It occurs to me that the Hottentots, whose ultimate derivation is Hamitic, might have brought with them the idea of a message sent by the Creator to assure men of immortality, and associated it with a Moon-myth borrowed from the Bushmen, who have exercised a strong influence on their language and probably also upon their thought.

The Bushmen say that the Hare was once a human being and that his mother died. When he was crying and mourning for her, the Moon tried to comfort him by saying that she was not really dead, " but will return, as I also do." The Hare would not believe this, and the Moon grew angry, hitting him on the face with his fist and, as already related, splitting his lip. He then turned him into a Hare and laid a curse upon him, that he should be hunted by dogs and caught and torn to pieces and " die altogether," and also on the whole human race, that they, too, should die without remedy.

The Nandi [22] say that a Dog one day came to the first human beings and said: " All people will die like the Moon, but unlike the Moon you will not return to life again, unless you give me some milk to drink out of your gourd, and beer to drink through your straw. If you do this, I will arrange for you to go to the river when you die and come to life again on the third day." There is no hint here of any one sending the Dog, or of how he became possessed of his information. The people laughed at the Dog and, though they supplied him with refreshment, they did not treat him with proper respect, but poured the milk and beer into the hollow top of a stool, for him to lap up, instead of giving him the one in a gourd and letting him drink the other through the tube [23] used for this beverage by the Nandi. So the Dog was angry, and, though he drank, went away saying, " All people will die and the Moon alone will return to life."

I heard from Abarea, headman of the Galla in the Malindi District of the East Africa Protectorate,[24] the account given by the Southern Galla of the way in which death entered the world. God (Wak) sent a certain bird (called by the Galla, from its cry, *Holawaka*, " the Sheep of God ") with a message to men. The bird, which I have not yet satisfactorily identified, though it may be the black and white hornbill, is black, with a white patch on each shoulder, and cries $a - a - a -$ like a sheep. (Abarea insisted much on its being black and white " like the sky " — perhaps the stormy sky — or, as the same word is used for black and blue, he may have meant the sky dappled with white clouds.) God gave him a crest, " like a flag, to show that he was a messenger," [25] and told him to tell men that when they felt themselves growing old and weak they had only to shed their skins and they would grow young again. The bird set out, but on the way saw a snake feeding on the carcass of a freshly-killed animal and was seized with a desire to share in the feast. He offered to tell the snake " the news of God " in return for some of the flesh, and, more especially, of the blood. (Abarea interpolated the remark that the snake was an enemy from the beginning.) The snake at first refused but, on being pressed, gave way, and the bird delivered his message in words to the following effect: " People will grow old and die; but you, when you grow old, all you have to do is to crawl out of your skin, and you will be young again." Consequently, men die and do not come back, but snakes shed their skins and renew their youth. Wak was very angry with the greedy and treacherous bird and cursed it with chronic indigestion, so that it knows no rest, but sits by itself in the trees, uttering its wailing cry, *Wakatia — a — a — a!,* which Abarea paraphrased: " My God! heal me, for I am perishing! "

Here we find the right message given, but to the wrong person — a variation I have not noted elsewhere. The idea that men could at one time renew their vitality by changing their skins is found among the Wachaga,[26] who relate that they might have continued to do so to this day but for the curiosity of two children. The parents, being about to accomplish their annual change, and wishing to get the children out of the way, sent them down to the river to fetch water in a basket, charging them not to return unless they could bring it full. After many trials, they grew tired and came back, but their father heard them outside the door and sent them away, so next time they came quietly and, getting in before they were heard, saw their mother half in and half out of her skin, as a result of which she died, and every one else has done so ever since. Several different stories appear to be current among these people. In one, a woman's child dies and she entreats her co-wife to carry the body out into the bush [27] for her and say: " Go and return again like the Moon "; but the woman, being jealous, said: " Go and be lost, but let the Moon go and return again."

PLATE XV

1. Abarea, the narrator of the *Holawaka* story.
2. In the lower photograph, he is shown struggling with a young man who was reluctant to be photographed and dragging him in front of the camera. The stick held by the young man (called hoko) is used for removing thorny branches from the path.

After photographs by Prof. A. Werner.

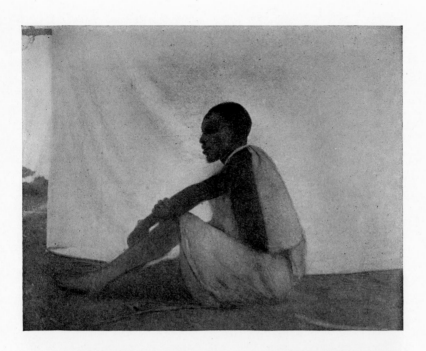

The Chaga substitute for the Chameleon story [28] is to some extent a reversal of the current type: it deals, not with the introduction of death, but with the saving of the human race from summary destruction. The Salamander went to heaven and complained that the earth was becoming over-populated; the friendly little House-lizard overheard him and, thinking: "If God (Iruwa) destroys men, where am I going to sleep?" went and said: "The Salamander is deceiving thee; there are only a few people in the world." So he remains a welcome inmate of the hut, but the spiteful Salamander was driven from human habitations and hides among the stones.

Before turning to the myth of Walumbe, referred to in our last chapter, which marks a somewhat different order of thought in contrast to those we have just been considering, we must refer in passing to a somewhat different notion found in some places, viz., that death, though universal, may in individual cases be remediable. The Wachaga have two legends illustrative of this belief. One is of a gigantic snail which could revive a dead man by crawling over and lubricating him. After this marvellous property had been accidentally discovered, people used to carry their dead friends into the forest and leave them to be crawled over by the snail. But a chief who was at war with the tribe and to whom the secret of their never-diminishing numbers was betrayed by a woman, sent men to hunt up the snail and spear it to death. [29]

The hyenas, too, [30] it is said, used to possess a magic staff called *Kirasa*, with which they could recall a dead man to life. They used it to revive dead men, whom they questioned as to the manner of their death, before eating them. [31] But a man once stole *Kirasa*, and the hyenas were in great straits; for, since every one who died recovered, there were no corpses to eat. At length they recovered it and, fearing lest the same thing might happen again, threw it into a deep pit where neither they nor any one else could ever get at it.

The Baganda have a Chameleon-legend of much the same character as those already mentioned, but, side by side with it and probably introduced by the Hamitic influence so visible in other parts of their national life, is a legend which shows Death as a person — in fact a son of Gulu (Heaven). When Kintu and Nambi left Gulu's presence to settle on the earth, carrying with them the domestic animals and plants which were henceforth to constitute the staple foodstuffs of the country, he warned them on no account to turn back should they find that they had forgotten anything. Walumbe (Death) was absent at the time, and Gulu was anxious that the couple should start before his return, as he would insist on coming with them. When they were about half way, they discovered that they had left behind the grain for feeding the fowl. Kintu insisted on returning for it, though Nambi remonstrated,[32] saying: " No, don't go back. Death will have come home by this time and he is execeedingly wicked; when he sees you he will want to come here and I don't want him, he does harm." But Kintu went back, and it fell out as Gulu and Nambi had said — the unwelcome brother-in-law followed him down to earth, though, for a time, he gave no trouble. When Kintu's children were growing up, Walumbe came and demanded one of the girls to cook for him. Kintu refused and Walumbe threatened to kill the children, but Kintu paid no heed to the threat, and the incident was repeated several times. At last the children began to sicken and die, and the father, now thoroughly alarmed, went and appealed to Gulu for help. Gulu answered as might be expected — and at considerable length — but afterwards so far relented that he sent another of his sons, Kaikuzi, to fetch Death back. Kaikuzi at first tried persuasion, but Death refused to come, unless his sister Nambi came too. Kaikuzi then seized him in order to take him away by force, but Death slipped from his hands and took refuge underground. Twice Kaikuzi succeeded in seizing

him and dragging him to the surface, and twice he escaped.
After a while, when Death seemed to be getting tired out,
Kaikuzi directed Kintu to give orders that every one was to
stay indoors for two days; the children were not to go out with
the goats, and if, by any chance, any one saw Death come out
of the ground, he was on no account to give the alarm. However, it seems that, in spite of the prohibition, some little boys
were out herding at Tanda (in Singo, the central district of
Uganda), and while they were playing in a meadow, they saw
Death appearing above ground and at once raised the shrill
cry, *ndulu,* which gives warning of danger. Kaikuzi hurried
up, but it was too late — Death had once more disappeared,
and Kaikuzi declared he was tired of hunting him and should
return to heaven. Kintu accepted this decision quite phil-
osophically: " Very well — since you cannot get the better of
Death, let him alone and return to Gulu's. If he wants to kill
men, let him — I, Kintu, will not cease begetting children, so
that Death will never be able to make an end of my people."
So Kaikuzi returned, reported his failure, and thenceforth
remained in heaven.[33]

There seems here a distinct notion that the reproduction of
the human species is necessitated by death. It is true that Kintu
already had several children before Death began to exercise
his power. But perhaps we are to understand that the family
would have increased up to a comfortable limit and then
stopped, had not the gaps made by Death called for indefinite
multiplication. Or it may be that the exigencies of the story
have betrayed the narrator into inconsistencies, as may happen
in more sophisticated literature.

Death also appears, under the slightly different name of
Olumbe (Orumbe) in the tale of Mpobe, the hunter, who,
following an animal into its burrow, found himself in the
country of the Dead. He found his dog and the game at a
village where there were many people, and he was asked by

the chief to give an account of himself. Having done so, he was allowed to depart, after being warned that if he spoke to any one of what he had seen, he would be killed. He returned home and successfully parried all inquiries, till at last his mother over-persuaded him and he told her. That night Mpobe heard some one calling him, and a voice said: " I saw you when you told some one. . . . Since you have told your mother — very well; if you have anything to eat, eat it," i.e. consume what substance you now possess. Mpobe made his property last out several years, and when Death came for him the next time, told him he had not yet finished. Death then went away, and Mpobe hid himself in the forest, thinking that so he might escape. Death tracked him down, and again he made excuse, saying that he had not yet consumed his property, whereat Death said: " Make haste and finish it then, for I want to kill you." Mpobe returned home and tried a fresh hiding-place every day, but finding all his efforts vain, went back to his house and resigned himself to his fate. Next time the inevitable question was repeated, he replied, " I have finished up everything," and his visitor rejoined: " Very good — since you have finished, die! " — and Mpobe died.

The Kingdom of the Dead is here called Magombe; the incident of the hunter reaching it through following an animal into a hole occurs elsewhere, e.g., in an uncollected Yao tale, which was mentioned to me in conversation many years ago, but of which I have never succeeded in obtaining a copy. But the idea is one so likely to suggest itself to the primitive mind that we need not look for evidence of derivation.

Death is also personified in a curious tale recorded by P. Capus [34] from the Basumbwa, a tribe living at the south-western corner of the Victoria Nyanza. Here Death is called Lufu or (with the augmentative) Lirufu. Men who die herd his cattle for him — apparently in the upper world. A man died and left two sons, the younger of whom took the inheritance to himself, giving his elder brother only three cows and two slaves, and making him the herdsman. While he was out with his younger brother's cattle, he met his father, who told him to drive his beasts home early on the morrow and meet him at the same place. The father was herding Death's cattle, and, in the evening, drove them home along a road which passed through a great opening in the earth. On arriving, they seem to have met with people, who asked: " Have you brought another? "— but nothing more is said about these, and he hid his son for the night. In the morning Death, the " Great Chief," came out. One side of him was entirely decayed, so much so that " caterpillars " (*nshimi*) dropped off it; the other was sound. His servants washed and dressed the wounds, and he uttered a curse: " He who goes trading to-day, will be robbed. She who is about to bring forth will die with her child. He who cultivates to-day will lose his crops. He who goes into the Bush will be eaten by a lion." On the following day, Death's servants washed his sound side, perfumed and anointed him, and he reversed the maledictions of the day before. The young man's father said to him: " If you had only come to-day, you would have become very rich. As it is, the best thing you can do is to return home and leave your brother in possession of the inheritance, for it is evident that your destiny is to be poor."

At first sight, one is tempted to think that Death regularly distributes good and evil fortune to mankind on alternate days. But in that case it is difficult to see why the father should have told his son to come on that particular day, and then deplored the fact, as though he himself had not been responsible. We must therefore suppose, either that the event was an exceptional one, or that the arrangement was not made known to all Lirufu's subjects.

Kalunga, or Kalunga-ngombe (" Kalunga of the Cattle ") is the name for Death (" the King of the Shades ") among the

Mbundu of Angola,[35] but it is also used for the place of the dead, the sea, and (as by the Herero and Kwanyama) for a Supreme Being. Heli Chatelain gives a story [36] in which a young hero, Ngunza Kilundu kia Ngunza, on hearing that his younger brother Maka is dead, announces his intention of fighting Kalunga-ngombe. He set a trap in the bush and waited near it with his gun, till he heard a voice calling from the trap: " I am dying, dying! " He was about to fire when the voice said: " Do not shoot, come to free me." Ngunza asked who was speaking, and the answer came: " I am Ka-lunga-ngombe." " Thou art Kalunga-ngombe who killed my younger brother Maka? " The answer was: " I am not ever killing wantonly; people are brought to me. Well, I give thee four days; on the fifth, go and fetch thy younger brother in Kalunga." Ngunza went and was welcomed by Kalunga-ngombe, who made him sit down beside him. One after another, the dead arrived from the upper world. One, on being questioned as to the cause of his death, said that some one who was envious of his wealth had bewitched him. Another, a woman, said her husband had killed her for un-faithfulness, and so on. Kalunga-ngombe said, not unreason-ably: " Thou seest, Ngunza Kilundu kia Ngunza, it is not I that am always killing mankind; the hosts of Ndongo " (in other words, " the people of Angola "), " they are brought to me. Therefore go and fetch thy younger brother." But Maka refused to come, saying that in Kalunga the conditions were much better than on earth. " What I have here, on earth perchance shall I have it? " So Ngunza had to return without him. Kalunga-ngombe gave him " seeds of manioc, maize, Kaffir-corn," and other things — a list too long to reproduce — to plant on earth, and told him: " In eight days, I will go to visit thee at thy home." When he arrived, he found that Ngunza had fled, going to the east, and he followed him from place to place till he came up with him, when he announced that he was going to kill him. Ngunza protested: " Thou canst not kill me, because I did no crime against thee. Thou ever sayest: ' People are brought to me, I don't kill any one.' Well, now, why dost thou pursue me to the east? " Kalunga-ngombe, for all answer, attacked him with his hatchet, but Ngunza " turned into a *Kituta* spirit," and so, presumably, passed out of his power.

Several points in the above are obscure, perhaps because the story was taken from " poorly-written " notes of an informant who died before Chatelain prepared his book for the press. It does not appear why Kalunga should have intended to kill Ngunza — perhaps the intimation of his visit was intended to convey a warning, which the latter disregarded; but, in that case, why does Kalunga fail to explain why he departs from his usual custom? Perhaps, as in the case of Mpobe, he had told Ngunza to say nothing about what he had seen in the underworld, and Ngunza had disobeyed him; but of this there is no hint in the story as it stands. The matter of the *Kituta*, too, calls for further explanation. A *Kituta* or *Kianda* [37] is a spirit who " rules over the water and is fond of great trees and of hill-tops "; one of a class of beings to be discussed in a later chapter.

The Ne (a Kru tribe of the Ivory Coast) [38] introduce a personification of Death into several of their folk-tales. In one he is an eight-headed monster, one of whose heads is cut off by a boy, on hearing that his mother is dead, a parallel to Ngunza's attack on Death. The boy escapes from the monster but is caught in a bush-fire and perishes, his soul escaping in the form of a hawk. This is why hawks are always seen hovering over bush-fires.

Another Ne story is a variant of many well-known tales dealing with cannibals. A young girl goes to Death's village and is sheltered in the hut of an old woman. Death, however, discovers her, and refuses to let her have anything to eat till she tells his name — a link with another group of stories [39] not specially well represented in Africa. She is helped by a bird, who betrays the name to her. Ultimately Death's big toe is cut off, and all the people he has devoured issue from it. This last incident is found in tales from such distant parts as Basutoland ("Masilo and Masilonyane") and Kilimanjaro, and we shall have to recur to it in a later chapter.

The Ne have another legend connected with Death which, as far as I know, has not yet been recorded from any other quarter. A man applied to Blenyiba, the great fetish of Cavalla, for a charm to make the approach of Death impossible. Blenyiba gave him a stone to block the path by which alone the enemy could approach; but as the man was transporting it to the spot, he met Nemla — the small antelope locally equivalent to Brer Rabbit, who offered to help him to carry it. The treacherous Nemla, while pretending to help, sang a spell which made the rock immovable, leaving the path open, as it is to this day, " and the rock is yet alive to testify of it."

In the next chapter, we shall meet with other legends bearing on the Underworld regarded as the abode of the dead. Perhaps some of those just recounted might seem to be more appropriately treated in connection with Ancestral Ghosts.

But, as already pointed out, the boundaries between the various departments of our subject are extremely difficult to draw, and the latter are apt to run into one another. No attempt has been made, throughout this work, to adhere to a rigidly scientific classification.

CHAPTER IV

THE ANCESTRAL SPIRITS

THE BELIEF in the continued existence of human beings after death, and their influence on the affairs of
the survivors is really the bed-rock fact in Bantu and Negro
religion. Even where there is a developed cult of definite
spiritual powers, as for example in Uganda and Dahome,
these have in many cases grown out of ancestral ghosts, and,
as has been already remarked, many beings which now seem
to be Nature Powers pure and simple, may have had a like
origin. This is not to deny that there are nature spirits which
have been such from the beginning, or that the two conceptions
may sometimes have been fused into one personality, as perhaps, for instance, in Leza, but only to repeat once more what
has so often been said as to the difficulty of exact classification.

Some Africans, for example, the Tẅi and Ewe, seem to
have arrived at something like a coherent philosophy of the
soul. There is the shade, which either haunts the neighbourhood of the grave, or sinks into the subterranean abode of the
ghosts (*kuzimu*), and the soul (called in Tẅi ' *kra* '), which
is reincarnated in one of the person's descendants.[1] But it
may be doubted whether this doctrine is everywhere consciously
and clearly held, and one must be prepared for vague and
sometimes contradictory statements. Sometimes it is only those
who have died a violent death who are said to haunt the upper
earth; sometimes those who have gone down to the Underworld are believed to come back from time to time. In Nyasaland, the ghost is thought to remain near the grave for some
time, perhaps a year or two, and then to depart, probably into
the Underworld.

Ghosts, apparently, are not immortal — indeed, if we may believe the account given to the Rev. J. Raum [2] by the Wachaga, they are kept alive by the offerings of the living. This account is one of the most detailed I have seen, and probably represents ideas current, though not recorded, elsewhere. The ancestral spirits are called in Chaga *warimu* (or *warumu*) and defined as the "shadows" (*sherisha*) of people who have died. (The shadow is often identified with the life, or soul, or one of the souls.) The ghosts are so called, say the Wachaga, "because they have no bones" — they look like living people, only you cannot take hold of them, and when you see them they are apt to vanish suddenly and instantaneously. Some are like old men, some like men in their prime; there are women and children among them: in fact, it would seem as if every one remained at the age he or she had reached at death. They live underground much as they had done on earth; they have their chiefs and their tribal assemblies; and when a man dies he passes to the dwelling-place of his own clan, while the clan remains with its own section of the tribe. But not all the ghosts are to be found in this abode — only the fathers, grandfathers, and great-grandfathers of the people now living. These are called the "upper" (or "recent") ghosts (*warimu wa uwe*) or "those who are known" (*waishiwo*), their names and standing being still remembered. They partake of the offerings made by their descendants, and it is implied that these keep them alive. The great-great-grandfather and previous generations get crowded out from the sacrifices by the later comers; they are unable to keep up their strength and sink down into a lower region. These are called *wakilengeche* or sometimes *warimu wangiinduka*, "the ghosts who turn back." Unlike the *waishiwo*, who freely communicate with the living, they never show themselves on the upper earth, though they haunt their old homes secretly and make people ill in order to get sacrifices out of them. But the oldest among them cannot even do this; they can no longer reach the sacrifices, and " their life is done "; they have " gone to pieces " and have no further connection with living men. These are called the *walenge*. The three regions of the dead are clearly distinguished in the legend of the Heaven-Tree.[3] One meets elsewhere with indications that the ghosts are not supposed to be immortal, but I do not think I have anywhere else found so clear and definite a statement on the subject as this. The usual name for the underground abode of the dead — *kuzimu* or some cognate [4] — is the locative form of a root very widely distributed in the Bantu languages, with the meaning of an ancestral ghost. Thus the Anyanja have the word *mzimu*, pl. *mi-zimu* (though, as we have seen, they sometimes use " Mulungu " in the same sense), and it survives in Swahili in the phrase *ana wazimu* (" he is mad " — literally, " he has spirits "), though otherwise obsolete. In Zulu, also, it is nearly obsolete, being used as a collective only in one particular phrase: the expressions now current are *ama-dhlozi*, of which the derivation is not very clear,[5] and *ama-tongo*, manifestly connected with *ubu-tongo*, " sleep," and applied to ghosts when they appear in dreams, while the other term is more generally used of spirits which show themselves in other ways, e.g. in the form of snakes, etc. The two names denote the same class of being, only viewed under different aspects, and, even so, no very exact distinction can be drawn between them, as Zulus use the words, to a great extent, interchangeably.

It should be noted that *mzimu* and its cognates are not, as a rule (Swahili is an exception) treated as belonging to the person-class — perhaps from a dim feeling that a ghost is not more, but less, than a human being. Such a feeling seems to come out in the Chaga beliefs already detailed, though it is not quite consistent with the dread entertained of the ghosts' maleficent power. But it may be that the change of concord merely indicates the idea of a disembodied *non*-human, but not necessarily *infra*-human personality. Animals, by the bye, are usually included in the person-class: *they* are intelligences invested with bodies, and we seldom, if ever, find them sharply contrasted with human beings.[6] This is a point to which we must return when speaking of Totemism.

We shall have to consider, later on, whether, and how far, we have to deal, in Africa, with spirits which were not, originally, the ghosts of the dead. Certainly, it is the latter which bulk largest in the people's imagination; and, as we have already seen in the case of local gods, some spirits which at first seem to have quite a different nature, may ultimately be traced back to such an origin.

We cannot say that ghosts are divided into benignant and malignant — except in so far as a man is supposed to retain after death the qualities which distinguished him during his lifetime. Less weight seems accorded to this consideration than one might expect, at any rate in the case of bad people — perhaps the maxim *De mortuis* is more thoroughly acted upon than by ourselves. At any rate, what is far more frequently and emphatically asserted is that the behaviour of the ghosts largely depends on the treatment they receive from their surviving relatives. When they send locusts — as Chipoka did to Mlanje in 1894[7] — or sickness, or other disasters, it is to remind the living of neglected duties.

It is hardly true to say that the predominant feeling with which the ghosts are regarded is one of terror and dislike, and that their cult is solely determined by fear. Many stories give evidence of affection surviving the grave and prompting interference on behalf of the living. The statements of Callaway's informants on this head are very interesting. On the other hand, the same evidence shows that their ethics, like those of their surviving descendants, have not outgrown the tribal standpoint. A ghost is not expected to care for any

PLATE XVI

1. Carved post (*kigango*) set up by the Giryama on or near the place where the head of the family is buried.

2. Giryama shrines for the spirits. Each small post represents a deceased member of the family. Offerings of beer are poured into a pot sunk in the ground (not visible in photograph).

After photographs by Prof. A. Werner.

outside his own family; and the family do not feel that any attentions are due to unrelated ghosts. This was avowedly the reason why Unkulunkulu was not worshipped — there were none living who knew themselves to be of his blood.[8] Of course, the ghosts of chiefs or famous medicine-men will be honoured by people outside their own families, and these, as we have seen in Nyasaland and Uganda, may attain the status of gods.

The Wachaga do not sacrifice to any ghost more than three generations back — that is, expressly and by name — for one gathers from the account already quoted that, if the Wakilengeche can by their own exertions secure a share in the offerings, it rests with them to do so. There is one exception, however: each clan sacrifices to the ancestor who first settled and planted in the Kilimanjaro country, when the tribe migrated thither from the north, and whose name, in some cases at least, has been preserved.[9]

The Wachaga believe, that while the spirits can influence the course of events on earth, they, in their turn, can be affected by revolutions in the affairs of the living. Thus, the coming of the Europeans to East Africa has made itself felt in the Underworld. What, exactly, Raum's informant meant by saying that "the white men, when they came here, also came to the ancestral spirits," and that the latter have to pay taxes to them, is not very clear, but no doubt he felt it to be a legitimate inference from the hard times experienced by the living. "It is said: Alas! even among the ghosts there is misery, O ye people! If you see an old woman of the spirits, she looks dirty; they are ragged, and they have grown thin. Those who are carried off by the spirits in dreams, by night, always say so, and so do the diviners." As to this carrying off of people — the ghosts of dead Wachaga are not content with merely appearing in dreams to their relatives — we shall have more to say presently.

The spirit-world is reached most easily, as we have seen, through caves or holes in the earth. The Wachaga speak of gates leading thither — some say there are two " in the east, where sky and earth join." [10] One of these gives entrance to heaven, the other " to the ghosts." The distinction is remarkable, and is also found in a legend already quoted, where the two gates are located, not on the distant horizon, but on Kilimanjaro mountain.[11] Here, those passing by the ghosts' gate see a blazing fire within, a touch which may be due to the infiltration of Moslem ideas from the coast; though, if there were any warrant for connecting this gate with the west (of which there is no hint in our authority) it might equally well be suggested by the flaming sunset.

A widow who had lost her only son once made her way to the eastern gate and was so importunate that the Chief of the Ghosts at length consented to restore her son, whom she found awaiting her on her return home. Tradition has preserved the names of various people who went to the spirit-land and returned, perhaps persons who recovered from cataleptic trances. There is a song sung by young girls:

> "Would I might go, like Kidova's daughter
> To seek the spirits beyond the water —
> To go I were fain,
> And behold, and return again." [12]

The Bapedi (a branch of the Bechwana living in the Eastern Transvaal) believed that the cave of Marimatle, from which the human race originally issued (as elsewhere from Kapirimtiya), was also the entrance to the spirit-world.[13] And we find in so many different places, that we may presume the legend to be or have been current all over Bantu Africa, accounts of men who, pursuing some animal into a burrow, have, like Mpobe, reached the abode of the dead. Thus the Zulus say that one Uncama [14] followed a porcupine into its

hole and, after a day and a night came upon a village, where
he saw smoke rising and people moving about, and heard dogs
baying and children crying: " all things resembled those which
are above, mountains, precipices, and rivers." He did not
wait to make a closer examination but said: " Let me not go to
these people, for I do not know them; perhaps they will kill
me," and returned with all speed, to find his own funeral being
celebrated when he reached his house. Another man, Umkatshana,[15] had a similar experience when hunting a buck, but
went on till he actually met " the people who are beneath "
face to face, saw them milking their cattle, and recognised
one of his own friends among them. " They said to him: ' Go
home! Do not stay here! ' So he went home again." The
Wairamba,[16] in Eastern Unyamwezi, also tell of a man who
followed a porcupine — this time a wounded one — underground, and came to the village of the dead, where he was
kindly welcomed and met various deceased relatives, while the
porcupine he had speared turned out to be his own sister. It
was explained to him that, while the ghosts enjoy a happy and
peaceful life in the Underworld, with cattle feeding in rich
pastures and abundance of almost everything they need, they
have no grain and therefore have to come up to earth in the
shape of animals and steal it from the gardens. He was therefore charged with messages to the living, desiring them to
bring offerings of porridge and beer to the graves from time
to time. (This is in marked contrast to several other stories of
the kind, where it is made a *sine qua non* that the visitor shall
never tell his experiences.) He was also assured that his sister
bore no malice, " because you did it in ignorance, and, besides,
her wound will soon heal down here."

This story is told to explain how the custom of offerings
to the dead was instituted; and the fact strikes me as peculiar,
because elsewhere it does not seem to be felt that the custom
needs any explanation. It is of immemorial antiquity, and, given

the belief that the dead continue to live, somewhere in or near their graves, a life not very different from their previous state of existence, its utility is surely self-evident.

The introduction of the porcupine is interesting, because we learn from Messrs Melland and Cholmeley [17] that the Waku-luwe have a sect or guild of porcupine-hunters (*waleli*) who own that they visit the village of the *fisinzwa* (ghosts) when they enter the porcupine's burrows, and " that the Chief of the village is called *Lungabalwa* and is most hospitable to them and never lets them go away empty-handed, always giving them a porcupine."

No doubt the appearance and habits of the porcupine are sufficient to account for this connection with the unseen world. He certainly looks uncanny; he burrows in the ground, and, while very destructive in the gardens, he is never, or rarely, seen by daylight. Natives firmly believe he has the power of shooting his quills at an assailant.

But the most usual mode of access to the spirit-world is through the lakes and smaller sheets of water in which the mountainous Chaga country abounds.[18] More especially does this apply to the deep pools or pot-holes under a waterfall. Through such a " linn," the ghosts are apt to ascend and seize on any sheep or goats found grazing within a convenient distance, and pick up any wooden troughs (used in making beer) which people may have left lying about. [19] Or if a man goes too near the bank, he may find himself seized and pulled into the water. It is not stated whether this means actual and final drowning, but we may infer such to be the case, for it is believed that, if you happen to have a knife or other sharp instrument by you, and can give yourself a cut in time, you will escape, since the ghosts will only accept an unblemished victim. Some say, however, that this never happens now [20] — at any rate in the districts of Kisangada and Ofurunye, where the ghosts were formerly a great nuisance, coming from the pools in the Msangachi valley to steal food from people's houses at night. It was proposed that a beast should be sacrificed to them, but some said that this would be no use in the end and that it would be better to find a childless man who should put a curse on the pools — not with " bell, book and candle," but with the " cursing-bell " and " cursing-pot." [21] (A childless man would have nothing to lose by the vengeance of the ghosts.) He accordingly took one of these implements in each hand and pronounced his commination:

" If ye will not cease from troubling the folk,
Perish and die away — sink down and rot. . . .
But if ye will cease and leave them in quiet,
Ye shall continue and be preserved! "

This ceremony had the desired effect.

But the ghosts are also believed to remove people temporarily to the Underworld and restore them. Sometimes during the night a sleeper will disappear, leaving only his clothes on the bed.[22] These must not be touched, nor must anyone call him, otherwise he will never come back. There is apparently no hostile intention; he is transported to the Underworld in order to be told what the spirits intend to do, or what they wish the living to do, and, if he behaves himself discreetly, no harm will happen to him. But he must not show undue curiosity or make remarks on what he sees: the shades are very sensitive to criticism — especially of their household arrangements. " For the Ancestors eat very nasty things. Their children go out to search for food and come home with crickets and moths " —presumably in the absence of offerings from above. Anyone who shows surprise at this or other details of the cooking will be detained for ever (and perhaps beaten as well) so that he may not talk and put the ghosts to shame among the living. More tactful visitors are sent back with whatever communications are deemed desirable, and it is from these and the diviners (*walashi*) that people get to know what is happening among the ghosts.

The lakes mentioned are personified in a very curious way. In old times, if wars or raids were going on, they could be heard shouting: " O–o–o! be easy. We shall drive away the enemy! " After the invaders had retreated, the shrill cries of joy raised by the spirit-women arose from under the water.[23] A story which in its present form must be quite recent, tells how a certain pool claimed human victims.[24] A child disappeared and was sought for in vain; at last a voice was heard from the pool, ordering the parents to bring offerings of food and leave them on the bank. Next day the offerings had disappeared and the child's dead body lay in their place. A certain European announced his intention of attacking the monster; he plunged into the pool and fired his rifle, when a door opened in the bottom. He fired again — seven times in all — and at each shot a door opened. He entered and engaged in a desperate struggle, from which he narrowly escaped with his life. He made another attempt and again penetrated the doors, but returned to the surface so badly burnt that he died in a few days. No precise details of the struggle are given, and we have no means of judging whether, and how far, the story is based on an actual occurrence. It might have been suggested by some accident to a daring climber in an active volcanic crater.

Nowadays, says the narrator of the cursing incident, the ghosts live in the pools and the " clan-groves," [25] in the latter case, apparently above ground. But it would seem that they sometimes come out to dance. A man heard them, one night, not far from his house, and, thinking it was a merry-making of his neighbours, went out to join them, in spite of his wife's protests. He soon discovered his mistake, but got home again with no worse experience than a fright.[26] The Wadoe (a tribe inhabiting the mainland opposite Zanzibar) speak of the

haunted woods of Kolelo, where " on some days the drums
sound, and you hear shrill cries like those raised by women
at a wedding." Certain open glades in this forest, where the
ground is smooth and covered with white sand, " just as if
people had gone there to sweep it," are the places where the
ghosts assemble.[27] The spirit-drums and other instruments
(horns and flutes) are also heard in Nyasaland [28] and in the
Delagoa Bay region, where people even profess to have heard
the words of their songs. Here the invisible performers would
stop when the traveller tried to catch sight of them, and the
music would begin again just behind him.[29]

M. Junod finds that Thonga ideas as to the abode of the
ghosts are " very confused, even contradictory." Some hold
to the notion of an Underworld — " a great village under the
earth, where everything is white (or pure);[30] there they till
the fields, reap great harvests and live in abundance, and they
take of this abundance to give to their descendants on the earth.
They have also a great many cattle." This may not seem com-
patible with the need for frequent offerings, but the Thonga do
not take the Chaga view that these are actually necessary to
keep the spirits in existence. " The gods do not ask for real
food or wealth; they only consider the *mhamba* (offering) as
a token of love from their descendants and as a sign that these
have not forgotten them, but will do their duty towards
them." [31]

Others think that the dead somehow continue to exist in
the grave, which is thought of as their house, and others, again,
that they live in the " sacred woods " (equivalent to the Chaga
" clan groves ") in much the same way as they did on earth.
They " lead their family life under a human form, parents
and children, even little children, who are carried on their
mothers' shoulders." They sometimes appear to the living in this way, though not very frequently nowadays;[32]
formerly they were often seen " marching in file, going to

draw water from the well. They had their own road. They were short of stature, the women carrying babies in the *ntehe* (prepared goat-skin), but, strange to say, head downwards."

These sacred groves are really ancient burial-places — among the Thonga, of the chiefs only — elsewhere, as, I think, in Nyasaland,[33] of people generally. Here one sees, dotted about the country, groves consisting of large and shady trees (they are carefully protected from bush fires), among which are the graves. Unless these are of recent date, there is nothing to distinguish them, except some earthen pots, whole or broken. These groves are avoided, as might be expected, by the natives; but I never heard of any special beliefs or traditions connected with them.

The Thonga groves are tabu to all except the " guardian of the wood," or priest, who is the descendant of the chiefs buried there and has charge of all the arrangements for sacrificing to and propitiating them. Terrible things have happened to unauthorised persons trespassing there. One woman who plucked a *sala* fruit [34] and cracked it against a tree-trunk, found it full of little vipers which addressed her as follows: " Go on, eat away! Haven't we seen you every day picking *sala*? And these *sala* are ours and not yours. What shall we gods have to eat? Have we not made this tree to grow? " " And she went home and died, because she had been cursed by the gods." [35]

The same fate — one cannot but think most undeservedly — befell another woman, who found, as she thought, a small child picking berries in a tree and carried him home on her back, as he seemed to be lost. But when she reached her hut and wanted to put him down to get warm by the fire, he could not be removed from her back. The neighbours came to the conclusion that he was no child, but a spirit, and sent for a diviner, who " threw the bones " and " at once knew what was wrong," but failed to get him off. So they suggested that she should carry him back where she had found him. The guard-

PLATE XVII

THE GHOST-BABY

ian of the forest, after a severe rebuke to the poor woman, sacrificed a white hen on her behalf, and interceded for her with the offended powers. " She did not do it on purpose. She thought it was a child; she did not know it was a god." While this sacrifice was being offered, the being suddenly " left her back, disappeared, and no one knew how or whither he went. As for the woman, she trembled violently and died."

This story offers no encouragement to those who would befriend waifs and strays.

Other legends tell what happened to people who cut wood, or killed snakes in the sacred places, or built their huts too near them. The old priest in charge of the Libombo forest was struck down, seemingly by apoplexy, when he went to see what was being done with a certain tree obstructing a road which was being made by the Portuguese authorities. His own account of the matter was, " The gods came to me, saying: ' What are you doing here? You ought to have stayed at home! ' I fell backward unconscious and remained in that state for four days. I could not eat; they had closed my mouth. I could not speak! My people picked me up and carried me home." He recovered after a sacrifice had been offered by his eldest son; but the gods were not entirely placated till after further ceremonies, and he carefully refrained from using the Portuguese road in future.[36]

From Kiziba,[37] on the western side of Lake Victoria, comes a tale connecting the sacred groves, in a somewhat unexpected way, with the tailed Heaven-dwellers. A certain man married a strange woman whom he met on the road as she walked alone, carrying a royal drum. (This circumstance is not further explained.) She told him not on any account to enter the Spirits' Wood, and, of course, he did so. There he met with people — no doubt the ancestors — who, whether out of impish mischief, or in order to bring about the punishment for his disobedience, informed him that his wife had a tail; and he could not rest till he had convinced himself that such was indeed the case. She then disappeared, never to return; but a voice from the haunted wood pointed the moral: " You listened to injurious reports against your neighbor and wanted to see the matter with your own eyes." This belongs to the familiar class of " Vanishing Wife " stories; but it contains some unusual features.

Nearly everywhere we find the belief that the dead some-times come back in the form of animals. There does not seem to be any idea of permanent reincarnation, only of occasional appearances, so that this does not constitute a distinct category of spirits — the animals may be supposed to come up from the Underworld, or out of the grave, or show themselves in the sacred woods, like the old chief of Libombo,[38] who appeared to his descendant, the sacrificing priest, in the shape of a green puff-adder. " I myself," said Nkolele, the priest in question, " went into the wood with the offering I had prepared for the gods, and then *it came out*. It was a snake . . . the Master of the Forest, Mombo-wa-Ndlopfu (Elephant's Face). He came out and circled round all those present. The women rushed away terrified. But he had only come to thank us. He didn't come to bite us. He thanked us, saying: ' Thank you! thank you! So you are still there, my children! You came to load me with presents and to bring me fruit. It is well! ' . . . It was an enormous viper, as thick as my leg down there " — at the ankle. " It came close up to me and kept quite still, never biting me. I looked at it. It said: ' Thank you! So you are still there, my grandson! ' "

Nkolele then made his prayer, which he gives at length. He may have meant that the snake's look and movement con-veyed to his mind the impression of the above words; but I am inclined to think, considering the quite genuine subjective experiences of some European children, that he fully believed he had heard it speaking. A friend of my own told me that, at the age of eight or nine, she was addressed by a cockchafer in a French garden. He said: " Petite fille, écoute! " but though she listened attentively, she heard no more; her imagination, she supposed, had not been lively enough to supply the matter of his discourse.

The serpent-shape is the one most frequently chosen by the ghosts — perhaps for the reason suggested by Wundt,[39] that these reptiles are associated in the native mind with the maggots found in decomposing corpses, and are supposed, e.g. in Madagascar, to be the form assumed by the soul on escaping from the body, a notion easily transferred, where classification is not very scientific, to all creeping things. But Madagascar is rather Indonesian than African in character, and I do not know that this particular belief is found anywhere in Africa itself. It seems simpler to take the view that any animal seen on or near a grave might easily be accepted as a new embodiment of the dead man, especially if, as a snake may sometimes do, it actually crawls out from the earth of the grave itself. One of Callaway's native informants says: " If he observe a snake on the grave, the man who went to look at the grave says on his return, ' O, I have seen him to-day, basking in the sun on the top of the grave! ' " [40]

The Zulus say that only certain kinds of snakes are *amadhlozi*. Some, including at least four poisonous kinds, " are known to be mere beasts: it is impossible for them ever to be men . . . they are always beasts." [41] (One of these is the puff-adder, which, we have seen, the Thonga of Libombo recognise as a spirit-snake, but it may be another species.) Of those which can " become men," some, but not all, are harmless; but not every individual of these species is necessarily an ancestor. Those which are, may be known by their behaviour when they enter a hut — and the fact that they do so at all is presumptive evidence of their character; they do not eat frogs or mice; they remain quiet until discovered, and are not afraid of men, " neither does a snake that is an *itongo* excite fear in men . . . but there is a happy feeling, and it is felt that the chief of the village has come." On the other hand, " A mere snake, when it comes into a hut looks from side to side and is afraid of men:. and it is killed, because it is known to be a wild snake." The " human " snakes, being fed and never molested, become tame — which may account for the behaviour of the puff-adder which was Mombo-wa-Ndlopfu. On the other hand, the Yao appear to think that when the dead come back as snakes, it is with the distinct intention of annoying the living — hence they may be killed without scruple, to stop the nuisance.⁴² If a Zulu, in ignorance, kills an *itongo*-snake, it comes back in a dream to complain, and " a sin-offering is sacrificed." ⁴³

Other creatures serving as the embodiments or vehicles of departed spirits are the mantis,⁴⁴ some lizards (one kind especially said to be the *amatongo* of old women), lions, leopards, hyenas (these are deceased wizards), etc.⁴⁵

CHAPTER V

LEGENDS OF THE SPIRIT-WORLD

ALMOST identical tales are told, as we have already had occasion to remark, about people who have ascended to heaven by means of a rope, or otherwise, and those who have gone down to the subterranean *kuzimu* and returned. Yet seldom, if ever, do we find it stated that the ancestral spirits live in the sky. Those who go there have some errand either to the Supreme Being or to a distinct set of Heaven-dwellers quite apart from ordinary human beings, and it is these whom they encounter and not their deceased friends. The country of the dead, on the other hand, is reached, usually, through a cave, or a hole in the ground, such as an animal's burrow, or by plunging to the bottom of a pool. The Wachaga speak of several gateways, probably caverns, which formerly existed in certain specified localities, but are now closed: this seems to be a tradition distinct from that of the gates on the eastern horizon, mentioned in the last chapter. In old times it was possible for a man who had lost all his children and feared the extinction of his line to enter one of these gateways and lay his case before the ghosts. They would hear his request and send him home, with the promise of another child. But the number of applicants became so great, that the ancestors grew weary of attending to them and closed two of the entrances — a statement which may preserve the memory of some volcanic disturbance. The third remained open for some time longer, but this approach, too, was finally cut off, and nowadays no one can even find the way to it.[1]

The details of the pilgrimage thus made by bereaved parents are interesting, because of their resemblance to some features of a story familiar to us all from childhood and already referred to in our first chapter — the " Frau Holle " of Grimm's *Kinder- und Haus-Märchen*. There are numerous African variants of this,[2] some of which will be discussed presently; their mythological background is unmistakably the same as that of the legend now before us. Having passed through the gateway, the father came to a door in a kraal-fence, where he sat down and waited till an old woman appeared. She led him into a hut and hid him in the sleeping-compartment. At noon " when the sun rests " — the hour for apparitions in hot countries — he saw a band of children passing, led by a man who seemed to be their guardian, and recognised among them his own lost little ones. He pointed them out to the old woman and then she sent him away, first asking him whether he would rather pass through the " sewage-door " or the " sugar-cane door." If he chose the latter, he was thrown up — in some way not explained in our text — through the fireplace, was burnt by the fire and cut by the sugar-cane and reached his home only to die. If he declared for the less inviting alternative, he found himself in his own house, unhurt, and lived for many years thereafter. Presumably, though this is not stated, he found his children awaiting him, or else one of them was re-born shortly after.

The belief that lakes and pools are entrances to and exits from the spirit-world is probably due to the frequency of deaths by drowning in a mountainous country where streams are swift and dangerous and their beds full of treacherous potholes. The mother who has been tricked into drowning her child throws herself into the pool after it and so reaches the spirit-country, as also does Maruwa, in the tale to be given presently.

But it is sometimes easier of access. Where the ghosts are believed to dwell in the sacred groves, there is at least no physical barrier to keep people from penetrating their haunts, though of course they do so at their peril. Junod gives a pretty story [3] of which the scene is laid at Machakeni, close to Lourenço Marques. The people had enjoyed abundant harvests for some years, but had become careless and neglected to sacrifice. So, one season, when they had as usual planted their sweet-potatoes and sugar-cane in the fertile marsh-land at the foot of the hills, they found that nothing would grow. Threatened with famine, they moved to the hills and planted there, but could get no crops. The men, one day, when out hunting, followed an animal down to the plain and found that their old gardens had produced abundantly, after all, but not a thing could they gather. Not one of them could get a potato out of the ground or detach a banana from the tree. Then the ghosts came out and chased them, so that they were glad to escape with their lives. The women, going into the forest to look for firewood found a bees' nest in a hollow tree. Every-one who put in her hand to take out the honey, had it broken off at the wrist. The only one who escaped was the chief's daughter, Sabulana, who refused to go near the tree. She tied up the bundles of wood for her companions and helped them to lift them to their heads. When they reached home, she advised that " the bones should be thrown " (the diviner con-sulted) to find out what should be done. The oracle directed Sabulana to go to the sacred grove and offer a sacrifice. Next morning, all the people assembled and sat down outside the grove: Sabulana alone dared to enter it. She found the spirits all seated in an open space, like the tribal chiefs and headmen when gathered for solemn deliberation. They asked her why she had come, and she replied in a song, which, as reported, does not seem to tell us much:

> " It is I, it is I, Sabulana,
> Daughter of the grass-land —
> It is I, the daughter of the grass-land,
> Sabulana, Sabulana."

The ancestors were delighted with her singing, and asked her to repeat it. They then (apparently without further questioning, but perhaps we are to take the dialogue for granted) gave her supplies of all sorts of provisions and called their children to carry the loads as far as the edge of the wood, where the people were waiting and transported them to the village. Then all the women had their hands restored to them. Sabulana returned to the place where the ghosts were seated, and they said to her: " Go and tell your people that they have sinned in that they tilled the ground and reaped the harvest without paying us any honour. But now let them come with their, baskets and bags and each one take away as much as he can carry on his head; for now we are glad that they have come back once more to pray to us. . . . We were angry with our children, because they ate but brought no offerings. Who, think you, prevented the maize from growing? It was because you sinned over and over again."

In return for Sabulana's services, she and her mother were made chiefs over the whole country.

A different and very curious conception of the spirit-world is found in the Zulu tale of *Unanana Bosele*.[4] Two children and afterwards their mother were swallowed by an elephant. " When she reached the elephant's stomach, she saw large forests and great rivers, and many high lands; on one side there were many rocks; and there were many people who had built their villages there; and many dogs and many cattle; all was there inside the elephant; she saw, too, her own children sitting there."

In short, as Tylor points out,[5] it is a description of the Zulu Hades. It also belongs, with a difference, to another group of tales which we shall have to study in some detail later on — that in which people and animals are swallowed, and subsequently disgorged by a monster. But instead of being released by a deliverer from outside, the woman cuts her way out of the

PLATE XVIII

Hut built for the accommodation of the spirits, Rabai Mpia, near Mombasa. After a photograph by Rev. K. St. Aubyn Rogers.

elephant after feeding, with her children, on his internal organs. The children having told her, in answer to her questions, that they had eaten nothing until she came — " she said: ' Why did you not roast this flesh? ' They said: ' If we eat this beast, will it not kill us? ' She said: ' No; it will itself die; you will not die! ' She kindled a great fire. She cut the liver and roasted it and ate with her children. They cut also the flesh and roasted and ate. All the people which were there wondered saying: ' O, forsooth, are they eating, whilst we have remained without eating anything? ' The woman said: ' Yes, yes, the elephant can be eaten.' All the people cut and ate."

This somewhat repulsive incident is quoted at length because it recurs more than once, among the animal stories, and will be noticed in that connection. The result is pretty much what might have been expected.

" The elephant told the other beasts, saying: ' From the time I swallowed the woman, I have been ill; there has been pain in my stomach! ' " (In another version it is stated that the elephant's groans, when slices were being cut from his liver, were so appalling that all the animals, feeding in different parts of the forest, came running to see what was the matter.) " The other animals said: ' It may be, O Chief, it arises because there are now so many people in your stomach! ' And it came to pass, after a long time, that the elephant died. The woman divided the elephant with a knife, cutting through a rib with an axe. A cow came out and said: ' Moo, Moo, we at length see the country.' They made the woman presents, some gave her cattle, some goats and some sheep. She set out with her children, being very rich."

The conception of the dead dwelling underground is illustrated in the traditions, already mentioned, of Umkatshana and Uncama, and also in the tale of Untombi-yapansi.⁶ Untombi-yapansi was the daughter of a chief, who also had a son,

Usilwane, and another daughter, Usilwanekazana. Usilwane appears to have practised evil magic, though the narrator does not expressly say so. On one occasion he returned from the hunt, bringing with him a leopard cub. He said: " This is my dog, give it milk; mix it with boiled corn and make porridge; and give it its food cold that it may eat; for it will die if you give it hot." His instructions were carried out, and the leopard throve and grew big, to the terror of the people, who said: " It will devour the people. Usilwane will become an *umtakati* (wizard). Why does he domesticate a leopard and call it his dog? " [7] His favourite sister, Usilwanekazana, was greatly troubled on his account; so, one day, when she happened to be alone at home, she gave the leopard hot food, and he died. When her brother returned he was very angry and stabbed her, not, apparently in the heat of passion, but in a cold-blooded and deliberate way which, with his subsequent proceedings, tends to suggest that the people's suspicions were not unfounded. He collected his sister's blood in a pot, and, after washing her wound and laying her out as if she were asleep, killed a sheep and cooked part of it with her blood. When his second sister came home, he offered her some of this food, and she was just about to eat it, but was warned by a fly which came buzzing noisily, again and again, " *Bu! bu!* give me and I will tell you." After vainly trying to drive it away, she gave it some food, and it told her what had happened.

She uncovered her sister's body, gave one look and rushed off to tell her parents. Usilwane pursued her with his spear and had nearly overtaken her, when, seeing no escape, she cried: " Open, earth, that I may enter, for I am about to die this day! " [8] The earth opened and swallowed her up, and Usilwane, utterly bewildered, went back again. Untombi-yapansi went on her way underground till evening, but nothing is said as to what she saw there; then she slept and started again next morning. At midday, she came out of the earth and, standing on a mound which overlooked her father's garden cried aloud: " There will be nothing but weeping this summer. Usilwanekazana has been killed by Usilwane; he says she killed the prince's leopard without cause." An old woman who heard her repeated the words, and the chief ordered her to be killed " for prophesying evil against the king's child." The same thing happened again next day, and this time an unfortunate old man who had heard the cry was sacrificed. But on the third day, all the people heard the girl's voice and ran towards her, asking " What do you say? " She told them, and they went to Usilwane's house, seized him and took him before the chief, asking what was to be done with him. The father, overwhelmed with grief, shame and despair, ordered them to close the doors — himself, his wife and his son being within — and set fire to the house. His daughter would seem to have accompanied the men, for he now turned to her and said, " You, Untombi-yapansi, go to your sister "—a married one not previously mentioned — " and live with her, for I and your mother shall be burnt with the house, for we do not wish to live, because Usilwanekazana is dead, and we too will die with her. . . . Take our ox, mount it and go. When you are on the top of the hill, you will hear the great roaring of the burning village; do not look back, but go on."

On the way to her sister's kraal, she met with an *imbulu* — described as a large lizard, but evidently able to assume a wholly or partly human form, which induced her, by a succession of tricks, to let it wear her clothes and ride on her ox.[9] They arrived at the village, where the *imbulu* was received as the chief's daughter and Untombi-yapansi, now called " Dog's tail " (*Umsilawezinja*), was supposed to be her servant and set to scare birds in the gardens. The girl who went with her was surprised to find that she got rid of the birds by merely singing — no doubt a magic song, though this is not stated, and the words, as given, would not seem to have any occult force. At noon, she left her companion, saying that she was going to bathe in the river. When she came out of the water, "with her whole body shining like brass" (this is supposed to be her usual appearance, but she had disguised it by smearing herself with earth), she struck the ground with a brass rod, saying, "Come out all ye people of my father and cattle of my father, and my food!" Immediately the earth opened, and many people, including her dead parents and sister, came out, bringing with them many cattle, also food for her, which she ate. Her own ox also came out (so that all who appeared were not necessarily dead); she mounted it and sang a song which all the people took up; she then dismounted, struck the ground again, caused the people and cattle to descend into it, and returned to the garden. Next day, her companion, whose curiosity had been aroused, followed her stealthily and saw what happened. She told the chief, who hid himself in the bushes near the river and watched her performing her incantations. The *imbulu* was then exposed and destroyed; and the chief married Untombi-yapansi in addition to her sister, after which "they all lived together happily." We are not told that the parents returned to life again after the brief apparitions above recorded — no doubt it was felt that, once their daughter's identity was established and she was settled in a home of her own, their intervention was no longer needed. It seems clear that they are imagined as living underground in very much the same way as they did on the surface of the earth, also that living people and animals can enter their abode and leave it without much difficulty.

In our first chapter, we have already mentioned some African analogues to the tale of which perhaps the best-known European type is Grimm's "Frau Holle."[10] This has a distinct mythological background, quite lost sight of in the English variant, where the ancient goddess Holda or Hulda[11] has become an unnamed "old witch," and the girl, instead of fall-

ing into the well, leaves her parents' house in order to look
for a situation. The older version does not expressly say that
she is drowned, but one can hardly doubt that she is supposed
to have entered the realm of the dead and to have returned
to life when dismissed through the golden gateway. The
African variants can scarcely be separated from those already
mentioned, where the oppressed or afflicted seek a remedy for
their troubles in heaven above.

Of these there are several types. The heroine may be an
ill-used step-daughter, whose step-mother is looking for a
pretext to get rid of her,[12] a child fearing her parent's anger
on account of some accident, or one of two or more wives,[13]
suffering from the jealousy of her rivals. It is perhaps worth
noting that, while the jealous co-wife figures pretty frequently
in folk-tales, the cruel step-mother is not so common: in general, it is assumed that the children of a polygamous household
will be as well treated by one mother as another, just as we
assume that, as a normal thing, brothers and sisters will live
together in harmony. The two step-mother stories I have
noted as belonging to this group, come from West Africa.
They also differ from the rest in more or less losing sight of
the spirit-world idea. In the one (Hausa), the step-mother
sends the girl to the " River Bagajun," reputed to be the abode
of cannibal witches, in the hope that she will never return;
in the other (Temne), she is despatched on an errand to " the
Devil "—probably, in an earlier form of the story, to the
other world, though of this there is no indication as it now
stands, and the " Devil " (the tale is told in Sierra Leone English, and the expression is obviously imported) might be a
forest demon. Perhaps he was originally an ancestral ghost
haunting a grove: in that case the link with the spirit-world
is obvious, though it is not located under the earth.

There is a very curious variation in another Hausa tale,[14] the
first part of which (like the opening of a Chwana " Holle "

story) [15] belongs to the class of " Ogre tales." A mother, whose daughter has been killed and eaten by a were-hyena, gathers up her bones and sets out with them for the town " where they mend men." On the way, she meets with various adventures through all of which she passes satisfactorily; when she arrives she behaves with courtesy and obeys the instructions given her, and her daughter is restored alive and well. Her co-wife, thinking that her own ugly daughter will be improved by the same process, purposely kills her and starts, carrying the bones; but she behaves exactly like the favoured but ill-conditioned child in " Frau Holle," and is fitly rewarded by receiving her daughter back " badly mended "— in fact, only half a girl, with one eye, one arm, and one leg. This same idea, strangely enough, recurs on the opposite side of Africa, where, in a Chaga tale already referred to,[16] the woman who has tricked her rival into drowning her baby and finds that she has got it back more beautiful than before, drowns her own child on purpose and gets it back with one arm and one leg. The notion of these one-sided beings seems to prevail throughout Africa — we shall have to come back to it later on, but these are the only instances known to me where it occurs in this particular connection.

In the most typical forms of this story, the girl meets with various adventures *en route*, usually to the number of three (as, with us, the corn, the cow, and the apple-tree). These are taken as tests of character, showing the first girl in a creditable, and the second in an odious light. Sometimes a service is required — in some cases of a repulsive nature, as when an old woman suffering from skin-disease asks to have her sores washed, or still worse, her eyes cleansed by licking out the purulent matter, in others, merely involving a little trouble. Sometimes, as in the " Route du Ciel," it is the girls' treatment of those who direct them on their way, that is decisive; so, in " The Devil's Magic Eggs " (Temne), the first one gives civil and respectful answers to the talking hoe-handles and the one-eyed man. The Hausa " How the ill-treated Maiden became rich " has a test of self-control in place of the tasks: the road leads past a river of sour milk, a river of honey and some fowls roasting themselves — all of which call out an invitation. The first girl, intent on her errand, says: " No, no, what is the use? " and passes on; the second rudely replies, " You are full of impudence, must I wait for you to ask me to take some? " Sometimes these tests or tasks are dispensed with till the girl has arrived, when she is either given some definite thing to do (the witch asks the Hausa girl to wash her, the " Devil " tells the Temne " Pickin " to relieve his head of its inhabitants) or set to work for a lengthened period, as is done by Frau Holle. Further, on leaving, there is usually either a choice of gifts, or a choice of means of exit. The Temne Devil tells the girls to help themselves to four eggs; the first takes the small ones, which, on being broken produce riches of all sorts; her sister chooses the largest, and finds them to contain bees, a snake, a whip, and fire, which consumes her wicked mother and herself. The Hausa witch gives each of the girls a basket, with directions when to open it — directions followed by the one and disregarded by the other, with results much as in the Temne tale.

In a Chaga variant,[17] the old woman asks, " Shall I strike you with the hot or with the cold? " The principle of this choice is not explained; but " the cold " is evidently the right answer. The girl who gives it is told to thrust her arms into a pot and draws them out covered with bangles. It should also be noticed that in two cases the successful candidate, if we may call her so, refuses the food offered by the spirits. This is a familiar incident in other mythologies, but it is sometimes curiously lost sight of — e.g., in the Iramba story mentioned in our last chapter.[18] As a specimen of these stories — none, so far as I can discover, unites all the features I have mentioned

—we may take that of "Maruwa," current among the
Wachaga.[19]

Maruwa and her little sister were set to watch the garden
when the beans were ripening. One hot afternoon, Maruwa,
being very thirsty, went down to the Kiningo pool to get a
drink. The little girl, left alone, saw a great troop of baboons
among the bean-plants, but she was afraid to drive them off by
herself; and when Maruwa returned she found that the whole
crop was gone. She was terribly frightened, thinking that her
father would beat her, so she ran down to the pool and jumped
in. Her sister ran home and told their mother, who came
down to the pool and found that Maruwa had not yet sunk,
but was still floating on the water. She called:

> " Ho! Maruwa, are you not coming back?
> Are you not coming back again?
> Never mind the beans, we will plant some more!
> Never mind the beans, we will plant some more."

Maruwa answered:

> " Not I! not I!
> The baboons came and ate the beans — *he*!
> The monkeys came and ate the beans "—

i.e. " they have stripped the garden quite bare, and I dare not
go back." The mother sang again and the girl answered
in the same words, and then sank. Her mother went home.

When Maruwa reached the bottom of the pool she found
many people living there, in houses much like those she had
left in her own village. They offered her food, but she
refused everything. Wanting to know what they could give
her, they asked: " What do you eat at home? "—and she,
trying to think of something unprocurable here, answered,
" Bitter fruit and emetic leaves! " She remained with them
many days, eating nothing all the time, and living in the house
of an old woman, who had a little girl to help her with the

PLATE XIX

1. View on Lake Kivu, in the volcanic region of Ruanda.

2. The Virunga Volcanoes, believed to be the abode of the Dead.

After photographs by Captain Philipps.

work. When the child went out to cut grass for the goats, the old woman said to Maruwa, " You may go with her, but don't help her — let her do the work."   Maruwa, however, did not act upon this advice, but cut the grass and carried it back, only giving it to the little girl when they were in sight of the house. It was the same when they went to draw water, and to collect firewood, and the child became very fond of Maruwa. One day she said to her: " You must not stay here too long; once you have got used to the place, they will begin to ill-use you. Go and tell the old woman you are homesick, and ask her to let you go. If she says: ' Shall I let you go through the manure or through the burning? ' say: ' Please let me go through the manure, mother! ' "   Maruwa did as she was directed and was thrown into the manure pit in the cow-stall. When she got out she found herself in the upper world again, not only quite clean, but covered with metal chains and bead ornaments. She reached her parents' house and, finding no one at home, hid herself in the compartment of the cattle. Her mother came, after a while, to fetch the milk-calabash, saw and recognised her, and stretched out her arm to touch her; but Maruwa cried: " Don't touch my ornaments! "   The woman ran and called her husband, " *He!*   Mbonyo! Mbonyo! " and asked him to fetch the milk-calabash from the cow-stall — an unusual thing for a man, which he was at first unwilling to do. Suspecting, hovever, that her request had some particular meaning, he went and found Maruwa who warned him also not to touch her or her ornaments.[20]   He understood, or at least supposed, that she had some serious reason for keeping him at a distance; he went at once, in great joy, to fetch a sheep, which he presented to her, " as a gift of welcome, so that she might come out and he could admire her properly in the courtyard. So, when Maruwa had been greeted with the sheep she came out into the yard in all her ornaments which she had acquired in the

Kiningo pool. The people came to look at her, and all of them wondered."

A neighbour's daughter was envious and, hearing where Maruwa had got all these things, ran to the Kiningo pool and threw herself in. She ate the food offered her, and, when received into the old woman's house, followed her instructions to the letter and left the little girl to do all the work. The latter, therefore, said to her one day: " We are very hard up here; you had better ask the old woman to let you go home." She then exactly reversed the advice she had given to Maruwa with the result that the old woman threw her into the fire, as requested. When she arrived in the upper world " fire was hidden in her body." She went home and hid in the cow-stall, as Maruwa had done. Maruwa was the first person to see her and held out her hand to her, but immediately fire burst from the girl's whole body. She ran away, plunging into stream after stream, but could not extinguish the flames. She cried to every river she passed to help her, but not one would do so. At last she came to Namuru and died in the Sere stream; so no one who knows the story drinks of its water to this day.

A Spider story from the Gold Coast [21] is related to this group of tales and may as well have a place here.

Once in a time of scarcity, Anansi or Ananu (the Spider) and his son Ananute, were looking for food in the bush, when the son found one palm-nut. Just as he was going to crack and eat it, it slipped from his fingers and rolled into a rat-hole. He crawled in after it and soon found himself in the presence of three very dirty spirits, one black, one red, and one white, who had neither washed nor shaved since the creation of the world. They asked what he wanted and were much surprised to hear that he had been taking so much trouble for the sake of a single palm-nut. They dug up some yams from their garden and gave them to him, telling him to peel them and cook the peelings and throw away the good part. He did so and found that they became very fine yams. He remained there for three days, getting plenty to eat, and became quite fat. On the fourth he took his leave, asking if he might carry back a few yams to his relations. The spirits gave him a large basket full, came with him part of the way, and taught him the following song:

(Solo)

" White spirit, ho! ho!
Red spirit, ho! ho!
Black spirit, ho! ho!

(Chorus)

Should my head disobey,
What would befall me?
The head he throws away —
The foot he throws away —
You, you offended the great fetishes! " [22]

This they said, he must not tell to anyone, or even sing it when by himself. Great was the rejoicing when he reached home, laden with supplies, which lasted the family for some time. When they were exhausted, he returned to fetch some more; and, as he was careful to obey the spirits' instructions, they allowed him to come again as often as he wished. His father's curiosity was aroused and he wished to come too, but his son — not unreasonably, when one remembers Anansi's character — would not hear of it. So next time yams were wanted, Anansi got up overnight, made a hole in his son's bag and filled it with ashes. This enabled him to follow his track and come up with him before he had reached his destination. The young Spider, seeing that he was determined, handed over the errand to him, with some well-meant hints as to his behaviour, and went home. Needless to say, he made a very bad impression. He burst out laughing when he caught sight of the spirits, remarked on their unwashed condition and offered to trim their beards for them. He then had the impudence to ask for yams, was given some and told to peel them and throw away the yams themselves, but said to himself that he was not going to be such a fool, and put the yams into the pot. He found, after waiting long past the usual time, that they were not done, nor likely to be, so he had to try the skins, which, as before, became very fine tubers. When he set out for home, the spirits taught him their secret song, and he began to sing it at the top of his voice, as soon as he was out of sight. Then " he burst from above, and broke down, then his head was cut off, and he also died, but still he went on singing! " The spirits, unwilling to proceed to extremities, restored him to life, but he repeated the offence a second and a third time, till at last they came after him, took away his yams and gave him a good thrashing. And his neighbours, when they heard what had happened, expelled him from the village.

There is one more group of legends which must be mentioned — that in which a murder is made known and avenged by means of a bird or other creature, which is usually, though not always, identified with the soul of the victim. There are a very large number of variants, one of the finest being the Zulu " Unyengebule,"[23] where a man kills his wife in a fit of irritation, and the plume of feathers which she was wearing in her hair turns into a bird. He kills the bird again and again, but it keeps coming to life and at last reveals the story to the murdered woman's parents. But a less well-known and less generally accessible form of the story is current among the Kinga people at the north end of Lake Nyasa.[24] It is called " The Heron's Feather," and relates how two youths went on a visit to their relations at a distant village. One of them wore a crow's feather in his hair, the other a heron's. They saw some girls on a hillside and shouted across the valley to them: " Maidens, which of us two do you prefer? " The girls answered: " We

like the one with the crow's feather best." The same thing
happened a second and a third time, and the young man who
had failed to attract admiration suggested to his companion that
they should change feathers, and he agreed. When they had
crossed the next hill, they met another band of girls and repeated their question, but the answer was, now, " The one with
the heron's feather is the handsomest." The other remarked,
" *Kwo!* they all despise me — I alone am the ugly one, for
they all like you, and I shall never get a wife! " and jealousy
rankled in his heart. After a while, they came to a dry water-
course in a deep ravine, and he suggested to his friend that
they should dig a pit to try and get some water. The other
agreed, and they dug for some time. When the pit was about
a man's height in depth, the envious youth snatched the other's
plume and threw it in, telling him to climb down and fetch it.
He did so, and his false friend, seeing that the pit was deep
enough, threw the earth in and buried him. He then went on
to his relatives' village and told them, in answer to their en-
quiries, that he had come alone. He remained with them for
some time and then went home. When he arrived, he was
asked where his friend was and answered: " Oh! I don't know,
he stayed behind; I suppose he is on his way." Next day, the
lad's parents enquired again and received the same answer,
which satisfied them for the time, but when he did not come
that evening or the following morning, they grew anxious.
Presently they noticed a bird sitting on the kraal fence and
singing: " Your son is not there; they blamed him for wearing
the heron's feather and buried him in the swamp." When
they heard this, they asked again: " Where did you leave your
friend? " but the young man insisted that he had only lingered behind and would most likely come next day. Apparently they were not quite certain they had understood the bird,
or were reluctant to apply its message to themselves, for they
accepted his assurance and waited another day. The lad did

not come back, but the bird did and sang the same words again. When he assured them once more that the missing one was on the way, they asked: " Well, then, what is that bird singing? " " Oh! " he answered, " I don't know, I expect he is drunk and singing some nonsense to himself, that is all! " Another day passed, and once more the bird came back, and this time the father and mother insisted on going to find out what had happened. They met people who had seen both lads go into the ravine but only one come out. They went on to the swamp and the mother remarked that the earth had recently been disturbed, so they dug down and found the body. They seized the murderer, dug another pit, threw him in and buried him.

Nothing is said here as to the identity of the bird, but we may be sure that, originally at least, it was the form assumed by the murdered lad's soul. How completely this idea has sometimes been lost sight of, is seen in a Mbundu story,[25] where Mutilembe, envious of his younger brother's success in hunting, kills him, the murder being reported by the two dogs, who witness it. He kills them both, as Unyengebule does the bird, but they return to life — a reminiscence of the idea that the accusing animal was the reincarnated (and indestructible) soul.

CHAPTER VI

HEROES

THE FIGURE of the Hero who is also the Demiurge, the institutor of the arts of life and, in another aspect, the " trickster-transformer," [1] is not very frequently met with in Africa, at least as far as our knowledge goes. However, we do, here and there, meet with traces of such a being, usually of a confused and fragmentary character. Hubeane (Hobyana) [2] of the Bavenda and Bapedi, said to be the son of the first man and the creator of other human beings (others call him the first ancestor of the race and the creator of heaven and earth), possesses many characteristics of the trickster. These appear very clearly in the Zulu Hlakanyana, [3] who also possesses magical powers of transformation, but does not seem to be credited with any share in the making of the world. In the present form of the tale, he is a human, or quasi-human being; but there are indications that he may be of animal origin, and some of his adventures are attributed to the Hare in Bantu folklore. The Hare never appears as a Demiurge; but the Spider, the arch-trickster of Western Africa, figures in the creation-legend of the Yaos, [4] and is connected with heaven in Angola, [5] by the Kongo people and by the Duala. [6] There are some miraculous circumstances about the birth of Hlakanyana, which he shares with Ryang'ombe, a hero of Kiziba: [7] both speak before they are born, and the latter eats a whole ox immediately after. Hubeane exhibits a mixture of cunning and real or assumed stupidity which recalls the Teutonic Tyll Owlglass and the Turkish Nasr-ed-din; his cunning is shown in the tricks played on others, but chiefly in his avoidance of the traps set for him after people have become convinced that he is too clever to be tolerated in the tribe.

This latter set of episodes is repeated in the story of Gali-kalangye,[8] found among the Wahehe, north of Lake Nyasa, among the Anyanja and Yaos farther south, and probably elsewhere. Here, the hero's mother promises, before his birth, to hand him over to a demon;[9] but it proves impossible to fulfil the bargain, as he can never be taken unawares. Some of the devices are the same as those employed against Hubeane; but all his stratagems are measures of self-defence — he plays no malicious tricks.

We have already mentioned Tsūi-goab, the "Wounded-Knee" chief, as a hero of the Hottentots, in process of deification, if not actually deified. This being may or may not be, as Hahn thinks, identical with Haitsi-aibeb;[10] if not, the latter must be set down as a distinct hero, about whom various legends have been preserved; though, unfortunately, it is now, apparently, too late to recover the connecting links between the records of isolated observers.[11]

Haitsi-aibeb's birth was miraculous;[12] and he was able to transform himself into various shapes. He fights with an enemy of mankind, Gaunab, or Gā-gorib,[13] the "Thruster-down," whose custom was to throw people headlong into a deep pit. He used to sit beside this pit and challenge those who passed to throw a stone at his forehead; but the stone rebounded, killing the thrower, so that he fell into the hole. At last Haitsi-aibeb was told that many men had been killed in this way and he went to the spot. He declined Gā-gorib's challenge, but presently drew off his attention and aimed a stone at him, which hit him under the ear, " so that he died and fell into his own hole. After that there was peace, and people lived happily."

Another version [14] represents the two chasing each other round and round the hole, crying alternately:

PLATE XX

A bowman of the Southern Bambala. He has
just parried with the back of his bow (note the
peculiar shape) an arrow shot at him, which is seen
flying over his head. After a photograph by E.
Torday.

"Push the Heigeip [Haitsi-aibeb] down! "
"Push the Gã-gorib down! "

till at last Haitsi-aibeb was pushed in.   Then he said to the
hole: " Support me a little! " and it bore him up till he was
able to get out again.   They chased each other as before, till
Haitsi-aibeb fell in again and again got out, but, the third
time, it was his adversary who was thrust in, " and he came not
up again."   " Since that day men breathed freely and had rest
from their enemy, because he was vanquished."   Gã-gorib is
by some identified with Gaunab, the enemy who wounded
Tsūi-goab in the knee.

The above story is also told of Tsūi-goab,[15] and, what is
even more remarkable, of the Jackal.[16]   This affords a presumption that Haitsi-aibeb, like other heroes, may originally
have been an animal.   The Jackal is the favourite hero of
Hottentot folklore, and many of his exploits are those attributed by the Bantu to the Hare.

At one time Haitsi-aibeb is said to have made friends with
a Lion,[17] and they used to go hunting together.   The Lion was
the more successful, but Haitsi-aibeb usually contrived to cheat
him out of the greater part of the booty, and then derided
him behind his back.   The Lion's daughter, to whom he carried home his prey, began to suffer from hunger.   Haitsi-
aibeb also had a daughter, and the two met one day at the
water-hole where they had come to fill their vessels.   The
Lion's daughter sat down to fill hers,[18] but the other told her
to get out of the way and, when she declined, taunted her with
her father's defeat, saying that he had been outwitted by
Haitsi-aibeb.   The Lion's daughter, on reaching home, told
her father, and he, during the next day's hunting, took care
to keep his spoil to himself.   Haitsi-aibeb then said to him:
" These two girls will cause us to quarrel: we had better kill
them both! "   The Lion agreed and killed his daughter, but

Haitsi-aibeb deceived him by beating with a club the skin on which he slept, his daughter being concealed elsewhere. When the Lion discovered the cheat, he pursued them both, but they escaped and took refuge underground. The Lion, in despair, entreated Haitsi-aibeb to restore his daughter to life, which at last he did.

The cairns found in many parts of South Africa were called Haitsi-aibeb's graves,[19] their number, when remarked on by a traveller, being accounted for by the assertion that he died and returned to life a great many times. That this is not merely an explanation called forth by a leading question seems clear from the legend given by Bleek [20] under the title " The Raisin-Eater."

Haitsi-aibeb and his family, on their travels, reached a certain valley, where they found ripe berries, of the kind called "wild raisins," in great abundance. Haitsi-aibeb ate of them and, becoming very ill, said to his son Uriseb:[21] " I shall not live, I feel it; thou must, therefore, cover me when I am dead with soft stones. . . . This is the thing I order you to do: — Of the raisin-trees of this valley ye shall not eat. For if ye eat of them, I shall infect you, and ye will surely die in a similar way." His wife said: " He is taken ill on account of the raisins of this valley. Let us bury him quickly, and let us go."

So they buried him, covering his grave with stones, as directed, and moved on to another place. While preparing to camp here, they heard, in the direction from which they had come, " a noise as of people eating raisins and singing." Then the words of the song became audible:

" I, father of Uriseb,
Father of this unclean one,
I, who had to eat these raisins and died,
And dying live."

The wife, noticing that the sound seemed to come from the old man's grave, sent Uriseb to look; and he returned, report-

ing that he had seen tracks which looked like his father's foot-
marks. So she said: " It is he alone," and told Uriseb to creep
up to him against the wind and cut off his retreat to the grave,
" and when thou hast caught him, do not let him go."

" He did accordingly, and they came between the grave and
Haitsi-aibeb who, when he saw this, jumped down from the
raisin trees and ran quickly, but was caught at the grave. Then
he said: ' Let me go! For I am a man who has been dead —
that I may not infect you! ' But the young wife said: ' Keep
hold of the rogue! ' So they brought him home, and from
that day he was fresh and hale! "

In Hubeane, the power of recovery from death has given
place to a marvellous fertility of resource in escaping from it.
He is described as the son of Ribimbi (Ribibi, Levivi), the
first man,[22] but so far as my information goes, nothing unusual is related in connection with his birth. He first distinguished himself by phenomenal stupidity, carrying out literally the directions he received, but always applying them
wrongly. Thus one day, he went with his mother to gather
beans.[23] She found a small buck asleep among the bean-plants,
killed it and put it into her basket, covering it over with the
beans as she picked them. She then sent Hubeane home with
the basket, telling him, " If you meet any one who asks
what you are carrying, say: ' My mother's beans,' but (you
know) in your heart (that it) is a bush-buck." Sure enough,
he met a neighbour, who asked what was in the basket. Hubeane answered: " I am carrying my mother's beans, but in
my heart it is a bush-buck."

When he grew older, he was set to herd the sheep and
goats. One day he came upon a dead zebra, and, when he came
home in the evening, being asked where the flock had fed that
day, he answered: " By the black and white rock." Next day,
going to the same place, he found that the hyenas had been
at the carcase, and, when asked the same question in the

evening, said he had driven the sheep to " the hyenas' rock." The men, already puzzled by the " black and white rock," could make nothing of this, so some of them went with him next day and found, to their disgust, that they had lost a valuable supply of meat. So they told him, that when next he found an animal, he must pile a heap of branches over it and come at once to call some people. Next day, he killed a small bird with a stone, covered it with branches and summoned the whole village — of course to their bitter disappointment. One or two took the trouble to explain to him that what he should have done was to tie the bird to his belt and so carry it home, and this, accordingly, he tried to do with a bush-buck which he killed, dragging it along the ground and quite ruining the skin. In short, he was the despair of his relations. His father took to accompanying him, so as to prevent disaster to the sheep, and Hubeane marooned him on the top of a high rock, telling him there was water to be found there, and, once he was up, taking away the pegs which he had driven in for him to ascend. He then ran home and ate the dinner prepared for his father, afterwards secretly filling the pot which had contained it with cowdung, and returning to the rock, helped his father down, pretending that he had only been to look after the sheep. When they reached home, he scolded the servants for being slow in dishing up the food, saying that, if they did not make haste, the meat would be turned into cowdung — which accordingly was found to be the case.

This and similar tricks at length so exasperated his father and the men of the village that they determined to get rid of Hubeane. They put poison into his porridge; but he insisted on eating from the bowl prepared for his brother; then they dug a pit in the place where he usually sat, planted sharp stakes in it and covered it over, but he went and sat elsewhere. Then they tied up a man in a bundle of thatching-grass, so that he could stab Hubeane with his spear when he came within reach. But again Hubeane was suspicious, and chose the grass for a target when practising javelin-throwing. So, finding that they could not catch him napping they decided to leave him alone.

Hlakanyana may originally have been the Hare, or possibly some creature of the weasel kind. The latter is suggested by the introduction to his story given in Callaway,[24] where it is stated that one of his names is Ucaijana, "Little Weasel," and " he is like the weasel; it is as though he was really of that genus, . . . he resembles it in all respects." But the narrator is clearly somewhat perplexed, and, since we do not find the Weasel otherwise prominent in Zulu folk-lore, it may be a recent substitution for the Hare. He is described by Callaway as a sort of Tom Thumb; but, though his smallness is insisted on in the introduction, it does not appear in the story itself. He is remarkable, however, in other ways. He speaks before he is born, and goes out immediately after to the cattle-kraal, sitting down among the men and eating beef. He plays tricks on his parents and others, but meets with more toleration than Hubeane, as the only hostile manifestation comes from the other boys who (not unnaturally) object to have him sleeping in their hut, though they do not otherwise molest him. After leaving home he has several adventures with cannibals, getting the better of them all in the long run. Except by getting rid of these nuisances — which is quite incidental in his career — he does not appear as a benefactor, unless we are to count a very curious incident which may be an indication of his once having figured as a culture-hero.[25] Having dug up some edible tubers (*umdiandiane*) he gives them to his mother to cook; she eats them herself, and when he demands them back, gives him a milk-pail instead. This he lends to some boys who were milking into broken potsherds; one of them breaks it and, on being remonstrated with, gives him an assagai in exchange. He continues the series of exchanges, each time getting an

article of greater value than the one lost, till he winds up with
a war-assagai, and " what he did with that, perhaps I may tell
you on another occasion." The two points to notice are, first,
that he is actually shown as introducing improvements: the
milk-pail instead of potsherds, an assagai for cutting meat
instead of sharp-edged slips of cane, an axe for cutting firewood, which women were presumably breaking off with their
hands, and so on. Secondly, the same story is told, with variations, of the Hare, who, in one place, finds people working with
wooden hoes, for which he substitutes an iron one, and again,
gives iron arrows for wooden ones.

In Kiziba, we have a more ordinary, human culture-hero
in Kibi, a mighty hunter who came out of Unyoro with his
dogs,[26] and the somewhat similar figure of Mbega in Usambara,[27] the founder of the Wakilindi house of chiefs. These
may typify the immigration or invasion of a more advanced
people. But we must pass over much interesting matter in
order to touch on a myth of great interest which is found all
over Bantu Africa and beyond its confines to an extent which
I have been unable to trace. The hero is often unnamed,
but the Basuto call him Moshanyana, or Litaolane. The story
is classed by Tylor [28] among Nature Myths and explained as
a dramatisation of the recurring phenomena of night and day:
the sun swallowed up by the darkness and re-emerging triumphant and unhurt; or perhaps of the more irregular and catastrophic disappearance of the sun or moon during an eclipse.
More recent observers have doubted whether we do find these
phenomena personified in just this way among very primitive
races.[29] Without attempting to decide this question, we will
tell the story of Moshanyana [30] as a fairly typical specimen.

The people — no doubt all the people of the world, as
far as the narrator is concerned — were swallowed up by a
monster called Kholumolumo,[31] and not only the people but
the cattle, the dogs, and the fowls. The only one who escaped

was a pregnant woman, who smeared herself over with ashes
from the dust-heap, and then went and sat in the calves' kraal.
Kholumolumo came and looked into the kraal, but took her
for a stone, " as she smelt like ashes," and left her. He went
on as far as the mountain pass by which he had reached the
village, but was unable to get through it again, after his meal,
and remained where he was.

In course of time, the woman's baby was born, and she left
it in order to go a few yards from the hut and fetch some food.
When she came back she found a grown man sitting there,
clothed, and armed with a spear. She said: " Hello! man!
where is my child? " and he answered: " It is I, mother! "
He inquired where the people were gone, and she told him
they had been eaten by Kholumolumo, as well as the cattle,
dogs, and fowls. He asked where the monster was. " Come
out and see, my child." She climbed with him to the
top of the calves' kraal and pointed to the pass (" nek ")
which gave entrance to the valley, saying: " That object which
is filling the nek, as big as a mountain, that is Kholumolumo."

He took his spears and, in spite of his mother's entreaties,
went to look at the monster, stopping by the way to sharpen
the spears on a flat stone. When it saw him coming, it opened
its mouth to swallow him; but, as it could not rise, he easily
kept out of reach of the jaws, went round behind it and stabbed
it twice, after which it died.

" Then he took his knife. A man cried: ' Do not cut me! '
He left and began at another place; a cow said: ' Muu! ' He
left and began at another place; a dog barked: ' Kwee! ' He
left and began at another place. ' Kokolokoloo! ' cried a hen.
This time he persisted and opened the belly of that animal.
All the people came out of it, also the cattle."

They made him their chief; but there were those who were
envious and stirred up discontent among the rest. After a
while, they planned to kill him, saying: " Let us take hold

of him, kindle a big fire in the public court and throw him into it." But " when they tried to seize him, he escaped them, and they took another man and threw him into the fire." Perhaps we are to understand that they were subjected, by supernatural means, to some delusion of the senses. " As for him, he was standing there and said: ' What are you doing to that man? ' "

They then tried digging a pit at the place where he habitually sat, but he escaped, not, like Hubeane, through refusing to sit there, but because he was miraculously prevented from falling in. Again, they tried to throw him over a precipice, but " he escaped them and they threw down another man," whom he recalled to life.

When they made their last attempt, he no longer thwarted them, but purposely allowed them to kill him. " It is said that his heart went out and escaped and became a bird."

This is a distinct and coherent narrative, some of whose features may have been grafted on to other themes, and it is found elsewhere, with variations *ad infinitum*. Sometimes the hero escapes death, sometimes though slain he returns to life, sometimes he is left undisturbed and " happy ever after " in the enjoyment of his well-deserved honours.

Moshanyana's rapid development (though his birth is not in itself miraculous) reminds us of Hlakanyana and is also found in other cases. But an interesting Ronga variant [32] attributes an actually abnormal birth to the hero, Bokenyane, whose mother, like the first ancestor of the Nandi, was afflicted with a boil on her shin-bone, from which, when it came to a head, the child issued. It was felt to be fitting that the Hero-deliverer, who accomplished what no human being could even attempt, should not come into the world in the ordinary human way.

Breysig [33] suggests another motive, which probably applies where the hero is also the ancestor of the tribe, viz. the desire to make him the actual starting point of the line, seeing that

PLATE XXI

A Swahili player on the sansa (chisanzi), Zanzibar. After a photograph by Dr. Aders.

to give him a human father would merely be carrying the ancestry higher up. This may be the case with some of the heroes we have been considering, though I have not found it stated anywhere except in the case of Hubeane, whose birth, so far as we are told, is not miraculous.

In connection with what was said above as to the hero being originally an animal, we may mention what is probably a very early form of the legend current among the Ne [34] of the Ivory Coast. Here a magic calabash swallows [35] up all men and animals except one ewe, who later on brings forth a ram lamb. When the ram has come to his full strength, he butts the calabash and breaks it.

The miraculous birth occurs in the case of Galikalangye, who has otherwise nothing in common with Moshanyana, except his repeated escape from death, in which he resembles Hubeane. Here the circumstances preceding the birth are entirely different, and also vary in the several versions of the tale, which, however, agree in making the mother promise her child to some being who has helped her out of a difficulty — in this case a Hyena. She has been gathering firewood in the forest and finds herself unable to lift the bundle to her head: the Hyena offers his assistance and asks what she will give him in return, and she replies, with somewhat startling readiness, that she will give him the unborn child. No sooner had she reached her home than he made his appearance and requested her to toast (*kalanga*) him over the fire on a potsherd — hence his name, and he developed with proportional rapidity. When the Hyena came to claim him, the mother told him to take him for himself, and promised to tie a bell round his ankle, so that he could be picked out among the other boys. Galikalangye got hold of a quantity of bells and tied them on to his playmates, instructing them to answer to the same name as himself; so the Hyena retired in perplexity. Next, his mother sent him to pick beans, at a place where the Hyena had hidden himself; he sent a beetle in his place, and went off to play. Then, having tied the Hyena into a bundle of brushwood, the mother sent Galikalangye to bring it in; but he looked at the bundle and remarked: " I can carry one three times as big as that," which so scared the enemy that he fled. This having failed, his mother told him to set a trap, and, after dark, when the Hyena has ensconced himself beside it, she said that it had fallen. " Has it? " said her son. " My trap always falls three times." Said the Hyena: " What sort of trap is this which falls three times? " and, once more, ran away. Finally, the mother shaved Galikalangye's head all down one side and told the Hyena to fetch him when asleep beside the fire; but the boy got up in the night, shaved his mother's head in the same way and retired to the back of the hut. The Hyena came, and, finding a person who answered the description asleep beside the fire, killed and carried off the mother.[36]

The Nyanja Kachirambe, however, after a series of escapes very similar to the above, forgives his mother, after killing the Hyena. The points of contact with the Hubeane legend are obvious; so are the important differences.

Ryangombe resembles Hlakanyana and Galikalangye in the mode of his birth, but without the circumstances preceding it in the latter case; otherwise he differs from all previously mentioned; he overcomes one famous champion and reverses the procedure of Moshanyana by swallowing the second, who cuts his way out and kills him. If correctly reported, this may be a late and corrupt form of the myth.

CHAPTER VII

NATURE MYTHS

NATURE MYTHS properly so called do not seem to hold a very conspicuous place in African thought, compared with what has been observed elsewhere. True, we have a certain number of stories in which the sun, moon, and other heavenly bodies play a part, speaking and acting as human beings — the Nama, indeed, expressly state that they were once men [1] — with others explaining the origin and character of natural phenomena. But, as we have seen, most of the creation-legends content themselves with accounting for mankind, taking the inorganic world more or less for granted.

The interpretation of myths as figurative descriptions of dawn, sunset, storms, and so forth, which was popularised, about the middle of the last century, by Max Müller and Sir George Cox, has perhaps been unduly discredited, owing to its injudicious and indiscriminate application. It is, however, now recognised that no one key will fit all locks, and that this theory may be valid in some cases though in others completely at variance with the facts. Breysig [2] points out that — at any rate in the most primitive stages of thought — divine or heroic figures are not personifications of natural forces, though, at a much later date, they may, by an afterthought, be identified with them. This seems to have been the case in ancient Babylon, with Marduk, sometimes explained as the sun-god, but also associated with the constellation Taurus, which seems to give us a clue to his real origin. It seems doubtful whether such identification has taken place in that part of Africa with which we are dealing. Those gods of the

Uganda pantheon who look most like nature powers may equally well be deified ancestral ghosts.

There are some widely current tales which have been explained as disguised Nature myths; but one is by no means convinced that this is necessarily the case. Thus, one of the most popular episodes in the story of the Hare is that in which he and the Hyena, in time of famine, agree to kill their mothers for food: the Hyena carries out the compact, but the Hare conceals his mother, conveying food to her by stealth, till at last the Hyena gets wind of the trick and kills her. The Ewe have a distinct Nature myth, which Meinhof [3] considers to be a variant — and presumably the oldest form — of the above. The Sun and the Moon each had a number of children and agreed to kill them. No reason is given, beyond the implication that they wanted a feast, nor do we find in the original native account [4] any hint as to the sex of either Sun or Moon. It seems most likely that, for the purposes of the story, they are both regarded as women. The Sun slaughtered her children and ate them, in company with the Moon; the latter, however, hid hers in a large water-jar and only let them out at night. So the Sun to this day is childless, while the Moon's offspring are visible every night in the shape of the stars.

The same tale is told, by the Somali,[5] of two human mothers, one red and the other black, the former being cheated by the latter. This may, as Meinhof thinks, be a development of the Sun and Moon myth given above, which afterwards reached the Bantu peoples and circulated among them in a variety of forms. (The Kinga attribute it to two men, but the Hare is usually the hero of the tale.) But it is possible that the development was the other way, and that the typical Bantu version with its animal protagonists, is the most primitive. Or, again, two or even three, distinct myths may have arisen independently and reacted on each other.

It has already been pointed out in the third chapter that

we sometimes find the Moon associated with the introduction of death into the world. In the Hottentot legend, the Moon, though not distinctly said to be the Creator, sends the Hare with the message of immortality to mankind. No genuine Bantu form of the legend assigns this function to the Moon, and it may be distinctly Hamitic, or, as suggested in the passage above referred to, derived from the Bushmen. These appear to have regarded the Moon as generally unlucky,[6] for: "We may not look at the Moon, when we have shot game. . . . Our mothers used to tell us that the Moon is not a good person, if we look at him." Some kind of "honeydew" found on bushes was supposed to emanate from the Moon, and it is this which "makes cool the poison with which we shoot the game; and the game arises, it goes on. . . . The Moon's water is that which cures it." But it does not appear to be efficacious, unless the hunter has looked at the Moon.

The Bushmen were in the habit of greeting the new moon with the following invocation, covering their eyes with their hands as they uttered it: "Kabbi-a yonder! Take my face yonder! Thou shalt give me thy face yonder! . . . Thou shalt give me thy face, with which, when thou hast died, thou dost again living return; when we did not perceive thee, thou dost again lying down come, that I may also resemble thee."

The Bushmen possess a much greater body of myths dealing with the heavenly bodies than the Bantu. They give two different accounts of the Moon. In one,[7] it was originally a hide sandal belonging to that mysterious being the Mantis, who flung it up into the sky on a dark night. In the other,[8] "the Moon is looked upon as a man who incurs the wrath of the Sun and is consequently pierced by the knife (i.e. rays) of the latter. This process is repeated until almost the whole of the Moon is cut away, and only one little piece left; which the Moon piteously implores the Sun to spare for his children. (The Moon is in Bushman mythology a male being.) From this little piece, the Moon gradually grows again and becomes a full moon, when the Sun's stabbing and cutting processes recommence."

When the Moon, as we say, " lies on her back," the Bushmen look on it as the sign of a death: " it lies hollow, because it is killing itself by carrying people who are dead." [9]

The Moon, when personified at all by the Bantu, is usually spoken of as masculine, and the Evening Star is sometimes said to be the Moon's wife. The Anyanja [10] say the Moon has two wives, not recognising the Evening and Morning Star as one and the same. Chekechani, the Morning Star, lives in the east and feeds her husband so badly that he pines away, from the day he arrives at her house, till he comes to Puikani, in the west, who feeds him up till he is fat again. Probably this myth exists in more places than have yet been recorded, for we find that the Girvama [11] call " a planet seen near the Moon," *mkazamwezi*, " the Moon's wife," and Bentley [12] says that the corresponding expression, *nkaza a ngonde*, is used in Kongo for a " planet — Jupiter or Venus."

The agricultural Bantu would be less likely to pay much attention to the stars — beyond those essential landmarks of the cultivator, the Pleiades and Orion, than the pastoral and hunting peoples. Accordingly they have few names — and those do not seem very certain — for any except the above and the planet Jupiter, which is known everywhere. The Lower Congo people have a little ditty [13] about the three stars in Orion's belt, which they call " the hunter " (*Nkongo a mbwa*), " the dog," and the *nshiji* (the rodent known to science as *Aulacodus* or *Thrynomys*). It runs somewhat as follows:

> " The gun — oh! the gun! —
> The hunter is following his dog,
> And the dog is after the palm-rat,
> And the palm-rat is up a tree,
> And the tree is too much for the gun: —
> So the gun is hung up again."

The star-lore of the Khoikhoi [14] greatly resembles that of the Bushmen. This is not the place to discuss whether they derived it from the latter, or whether it is Hamitic in origin. Hahn says that the Pleiades (Khunusiti), Orion's Belt (called "the Zebras"), α-Orionis ("the Lion"), and Aldebaran, were known to them before their separation. The Pleiades are the wives of Aldebaran. Once they asked him to go to shoot the three Zebras for them, telling him that he must not come home again till he had done so. He took only one arrow with him, and, having missed the first shot, could not go to pick it up, as the Lion was watching the Zebras on the other side. "And because his wives had cursed him, he could not return, and there he sat in the cold night, shivering and suffering from thirst and hunger."

The Pokomo, who call the Pleiades *vimia*,[15] speak of the male and female *vimia*, the former being, as pointed out to me at Kulesa in 1912, the stars of Orion's Belt. It is possible that this is a confusion and that the name originally belonged to the Hyades, of which Aldebaran is the most conspicuous star. The Pokomo are agricultural Bantu, but largely mingled with aboriginal hunting tribes who appear — allowing for differences of environment and circumstances — to have had much in common with the Bushmen.

Certain stars in the Hyades were regarded by the Khoikhoi as the sandals and the cloak of Aldebaran (called *Aob*, "the Husband"), and two of the smaller stars in Orion were his bow.

The Bushmen called the planet Jupiter, "Dawn's Heart." [16] He had a wife named Kogniuntara, who is now the Lynx. One day, Dawn's Heart, who had been carrying the baby, hid it under the leaves of a plant thinking that his wife would find it when she was out collecting roots. But before she came, it was discovered by various animals and birds, each in turn offering to act as its mother, but the child refused them all.

At last came the Hyena, who took offence because the baby would not come to her, and poisoned the " Bushman rice " (ants' larvae — a favourite food) which Kogniuntara was about to collect. The latter, having found her child, took it up and went with her younger sister to look for " ants' eggs." Having found the poisoned supply, she ate some and was bewitched, turning into a lioness. She ran away into the reeds, while the Hyena, assuming her shape, took her place in the home. Her younger sister followed her to the reed-bed entreating her to feed the child before she left; Kogniuntara's answer seems to show either that the whole transformation was gradual, or that the mental process did not keep pace with the bodily: " Thou shalt bring it that it may suck; I would altogether talk to thee while my thinking-strings still stand " — i.e. while I am still conscious. Twice more the younger sister carried the baby out to the reed-bed to be nursed, the Hyena meanwhile living in the hut unrecognised by the husband, but the second time, the mother said: " Thou must not continue to come to me, for I do not any longer feel that I know." The girl returned home, and that evening, when her brother-in-law asked her to be his partner in the *Ku* game (in which the women clap their hands rhythmically, while the men nod their heads in time with them), she said, angrily, " Leave me alone! your wives, the old she-hyenas, may clap their hands for you! " He at once seized his spear and sprang to stab the Hyena, but missed her and only pierced the place where she had been sitting. In escaping, she stepped in the fire outside the hut, and burnt her foot, wherefore she limps to this day. Next morning, Dawn's Heart and his sister-in-law went down to the reed-bed, taking a flock of goats with them. The girl told the husband and the other people to stand back, while she stood beside the goats and called her sister. The Lioness leaped out of the reeds, ran towards her sister and then turned aside to the goats, of whom she seized one, whereupon the husband

PLATE XXII

Zulu " Lightning-Doctors." They stand on the
wall of the cattle-fold, holding shields and specially
medicated spears and staves and address " words of
power," to the storm, that it may pass by their village.
After a photograph by Ferneyhough (?) Pietermaritzburg.

and the rest took hold of her. They then killed the goats and anointed Kogniuntara with the contents of their stomachs — a favourite African medicine — and then rubbed her till they had removed the hair from her skin. But she asked them to leave the hair on the tips of her ears, " for I do not feel as if I could hear." With this exception, she was restored to human form; but, having been bewitched by means of " Bushman rice," she could no longer eat that standing dish and to avoid starvation, turned into a Lynx, which eats meat. (Perhaps we are to understand that the Lynx was a new animal, previously unknown, for which the furry ears formed the starting-point.)

This story explains why the Dawn's Heart frightens the jackals when he returns home in the early morning, sticking his spear into the ground, and with an arrow ready on his bowstring — " His eyes were large, as he came walking along, they resembled fires."

This tale has some interesting points of contact with the Xosa one of *Tanga-lo-mlibo*,[17] which, however, has nothing to do with the stars: the common element being the return of the mother (in this case drowned, not changed into an animal) to nurse her child, and her ultimate recapture by the husband, who drives cattle into the river.

The Milky Way is said by the Bushmen[18] to have been made by a girl belonging to " the early race," who threw up some wood-ashes into the sky. She subsequently produced the stars by throwing up some of the edible roots called *huin*, the old ones, which are red, becoming red stars, the young roots, white stars. The Pokomo in former times thought that the Milky Way was formed by the smoke from the cooking-fires of the " ancient people "; in later times, after they had suffered from Somali raids, they called it *njia ya Wakatwa*, " the road of the Somali," because these used to come to them from the north-east. The Wachaga seem to have something of the same notion,[19] for they say that, when the Milky Way is clearer than usual, God is warning them of an approaching raid.

The Bushmen held that the Sun and Moon were once human beings and lived on the earth;[20] their presence in the sky is due to the mysterious " early race," who " first inhabited the earth." The Sun, who did not belong to this race, lived among them, shedding light from under his arm intermittently, as he lifted or lowered it, and only on a small space round his own hut. Some children, at the suggestion of their mother, stole up to him while he was asleep and, by a concerted effort, flung him up into the sky, so that he might " make bright the whole place." After this, he " became round and never was a man afterwards."

We do not here get any hint of the Sun and Moon being regarded as man and wife. This view seems to be held by the Nandi [21] and also by the Wachaga,[22] who have a common saying: " Now," i.e. at sunset, " the Sun-Chief is handing his shield to his wife."

These people, who use the name *Iruwa* (" Sun ") for their High God — a conception they may have borrowed from the Masai, as they make a very clear distinction between Iruwa and the ancestral ghosts — certainly seem to associate him with the Sun. Some kind of worship is paid to the latter: at sunrise they spit four times towards the east [23] — this suggests Masai influence — and utter a short prayer: " O Iruwa, protect me and mine! " The New Moon is greeted in a similar way. Gutmann thinks that these ceremonies are relics of a primitive sun-cult; but it seems more likely that they were adopted from the Masai and superimposed on the Bantu ghost-worship. The greeting of the New Moon is of fairly frequent occurrence among the Bantu, but there does not seem to be any developed system of moon-worship.

Various legends show us Iruwa endowed with the attributes

of the personified sun. We have the tale of Kyazimba,[24] who was " very poor " and, in his sore extremity, set out for " the land where the sun rises." As he stood gazing eastward, he heard steps behind him and, turning, saw an old woman who, on hearing his story, hid him in her garment and flew up with him to mid-heaven, where the sun stands at noon. There he saw men coming, and a chief appeared and slaughtered an ox and sat down to feast with his followers. Then the old woman, whose identity is not revealed, asked his help for Kyazimba, whereupon the chief blessed him and sent him home, and he lived in prosperity ever after. Still more striking is the story of a man who having lost all his sons, one after another, said, in his rage and despair: " What has possessed Iruwa to kill all my sons? I will go and shoot an arrow at him." So he went to the smiths and had a number of arrow-heads forged, filled his quiver, took his bow and said, " I will go to the edge of the world, where the sun rises, and when I see it I will shoot — *ti-chi!* " (a sound imitating the whistling of the arrow). So he arose and went, till he came to a wide meadow, where he saw a gate and many paths — some leading to heaven, others back to earth. Here, he waited for the sun to rise; and suddenly, in the silence, he heard the earth resounding as if with the march of a great multitude, and voices cried: " Quick! open the gate, that the King may pass through! "

Then he saw many men coming, goodly to look on and shining like fire, and he was afraid and hid himself in the bushes. Again he heard them cry, " Clear the road for the King! " and another band passed. Then appeared the Shining One himself, radiant as glowing fire, and after him yet another troop. But those in front said: " What stench is here, as if a son of earth had passed? " They searched about, found him and brought him before the King, who asked him, " Whence come you? and what brings you to us? " The man answered: " Nothing, lord — it was sorrow which drove me from home;

I said to myself, ' Let me go and die in the scrub.' " The King said: " How is it, then, that you said you were going to shoot me? Shoot away! " But the man did not dare. Then the King asked him what he wanted. " You, O Chief, know without my telling you." " Do you want me to give back your children? There they are "— and the Sun pointed behind him — " take them away and go home."

The man looked and saw his lost children, but they were so changed, so beautiful, that he could scarcely recognise them, and said: " No, lord, these are yours. Keep them here with you! " So the Sun said: " Go home, and I will give you other children instead of these. Moreover, you will find something on the way which I shall show you."

So he went his way and found game in such abundance, that he had enough to eat till he got home, and also many tusks, which he buried, till he should be able to come back for them with his neighbours. With this ivory he bought cattle and became rich; and in due time sons were born to him, and he lived happily.

The Rainbow, as is natural, has attracted attention everywhere; it is looked upon as a living being — usually a snake, and, curiously enough, often dreaded as a malignant influence. The people of Luango, however, believe in a good and an evil rainbow.[25] Sometimes it is not itself the snake, but merely associated with it; the Ewe [26] look on it as the image, reflected on the clouds, of the great snake Anyiewo, when he comes out to graze or, according to others, to seek for water in the clouds. His ordinary abode is in an anthill, out of which he arises after rain and to which he returns. If he falls on any person he at once devours him, for which reason both rainbow and anthills are regarded with dread. But if any one can find the spot where either end of the rainbow has touched the earth, his fortune is made, for these are the *caches* of the famous " Aggry " and " Popo " beads, which are so prized, as they cannot be manufactured now, but are only dug out of the earth — from old graves and forgotten sites.[27] The Subiya [28] also associate the Rainbow with anthills though they do not seem to figure it as a serpent, but as a "beautiful animal" not further described. If you come across him, you must run in the direction of the sun, for then he cannot see you; if you run away from the sun, he catches you and you are lost. But those who know how to take the proper precautions can sometimes see him come out of his ant-heap and frolic about with his children — " C'est comme de jeunes chiens qui jouent agréablement," says M. Jacottet translating from his native informant.

The Zulus [29] appear to have given various accounts of the rainbow, which they call either *umnyama*, "the animal," or *utingo lwenkosikazi*, "the Queen's Bow " or rather " Arch," that is, one of the bent rods or wattles forming the house of the Queen of Heaven. Some say that it is a sheep — which does not seem easy to understand; others that it lives with a sheep, or that it lives with a snake — in any case, its dwelling-place is a pool. Its influence is peculiarly unpleasant. Utshintsha's testimony, as related to Bishop Callaway, is as follows:

" I had been watching in the garden when it was raining. When it cleared up, there descended into the river a rainbow. It went out of the river and came into the garden. I, Utshintsha, the owner of the garden, ran away when I saw the rainbow coming near me and dazzling in my eyes; it struck me in the eyes with a red colour. I ran away out of the garden . . . because I was afraid, and said: ' This is disease; why does it come to me? ' Men say: ' The rainbow is a disease. If it rests on a man, something will happen to him.' So, then, after the rainbow drove me from the garden, my body became as it is now, that is, it was affected with swellings."

At the beginning of the rainy season in the tropics — especially where, as in Natal, it coincides with the hot weather, people often suffer from boils, prickly heat, or some equally distressing complaint. This particular witness had " a scaly eruption over his whole body," which, whether caused by atmospheric conditions or not, no doubt coincided with the appearance of the rainbow.

There is a curious Chaga tale [30] of a Dorobo who set out to ask God for cattle and, coming to the place where the rainbow touches the earth, remained there praying for many days. But no cattle appeared. When, at last, it became clear that his prayers were in vain, " his heart swelled," and he took his sword and cut through the rainbow. Half of it flew up to the sky; the other fell down and sank into the earth, leaving a deep hole. Some people, who had the curiosity to climb down into this hole, found that it gave access to another country so attractive that they felt disposed to stay there. But they were soon driven away by lions — it is not stated whither they fled or what became of them, and when a further contingent of settlers arrived, they found the first-comers gone, heard the lions growling, and returned. No one has ventured down since.

Some young Masai warriors [31] are said to have killed a rainbow, which came out of Lake Naivasha by night and devoured the cattle at their village. On the third night of his coming, they heated their spears in the fire and waited for his appearance, when they stabbed him in the back of the neck, just behind the head — his only vulnerable part.

An interesting Kikuyu [32] legend makes the Rainbow, Mukunga Mbura, figure in the " Swallower " myth referred to in a previous chapter. A curious point in the story is that, when the hero is about to kill Mukunga Mbura, the latter says: " Do not strike me with your sword over the heart, or I shall die, but open my little finger, . . . make a big hole, not a little one." When the boy did so, all the people and cattle whom the Rainbow had eaten came forth from the incision, just as the cows came out of the old woman's toe in " Masilo and Masilonyane," [33] a story which does not otherwise belong to the same group. Another feature connecting this story with the ogre tales to be dealt with in our next chapter is that, when it was decided, after all, to destroy Mukunga Mbura, lest he should come again to eat people as before, and the warriors hacked him to pieces, one piece went back into the water. The warrior then went home and said that he had killed Mukunga Mbura, all but one leg: " but tomorrow I will go into the water and get that leg and burn it. " But when he came back next day, the water had disappeared; there were only a number of cattle and goats grazing on the plain. "What remained of Mukunga Mbura had gathered together his children and taken all the water and gone very far — but the beasts he had not taken but left behind."

Of myths connected with thunder and lightning, perhaps the most remarkable is that of the Lightning-bird, which is best known from the Zulu accounts;[34] but we find that the Baziba [35] also think that lightning is caused by flocks of brilliantly-coloured birds, which are flung down to earth by Kayurankuba, the spirit presiding over storms; the thunder is the rushing sound of their wings. The Zulu Lightning-bird is described by Callaway's informant as red and glistening; it is sometimes found dead where the lightning has struck the earth and is greatly prized by medicine-men as an ingredient in powerful charms. But the Lightning-bird has also been directly identified as a kind of heron, called by the Boers *hammer-kop* (*Scopus umbretta*), the destruction of whose nest is said to cause rain. Some say that the Lightning-bird buries itself in the ground where it strikes and has sometimes been dug up by an *isanusi* (doctor); others [36] that it lays a large egg, which the *isanusi* tries to dig up, though none has ever yet found one.

Thunder is more often spoken of as a person than lightning, which is sometimes called a weapon or instrument — the Wachaga [37] call it "God's axe," and the Lower Congo people [38] say that it is made by a blacksmith, living in the centre of Ka-kongo. The Thunder is by them called Nzasi and goes about hunting, with twelve couples of dogs. A native told Mr. Dennett how he had once seen Nzasi's dogs. " It was raining, and he and his companions were under a shed playing at marbles, when it began to thunder and lighten. It thundered frightfully, and Nzasi sent his twenty-four dogs down upon them. They seized one of the party who had left the shed for a moment, and the fire burnt up a living palm-tree.

This recalls a curious experience related by an old Chaga woman to Gutmann and probably to be explained in the same way — illusory images impressed on the retina dazzled by the lightning-flash and shaped by sub-conscious thought. She said she saw God (Iruwa), apparently in human shape, but " as large as a cow," one side of his body shining white, the other red as blood. He had a tail, which was also parti-coloured — red and white. It is a remarkable fact that the Heaven-dwellers are sometimes represented as tailed.[39]

Another Congo man had a disastrous encounter with Nzasi.[40] Going through the bush he was caught in the rain, and, hastening home, met a beautiful dog, wet through, like himself. He took it into his hut, meaning to keep it as his own, and lit a fire to dry and warm it, but " suddenly there was an explosion, and neither man, dog, nor *shimbec* (hut) was ever seen again." The dog, Antonio said, was Nzasi himself — but thunder and lightning are often spoken of as one.

A different aspect of the lightning appears in another incident related as true by the same Antonio: [41] " There is a man still living who declares that he was translated to heaven and saw Nzambi Mpungu. He lives in a town not far from Lo-ango. He says that, one day, when it was thundering and lightning and raining very heavily, and when all the people in his village, being afraid, had hidden themselves in their *shimbecs*, he alone was walking about. Suddenly, and at the

PLATE XXIII

1. Majaje, a famous chieftainess and rain-maker in the mountains of North Transvaal. She was believed to be immortal and is said to have suggested to Rider Haggard the idea of his romance *She*. The truth seems to be that there was a succession of "Majajes," and the death of each one, when it occurred, was kept secret by her councillors.

2. The "New Yam" ceremony in the Calabar country; chiefs pressing forward to partake of the offerings. Analogous "feasts of first-fruits" are found, probably all over Bantu and Negro Africa — e.g. the *ukutshwama* of the Zulus. The idea seems to be that it is not safe to make use of the new crops till the chief has "taken off the tabu" by tasting them.

moment of an extraordinarily vivid flash of lightning, after a very loud peal of thunder, he was seized and carried through space till he reached the roof of heaven, when it opened and allowed him to pass into the abode of Nzambi Mpungu. Nzambi Mpungu cooked some food for him and gave him to eat. And when he had eaten, he took him about and showed him his great plantations and rivers full of fish, and then left him, telling him to help himself whenever he felt hungry. He stayed there two or three weeks, and never had he had such an abundance of food. Then Nzambi Mpungu came to him again and asked him whether he would like to remain there always, or whether he would like to return to the earth. He said that he missed his friends and would like to return to them. Then Nzambi Mpungu sent him back to his family."

Leza [42] is sometimes identified with the lightning, and the " red " and " black " gods of the Masai [43] with the lightning and the rain-cloud. Elsewhere, we do not often find the rain regarded as a distinct personality, except among the Bushmen, who record various instances of the Rain being made angry by inconsiderate conduct. Miss Lloyd on one occasion found a curious and beautiful fungus, which she carried home and kept for some days. Subsequently, as she feared it was going bad, she desired the Bushman, Hankasso, to throw it away.[44] He demurred, but finally removed it, explaining afterwards that he had not thrown it away, but laid it down gently, as it was " a rain's thing," and must not be treated roughly. His care did not prevent a tremendous downpour, which he attributed to the displeasure of the rain at the ejection of the fungus.

In general, stories about rain are concerned with the producing or withholding of it: it is well known that (as is only natural in a country where water is scarce) the rain-maker's is a most important profession among the Bantu. The Giryama, in time of drought, practise incantations at the grave of a woman, Mbodze, who was a famous rain-maker in her day, and who — inconsistently enough — is said to have been caught up to heaven in a thunderstorm.

The late Bishop Steere published, in the *South African Folk-Lore Journal*,[45] a story which would appear to be connected with some myth of this sort. It was related, as current among her own people, by a girl in one of the mission schools at Zanzibar, a freed slave who had been brought from the Chipeta country, west of Lake Nyasa. At a time when water was scarce, though food was plentiful, some little girls went to play in the scrub outside their village, carrying with them their miniature cooking-pots and some provisions. Among them was a child whose parents were both dead. She said to her companions: " I will show you something, but you must not tell any one." They all promised to be silent. Then she stood and looked up at the sky, and presently clouds began to gather, and in a short time there was a heavy shower, which filled their water-jars, so that they were able to cook their food; but it did not reach the village. When they went home, they took some of the cooked food with them, but refused to answer any questions as to how it had been obtained. Next day they went out again, and the orphan girl procured rain as before; but this time one of the other children secretly brought a second water-jar, and, when she had filled it, hid it in the bushes, while she used the other for cooking. That night she told her mother, under promise of secrecy, and showed her where she had hidden the water-jar, which they brought back to the house. As might have been expected, the story was soon all over the place, and at last reached the ears of the chief. He sent for the child to the council-place, loaded her with gold ornaments, and directed her, in the presence of the assembled people, to bring rain. (We may perhaps infer that there had been ineffectual attempts at persuasion. The " gold ornaments " are probably a touch only introduced after the story had reached the coast region.) She asked all the bystanders to retire to a distance, but they refused. Then she looked up at the sky and sang; the clouds collected, and presently there was a great rain, with lightning and thunder, and, in the midst of it, the child was caught up to the sky and never seen again.

Not very long ago, I read over the orginal Swahili of the above to a Zanzibar man, who was a Zigula by birth, and fairly versed in his native folklore, though he had been at sea, and out of touch with his own country for years. He did not profess to recognise it, but remarked at the end that the little girl who brought the rain was *mtoto wa malaika*, " a child of the angels "; which may have been a Moslem way of saying that she belonged to the Heaven-dwellers referred to in previous chapters. It seems likely, too, that the explicit statement of her parents having died was inserted by some narrator who did not fully understand the story, and that the original merely said either that she had no parents or that no one knew who they were, as was the case with Vere.

The sea does not figure very largely in Bantu mythology: it is only a few tribes who have been long enough in touch with it to have any ideas on the subject.[46] The tribes of the Guinea coast include sea-gods and goddesses in their pantheon, but do not seem to personify the element itself; and, in general, we may repeat what has been said on previous occasions, that sea-spirits, like river-spirits, lake-spirits, tree-spirits, etc., are not so likely to be personifications of these phenomena, or even powers specially and exclusively attached to them, as, in the last resort, ghosts of mortal men.

That there may be spirits of another sort, who are not ghosts, nor exactly what we mean by Nature Powers, is not disputed; and these, as " Haunting Demons," will come within the scope of the next chapter. But some, even of these, can be shown to have started in life as ghosts.[47]

CHAPTER VIII

TALES OF DEMONS AND OGRES

WE FIND, all over Africa, more or less, the notion of beings which cannot be explained either as ghosts or personified Nature-powers and which perhaps may be most appropriately called "Haunting Demons." Not all of those can be properly described as monsters, though many have more or less monstrous characteristics. Some are, no doubt, nightmare-phantoms originating in the horror of lonely places: the dark recesses of the forest, the poisonous swamp, the blazing heat of noon over the sandy scrub. But even here the line is very difficult to draw. Klamroth,[1] for instance, after making a very careful study of the spirits or demons extant in Uzaramo, came to the conclusion that many, if not all of them, such as Mwenembago, the "Lord of the Forest," were ghosts who had taken to haunting the wilds. On the other hand, Azizā, the Hunter's God or Forest Demon of the Ewe,[2] is clearly (if we may say so), an intensified chimpanzee.

The Pokomo describe a being which haunts the forests of the Tana and the open bush-steppe bordering on them, to which they give the name of *Ngojama*.[3] It has the shape of a man, but with a claw ("an iron nail," said my informant) in the palm of his hand, which he strikes into people if he catches them. He then drinks their blood. This creature has by some Europeans been supposed to be an anthropoid ape [4] — no species of which has hitherto been recorded from East Africa. I think he is more likely to be purely mythological.

From a Musanye at Magarini (in the Malindi district), I learnt that the *ngojama*, though something like a human being,

has a tail, like certain Masai " devils." [5]   A man of the narrator's tribe, long ago, came to grief through mistaken kindness
to a *ngojama*.   He came across him in the bush, wandering
about and eating raw meat: he took him in hand, taught
him to make fire and to cook, and had to some extent civilized
him, when suddenly, one day, the *ngojama* reverted to type,
turned on his benefactor and ate him.

The Nama Hottentots of the Kalahari tell of queer and
monstrous shapes haunting the scrub and the sand-dunes: the
Aigamuchab [6] who have eyes on their feet — on the top of the
instep — instead of the usual place.   They walk upright, their
eyes looking up to the sky; if they want to know what is going
on around them, they progress on hands and knees, holding
up one foot, so that the eye looks backwards.   They hunt men
as if they were zebras, and tear them to pieces with their
terrible, pointed teeth, which are as long as a man's finger.
These cannibals are not solitary, like the *ngojama*, but live in
villages, with their wives and children.   There are stories of
people straying into an *Aigamuchab* village and escaping with
difficulty.   Another mythical tribe of the same sort are the
" Bush-jumpers," *Hai-uri*, [7] who progress through the scrub by
jumping over the clumps of bush instead of going round them.

Another denizen of the Pokomo forest is the *Kitunusi*, who
seems to be related in some degree to the Giryama *Katsumbakazi*, who, again, has points of contact with the " Little
People " discussed in our next chapter.   The *Katsumbakazi*
is said to be of very low stature; [8] so is one kind of *Kitunusi*
(there are two) [9] — according to my Pokomo informant's indication, he stands about two feet six.   The other is of normal
human height, but does not appear so, as it is his habit to move
about in a sitting position.   Thinking he must be some primitive kind of *cul-de-jatte*, I enquired whether he was devoid
of legs, but was assured that he had them.   He is greatly
feared, for those who meet him are apt to be seized with severe

illness and perhaps lose the use of their limbs. But in old times people sometimes wrestled with him, and, if they could succeed in tearing off a piece of the *kaniki* waist-cloth which is his usual wear, their fortunes were made. A man would put away this bit of rag in the covered basket in which he kept his choicest possessions, and he would somehow or other (my informant did not enter into particulars) become rich.

Here is a link with the *Chiruwi*,[10] who haunts the woods in Nyasaland, and to whom we shall presently return. The Swahili of the coast seem to be acquainted with the *Kitunusi* but to have a different conception of him.[11] He lives in the sea, and is dreaded by fishermen. He is variously described as " a large fish which devours men who are bathing or diving in the sea," or as the spirit possessing such a fish — as Krapf quaintly says, " the natives believe that a ghost or Satan sits in the fish and instigates him " (without the fish's knowledge, we are elsewhere informed) " to swallow a man."

This might suggest that the Pokomo *Kitunusi* is really a water-sprite, like the Zulu *Tokolotshe* or *Hili*.[12] This would not be surprising, when we remember how the River Tana is bound up with the life of this tribe, and how much of their time they pass either on or in the water; but I have met with nothing to support this notion. On the contrary, the *Kitunusi* seemed rather to haunt the sandy scrub away from the river.

The *Chiruwi* just mentioned belongs to a very numerous family, who figure in the mythology of other continents besides Africa and who might be called " half-men," as they are usually more or less human in shape. Their body is split longitudinally:— they have only one eye, one ear, one arm and one leg — only in one instance do we find an obscure mention [13] of a person divided transversely. They may be malevolent or the reverse: a Nyanja tale [14] relates how, some children being cut off by a river in spate, they were carried across by a " big bird, with one wing, one eye, and one leg."

PLATE XXIV

Masks used in initiation ceremonies by the Bap-
ende. Probably intended, in the first instance, to
represent the spirits of the dead. After photographs
by E. Torday.

Chiruwi (*Chitowi* of the Yao)[15] is a being of this class, who haunts the forest, carrying an axe of the ornamental kind which is borne before chiefs. Some say that one side of him is made of wax, others that it is missing altogether, and " he is invisible if viewed from the off-side." If any one meets the *Chiruwi*, the latter says: " Since you have met with me, let us fight together." They then wrestle, the odds being on *Chiruwi*, who is " very strong," and, if the man is overcome, he " returns no more to his village." If, however, he is able to hold out, till he throws *Chiruwi* down, the latter shows him all the valuable medicinal herbs in the bush, and he becomes a great doctor. The Baila of the Middle Zambezi [16] have a similar belief, but their *Sechobochobo* is of kindlier mould, " he brings good luck to those who see him, he takes people and shows them trees in the forest which can serve as medicine "— without any preliminary conflict.

The Subiya [17] also have their *Sikulokobuzuka* (" the man with the wax leg "). A certain man named Mashambwa was looking for honey in the forest, when he heard *Sikulokobuzuka* singing, but did not at first see him. He heard a honey-guide calling, followed him to the tree where the bees had their nest, lit his torch, climbed the tree and took the honey. He had scarcely done so when he saw *Sikulokobuzuka* coming. He came down with his wooden bowl of honey, and the goblin immediately demanded it of him. Mashambwa refused, and the other challenged him to wrestle. They struggled for a long time, and Mashambwa, finding his opponent very strong, and despairing of victory as long as they were on the grass, into which *Sikulokobuzuka* could hook his foot, pulled him off on to the sand and threw him down. He then said to him: " Shall I kill you? " The other replied: " Don't kill me, master; I will get you the medicine with which you can bewitch people to death." " I don't want that medicine — is there no other? " " There is another — one to get plenty of meat." " I want that one." So *Sikulokobuzuka* went to look for it and showed him all the medicines good for getting supplies of food, and also that which gains a man the favour of his chief. Then they parted. Mashambwa lost his way and wandered about till evening, when he once more met the wax-legged man. The latter guided him home to his village and left him, telling him on no account to speak to any one. So Mashambwa went into his hut and sat down on the ground, and when his friends addressed him, he never answered; and at last they said to each other: " He has seen *Sikulokobuzuka*." Then he fell ill and remained so for a year, never speaking throughout that time. At the end of the year, he began to recover, and one day, seeing some vultures hovering over a distant spot in the bush (this seems to have been a sign that his probation was over), he said: " Look! those are my vultures! " and sent some men off to the place. They found a buck freshly killed by a lion, and thenceforth Mashambwa never wanted for food or any other necessaries.

These half-men can scarcely be classed as ogres; but there are various tribes of ogres having only one arm and one leg, while others, though in various ways monstrous and abnormal,[18] have not this peculiarity. The Basuto call the former class of beings " Matebele " [19] — probably from having come to look on their dreaded enemies, the Zulu tribe of that name, as something scarcely human. The tale of Ntotwatsana relates how, while a chief's daughter was out herding the cattle on the summer pastures, a whirlwind caught her up and carried her to a village of the Matebele " who had but one leg, one arm, one ear and one eye." They married her to the son of their chief, and, to prevent her escape, buried a pair of magic horns in her hut. One night, she tried to run away, but the horns cried out:

" U–u–u–e! it is Ntotwatsana, who was carried away by a whirlwind
  in the pastures,
When she was herding the cattle of her father, of Sekwae! "

Then the Matebele came running up and caught her.

As time went on, she had two children, twin girls, who were
like their mother, with the usual number of limbs. Years
passed, and one day the maidens went to the spring to fetch
water, and found there a warrior with his men. He called to
them and asked: " Whose children are you? "

" We are the children of the Rough-hided One."

" Who is your mother? "

" She is Ntotwatsana."

" Whose child is she? "

" We do not know — she has told us that she was carried
away by a whirlwind in the pastures."

So he said: " Alas! they are the daughters of my younger
sister."

Then some of his men drew water for them, while others
cut reeds and trimmed them neatly with their knives. Their
uncle said to them: " When you get home, ask your mother
to go and get you some bread, and, when she is gone, hide the
reeds under the skin she sits on."

So they went home, put down their water-pitchers, and
began to cry, telling their mother, who was sitting outside the
hut, that they were very hungry and asking her to get them
something to eat. She got up to fetch them some bread, and
as soon as her back was turned, they slipped the bundle of
reeds under her rug. When she came back, she sat down on
the reeds and crushed them: the girls began to cry again, and
when their mother found out what was the matter, she said
she would send a young man to get other reeds for them. As
they had been instructed, they acted like spoilt children, and
insisted that no reeds would do unless their mother picked them
herself. So she went to the spring and of course found her

brother there, whom she recognised at once, and who asked her when she would come home. She explained that she was unable to come, on account of the horns, and he said: "If you are wise, warm some water, and when it is boiling pour it into the horns, then stop up their openings with dregs of beer, and lay some stones on top of them, and when it is midnight, take your two children and come here."

She did as directed, and at midnight called her daughters, and they went down to the reed-bed by the spring, taking with them a black sheep. The horns tried to give warning, but, being choked could only produce a sound "*U–u–u*"— which the villagers took for the barking of the dogs. They had gained a considerable start before the horns succeeded in clearing their throats and cried:

"U–u–u–e! it is Ntotwatsana, who was carried away by a whirlwind in the pastures,
When herding the cattle of her father, of Sekwae!"

The Matebele started in pursuit, hopping on their one leg. It was beginning to dawn, and they were drawing near to the travellers, when the sheep lifted up its voice and sang:

"You may as well turn back, for you have no part nor lot in us." [20]

The Matebele stood still in astonishment, gazing at the sheep, which then began to dance, raising its tail and digging its hoofs into the ground. When Ntotwatsana and her companions had again got the start of their pursuers, the sheep disappeared and, by some magical means, overtook its friends.

"The Matebele departed, running as in a race; they ran wildly through the open country, one before the other. They arrived near Ntotwatsana. The sheep sang and danced again, then disappeared. When the Matebele departed, they said: 'By our Chief Magoma! we will go, even if we were to arrive at Ntotwatsana's village; that little sheep, we must simply pass it, even if it dances and sings so nicely.' They went on."

However, when the incident was repeated, they grew weary and gave up the pursuit. Selo-se-Magoma, the Rough-hided One, went home sad; but the brother and sister reached their village in safety and found every one mourning Ntotwatsana as dead. So the story ends happily.

A favourite character in the tales of the Zulus and the Basuto is the *Izimu* (*Lelimo*), usually rendered " cannibal "; but his characteristics suggest that " ogre " is a more appropriate term. It is quite clear that what is meant is not a man who has taken to eating his fellow-men — as did certain unfortunate people in Natal, during the famine that followed on Tshaka's wars [21]— but something decidedly non-human. This word, as has been remarked in a previous chapter,[22] is found in closely allied forms in most Bantu languages; but the creature connoted is not always the same. Sometimes he belongs to the class of half-men; sometimes he seems more akin to the monsters *Kholumodumo*, *Usilosimapundu* and *Isikqukqumadevu*. There is a strange Chaga tradition of a man who broke a tabu and became an *Irimu*.[23] Thorny bushes grew out of his body, till he became a mere walking thicket and devoured men and beasts. He made himself useful, however, by swallowing a hostile war-party who were raiding the country, and was finally disenchanted, under the advice of a soothsayer, by his brother, who came up behind him and set the bushes on fire.

The name *Dzimwe*, used by the Anyanja, is evidently the same word, and is somewhat vaguely defined as meaning " a big spirit," but in their tales, he seems somehow or other to have got confused with the elephant, and figures chiefly as the butt and victim of the Hare, filling in some instances, the exact part played by the Hyena, or, in the New World by Brer Fox and Brer Wolf. The Swahili have not departed so far from the original conception of their *Zimwi*, but the word has been to some extent displaced by the borrowed terms *jini* and *shetani*. The Swahili version of a very popular story runs as follows: [24]

Some girls had gone down to the beach to gather shells. One of them picked up a specially fine cowry, which she was afraid of losing, and so laid it down on a rock till they returned. On the way back, she forgot her shell till they had already passed the rock, when she asked her companions to go back with her. They refused, but said they would wait for her, and she went back alone, singing. There was a *Zimwi* sitting on the rock, and he said to her: " Come closer, I cannot hear what you say! " She came nearer, singing her petition: " It is getting late! let me come and get my shell which I have forgotten! " Again he said: " I can't hear you! " and she came still nearer, till, when she was within reach, he seized her and put her into the drum which he was carrying. With this he went about from village to village, and, when he beat the drum, the child inside it sang with so sweet a voice that every one marvelled. At last he came to the girl's own home and found that his fame had preceded him there, so that the villagers entreated him to beat his drum and sing. He demanded some beer and, having received it, began to perform, when the parents of the girl immediately recognised their child's voice. So they offered him more beer, and, when he had gone to sleep after it, they opened the drum and freed the girl. Then they put in " a snake and bees and biting ants," and fastened up the drum as it had been before. Then they went and awakened him, saying that some people had arrived from another village, who wanted to hear his drum. But the drum did not give forth the usual sound, and the *Zimwi* went on his way disconcerted. A little later, he stopped on the road to examine his drum; but, as soon as he opened it, he was bitten by the snake and died. On the spot where he died,

PLATE XXV

Dance of Yaos (near Blantyre), both men and women taking part.

pumpkins and gourds sprang up, and in due time bore fruit. Some children passing by stopped to look at them and said: "How fine these big pumpkins are! Let us get father's sword and split them open!" One of the pumpkins, we are told, "became angry" and pursued the children, who fled till they came to a river, where they got an old ferryman to take them across, and, passing on, reached a village where they found the men seated in the council-house and asked for help. "Hide us from that pumpkin! The *Zimwi* has turned into a pumpkin and is pursuing us! When it comes, take it and burn it with fire!" The pumpkin came rolling up and said: "Have you seen my runaway slaves passing this way?" The men replied: "What sort of people are your slaves? We do not know them!" "That's a lie, for you have shut them up inside!" But they seized the pumpkin and, having made a great fire, burnt it to ashes, which they threw away. Then they let the children out, and they returned home safely to their mothers.

In parts of West Africa, such as Sierra Leone, where English (of sorts) has almost become the vernacular, the *Zimwi*, or whatever his local representative may have been called, has become a "devil" (or, more usually, "debble"). Thus we find, among Temne stories,[25] "The Girl that Plaited the Devil's Beard" and "Marry the Devil, there's the Devil to Pay." The latter introduces a theme which recurs again and again in "were-wolf" stories: a girl who had refused all suitors is at length beguiled by a handsome man who is really a disguised "debble." Like some varieties of the *Zimwi*, he has only half a body; but he borrows another half for the occasion: "he len' half-side head, half-side body, all ting half-side." On the way to his home, his wife sees the borrowed parts drop off one by one. The husband prepares to kill and eat her, but she is saved by her little brother, who had insisted on following her, though sent back again and again.

Among the Kikuyu, " the *Ilimu* takes the form of a man, either normal or abnormal in shape, and talks like a man, ' but is a beast.' His body is either wholly or in part invulnerable. His great characteristic is that he feeds on human flesh." [26] In one of the stories, he is described as having one foot and walking with a stick, " and his other foot comes out at the back of his neck, and he has two hands." If this is correctly reported, it looks like a distorted recollection of the Half-man.

The Wachaga seem to attribute various forms to their *Irimu*. One has already been mentioned. He seems sometimes to be associated with the idea of a leopard: in fact Gutmann calls him " the were-panther " (*Werpardel*),[27] but this description certainly will not always fit — for instance, in the following story.[28] Here, presumably, we are to understand that the dog's nature became changed after drinking the child's blood: the indestructible part (here, the skull) is a feature occurring elsewhere; but it is not clear how far the creature developed out of it is the same as the original dog.

There was a certain young married woman, named Mukosala, who had a small child. She had no one to help her in looking after it; but, one day, a strange dog appeared at the homestead, and took to coming regularly, as Mukosala fed him. She grew so used to him that one day, when she wanted to leave the house, she said: " I will give you this bone, if you watch the baby nicely till I come back." The dog agreed, and performed his task well for a time; but, growing impatient, he took the bone and cracked it, and a splinter flying from it hit the baby's neck and drew blood. Unable to resist the sight of the blood, he sucked at it till he had killed the child, which he then devoured. He took the bud of a banana-tree (which may be quite as large as a small baby), laid it on the bed and covered it with a cloth, saying to the mother, when she returned: " Take care not to wake him: I have just fed him."

But she very soon discovered what had happened and, sending him away to fetch dry banana-leaves, called her husband. When the dog came back, they seized him, bound him securely and threw him on the heap of dried leaves, which they set on fire, so that he was consumed, even to the bones, all except the skull. This rolled away, first into an irrigation-channel and thence into the river, which washed it up into a meadow. Some girls, coming down to cut grass by the river, and chewing sugar-cane as they walked, saw the skull and took it for a white stone. Some of them cried out: " What a beautiful white stone! — as pretty as baby brother! " and threw it some of their sugar-cane as they passed. But one laughed at her friends, and said: " How silly! how can a stone be like your baby brother? " They finished cutting the grass, helped each other up with their loads and turned to go home. But when they came back to the skull, they found that it had grown into a huge rock which barred their path. So they began to sing spells in order to remove it. The first one sang:

> " Make room and turn aside!
>   Let us pass! Let us pass!
> She who laughed in her pride
> Is far behind — turn aside! —
>   We come with our bundles of grass —
>   Let us pass! Let us pass! "

The rock moved aside and let her through. Each of her companions in turn sang the same words and went on. Last of all came the girl who had jeered at the skull, and she, too, sang the magic song, but the rock never stirred. So she had to wait there till evening. Just as it was growing dark, a leopard appeared and asked her: " What will you give me, if I carry you over? "

" I will give you my father."

" That won't do! "

" Or my mother! "

" No use."

" I'll give you the ox next the door, at home."

" No."

" The one in the middle — the one next the wall? "

" I don't want any of them."

" Then I will be your wife."

" I agree to that," said the Leopard. " Now hold on to my tail! "

She did so, and he climbed the rock, pulling her after him. But, just as he had got half-way, his tail broke, and she fell down. Other leopards came, one after another, but the same thing happened to each. At last came a leopard with ten tails, who made the same bargain as the rest. She seized all his tails at once and was carried safely over. After he had gone a little distance with her, he asked if she could still see her father's house. She said that she could, and he went on, repeating the question from time to time, till she answered: " I can still see the big tree in the grove by my father's house." Still he kept on his way up the mountain side and soon came to a rock, where he stopped and cried: " House of the Chief, open! " The rock opened, and they entered the leopard's dwelling, which consisted, like a Chaga hut, of two compartments, one for the people and one for the cattle. He took up his quarters in the latter, leaving the other to his wife, whom he kept well supplied with fat mutton and beef. He himself lived on human flesh, but he always brought his victims in by night and hid them in the cow-stall, so that his wife never saw them.[29] After some months, when he considered her fat enough (a fact ascertained by stabbing her in the leg with the needle or awl used in thatching and mat-making), he went out to invite his relatives to the feast, telling them to bring a supply of firewood with them. While he was gone, her brothers, who had been searching for her, reached the rock. She heard their voices and called out to them the magic words

which would open it. They came in and she set food before
them, but the husband came home suddenly, and she had only
time to hide them in the spaces under the rafters, where the
young leopards slept. The cubs began to growl, and the
Irimu became suspicious, but his wife pacified him by saying
that they were hungry. The brothers escaped during the
night, while he slept. Next day, after he had gone out, the
wife smeared herself all over with dirt, and also plastered
dirt on the threshold, the cooking-stones, the posts to which
the cattle were tied, and the rafters of the roof. To each of
these she said, " If my husband calls me, do you answer,
' Here! ' "

Then she got out of the house [30] and hastened homeward.
On the way, she met one after another of the *Irimu's* kinsfolk,
each one carrying a log of wood on his shoulder. Each one, as
he passed her, asked: " Are you our cousin's wife? " and she
answered: " No, his wife is sitting at home, anointing herself
with mutton-fat! "

They suspected nothing and passed on, to be met by the
Irimu, who conducted them to the rock and called his wife.
The threshold answered " Here! " but no one came, and he
called again. This time the voice answered from the fireplace, and so on, till he had searched the whole house in vain
and come to the conclusion that his wife had escaped. He
then heard from his guests how they had met her and been
deceived by her and, leaving them to make the preparations
for the banquet, he set out in pursuit.

Meanwhile the wife had reached a river too deep to ford
and cried: " Water, divide! Let this stand still and that
flow! " Immediately the stream divided, and she went
through dryshod, and, having gained the further bank, said:
" Water, unite and flow on! " The water did so, and she sat
down to rest and cleanse herself. Presently the *Irimu* appeared
on the other side and asked her how she had got across. She

answered: " You have only to say to the water, 'Divide! Let this stand still and that flow! ' But when you are in midstream, say, ' Come together again! ' " The *Irimu* did as he was told and was carried off by the current. As he was being swept out of sight, he cursed her, saying: " Wherever you go, you shall only see people with five heads! " She called after him: " Go your way and take root as a banana-tree! "

The woman went on, and soon came upon some people who had five heads. When she saw them, she burst out laughing, and four of each person's heads dropped off. They said: " Give us back our heads! " So she gave them strings of beads and passed on. The same thing happened over and over again; but at last she reached her parents' village in safety. The *Irimu*, for his part, was washed ashore by the stream, took root on the bank and became a banana-tree.

The concluding incidents, as we have them, are not very clear, but we may perhaps connect the last one with another Chaga story,[31] where a woman, carrying her baby with her, goes to the river-bank to cut grass, and finds a banana-tree with ripe fruit.[32] She says: " Why, these are my bananas! " and the bananas reply: " Why, that is my son! " The little child breaks off a banana and one of his fingers drops off. Subsequently, they meet an *Irimu*, who tears the child to pieces. The relation between the *Irimu* and the banana-tree is not stated, but may be guessed without difficulty, when we recall the preceding story, and the pumpkin-plant which sprang from the dead *Zimwi* in the Swahili tale.[33]

The latter part of the " Irimu's Wife " belongs to the numerous tales which have been classified under the heading " Flight from Witchcraft." It is found here in a comparatively simple form, the obstacles occurring in most of them being reduced to one — the river. And here we may remark that the dividing of a river — either by a mere " word of power," as here, or by striking it with a staff — is too common an incident in African folklore to be ascribed to echoes of missionary teaching. It occurs, not only in fairy-tales, but also e.g. in the traditions of the Zulus, who bring it down to so recent a period as the northward migrations of Zwangendaba, about 1825. The Basuto,[34] in the tale of "The Nyamatsanes," describe a man flying from ogres, who throws a pebble behind him. This becomes a high rock, which they cannot pass. Where the obstacles are multiplied, as in the Swahili "Kibaraka" (thorns, rock, swords, water, fire, sea), outside influence would seem to have been at work.

The theme is exemplified in nearly every part of Africa, sometimes in a very close parallel to "Hänsel and Gretel," but more usually in the case of a girl married to an ogre (or were-wolf) and saved by a younger brother or sister. Some of them we shall have to notice in a later chapter.

CHAPTER IX

THE LITTLE PEOPLE

WE HAVE mentioned Kitunusi and Chiruwi among the uncanny denizens of the wood and wild in Tanaland and the Shire Highlands respectively. Both these beings link on to a set of legends, which seem, like those of the elves and "Good People" in Europe, to refer, ultimately, to some former inhabitants of the country, of smaller stature and lower culture than the later invaders, yet possessed of knowledge and skill in certain arts which gave them a reputation for preternatural powers. Some had a knowledge of metal working, others a familiarity with the ways of wild animals and the properties of plants, which might seem little short of miraculous to the more settled agricultural or even the pastoral tribes. The mystery of their underground dwellings; their poisoned arrows; their rock-paintings and sculptures (which, moreover, seem to have served some magical purpose) — all had a share in building up their mythical character. As regards Europe, the subject has been fully treated by Mr. David MacRitchie in *The Testimony of Tradition* and other works.

The Giryama, whose country adjoins that of the Pokomo, have the Katsumbakazi, who appears to be in some respects akin to the Kitunusi. He is, says the Rev. W. E. Taylor,[1] "a *p'ep'o* or jinn, said to be seen occasionally in daylight. . . . It is usually malignant. When it meets any one, it is jealous for its stature (which is very low) and accordingly asks him: 'Where did you see me?' If the person is so unlucky as to answer: 'Just here,' he will not live many days; but if he is aware of the danger and says: 'Oh, over yonder!' he

will be left unharmed, and sometimes even something lucky will happen to him."

This sensitiveness as to their size appears to be a common trait among similar beings.   Mr. Mervyn W. H. Beech [2] heard from the Akikuyu elders in Dagoreti district that the country was " first inhabited by a race of cannibal dwarfs called Maithoachiana."   These were followed by some people called Gumba, said to have been the makers of the old pottery now sometimes dug up, and also to have taught the Akikuyu the art of smelting iron.   Mr. Beech was informed by the District Commissioner of Fort Hall that "the Maithoachiana appear to be a variety of earth-gnomes with many of the usual attributes; they are rich, very fierce, very touchy, e.g. if you meet one and ask him who his father is, he will spear you, or if he asks you where you caught sight of him first, unless you say that you had seen him from afar, he will kill you. . . . Like earth-gnomes in most folklore, they are skilled in the art of metal working."

There seems to be some difference of native opinion here, as some say it was the Gumba who were the metal-workers. Stone implements are found everywhere in the Kikuyu country.   Again, some say it was the Gumba who lived in caves, as many of the people round Mount Elgon still do; others that it was the Maithoachiana who lived in the earth. Maithoachiana means, in Kikuyu, " eyes of children."

There are legendary dwarfs called by the Swahili Wabili-kimo.   Krapf says [3] that they are said to live four days' journey west of Chaga, "they are of a small stature, twice the measure from the middle finger to the elbow."   Krapf, or his Swahili informant, endeavours to derive the name from -*bili* (-*wili*), "two," and *kimo*, "measure"; but it very likely belongs to some language of the interior, and the Swahili may have followed the practice of popular etymologists all over the world in trying to get a meaning, by hook or by crook, out of an otherwise unintelligible word. In Giryama, *mbiri-kimo* is " a member of the rumoured race of Pygmies," [4] and I have myself heard of them, quite accidentally, from a Gir-yama; at any rate it seems clear that the name and the story came from the interior. Krapf says: " The Swahili pretend to get all their knowledge of physic from these pygmies " (this is his gloss on the statement that they go to " Mbilikimoni *ku tafuta uganga,* ' to search for medicine ' "), " who have a large beard and who carry a little chair on their seat which never falls off wherever they go." Krapf goes on to make severe re-flections on the fables invented by the " credulous and design-ing Swahili "; but the last statement has some foundation in the fact that several tribes of the interior are in the habit of carrying their little wooden stools slung at their backs by a hide thong, when they travel; and, seen at a distance these might be taken for a fixture of their anatomy.

" All medicine " (*uganga,* generally understood as refer-ring to the occult department) " is in their country "; and herein, they resemble Bushmen, Lapps, and elves. But it is not clear whether they are the same people as the Kikuyu Maithoachiana.

In Nyasaland, Sir Harry Johnston [5] found, twenty-five years ago, that the natives had a tradition as to " a dwarf race of light yellow complexion," living on the upper part of Mlanje mountain. These may have been actual Bushmen, and, indeed, a careful study of the population in some parts of the Protectorate suggests that there must have been a con-siderable absorption of Bushman blood in the past. " They gave' these people a specific name, ' A-rungu,' but I confess this term inspired me with some distrust of the value of their tradition, as it was identical with that used for ' gods.' "

It *may* only have meant that these " little people " were passing into the mythical stage which they, or some like them, have already reached in other parts of Nyasaland. Dr. H. S.

Stannus⁶ found that, while the Yaos in some parts of the Protectorate use the word *Chitowe* (pl. *Itowe*) in the sense already mentioned (as equivalent to *Chiruwi*), others apply it as follows:

"Among the Machinga Yao the *Itowe* are 'the little people' of the Leprecaun order. They rob the gardens and cause rot among the pumpkins; their little footprints can be seen where they have passed hither and thither; fruits and vegetables that they touch will become bitter. To prevent these disasters, the Yao, at the time when their crops are ripening, take some of their different kinds of vegetables and place them at cross-roads, hoping thereby to satisfy the *Itowe* and prevent them coming into the gardens. The *Chitowe* is variously said to be like a man but rather like an animal. He has two legs, but goes on all fours. The Yao describe another legendary race of 'little people' who 'used to live in the country and may still be met with — who knows'? He was of very small stature, grew a long beard, was very touchy, quarrelsome and fierce, and carried spears as his weapons. When anyone met one he was immediately asked: '*Mumbo-nelekwapi?*' (From how far did you see me?) and it was always as well to pretend to have seen the little man coming a long way off and make him believe he was considered quite a big person; if you said, 'Hello, I have only just spotted you!' he would immediately spear you. They are commonly supposed to dwell on the tops of high mountains and are iron-workers. They are called the *Mumbonelekwapi.*" The Machinga Yao dwell on the upper side near the outlet of Lake Nyasa.

The going on all fours may remind us (though it is not the same) of the Kitunusi's mode of progression.

Dr. Stannus goes on to say that the same legend is found, not only among the Anyanja and Yao, but among the Henga and Nkonde at the north end of Lake Nyasa, and everywhere the same name, the equivalent of " Where did you see me? " is in use. And here, at the risk of wearying the reader with another parallel, we will pass on to the Zulus, and reproduce the account of the Abatwa given to the late Bishop Callaway by Umpengula Mbanda.[7]

" The Abatwa are very much smaller people than all other small people; they go under the grass and sleep in anthills; they go in the mist; they live in the up-country, in the rocks; they have no village of which you may say ' There is a village of the Abatwa.' Their village is where they kill game; they consume the whole of it and go away. That is their mode of life."

" But it happens if a man is on a journey and comes suddenly on an Umutwa " (singular of Abatwa), " the Umutwa asks, ' Where did you see me? ' But at first through their want of intercourse with the Abatwa a man spoke the truth and said, ' I saw you in this very place.' Therefore the Umutwa was angry, through supposing himself to be despised by the man, and shot him with his arrow, and he died. Therefore it was seen that they like to be magnified and hate their littleness. So then, when a man met with them, he saluted the one he met with, ' I saw you! ' " (the customary Zulu greeting, Sa-ku-bona). " The Umutwa said, ' When did you see me? ' The man replied, ' I saw you when I was just appearing yonder. You see yon mountain? I saw you then, when I was on it.' So the Umutwa rejoiced, saying, ' O, then, I have become great.' Such then became the mode of saluting them."

There is a little addition to this account, which, whether originally a part of it or not, belongs to a comparatively recent period, since it assumes, as a matter of course, that the Abatwa possess horses.

" It is said, when Abatwa are on a journey, when the game is come to an end where they have lived, they mount on a horse, beginning on the neck, till they reach the tail, sitting one behind the other. If they do not find any game, they eat the horse."

Their "dreadfulness," according to Umpengula, lies in their very insignificance: "They are little things, which go under the grass. And a man goes looking in front of him, thinking, ' If there come a man or a wild beast, I shall see.' And, forsooth, an Umutwa is there, under the grass; and the man feels when he is already pierced by an arrow; he looks, but does not see the man who shot it. It is this, then, that takes away the strength."

Their arrows, too, are always poisoned, so that the slightest wound is fatal, and thus it is no wonder if they were felt to be something not altogether human. The sense of horror and mystery which they inspire is admirably rendered in a sketch of Frederick Boyle's,[8] describing some uncanny Bornean forest-folk whom he calls *Ujit;* but what authority there is for this, I do not know. I remember, when passing through the forest which clothes the range of hills a few miles inland from Mambrui, on the East Coast, a little to the North of Malindi, one of the porters suddenly remarked: "*Wasanye!*" I heard a cry of "*Dungich!*" ("the European") from among the trees, caught one glimpse of moving shapes, and all was still. Presently I noticed the peculiarly insistent call of some bird, repeated again and again and answered by another. "Is that a real bird, or the Wasanye?" I asked the man nearest me. "The Wasanye," he answered. We saw and heard no more of them at that time.

These were perfectly harmless people and so, in many cases, are the Bushmen. "Some are of gentle disposition, ready to do any service," says Father Torrend; [9] "others wage war on all living beings and cannot be trusted with anything." It would have been only fair to add that the disposition of these latter is consequent on the treatment that they have met with.

Bishop Callaway adds in a note: " But they are not Bush-men which are here described, but apparently pixies or some race much more diminutive than the actual Bushmen. Yet the resemblance is sufficiently good to make it almost certain that we have a traditional description of the first intercourse between the Zulus and that people."

Further comparative research shows that the doubt here conveyed was needless. These Abatwa are certainly the real Bushmen, though they have passed into the region of myth-ology.

This name, under various easily recognisable forms, is found in many parts of Africa; sometimes applied to actual pygmies, sometimes to people who are not particularly dwarfish, but also resemble the Bushmen in their mode of life, or have other characteristics in common with them. Thus the (Bantu) Pokomo of the Tana River call the Wasanye Wa-hwa, and there are people called Batwa living in the marshes of Lake Bangweolo, who cannot be described as pygmies.[10]

But everywhere, the name seems to be given by the present population of the country to some earlier inhabitants. The Watwa of Urundi consider themselves, says P. Van der Burgt,[11] " the true aborigines of the country. They are . . . hunters, smiths, potters, . . . nomad, timid, cruel, irascible, *greatly given to magic arts,* very black, lean, below the mid-dle height, hairy. . . . The Warundi despise them, *consider-ing them not men but beasts.*"

On the writer's own showing, however, this can scarcely be accepted as an exhaustive description of the Warundi's atti-tude, since the Watwa seem to have the same uncanny attri-butes as their congeners elsewhere. In their own ritual chants, they call themselves " sons of the stone-men," which, whatever it may mean, seems to hint at a different origin from that of the people among whom they dwell. It is a pity that no further explanation is forthcoming. We have seen that, when African cosmogonies take any account of people other than the narrators, these are frequently said to have " come otherwise "— like the stars in the idea of Browning's Caliban — also the Hill Damara and the Bushmen.

The Pygmies (Batwa) of the Kasai also " came otherwise " — their progenitors are held to have been the offspring ⸢of trees, and the Bangongo informed Mr. Torday [12] that you can still see the great cracks in some trees from which they came out. Tradition tells that Woto, the fourth chief of the Bushongo, having left his people and retired into the forest, on account of the misdeeds of his relations, found himself very lonely and uttered an incantation. Thereupon the trees opened and sent forth a multitude of little beings who, when he asked them what people they were, answered: " *Binu batwe!* " (" we are men ") — whence their name. " At the present day," said the informant, " they, are human beings and have children like other people, but at that time they were only phantoms in human shape, being the children of the trees."

They are regarded with superstitious terror; even those who have left the forest and settled down to agricultural life are considered more or less dangerous, and the other tribes never intermarry with them.

However, there seems to be one place at least, where the Little People are friendly and helpful. This is on Kilimanjaro, where some suppose them to live in a world of their own, within the mountain, with their banana-groves and herds of cattle. Poor or distressed people who find the entrance to this world are kindly received and dismissed with generous gifts, while the well-to-do, who come in hope of getting still richer, are driven out in disgrace. This reminds us of the numerous " Holle " stories (see Chapter V), though these belong rather to the Kingdom of the Dead, and indeed this is expressly stated in tales of this kind told by these very people, the Wachaga. It seems pretty clear, however, that the kindly

Underworld folk are not the ancestors (*warimu*), but "the legendary earliest inhabitants of the country." Some localise them, not inside the mountain, but on the top of Kibo — the huge, rounded, snowy dome of which you catch a distant view from the train, approaching Voi, as you come from Mombasa.

"They are dwarfs with great, misshapen heads, who have retreated before the advancing tribes and taken refuge on the inaccessible height. They are called Wadarimba or Wakonyingo. They have a kind of ladders, like the rafters in the roof of a native hut, fixed against the rocks, by which people can climb up to them, and which do not stop short there but reach straight up into the sky. These dwarfs, too, take pity on those in trouble as is related in many legends. The bits of meat which they lay out in the banana-groves when sacrificing to their ancestors, roll down the slopes of the mountains and turn into ravens." [13] Perhaps this is an attempt to account for the fact that the white-necked raven, fairly common on Kilimanjaro, is seldom, if ever, seen as high as the snow-limit.

The Wakonyingo are said to be no larger than human children, but to have enormous heads. They never lie down to sleep, but sit, leaning against the wall of the hut, for if they were to lie down, they could never get up again, being so topheavy. If one of them falls, he has to wait for his friends to help him up, and therefore every Mkonyingo carries a horn at his belt, so that he can blow it to call for aid, if necessary.[14]

They tell a story of the Wakonyingo,[15] somewhat to the following effect:

There was a poor man with two sons, Mkunare and Kanyanga. As they had not even one cow, Mkunare said: 'I will go up to Kibo. They say that a chief dwells there who has pity on the poor.' He took food with him and went up the mountain. First he came to an old woman sitting by the wayside, whose eyes were so sore that she could not see out of

PLATE XXVII

The Dwarfs with the Big Heads

them. He greeted her, and she thanked him, saying: ' What brings you up here? ' He told her, and she said: ' Lick my eyes clean first, and then I will tell you how to reach the chief.' He could not bring himself to do this and went on till he came to the Wakonyingo and found all the men sitting at the Chief's kraal. None of them was bigger than a little boy who herds the goats (which the youngest do, before they are considered capable of going with the cattle). So he took them for children and said: ' Good-day, youngsters. Just show me the way to your fathers and big brothers! ' The Wakonyingo answered: ' Just wait till they come! ' He waited, but no grown men appeared, and, as the evening fell, the Little Ones drove in the cattle and killed a beast for supper; but they gave him no meat, only saying: ' Wait till our fathers and brothers come! ' So he had to go away hungry, and, when he reached the old woman once more, she would answer no questions. He lost his way and wandered about for a month before getting home, where he reported that a great tribe with many cattle lived on the top of Kibo, but they were inhospitable and would give nothing to strangers. But as their case continued desperate, the younger brother, Kanyanga, resolved to try his fortune. He set out, found the old woman and performed the charitable office requested of him. The grateful old woman then said: ' Go straight on, and you will come to the Chief's green, where you will find men no bigger than the goat-boys. But you must not think they are children, but greet them respectfully, as the Chief's councillors.' Kanyanga did as he was directed, and the Wakonyingo welcomed him and took him to the chief, who, on hearing his story, at once supplied him with food and shelter. In return for this generosity, Kanyanga taught the Wakonyingo the proper charms for protecting their crops against insect and other pests and also those for ' closing the roads ' so that no enemy could enter their country. This is

remarkable, as showing that certain kinds of magic may have
been known to the later comers and not to the aborigines.
These dwarfs were so delighted that each of them gave
Kanyanga a beast and he returned home in triumph, driving
his cattle before him and singing the Herding-Song:

" Bring me an axe to strike the tree —
   The Talking Tree that talks to me:
Bairns, says he, and kine, says he —
   And where shall I graze those kine? tell me!
They shall graze on Kibo, till Kibo is burnt off.
   They shall graze on Mawenzi, till the fire has swept the peak —
They shall feed o'er Lalehu and on Kimala side,
   And in Leruhu swamp, till there's no more grass to seek.
On Mamkinga meadows, by Makirere banks —
   Down Kinenena slopes, till the grass is burnt and done . . .
Down, down, to the pools of Kikulo and Malaa —
   And then they'll be at home, every one! "

So Kanyanga grew rich and restored the fallen fortunes of
his clan. But the people made a song about his brother,
which is sung to this day:

    " O Mkunare, wait till the fathers come!
    What right have you to despise the Little Folk! "

Here we find the Wakonyingo less aggressively sensitive
about their small size than the Abatwa, and less extreme in
their retaliation, though by no means disposed to overlook
slights. Another story,[16] partly to the same effect, describes
their country as reached by a gateway — no doubt like those
which lead to the fortified *kayas* of the Wanyika. Near the
top of Kibo are two doors side by side, one giving access to
the Wakonyingo's ladders, the other leading downwards.
Any one ill-advised enough to go through the latter would
perish miserably, for those who come down again perceive
what they were unable to see when going up — ghosts and

a great fire. This story also describes the Wakonyingo women going down the mountan to cut grass, each with a gourd of cream tied to her back, to be shaken up as she walked, which was their method of churning.

It thus appears that, if the Wakonyingo are not actually Heaven-dwellers, yet they resemble them in some respects. But the Thonga, as we have seen, believe in dwarfs actually living in the sky, who sometimes come down in thunder-storms,[17] but, from their connection with rain, they would have come more appropriately into the chapter on Nature Myths.

On the other hand, Duff Macdonald [18] quotes a confused little tradition that " people died and went to the graves and became Itowe," but there is nothing to show that these are the same as the pixie-like Itowe described by Dr. Stannus.[19]

CHAPTER X

TOTEMISM AND ANIMAL STORIES

TOTEMISM seems to exist, or to have existed, all over Africa south of the Sahara. Sometimes we meet with it in a clear and unmistakable form, sometimes only in a state of survival, no longer understood — or only partly so — by the people themselves.

This is not the place to discuss the nature and origin of totemism, or to compare its African manifestations with those found in other parts of the world. We are concerned with it only as a factor in mythology; and here it is of considerable importance. It may be well, for the sake of clearness, to start with Frazer's definition [1]— the most recent and satisfactory known to me:

" A totem is a class of material objects which a savage regards with superstitious respect, believing that there exists between him and every member of the class an intimate and altogether special relation. . . . The connection between the man and his totem is mutually beneficent; the totem protects the man, and the man shows his respect for the totem in various ways, by not killing it if it be an animal, and by not cutting or gathering it if it be a plant. As distinguished from a fetish, a totem is never an isolated individual, but always a class of objects."

A totem may be an animal or plant, more rarely an inanimate object, still more rarely an artificial object. There are " rain " and " sun " totems among the Nandi and the Herero; a " hill " totem in Nyasaland, and the Barolong (Bechuana) have an " iron " totem (*tshipi*). The way in which this originated (as related to me by a member of the clan, Mr. Solomon Tshekiso Plaatje) may throw some light on other seemingly anomalous totems. The Barolong formerly " danced " (as the Bechuana say) [2] the kudu, and therefore could not eat its flesh. Once, in time of famine, it appears that a kudu was accidentally killed by some one; no one, however, dared to eat its flesh, though sorely distressed. The chief came to the rescue, by suggesting that the totem should be changed and that they should thenceforth venerate, not the kudu, but the spear which had killed it. (This suggests that the " iron " totem belongs to the class, not merely of inanimate, but of artificial objects.)

Totems, as Frazer points out,[3] are never worshipped in any real sense; the relation " is one of friendship and kinship." The man " identifies himself and his fellow-clansmen with his totem . . . he looks upon himself and his fellows as animals of the same species, and on the other hand he regards the animals as in a sense human." Totemism may sometimes develop into worship of animals or plants, as may have been the case in ancient Egypt. The Baganda have a " python-god," Selwanga, whose temple is in Budu. His priests are members of the " Heart " clan, and there is nothing in Roscoe's account to suggest that he is a totem;[4] but, when we find that a tribe to the northeast of Lake Victoria (the Kamalamba)[5] have a python totem, and that the two clans owning this totem pay special honours to the python, his origin is pretty evident. The Wawanga, a tribe allied to the Kamalamba, " have certain sacred rites connected with the python. . . . Straw images of these snakes, with a pot of porridge or beer, and perhaps a few feathers stuck into the ground beside them, are often to be seen in the villages. In such a case, some one in the village has recently met a python and offered it food, or a fowl, and on his return has made this image of it." [6] This applies to the whole tribe — not to any particular clan, and would appear to be a transition stage between the practice of the Kamalamba and that of the Baganda.

Again, totemism appears to exist, though becoming obsolete, among the Ewe,[7] and three Ewe totems, the Python, the Crocodile, and the Leopard, are enumerated by Ellis among " tribal deities." It is true that he does not mention a Python clan, but his list is admittedly incomplete, and it does include a Snake clan (Ordañh-do; the Python god is Dañh-bi), which may be the same thing.

Totemism is sometimes confused with the idea that the dead are re-incarnated in the form of animals; but the two notions are really quite distinct, as is quite clear when we consider what the Zulus say about the *amadhlozi* coming back as snakes. All animals of a given class are totems; but only a diviner can tell for certain whether any individual snake is or is not an *idhlozi*. Again, while other creatures besides snakes may be re-incarnated ancestors, there appears to be no case of their being appropriated to the particular clans, as they would be if they were totems.

The Wachaga seem to be losing their hold on totemism — at least only three totems are recognised nowadays — viz., the Baboon, the Elephant, and the Python.[8] There are probably others, e.g. the Wild Boar clan explain their name by saying that their ancestor was once knocked over by a wild boar, and they do not consider it an honour to be addressed by it. But this seems to show that the real meaning has been forgotten. The clans above mentioned believe themselves to be descended from their namesakes, but whereas most peoples who still retain a conscious belief in totemism think that their ancestor was actually an animal — usually, one who took human shape in order to found the family — the Wachaga represent the human ancestor as having afterwards turned into an animal. This alone is a sufficient indication that the idea has undergone some change, and that totemism, as such, is more or less obsolete.

A seeming exception to this last remark is the case of the Baboon clan. Their ancestor was a Baboon pure and simple who, having quarrelled with his fellows, went and settled in a village. However, the exception is only apparent, as the Wachaga believe these apes to be degenerate human beings. Certain people, being hard pressed by their enemies, fled into the jungle, and finding, after a time, that their huts had been burnt down and their fields wasted, gave up the attempt to lead a settled life and have remained wild ever since. Hence the founder of the clan was only returning to a state from which his ancestors had fallen.

I think the notion of apes as degenerate men has been reported from various parts of Africa, but the stories I have myself come in contact with, rather suggest the notion that they are inferior beings trying to raise themselves to human status. An East African tale relates how the Baboons, tired of being driven away from people's gardens, chose one of their number, cut off his tail (by way of disguise), and sent him to settle in the nearest village, directing him to marry a woman of the place and then cultivate seven gardens, of which five were to be left for his relations, while he and his wife were to live on the other two. The arrangement worked well for a time; but at last the wife grew tired of working so hard, " hoeing for those apes only! " Her husband agreed with her; but his kinsmen overheard them talking in this way and hastened back to the Bush, where they informed the rest of the tribe. It was resolved that his tail should be restored to him: so the whole party set off for the village, carrying it with them and singing:

" *Nyani, hge nyani, hala muchirao!* "
" Baboon, ho! baboon, come and take your tail! "

When they arrived at his abode, he was not at home, having gone to thatch his father-in-law's house; but they followed him thither and kept on singing till the import of their song reached him where he was, perched on the ridge-pole of the hut. He seems to have thought no protests would serve him, for he merely asked them to let him finish the roof, and then descended and resumed his tail, much to the astonishment of his wife and her family — this being the first intimation of his real nature.[9]

The Elephant totem of the Wachaga [10] belongs to the Wakonadai clan. The legend has it that a girl of this clan was once given in marriage against her will to a man of the Wakosalema. She refused to eat ordinary human food, subsisted on leaves and grass, and finally turned into an elephant, escaping into the forest. Since that time, elephants have greatly increased and have taken to feeding in people's gardens which they formerly avoided. They never harm one of their own clan, but if they meet a Mukosalema, they instantly kill him or her.

There does not seem to be a legend about the origin of the Python totem, which seems to have existed in many parts of Africa, but Gutmann's account is a very good illustration of the way in which these people treat their totems. Whenever a marriage has taken place, a feast is made for the Python, and the young wife sweeps and adorns the hut with especial care. It is said that the reptile always appears and throws down in the court-yard some of the yellow berries which are looked on as its peculiar treasure. It then enters the hut, where the wife is seated on the ground, glides over her outstretched legs and, after helping itself to the milk and other refreshments placed ready for it on a stool, passes out at the door and disappears in the scrub.

Gutmann says that this great serpent is regarded as an embodiment of an ancestor; but this, as already pointed out, is not the same thing as a totem: moreover, he adds that they never pray or sacrifice to it, as they do to their ancestral spirits.

The relation between a man and his totem is further exemplified by an experience of Mr. Hollis's [11] among the Nandi — a Hamitic tribe of East Africa. I give it in his own words:

" In March, 1908, I was on the point of encamping at the foot of the Nandi escarpment. The porters were pitching the tents, the cook had lit his fire, and I was having lunch. All at once an ominous buzzing warned us that a swarm of bees was near at hand, and in less than a minute we had to leave our loads and fly, hotly pursued by the bees. . . . During the course of the afternoon we tried two or three times to rescue our loads but without success, some of the porters being badly stung in the attempt. At four o'clock, when I had just decided to do nothing more till dark, a Nandi strolled into camp and volunteered to quiet the bees. He told us that he was of the Bee totem, and that the bees were his. He said we were to blame for the attack, as we had lit a fire under the tree in which their honey-barrel hung. He was practically stark naked, but he started off at once to the spot where the loads were, whistling loudly in much the same way as the Nandi whistle to their cattle. We saw the bees swarm round and on him, but beyond brushing them lightly from his arms he took no notice of them and, still whistling loudly, proceeded to the tree in which was their hive. In a few minutes he returned, none the worse for his venture, and we were able to fetch our loads."

The Nandi have a Baboon and a Leopard clan, but (unless it is included under the general designation of " Snake ") there does not appear to be a Python among their totems. The Hyena clan has some curious privileges and restrictions and is very highly esteemed. I mention this, because the hyena is to a certain extent respected by all Nandi, not merely by those whose totem he is, and is also the object of what might be called a cult among the Giryama and other tribes, who, as far as one knows, have no such totem. This may be a case of totemism developing into zoölatry, as seems to have happened with the Python.

The Thonga, according to Junod,[12] are not totemic, but two tales [13] which he gives afford a strong presumption that they once were. As these form excellent illustrations of the subject, they may be given here. A young man married a girl named Titishana, and, when the time came for him to take her home, her parents said: " Take an elephant with you! " (There is nothing in the tale, as it stands, to lead up to this astonishing offer, but it seems to be assumed that she would take some animal with her to her new home; perhaps she had begun by demanding the totem, and the parents made futile attempts to buy her off.) She refused, saying: " Where should I keep him? there is no forest near my husband's village." They said: " Take an antelope! " but again she would have none of it. " No! give me your cat! " They would not consent. " You know that our life is bound up with the cat! " But the heartless daughter replied: " That does not matter to me! I may meet with bad luck if you refuse! " So they yielded and gave her the cat. When the young couple left next day, the bride, without her husband's knowledge, carried the cat with her. On reaching their home, she secretly constructed a kraal for it and kept it there. When, subsequently, she went out to cultivate her garden at a distance (no one being left at home in the hut), she told the cat he might come out and eat the cooked maize left in the pot. He did so, and, after scraping out the pot, took down the kilt belonging to her husband, and his rattles, put them on and began to dance, singing:

" Oh ho! Titishana! Where have you gone, Titishana?
You have gone away — *va! va! va!* "

Then, fearing he might be caught, he restored the things

to their places and returned to his enclosure. He did the
same every morning as soon as Titishana had left for the
gardens, till, one day, he was overheard by some children,
who went to tell the master of the house. The man refused
to believe them, but hid himself near the door, and presently
saw the cat, wearing his own kilt and ornaments, begin to
dance. He fired at it and killed it, and, at the same moment,
Titishana, hoeing in her garden, fell down, as if seized by
sudden faintness. She called out: " They have killed me at
the village! " and went home, crying aloud all the way. She
sat down by the door of the hut, telling her husband to wrap
the body in a mat — since she would die, if she saw it uncovered — so that she could carry it to her own village. She
set out, her husband following behind, and on arriving, laid
the bundle down in the middle of the public place. It seems
there was no need to explain what had happened, for a woman
came up to her and said: " We offered you an elephant — you
refused; we offered you an antelope — you refused; have
you not now killed us all? — tell me! " All the inhabitants
of the village assembled there saying: " We, the Cat-clan,
are undone! "

Then they unrolled the mat and, one after another — the
culprit being the first to do so — went to look at the dead cat,
each one falling down dead, as he or she caught sight of it.
The son-in-law went out, closed the gateway (the entrance
to the circular stockade surrounding the village) with a heap
of thorn-bushes, and went home, leaving the corpses to decay
unburied. He told his friends that, by killing the cat, he
had killed all these people, as their life depended on that
of the beast. Moreover, he lost the dowry he had paid for
his wife, since there was no one left alive from whom to
claim it.

It seems clear that this cat was a totem, and several points
in the tale are interesting. The wife wants to keep her own

totem, but is evidently not expected to do so, and disaster follows. Does this preserve an obscure memory of the change from female to male kinship? The fact of the clan's life depending on the cat seems to favour the theory of the totem as external soul, which Frazer one time adopted, but afterwards saw reason to reject.[14]

The same idea comes out in the story entitled " Le Gambadeur de la Plaine "— a translation of *Matlangu wa libala*, the *shibongo* or " praise-name " of the totem, which is here a buffalo. The incidents are much the same as those given above: the totem is kept secret from the husband, who finally kills it in ignorance. There are some differences: the buffalo is invisible to all except the wife [15]; the wife, unable to feed him without betraying his presence, tells him to hide in the forest and come out at night to graze in the gardens and he performs various tasks for her — fetching wood and water, cultivating, etc. When he is killed, the wife tries to revive him by magical ceremonies, and would have succeeded, but that she was interrupted at critical moments. Finally, the members of the totem-clan, on hearing of the buffalo's death, kill themselves and their children, which seems a less primitive conception than the other.

According to Dr. Mansfeld,[16] the Ekoi of the Cameroons not only look on their totem animals as helpers and protectors, but can influence them to do their bidding, e.g., attack their enemies. The totem-group usually coincides with the village, i.e., it has become a matter of locality rather than of descent. The commonest totems are the hippopotamus, elephant, crocodile, leopard, and gorilla — also fish and snakes. This author gives a remarkable and beautiful photograph of a stream frequented by the totem of the Hippopotamus clan, where the monsters, being left undisturbed, are (or were) perfectly tame: the illustration shows sixteen heads calmly floating on the smooth surface quite regardless of the white

PLATE XXVIII

Harry Kambwiri (a native teacher of the Blantyre Mission and excellent narrator of folk-tales), with his wife Lucy. Both are mixed Yao and Nyanja stock.

man and his camera.   They came at the call of the chief who
acted as Dr. Mansfeld's guide, and followed the party as
they walked along the bank.

The Ekoi theory seems to be that half of every man's soul
lives in an animal of his totem species, therefore it is only
one particular animal which is his individual totem.   Men
of the Elephant clan will hunt elephants and kill them with
impunity, so long as they spare those which are totems, for,
apparently, not all elephants are totems.   A man and his own
totem will always instinctively recognise and avoid each other:
as for other men's totems, if the hunter, as he should do, has
properly sacrificed to the elephant-fetish before starting, any
totem-elephant he meets will make himself known by holding
up one forefoot.   Should he have omitted to sacrifice, he may
wound or kill a totem, and the man to whom that totem belongs
falls ill or dies, as the case may be.   A man, it appears, can
change himself into a crocodile or a hippopotamus, or whatever his totem animal may be, and then make himself invisible, in order to revenge himself on an enemy.   But, at the
same time, he can send the second half of his soul, embodied
in the totem, on a similar errand.   This seems a superfluous
doubling of parts, and it is not explained why, given the power
of assuming the animal form, it should also be necessary
to become invisible.   But the account comes from a careful
observer, who knew the Ekoi language and was able to get
his information at first-hand.   It is possible that this particular
form of totemism may have been modified through contact
with the doctrine — so fully developed in West Africa —
of the Bush-Soul.

In many cases, totem-clans, besides being bound to respect
their totems, are subject to various ceremonial prohibitions
whose connection with the totem it is difficult to conjecture.
Thus the Nandi clan called Kipoiis,[17] whose totems are the
jackal and the cockroach,[18] " may not make traps, although

they may hunt; they may not build their huts near a road; and they may not wear the skins of any wild animal except the hyrax." This last prohibition applies to several other clans, while one (the Kipkenda) *may* wear the skin of any animal except the duiker. Their totem, however, is not the duiker, but, for one division of the clan, the bee, for the other, the frog. (The duiker is the totem of the Kipamwi clan, but — though of course they are not allowed to eat it — nothing is said as to the wearing of its skin.) People of the duiker totem may not plant millet, nor those of the bush-pig totem touch a donkey. The nature of these tabus is obscure, but they might possibly have originated in individual prohibitions, such as those issued by the Congo medicine-man to a woman before the birth of her child.[19] He orders a feast, prescribing the food — both animal and vegetable — to be prepared for it, and the child must abstain, either during life or for a certain fixed period, from the flesh of any animal or fish eaten at the feast. The restriction applies to animal food only, not vegetable; and we hear nothing of tabus other than dietetic. But there seems no reason why such should not be imposed, and probably they might be. Duff Macdonald [20] gives a Yao story of a girl who was only allowed to marry on condition that she should never be asked to pound grain or anything but castor-oil beans. Her co-wife, in the husband's absence, insisted upon her pounding the maize; as she did so " water appeared up to her loins, she pounded again and it was at her neck, as she tried again, she was covered over." A similar incident occurs in a story of the Chameleon narrated by Junod,[21] with the additional touch that the water became a lake. Again, we have a Kinga tale [22] in which a boy is buried alive, close to a river, by some of his companions. His sister came to the river to fetch water, and, as she stooped to fill her gourd, she heard a voice saying: " If you are my sister, tell my mother that they have buried her eldest son! " The girl ran home terrified, and said nothing of what she had heard. The same thing happened three days running, but, on the fourth day, she told her mother, who went down to the river with her, and hid herself, while the girl drew water. The mother heard the voice, went to the spot whence it seemed to come and lifted away the loose earth, uncovering the boy's head. Then she fetched a hoe and dug him up. He was alive, but the flesh of one side was decomposed. They carried him home, and stayed with him three days. On the fourth, the parents went out to hoe their garden, and, before leaving, told the boy on no account to fetch fire, if asked to do so. When he was left alone in the hut, some chiefs came by and sat down to rest in the shade, telling the boy to bring some fire, as they wished to smoke. He refused several times, but, being threatened with a stick, complied, when he was immediately turned into water, and a large pool occupied the site of the hut. The chiefs fled in terror, and the parents, when they returned, went and hanged themselves in the hut of the people who had tried to murder the lad.

Several points in this tale need clearing up, and it is probably imperfect as we have it. But if the boy's totem was water, there would be a reason for the prohibition against meddling with fire, and also for his turning to water when the tabu was contravened. In the present form of the story, the motive is obscured, if not entirely lost; but perhaps a hint of it may be preserved in the statement that he was buried close to the river and discovered by his sister when drawing water. In the two preceding examples, there is no discoverable connection between the tabu and the water-totem, if it is such.[23]

But it is only here and there, if at all, that we can trace any direct connection with totemism in the animal-stories which may be said to make up the great mass of African mythology. They are not so much a product of totemism as an outgrowth of the state of mind which gives rise to totemism, though, while the latter is more or less falling into oblivion, they continue to flourish and everywhere are the primary channel of the people's budding literary instincts. The three branches of Africans whom we have envisaged in this study all possess them in enormous abundance, and while some themes, common to all three, may have been diffused from a common centre, others may very well have originated independently and been developed by each in its own way.

The principal hero of the Bantu animal-story is the Hare, who has reached America as Brer Rabbit. The bulk of the Negroes in the Southern States are descended from Bantu-speaking tribes — most of them, I understand, from the Congo region. This is rather curious, in view of the fact that the Hare is not conspicuous in the folklore of the Congo people; but Mr. Weeks [24] suggests the solution, when he says: " Brer Rabbit is the Gazelle (*nsexi*) "— either Neotragus or Dorcatherium, the Water Chevrotain, appears to be meant — " [It] is very agile, and I suppose the slaves from Congo, finding no such animal in America, used the rabbit as a substitute." But the real hare, found in most parts of eastern and southern Africa, is undoubtedly the animal which figures in the folktales of those regions and some of whose adventures, in all their details, are attributed to the little antelope who takes his place in the west — from the Congo northwards to the Cameroons and beyond the Bantu area as far as Sierra Leone. That this antelope should be called by English-speaking negroes " Cunnie Rabbit " is something of a puzzle, perhaps to be explained by the great mingling of tribes which took place through the settling of freed slaves at Sierra Leone. Koelle's vocabularies, collected there, include a number of Bantu dialects, some of them spoken by people whose tales deal with the Hare. English, of a sort, became the common language of all the Sierra Leone settlers, and it would be quite natural if, in the interchange of thought, the name " Cunnie Rabbit " was transferred from the hero of the eastern tales to the protagonist of the western — the tales themselves being, in many cases, almost identical. I cannot help thinking that the Hare has the prior right, and that the so-called " Cunnie Rabbit " took his place in regions where no hares are to be found; "no form of hare has yet been recorded from the central or heavily forested regions of the Congo basin." [25]

The Hare (Kabulu) reappears in the folklore of Angola,[26] where he is one of the heroes of the celebrated Tar Baby story. Further south, among the Nama, his place is taken by the Jackal, who really belongs to Hamitic tradition, though he is occasionally found in Bantu tales.[27] The Basuto, who attribute to the Jackal an adventure elsewhere belonging to the Hare, may have borrowed the former from the Hottentots. The Zulus are not altogether unmindful of the Hare (*umvundhla*), though they have given his glory in great part to Hlakanyana; but he comes into his own again all over East Africa, not only among the Bantu, but with the Nilotic peoples north of Lake Victoria, even as far north as Darfur. The Hamitic Galla and Somali will have none of him, in his capacity of hero, counting him an unlucky beast — so much so that if he crosses a hunter's path in the morning, the man will turn back at once, knowing that he will only meet with bad luck if he goes on.

Abarea, whom I questioned at Mambrui in 1913, was very explicit on this point; and when I asked why it was that the Hare, if so abhorred, enjoyed so great a reputation and had so many tales told about him, he repudiated the suggestion and affirmed that it was not the Hare who, e.g., got the better of the Lion by inducing him to swallow a hot stone, but the Gedal (jackal). This is quite in accordance with the traditions of the Nama, at the other end of Africa, and of the Masai, who also are partly Hamitic. The latter, accordingly, have two tales at least [28] which elsewhere are given to the Hare. But we also find a Hare story [29] (containing the " Uncle

Remus" incident of " Tu'n loose dat stump-root en ketch hole er me ")[30] which the Galla tell of the Jackal.

The Tortoise is common to " Bantu " and " Negro " Africa; he is the one creature who is a match for the Hare in the first, and the Spider in the second. He, too, has crossed to the New World — as Brer Terrapin. He sometimes appears as the embodiment of experienced wisdom and shrewd benevolence, but sometimes also as a cold-blooded old Shylock, tracking down his victims with infinite patience and persistence, and making them pay up, to the uttermost farthing.

The Spider makes occasional appearances in the folk-lore of Bantu Africa, where some have explained him as an *alias*, if one may say so, of the Sun — the rays of the latter being compared to his web.[31] If it is correct that the Duala word for " spider," *dibobe*, is also used for the sky, there is certainly some ground for this assertion, but it is difficult to see how it applies to Anansi, the Spider, as he figures in the folk-tales of Sierra Leone and the Gold Coast. The latter can scarcely be said to represent the Hare in this region, as he has none of the latter's better qualities — his cleverness has a wholly malignant character, and he is altogether without redeeming traits. In fact, we find him side by side with, and sometimes defeated by, Cunnie Rabbit.[32]

These five are the principal characters in the beast-fable, as we have it in Africa. There are other protagonists, who appear less frequently: the Chameleon,[33] the Crocodile, the Python, various birds, the Frog (and particularly, in the Delagoa Bay region, the curious little species known to science as *Breviceps mossambicensis*) [34] and others.[35]

Then we have, *en second plan*, those who serve as butts, victims, or foils to the hero of the tale, and these are usually creatures of much greater size, strength, and apparent importance: the Lion, the Elephant, the Hippopotamus, the Rhinoceros, the Leopard, and the Hyena.

The sense of fair play which delights in the confounding of the mighty by the weak things of the world, is, one hopes, common to human nature everywhere; but it seems to be specially marked in Africa — perhaps because its peoples have always been the prey of stronger and less scrupulous races. M. Junod, in classifying his Ronga tales, calls one division "*La Sagesse des Petits*" — but the trait is not confined to any one group: it could be as fully illustrated from his other classes of "*Contes d'Animaux*" or "*Contes d'Ogres.*"

It is hardly fair, one may remark in passing, to say, as McCall Theal does:[36] "There was nothing that led to elevation of thought in any of these stories, though one idea that might easily be mistaken for a good one, pervaded many of them: the superiority of brain power to physical force. But on looking deeper it is found that brain power was always interpreted as low cunning; it was wiliness, not greatness of mind, that won in the strife against the stupid strong."

This, on the one hand, is far too sweeping, and, on the other, takes no account of the fact that you must not look for ethical ideals in fairy-tales, which are the playground of irresponsible fancy. What sort of ethical code could be inferred from "Jack the Giant Killer," "Tom-Tit-Tot," and others of our most popular tales, taken as they stand?

To return to our subject: the Hyena, in his association with the Hare, is the most likely original of Brer Fox, possessing at the same time, some characteristics of Brer Wolf. He is cunning as well as brutal, makes friends with the Hare and takes advantage of his good-nature, but is no match for him, once his suspicions are aroused. The Lion is tricked over and over again, by Jackal and Hare. The Elephant likewise cuts a very poor figure, so, as a rule, does the Hippopotamus, though one Ronga story,[37] curiously enough, represents him as a benevolent fairy god-father — a kind of subaqueous Dr. Barnardo, who receives lost or deserted children and in due course restores them to their sorrowing parents, if any. We are not informed what ultimately becomes of the unclaimed ones.

In the following chapters an attempt will be made to group the principal tales relating to the Hare and Jackal, the Tortoise, and the Spider.

There is a distinct type of tale (that on which Kipling's *Just-So Stories* are to some extent modelled), which professes to explain the origin of certain animals, or of their peculiarities. Thus we learn why the Hare has a short tail and long ears (one version has it that his ears became elongated through so many people stroking them in their delight at his cleverness), why the Spider has a flattened body and lives in dark corners, why the Parrot has bright red tail-feathers, and so on. The Rock-Rabbit has a little stump of a tail because, when tails were being given out, he stayed at home, as it was a wet day, and sent some one to fetch his for him. The Snake has no legs and the Millipede (so the Swahili believe) no eyes, because the latter, wishing to attend a wedding dance, and having in those days no legs, borrowed the Snake's, who lent them, on condition of receiving the Millipede's eyes during his absence; but when the Millipede returned from the dance, the Snake refused to restore his eyes, so he has kept the Snake's legs to this day. This reminds one of the exchange of feathers between the Fowl and the Parrot, as reported by the Benga.[38]

Stories of this kind, though not uncommon, are comparatively few, when viewed in relation to the vast mass of Bantu animal folk-lore. It seems as though the African mind took the animals for granted, being more eager to relate their adventures than to inquire how they came to be as they are.

A charming Yao "Just-So" story [39] is concerned with a little brown bird, as to whose scientific identity I have no information. He is called by the natives "Che Mlanda" and is

PLATE XXIX

The Story of Che Mlanda

remarkable for his restless habits — always running up and down, cheeping and twittering fussily, as if determined to attract attention at all costs. In the beginning, it appears, all birds were alike white. They thought this state of things very dull and accordingly petitioned Mulungu to make them of different colours, like the flowers and insects. Mulungu heard their prayer and commanded them all to attend on a certain day. The birds gathered in the *bwalo*, where Mulungu sat on his stool, like a Yao chief dispensing justice, with his pots of paint at his feet. They ranged themselves in concentric semicircles and stood waiting their turns, as he called them up one by one, letting each bird hop on his finger and then setting him on his knee. He took up his little painting-stick, chose his colors, decorated the bird and let him go, calling up the next. Che Mlanda's place was some way from the end of the row, but he was too impatient to wait till called, and behaved like a spoilt child, dancing up and down and chirping: " Me next! paint me next! " Mulungu at first took no notice, beyond bidding him wait, and went on with the other birds — the black bishop-finch with his scarlet wings, the little jewelled emerald and sapphire king-fisher, the gorgeous plantain-eater, blue and green and purple, and the rest. But Che Mlanda would not be denied and kept clamoring to be taken out of his turn, and at last Mulungu beckoned to him, saying: " Well then, you shall have your way! " The little bird hopped up, full of self-importance, and Mulungu dipped his stick in the pot of brown paint, hastily brushed him all over with a uniform, dull tint, and dismissed him. So he runs up and down, to this day, in his sober coat, among the brilliant-plumaged fowls who adorn the African bush.

This chapter would not be complete without a reference to the Mantis, who is a prominent figure in Bushman folk-lore. Indeed, he may be called a sort of divinity — whether originally a totem, we cannot say, because we know so very little about Bushman totemism.[40] I have not met with any Bantu myths concerning this creature; but it is probably everywhere the object of various superstitions, which is not strange, considering its uncanny appearance and habits. The Northern Swahili call it *Kukuwazuka*, " fowl of the Ghosts," [41] and the Thonga people say that, in old times, it was considered a god, or rather an emissary of the ancestor-gods.[42] " Young shepherds, when they meet with a Mantis, tear out a little hair from the skins of their belt and offer it to the insect, saying: ' Take, Grandfather!' " Formerly, " when one entered a hut, no one interfered with it, as it was thought that perhaps some god had come to pay a visit to his descendants. These ideas seem to be disappearing now, and the offering is but a little children's game." The Baronga think that the ancestral spirits (*psikwembo*) sometimes take the form of this insect.[43]

The South African colonists usually call the Mantis the " Hottentot god," and it is sometimes said that the Hottentots used to worship it. Hahn [44] confirms the assertion of Peter Kolben on this point, adding: " The Namaquas believe that this insect brings luck if it creeps on a person, and one is not allowed to kill it." But this hardly amounts to worship, and, though Thunberg says, " the people here believe that the Hottentots offer prayer to it," the statement is too vague to accept unsupported, and Bleek, as we shall see, distinctly controverts it.

The Zulus divine by means of the Mantis — disturbing it when sitting on a stalk of grass, and then noting the direction of its head when it settles again. This is done especially by herd-boys trying to discover the whereabouts of strayed cattle.[45] Sometime it is called [46] by names meaning " break the pot," which are explained by saying that if you see one when you are carrying a pot, you are sure to drop and break the latter.

Whatever the ideas underlying the above, it seems clear that

the Bushmen held the Mantis (Kaggen, Cagn) to be a divine
or quasi-divine being.[47]   He was concerned in creation; the
moon is his old shoe, which he flung up into the sky;[48] he makes
an eland and restores it to life when killed.   " Besides his own
proper name (Kaggen) he possesses several others, and so also
does his wife. . . . Their adopted daughter, the Porcupine
(whose real father is a monster named Khwai-hemm, the All-
devourer . . .) is married to Kwammang'a and has by him a
son, the Ichneumon, who plays an important part, particularly
in advising and assisting his grandfather, the Mantis, and in
chiding him for his misdeeds. . . . It does not seem that he
is the object of any worship, or that prayers are addressed to
him." [49]

This seems to conflict with Mr. Orpen's account, which contains the touching prayer versified by Andrew Lang.[50]   Still, it
is not surprising to find a different development of the idea in
people inhabiting areas so widely separated as those of the
respective informants.   But, in any case, Kaggen's character is
" ondoyant et divers ": sometimes he appears creative and
beneficent, sometimes as tricky as Hubeane, for instance, when
he turns himself into a dead hartebeest and frightens out of
their wits the little girls who, delighted at finding such a prize,
skin and cut him up with their flint knives.[51]   The head com-
plains of being uncomfortably carried on the back of the child
who is taking it home, and, when she drops it, calls out: " Oh!
oh! my head! Oh! bad little person, hurting me in the head! "
Then all the joints reunite and the revived hartebeest assumes
the shape of a man and chases the girls home.   " Have you
been and cut up the old man, the Mantis," asks their father,
" while he lay, pretending to be dead, in front of you? "

The Mantis has three children, one of whom, Gaunu-
Tsachau, was killed by the Baboons and afterwards brought
to life by his father — a process described at great length, and
remarkable because the dead child's eye is treated as a kind of

germ or seed and kept in water till the whole body has grown from it.[52]

Finally, Kaggen and his son-in-law (by all accounts a less exemplary character even than himself) are to be seen in the rainbow,[53] Kaggen above and Kwammang'a underneath; and the Moon (for which, as we have already seen, he is responsible) " can talk, because he belongs to the Mantis, all of whose things talk." [54]

PLATE XXX

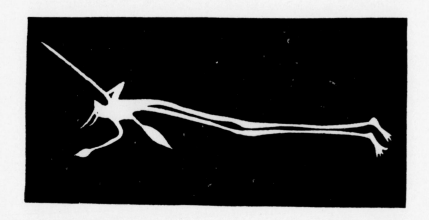

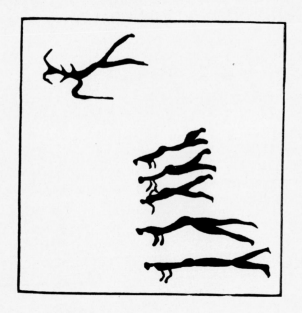

CHAPTER XI

HARE AND JACKAL STORIES

THE HARE, in one part of Africa the favorite hero of folklore, is in others held to be distinctly unlucky. The Abyssinians will not eat hare's flesh, neither will the Galla, and a hare crossing the path is by them considered the worst of omens. The Hottentots, as already stated, connect him with the Moon in a myth which relates how his blundering brought irreparable disaster on mankind. The Bushmen say that the Hare was once a human being, who assumed his present shape when cursed by the Moon for his imbecility. They have no objection to eating the Hare, but always carefully avoid one particular muscle in the leg which, they think, was taken over unchanged from his human form.[1]

Various reasons have been given for the popularity of the Hare in general Bantu tradition. Natives have sometimes said that his habit of moving his mouth, as if talking to himself, indicates great wisdom. Something must be allowed for the sympathy naturally inspired by the cleverness shown by a weak and insignificant creature in escaping the pursuit of the more powerful and ferocious beasts. And he is undoubtedly among the most beautiful and attractive of " small deer."

It is sometimes denied that the African native is at all sensitive to beauty in nature, living or inanimate; but a little first-hand research is sufficient to show that this opinion is, at best, only partially true. The Pokomo women, for instance, habitually make songs in praise of various birds — songs which, simple as they are, show both observation and sympathy.

Some of the tricks and adventures attributed elsewhere to

the Hare are told by the Zulus of Hlakanyana, a quasi-human being who, in some respects, resembles our Tom Thumb, or perhaps may be looked on as a sort of elf or pixy, though born of human parents. It seems reasonable, in this case, to think that the animal version of the story is the older one and the other a later development [2] — favoured, no doubt, by the story-teller's inveterate habit of assuming that the animals are the same as himself and his audience, or rather, of forgetting that any points of difference exist: the Hare and the Hyena hire themselves out to hoe a man's garden; the crow casts lots like a diviner; a bird makes a drum and plays on it, and so on, *ad infinitum*. " Uncle Remus " somewhere explains that " beasts " were once upon a time just like " folks "; the necessity for such an explanation would never occur to the genuine African.[3]

Having mentioned " Uncle Remus," we may remark here that for many of the " Brer Rabbit " stories African originals have actually been found, and probably many, if not all, of the remainder, can be similarly traced to their sources, though, of course, they have all been adapted to American surroundings. Brer Fox and Brer Wolf have replaced the Hyena; Brer B'ar is substituted for the Elephant; while the Lion makes a few appearances in his own person, though under greatly altered circumstances.

Whether or not Hlakanyana be considered as a development of the Hare, the latter has a curious tendency to attract to himself imported incidents belonging to other characters. This is especially observable in East Africa, where there is a certain confusion between the Hare and Abu Nuwâs, the Arab jester and hero of many more or less discreditable adventures. Thus, when the personality of Abu Nuwâs has been forgotten, *banawasi* has become a common noun in Swahili, meaning " a man who always has an answer ready,[4] who excels in repartee." Indeed, the name — if we may trust a somewhat perplexing entry in Krapf's *Dictionary*, has become associated with the Hare, as is also evident from an instructive parallel obtained by M. Junod at Lourenço Marques. Here, some of the best-known adventures of Abu Nuwâs [5] are related of one Bonawasi — a name which Junod, influenced by the idea that the story is Portuguese, explains as a corruption of Bonifacio. One of the characters remarks, in admiration of this man's cleverness: " Truly, he is *Nwachisisana!* " — the usual *shivongo* (honorary title) of the Hare.

In South Africa the contact of races has tended to produce a certain confusion about the Hare, which, however, is easily cleared up. The Basuto attribute one of his best-known adventures to the Jackal — " probably through direct or indirect Hottentot influence." [6] Here the Hare appears as one of the Jackal's victims, a fact explained by the Hamitic view. " He — he's not clever," said Abarea the Galla, " his cleverness is only in running away! " And when I asked why, then, so many tales were told about him — as, for instance, of his killing the Lion by getting him to swallow a hot stone — the answer was, " Oh! *that* was not the Hare, it was the *Gedal* (jackal)."

Conversely, a story told me by Abarea about the Jackal (which will be given later on) is told, by some Masai at least, about the Hare.[7]

The Basuto call the Hare *'mutla*, or, usually in the tales, by the affectionate diminutive *'mutlanyana*. He is sometimes opposed to an animal called *hlolo*, translated " rabbit " in Jacottet's version, and described by Brown as " a small red animal like a hare," but apparently distinct both from the rock-rabbit (*pela*) and the spring-hare (*tshipo*).[8] The point is of interest, because it seems to mark an attempt at something like compromise between the two views. The Bantu, unable to conceive their beloved Hare in the *rôle* of a dupe and victim, have insisted on his retaining his place, and put in some less esteemed congener to be a foil to him. Such might conceivably

be the genesis of the " March Hare," as Madan calls him,⁹
who plays the part elsewhere assigned to the Hyena or Brer
Fox. A tale, " The Wise and Foolish Hares," preserved in
Campbell's *Travels*,¹⁰ may be an indication of the same thing.
It would appear from the opening that the two hares in question were both of the same species, " accustomed to dwell on
the mountains in holes dug by themselves. " The wise one
made several entrances to his burrow, the one who was not so
wise " made a passage that went straight in, neither crooked
nor divided." Consequently, when some ill-disposed person
" kindled a fire on the outside in the direction of the wind,"
the foolish hare was suffocated. When she " felt the smoke
and heat entering her cell, she cried out loudly: ' Brother,
brother! come and help me, for I am almost suffocated! ' but
the other paid no attention to her screams; he only laughed
and in sport desired her to stand on her head, which, while attempting to do, she died. On entering the hole afterwards,
the live hare took the dead one by the ears and called out:
' Stand up, my sister, or I shall eat you up '; but he found
she was dead. After this, the wise hare, that had horns on his
forehead, began to talk of his wisdom in providing against
evil; but while he was boasting, a creature came down from the
heavens and snatched away his horns."

They were ultimately restored to him, so he has presumably
kept them; and the author adds this curious note: " There is
an animal, resembling a hare, which has horns about four
inches long. The scull (*sic*) and horns of one is in the Missionary Museum."

This, if not *Neotragus*, may be some small species of antelope which has the same reputation as " Cunnie Rabbit." There
may be a further hint of some association or confusion between
it and the Hare in the fact — if fact it be — that *Kalulu*, the
name for " hare " in Chinyanja and many allied languages,
is elsewhere the name for some small antelope.

It is also remarkable that the Hare in this story, after losing his horns, is persecuted by mysterious unnamed beings whose efforts to destroy him — though the methods employed are different — recall the adventures of Hubeane and Kalikalanje. It is difficult to resist the suspicion that these heroes, like the Algonkin Ioskeha in America, were originally identical with the Hare. Perhaps the same might be said of Hlakanyana, though the descriptions given by Callaway's informants rather suggest some sort of weasel. Hlakanyana, by the bye, kills the Hare and makes a whistle out of his bones — as the Hare is elsewhere said to do to other creatures. This may mark a stage in the transition from the Bantu to the Hamitic hare.

In another tale given by Campbell, the Hare appears incidentally as a rain-maker, which may be a link with the older mythological conception hinted at above.

No one has yet attempted to weave the " faicts et gestes " of the Hare into a connected whole, as was done by the unnamed mediaeval poet, or poets, for Reynard the Fox. But it would not be a difficult task and may well be accomplished some day. M. Junod points out that the two tales to which he has given the common title of " Roman du Lièvre " [11] have more or less of literary coherence, and each leads up to a distinct climax; but they include only a few of even the most typical incidents.

The first begins with a trick played on the Gazelle, the Hare inducing her to get into a cooking-pot and boiling her to death, as Hlakanyana does the Cannibal's mother. He then makes her horns into a musical instrument,[12] on which he plays, frightening the whole country-side. The Hippopotamus lies in wait for him and catches him, but is induced not to betray him by the promise that the Hare will teach him to blow the horns. He tries, but without success, and the treacherous Hare persuades him to have first one lip and then the other cut off, on the pretext that their thickness prevents his blowing properly.[13]

The Hippopotamus, in revenge, swallows the horns and the Hare attempts to kill him, but is frustrated by the Dove, who repeatedly warns the intended victim, till the Hare shoots and destroys her, even to the last feather; he then shoots the Hippopotamus, cuts him open and recovers his trumpet. While he is washing it in the river, a Civet-cat steals the meat which he has left on the ground; he smokes her out of the tree in which she has taken refuge, kills her, and sells her skin, living for some time on the proceeds. When these are exhausted, he takes to stealing from people's gardens, frightening the owners away by raising a cry that the enemy are coming.[14] This trick works for some time, but at last the villagers catch him by setting up the image of a woman covered with some sticky substance — a Tar Baby, in fact.[15] They determine to kill him, but only succeed in killing their own chief, while the Hare escapes.

The next story opens with an episode which occurs elsewhere in other connections, even in European folklore. The Hare, frightened (or pretending to be so?) by a sudden noise, runs away, communicating the alarm to every one he meets, till the whole population of the forest is running.[16] The connection between this and the next episode is not very clear: they reach a tree, covered with sweet fruit which they eat, leaving, at the Hare's suggestion, one bunch for the use of the chief. He steals this fruit himself during the night and contrives to put the blame on the Elephant — much as Brer Rabbit brings home to the innocent Brer Possum the theft of the butter [17] — and the Elephant is accordingly put to death. But the Hare cannot refrain from boasting of his exploit, is pursued, takes refuge in a burrow, is caught, but escapes by the device of calling out the equivalent to " T'un loose dat stump-root en ketch holt er me! " [18] However, the pursuers stop the opening of the burrow and leave him. He makes his way out at last, nearly starved, and sets to work to weave a number of baskets.

He then (by way of disguise) makes himself a wax head-ring[19] and goes away to peddle his baskets at the Elephant's village. He is detected when the sun melts the wax, but runs away, shaves his head, and coming back unrecognised, enters into conversation with the village chief and, persuading him to take a vapour bath, scalds him to death and makes his skull into a drum, which he beats to call the villagers together, himself remaining hidden. He plays at hide and seek with them for some time and finally escapes — it is not clearly stated how.[20]

But this is not an epic close — it is merely a pause in the development of the story. There are endless additional incidents, some of which may be placed before and some after the above, while some, no doubt, are alternative versions. I will content myself with recounting some of the most famous, before passing on to the tragic climax which so artistically rounds off the whole.[21]

At a time of drought, the animals agreed to dig a well, being summoned for the purpose by the chief, sometimes — but not always — specified as the Lion. The Hare, however, refused to take his share in the task and, consequently, was not allowed to draw water when the well was finished.[22] All the animals resolved to take turns in watching the well. The Hyena took the first watch and, after waiting about three hours, heard the voice of the Hare, who strolled along carrying two gourds, one empty and one full of honey, soliloquising aloud: " I don't want any water — I don't care for the water of this well. I have sweet water of my own! " Having raised the Hyena's curiosity, he gratified it by giving him a taste of the honey, but, when he asked for more, refused it except on condition of his allowing himself to be tied to a tree — alleging that, such was the strength of the drink, he would otherwise be unable to keep his feet. The Hyena consented and was tied up; whereupon the Hare, instead of giving him the honey, laughed in his face, took all the water he wanted and went his way. When the other animals came back in the morning and found the Hyena tied up, he made some attempt to save his face by declaring that he had been overpowered by numbers, but no one believed him. The Lion undertook the next watch, but was similarly beguiled, and the Hare added insult to injury by bathing in the well after supplying himself with water. Other animals tried their luck (one account mentions the Elephant and the Buffalo) with no better result, till at last the Tortoise volunteered. He hid under water and kept quiet, never answering when the Hare shouted his noisy greeting. The latter, after waiting and getting no answer, concluded that the animals were now thoroughly frightened, and stepped into the water, putting his foot on what he took for a stone but which was in fact the Tortoise. When he stooped to dip out the water, the Tortoise caught his " hand," then, in spite of his struggles, the other; then both feet, and so held him till the animals came up. They carried him before the chief and began to discuss the manner of his death, when he spoke up, and — less subtle than Brer Rabbit — suggested that the way to kill him was to tie him up with banana-leaves and throw him down in the sun. This was done, and he lay quiet, till — the sun being high — the banana-leaves dried up and began to crack. Some of the animals heard it and reported to the chief: " The Hare will break loose! " The Hare heard and groaned languidly: " Leave me alone — I am just about to die! " In a little while, he felt that the drying process had gone far enough, stretched himself vigorously and, as his bonds fell off, sprang away too quickly for any one to catch him.

In some versions the tale ends here: others carry it further and relate how the Hare, pursued by the other animals, crept into a hole in an ant-heap. The Elephant put in his trunk and seized him, but let him go again (all the animals in their

PLATE XXXI

1. Bwana Ahmadi, a Swahili of Mambrui, whose grandfather was miraculously cured of his blindness. (See page 349.)

2. A group of Akamba in Rabai market-place. The woman on the right is wearing a quantity of the fine copper chains alluded to in the text. (See page 300.)

After photographs by Prof. A. Werner.

native wilds seem singularly credulous) when informed that
he had got hold of a root. The animals left the Crow to watch
the hole, while they went to fetch fire. As soon as they were
gone, the Hare called out to the Crow: " Would you like
some white ants? "

" Yes, give me some! " said the Crow.

" Open your eyes as wide as you can, so that you can see
them! " and the Hare scratched up some earth and threw it
into the Crow's eyes, taking advantage of his predicament
to escape.[23]

Some time after this, he made friends with the Hyena, and
they agreed to go on a journey together. On the way, they
stopped to set a trap in the bush, and caught a guinea-fowl.
The Hare left the Hyena to roast it, while he lay down to
sleep. The Hyena, unable to resist the savoury smell of the
roast, devoured it as soon as it was done; he then put the
feathers and legs into the fire and lay down, pretending to be
asleep. The Hare was awakened by the smell of burning
and called the Hyena, asking what had become of the guinea-
fowl. The Hyena ruefully confessed that he had gone to sleep
and let it burn. The Hare did not believe him, but said
nothing.

A little later, the Hare proposed that they should both
visit his parents and the Hyena agreed. But the Hare led the
way to a strange village and left his companion behind in the
banana-gardens outside it, telling him to take as many bananas
as he wanted, while he (the Hare) went to announce their
arrival. As soon as he reached the village, he told the people
that there was a thief among the banana-trees, and made off.
The villagers rushed out, caught the Hyena, tied him and
beat him soundly. When they had left him, the treacherous
Hare appeared on the scene, showed his great surprise and
distress and condoled with his friend as he released him.

They then went on their way and in a little while arrived

at a village where a dance was going on. The Hyena retired apart, bathed and adorned himself, wearing on his head an egg-shell into which he had stuck some feathers saved from the guinea-fowl. He then danced, while the Hare sat and looked on, and presently began to sing a riddling ditty:

" The whole guinea-fowl was scorched up in the fire, *ti! ti! ti!* "

The Hare, guessing the sense of the words, took a drum and began to beat it singing:

" I got him tied up with banana-leaves and beaten, *pu! pu! pu!* " [24]

This quarrel appears to have been made up, for a little later, we find the two, in time of famine, making a bargain to kill and eat their respective mothers. The Hyena carried out his part of the contract, and the two feasted on the meat thus provided; but the Hare hid his mother and, when the time came to produce her, declared that she had been killed by a lion. The Hyena believed him at first, but, finding that he went away secretly every day and would give no account of his movements, followed him, discovered the mother hidden in a cave, gained admittance by a trick, killed and ate her. [25]

The Hare said nothing at the time, but " went away and grieved by himself," nursing thoughts of revenge. After a certain interval, he appeared at the Hyena's abode " very fine — just like a Kamba," i.e., adorned with bright brass and copper chains, armlets and anklets, such as the Akamba make and wear. The Hyena was overwhelmed with admiration and envy. " Do you know how I got all these fine things? " asked the Hare. " I had a nail made red hot and driven into the top of my head." The Hyena did not stop to inquire into the logic of the process, but was quite willing to undergo the operation. So the Hare heated a nail and paid off old scores, killing the Hyena outright. [26]

On another occasion, the Hare made friends with the Lion, at a time when the latter was weak and low after a run of bad luck in hunting. He proposed a scheme for providing him with food and helped him to build a large house, with a *baraza* (verandah or porch). Inside, he dug a hole and, having induced the Lion to lie down in it, covered him up with sand, so that nothing showed above ground but one of his teeth. Then he beat his drum and called all the animals to a dance. The Rhinoceros came up to him and asked him to start the tune; and, accordingly, he began to sing:

> " All you elephants, all you wild boars,
> You shall dance in the inner house!
> All you buffaloes, you shall dance in the inner house!
> All you hippos, you shall dance in the inner house! "

After the animals had entered and shown some alarm on perceiving the Lion's tooth projecting from the ground:

> " This is only the tooth of a dead camel —
> Tooth, tooth, tooth, tooth of a camel! —
> I and the Civet-cat, we will dance in the outer house!
> Tooth! tooth! tooth! tooth! of a camel! "

The animals took up the refrain and shouted in chorus:

> " *Hidyo ni gego, gego, gego, gego dya ngamia!* "

And, while the fun waxed fast and furious, the treacherous Hare and the Civet-cat barred the door on the outside and ran away. When the singing was at its height, the Lion suddenly leapt from the ground and began to lay about him. Not one escaped, and the Lion had a full supply of meat. Then the Hare came back and opened the door. But the Lion was ungrateful and consumed the meat by himself, and the Hare soon grew tired of providing for him. So one day he heated a stone in the fire, wrapped it up in the kidney-fat of the animal just killed, and called on the Lion to open his mouth for the reception of a specially dainty morsel. The Lion swallowed it, and that was the end of him.

This is told by Hottentots of the Jackal [27]; the Basuto, in a similar story about the Hare, describe a different trick: he gets the Lion to help him to thatch a house and fastens his tail into the thatch, leaving him on the roof to perish, as Hlakanyana does the Cannibal.

In some versions, having killed the Lion, he uses his skin to play tricks on the Hyena. This need create no difficulty in view of the latter's death as already narrated — we are at liberty to arrange the chronology of the incidents as we please, or to suppose that the one just mentioned concerns a different Hyena.

And now, passing over other adventures too numerous to specify, we come to the last tragedy which proves that — as the Giryama story-teller puts it — " Harey (*Katsungula*) was clever, but he met with his match at last." [28]

The Cock and the Hare became very friendly and frequently visited one another. But the Hare, finding it advisable to conceal his whereabouts from his enemies, built himself a great many houses, omitting to tell his friend in which of them he was to be found. Consequently, one day when the Cock came to see him, he was put to a good deal of trouble in finding him, and took offence, though he refrained from expressing his annoyance and only said: " To be sure it was a very clever device, such as no one else is in possession of! "— and they " conversed and ate their meal," till at sunset the Cock took his departure, after arranging that the Hare was to return the visit " the day after to-morrow, when the cattle go to graze."

The Cock went home, nursing his grievance, and, when the appointed day came, he said to his wives: "That friend of mine went and put me to trouble by a device of building many houses, and so I too have thought of a trick to play on him to-day, in order that he too may come to wait about." So he gave them full instructions, and sent scouts to watch for the Hare's approach. As soon as he was reported coming, the Cock tucked his head under his wing and went to sleep. When the visitor arrived, the women told him that his friend had gone out to the pasture with the herd-boys and would return with them in the evening. On his expressing his astonishment at such inhospitable behaviour, they explained that he had not really gone away altogether — he had sent his head away with the herd-boys, while his body remained in the house; and in proof of this they showed him the apparently headless form of the Cock. The Hare was greatly impressed and asked the women to " wake him that we may come and have a talk," but was given to understand that he must wait till afternoon. At last, when the herd-boys came home, their mother said to them: " Just rouse your father there where he is sleeping." So they roused him, " and he woke with a start, saying: ' Ah! so then, my friend, you have come? ' " And the Hare rejoined, reproachfully: " I have been come a long time." However, the Cock succeeded in placating him, and they dined together, chatting as usual, till, when about to leave, the Hare, unable any longer to repress his curiosity, inquired about the " device." The Cock replied: " Now, my dear friend, is it so very much of a device? If you think you would like to do it, it is done merely by those herd-boys of yours cutting off your head, so that they may go with it to pasture, and then, when they see you have come home, for them to hit you, and you will awake! "

The Hare hastened home full of excitement, and related the wonder to his wife and next morning told his boys to cut off his head and take it with them when they went out with the cattle. They demurred at first but, on his insisting, said: " Well, we know your cleverness! " and gave in. So, when the time came for them to go out, they said: " Now then, we are ready. Come, Sir, and let us cut the head off, as you said," and he went outside and they cut off his head, piercing the ears to run a string through for carrying it. And when he was quite dead, the women picked up the body and laid it on his own bedstead. The Cock was not long in coming round to see how his suggestion had borne fruit, and, of course, when shown the body, jeered at his friend's credulity, but said he would wait till the boys came home and see what happened.

" And on arriving they asked: ' But where is father? ' And their mother said to them: ' Is not that he, yonder on his bed? ' And they went up to him and struck him, but he did not get up and they struck him again — he did not get up! And the children burst out crying. And the mothers of the family cried. And folks sat a-mourning. And all the people that heard of it were amazed at his death: ' Such a clever man! who built so many houses, you know — and for him to have met with his death through such a trifling thing! Well, who will get his property? Let that friend of his inherit it. Yes, he is the clever one! ' And the Cock took the property left by his friend."

We may share the surprise of the mourners that one so acute should so easily have been taken in — but there is a touch of shrewd observation here. We are familiar with the fact — however psychologists may explain it — of some inexplicable oversight, some momentary lapse of perception or memory, wrecking the carefully thought-out plans of a powerful intellect.

As already mentioned, the story of the Lion and the hot stone is given by the Hottentots to the Jackal; so is that of the well — the Basuto, apparently, having adopted that form of the tale, though in some other cases they have retained the adventures as the Hare's. Another well-known jackal story I will give as obtained from a Galla informant, premising that it shows the Lion in a much more favourable light than do the Hare stories and thus makes his treatment by the Jackal quite inexcusable.[29]

The Jackal (*gedal*) sat by himself out in the Bush, crying. The Lion passed by and asked him what was the matter. " My father and mother are dead, and I am here all alone, with no one to take care of me." The Lion said: " Don't cry, I will look after you," and took him along to his village, where he set him to herd his cattle. One day the Lion killed a bullock and said he would go to herd, directing the Jackal to stay at home and cook the beef for him. The latter did so, but at the same time put a stone into the fire and, when it was red-hot, wrapped round it a very fat piece of meat. When the Lion came home hungry, Gedal told him to open his mouth as wide as he could and threw the stone down his throat.

The narrator here described very graphically how the fat sizzled on its passage down and how, " his bowels being cut through," the unfortunate Lion died. (This climax was expressed by putting both hands under his left cheek and drooping his head over them.)

Soon after, the Hyena, attracted by the smell of the roasting meat, came up and asked for a share. Gedal gave him some bones, telling him to make no noise, as the Lion was asleep; then he sat down between the Hyena and the dead Lion and — as if he had nothing better to do — asked the former to let him play with his tail. The Hyena, busy with the bones, made no objection, and never noticed that Gedal was tying his tail to the Lion's. Presently he shouted a caution: " Look out! the Lion is awake! " — and the Hyena started at a run, dragging the dead Lion after him, reached his burrow and crawled in. The carcase, of course, blocked the entrance, and the Hyena waited, not daring — and indeed unable — to move, till, in the course of nature, the truth became evident, and the Lion's tail came away when he pulled at it. Then, after a time, he made his way out. Meanwhile Gedal, having finished up the beef, and being again in want of an easy subsistence, tried the same trick a second time, and sat in the bush weeping and waiting for some charitable stranger to pass. This time it was the Elephant, laden with a bag of honey, who listened compassionately to his story and — when Gedal added, as a final touch, that "Father always used to carry me on his back" — said: "All right, up with you!" While enjoying his ride, Gedal fell to eating the honey from the Elephant's bag. The latter, feeling the drops which he let fall from time to time, asked if it was raining, and the disconsolate orphan replied that the drops were his tears, which he could not keep back, whenever he thought of his mother. Having finished the honey he next remarked that his father, when he took him for a ride, was always considerate enough to pass under the trees, so that he could pick fruit without dismounting. The good-natured Elephant, seeing a fruit-tree with conveniently overhanging boughs, walked under it, and Gedal sprang into the branches and took himself off. We do not press the question of his arboreal habits too closely. "When the Elephant got home, his wife took down the bag and found it empty." The domestic sequel is left to the imagination.

As already remarked, the Jackal is the favourite hero of the Hottentot stories. Schultze has summed up his characteristics in the following passage:[30] "The Jackal's cunning is most conspicuously successful where it is combined with personal courage, or cleverly takes advantage of his adversary's cowardice — as here in the case of the hated Leopard or the more harmless Baboon. Where the adversary is both stupid and greedy — as in the adventure of the Jackal with the Boer, the sly rascal makes good his escape at the last moment. Where his opponents show irresolution, or ill-judged leniency (like the missionary who, in a tale of recent origin, employs

PLATE XXXII

1. The Nyanga, an elder of the Bushongo (Bangongo tribe) presiding over the initiation ceremony.
2. House in which a death has occurred, which is abandoned and left to decay (Babunda).

After photographs by E. Torday.

him about the farm and is wofully cheated), his most serious offences are allowed to go unpunished. Yet the old rogue sometimes comes in for a good beating . . . for instance, when he behaves with excessive arrogance towards the Flamingo family. When persecuted by powerful enemies and defeating them by his own ready wit, he enjoys the Hottentot's unlimited sympathy — still more so, when he avenges the wrongs he has himself suffered; but most of all, when he appears as avenger and benefactor of the weak in general."

There is a curious story [31] which represents the Jackal as falling in love with the Sun (here, of course, feminine) and trying to carry her off on his back, with the result that his fur got burnt and remains black to this day (this of course, is the South African variety known as the black-backed jackal). Other versions [32] represent the Sun as a baby, apparently forsaken by the wayside, which the Jackal picks up and carries off. "When it burnt him, he said: 'Get down,' and shook himself, but the Sun stuck fast to his back."

We all remember the delightful episode in *Uncle Remus*, when Brer Rabbit presents Brer Fox in the character of " my fambly ridin' hoss." This appears to be a genuine jackal-story, perhaps because the peoples who have made the Hare their hero do not ride, or have only learnt to do so recently.[33] The Hyena is the victim. Both were invited to a wedding, but the Jackal pretended he was too ill to walk and so induced the Hyena, not only to take him on his back, but to provide him with saddle, bridle, and spurs, on the plea that he would be unable to keep his seat without them.[34]

We cannot conclude this chapter without a reference to the remarkable parallels contained in the Indian story of Mahdeo and the Jackal.[35] The Jackal gets himself himself carried on the Elephant's back; he is caught by Mahdeo (who hides under water and seizes him by the leg), and calls out that Mahdeo is holding the root of a tree. Mahdeo then catches him by means of a Tar-baby figure and ties him up, but he escapes by a trick, inducing another jackal to take his place, and Mahdeo is so delighted with his cleverness that he makes him his watchman.

I do not think it is necessary to suppose that all the Hare and Jackal stories migrated from Africa to India; indeed, it seems to me that an independent origin is indicated for the Tar-baby, to take only one instance; but I should prefer to abstain from theorising, till the materials have been more fully studied.

CHAPTER XII

TORTOISE STORIES

ON THE few occasions — apart from the last disastrous encounter with the Cock — when the Hare does not come off victorious, it is the Tortoise who circumvents him. We have seen how this happened in the story of the Animals and the well,[1] and it is scarcely necessary to mention the two most famous exploits of " Brer Terrapin "[2]— of which the African versions will be given presently.

It is not difficult to see why the Tortoise should have gained the reputation he bears in African and other folklore. His ability to exist for a long time without food, the difficulty of killing him, the ease with which he conceals himself, together with his slow movements and uncanny appearance all combine to suggest infinite watchfulness, patience, endurance, and wisdom, a grim sense of humour, and magical or preternatural powers of some sort. I say advisedly wisdom, rather than cunning, because, though in some cases the Tortoise's intellect serves the purposes of malice and vindictiveness, in others we find him applying it to harmless fun or actual beneficence.

It is to be noticed that the Tortoise appears in all three divisions of African folklore — i.e., side by side with the Hare (or the antelope which sometimes takes his place), the Jackal, and the Spider. Sometimes the land-tortoise, sometimes the turtle, or one of the fresh-water species, appears to be meant — no doubt according to locality. One or the other, at least, is found in every part of Africa.

The Baronga do not take much notice of the Tortoise in their folk-tales; its place is taken by the strange little batrachian called by them *chinana* and by zoölogists *Breviceps mossambicensis*.[3]

In Sierra Leone,[4] we find the Turtle (" Trorkey ") making a riding-horse of the Leopard — a feat ascribed in the West Indies to Anansi. Here the Turtle, by a refinement of astuteness, induces the Leopard to offer the ride and even press him to let himself be carried. However, when he finds himself tricked, he has his revenge, ties Trorkey to " one big 'tick," and beats him so severely that the marks show on his shell to this day. This is an ending I have not met with elsewhere — though there are other stories accounting for the conformation of the Tortoise's shell by relating how he got it broken to pieces and mended again.

The famous race story as told in Aesop is probably a moralisation of comparatively recent date. The primitive tale, which seems to be so universally diffused as to create a presumption that it originated independently, is both less edifying and more amusing. The Akamba[5] say that the contest took place between the Tortoise (*Ngu*) and the Fish-eagle (*Haliaetus vocifer*) called by these people *Kipalala* and by the Swahili *Furukombe* or *Chalikoko*. Both creatures had asked for a Kamba girl in marriage, and had been told by her father that the condition of winning her was " to start at daybreak for the coast and return before nightfall with some sea-salt."

The Eagle was quite willing; the Tortoise showed some reluctance, but consented to compete if the race were put off for ten months, to which the Eagle agreed. " Next day, unknown to the Eagle, he started for the coast to fetch some salt; it took him nearly five months to go and five to return, and he hid the salt in his house. Now during his journey to the coast he arranged with all the tortoises he met on the way to station themselves at intervals along the route between Ukamba and the coast, one at each of the various camps, streams and water-holes, and he told them all to look out for the Eagle as he flew past . . . and, when he called out: ' Tortoise, are you there? ' each one was to reply in turn, ' I am here.' On the appointed day the Eagle started off on his flight to the sea; at intervals he called out: ' *Ngu iko?* ' and at various points *en route* he received the prearranged reply. He was much surprised to find the Tortoise getting on so quickly, and still more so when he reached the shore and found a Tortoise there in the act of collecting some salt. He, however, quickly picked up his own salt and flew back at full speed, and not knowing that the Tortoise which he had left on the beach was not his competitor, felt confident that he had won. About four o'clock in the afternoon the original Tortoise, who was on the look-out, saw the Eagle like a speck in the distance, so he emerged from where he had hidden throughout the day and waddled up the road to the village, announced his return from the coast and handed the packet of salt to the girl's father."

The Eagle, when he arrived and found that he had been outwitted "was very angry and flew off in a great temper." The Mukamba said to the Tortoise: " It is true that you have won, but if I give you my daughter, where will you live in safety? for the Eagle is so angry that he is sure to find you out and kill you." The Tortoise answered: " Oh! that is all right, do not be anxious for my safety. My home will in future be in the water, and the Eagle will never get me."

We have no information as to the various species of Tortoise to be found in Ukamba; but this suggests that at least one of them lives in fresh water, or is amphibious.[6]

There is a curious little Hottentot story recorded by Krön- lein [7] which seems to be based on the same idea as the above, though the race motive is absent.

" One day, it is said, the Tortoises held a council how they might hunt Ostriches, and they said: ' Let us, on both sides, stand in rows near each other, and let one go to hunt the

Ostriches, so that they must flee along through the midst of us.' They did so, and as they were many, the Ostriches were obliged to run through the midst of them. During this they did not move, but remaining always in the same places, called each to the other: ' Are you there? ' and each one answered: ' I am here.' The Ostriches, hearing this, ran so tremendously that they quite exhausted their strength and fell down. Then the Tortoises assembled by and by at the place where the Ostriches had fallen, and devoured them."

This does not seem very clear, but no doubt means that the Ostriches thought the pursuers were at their heels all the time instead of being — as in fact they were — stationary, and so rushed on madly to their destruction. An ostrich, as is well known, cannot see distinctly what is close to him.

Another Tortoise story, printed by Bleek [8] from a MS. of Rath's (the original is in Herero), represents the Tortoise as placed by the Elephant in charge of a pool of water, while he went off to hunt. The Elephant had previously quarrelled with the Rain, which consequently left the country; he then asked the Vulture to work a rain-charm, but the latter refused. The Crow, however, consented, and rain fell " at the lagoons, but they dried up, and only one lagoon remained." During the Elephant's absence, the Giraffe, the Zebra, the Gemsbok and several other animals came and demanded water, but the Tortoise refused them all, saying: " The water belongs to the Elephant." Last of all came the Lion, who, without waiting for an answer to his request, seized the Tortoise and beat him and drank of the water. " Since then the animals drink water " — as though it had not been their custom before. " When the Elephant came back from the hunting, he said: ' Little Tortoise, is there water? ' The Tortoise answered: ' The animals have drunk the water.' The Elephant then asked: ' Little Tortoise, shall I chew you or swallow you down? ' The little Tortoise said: ' Swallow me, if you please '; and the Elephant swallowed it whole. After the Elephant had swallowed the little Tortoise and it had entered his body, it tore off his liver, heart and kidneys. The Elephant said: 'Little Tortoise, you kill me!' So the Elephant died; but the little Tortoise came out of his dead body, and went wherever it liked."

I have given this latter part at length because of its possible bearing on a curious unexplained point in the Swahili story which describes the animals as " singing " in order to obtain water.[9] There it is said that, after the rest had been unsuccessful, " the Tortoise appeared, and the Elephant saw him and caught him and put him into his mouth, and he came out at his nose, and his (the Elephant's) companions said to him: ' Let him go, perhaps he will get water.' And they let him go. And he went and sang and got much water."

This looks as though the well-known story related in our last chapter had got mixed up with some rain-making legend like the one given above, and one may conjecture that the Tortoise proved his magical powers by coming out unharmed in the way described.[10]

Another point to notice is the eating of the Elephant from inside, which we have already seen in " Unana-bosele." In a Mandingo tale,[11] the Hyena having discovered a way to introduce himself into the Elephant's internal economy, feeds on him and grows fat, but is always careful to avoid touching the heart. The Hare, having got the secret out of " Uncle Hyena," accompanies him and, paying no heed to his directions, seizes on the heart and kills the Elephant. When the chief's servants come to cut up the carcase, the Hare hides in the gall-bladder, which is at once thrown into the bushes, and so he escapes, while the Hyena is killed.

The Mpongwe Tortoise and Leopard [12] act in a similar manner towards the Giant Goat, who, however, is good-natured enough to permit this parasitism, so long as the limits are observed, and the incident also figures among Anansi stories.[13] It seems possible that it may have originated in the idea — common and quite natural among primitive people — that some animal is the cause of internal pains not otherwise accounted for.

The famous " Tug-of-War " — usually between the Elephant and the Hippopotamus — is found in various parts of Africa. In the American version, it will be remembered, Brer Tarrypin ties the rope to a stump under water, after giving the other end to Brer B'ar. This is probably owing to the difficulty of finding in the New World two equally matched competitors.[14]

The tale as told by the Mpongwe (Gabun) is as follows: [15] The Tortoise, having worsted the Leopard in several encounters and finally caused his death, began to consider himself equal to the Elephant and to the Hippopotamus and to say: " We three who are left are of equal power; we eat at the same table and have the same authority." The people who heard this and similar speeches went and reported them to the animals mentioned, who only laughed and said that they could afford to despise him.

One day, these two met in the forest, and the Hippo asked the Elephant if he had heard of the Tortoise's boasts. The Elephant replied: " Yes, I have heard. But I look upon it with contempt. For I am Njagu. I am big. My foot is as big as Ekaga's body. And he says he is equal to me! But I have not spoken of the matter, and I will not speak, unless I hear Ekaga himself make his boast. And then I shall know what I will do." The Hippopotamus agreed to do likewise.

When the Tortoise heard of their threats, he set out to look for the Elephant and, when he found him, addressed him familiarly as " *Mwera* " — about equivalent to " Mate! " The Elephant, in great indignation asked: " Whom do you call Mwera? " and the other coolly replied: " You," and pro-

ceeded to assert his claim of equality and suggested that they should test it by a tug of war on the following day. To this the Elephant unwillingly consented. It was agreed that " if one overpulls the other, he shall be considered the greater, but if neither, then they were Mwera."

The Tortoise then cut a long creeper in the forest — such as in West Africa is called a " bush-rope " — and, handing one end to the Elephant, went into the forest with the other, telling him to begin pulling when he should give the signal next day. He then went to find the Hippopotamus and, after challenging him in like manner, and getting him to agree to the contest, gave him the other end of the rope, saying, " To-morrow when you feel the vine shaken, know that I am ready at the other end, and then you begin, and we will not stop to eat or sleep until this test is ended."

Each of the competitors — not very consistently, considering the confidence they had previously expressed — went into the forest " to gather leaves of medicine with which to strengthen his body." Next morning, the Tortoise went to a spot half-way between the two, where he had made a mark on the ground, and shook the creeper, first towards one end and then towards the other. The two then pulled with all their might, and the Tortoise laughed as he sat and watched them. When he felt hungry, he went off and ate his fill of mushrooms, after which he returned home for a sleep, awoke late in the afternoon and went back to the forest to see how the contest was going. He found the rope stretched quite taut, and though, from time to time, it was pulled a little way in one direction or the other, yet this was soon neutralised by a pull from the opposite side, and neither gained any advantage.

At last the Tortoise, growing tired, nicked the creeper with his knife, whereon it parted and each of the combatants fell violently to the ground, the Elephant bruising his leg badly and the Hippopotamus his head. The Tortoise visited each of them in turn, and in each case was acknowledged as an equal. "After that, whenever they three and others met to talk in palaver, the three sat together on the highest seats."

The Tortoise also figures in a tale of a somewhat unusual kind, occurring in widely separated regions. The examples hitherto collected are not numerous, and of the five which I have noted, one has the Hare and another Hlakanyana in place of the Tortoise. But there is a surprising agreement between two forms collected at opposite ends of the Bantu area — one from the Basuto, the other from the Benga of the Cameroons.

Jacottet [16] thinks it may be a remnant of some ancient religious tradition, which is probably indigenous. It centres about a tree whose fruit cannot be eaten without the permission of the owner and then only by those who know its name. (This is not expressly stated in any of the versions before me, but the importance attached to the knowledge seems to imply something of the kind.) [17] Messengers are sent to the owner of the tree, who in each case gives the required information, but every one forgets it on the way back — usually in consequence of some accident — till at last the Tortoise (or, in one case, the Hare) is more successful. In some instances, the successful animal takes an unfair advantage of the others and robs them of the fruit, throwing the blame on some innocent party, and this is sometimes found in connection with other incidents and without the episode of the name, as for instance, in the story of the Hare already referred to, [18] where it follows on the panic of the animals caused by the dropping of a fruit.

In two cases the owner of the tree is expressly stated to be God (Leza, Maweza). In another, it is said that he, or more probably she, for the word means "grandmother," was named Koko. Elsewhere it is said to belong to "the chief of the animals," and in the Ronga variant a woman, unnamed and otherwise unaccounted for, appears to be in charge of it. One

more point should be noted: the name of the tree is sometimes said to be quite meaningless,[19] or else the narrator is
unable to explain it. Perhaps it is an archaic word whose
meaning has been lost, and it is possible that its original form
had some forgotten mythological significance.

Dr. Nassau collected a very interesting version of this tale
from the members of the Benga tribe at Batanga in the Cameroons. It runs somewhat as follows:

In old times all beasts lived together in one part of the
country, with the exception of the Python, Mbama, who
dwelt by himself in a place about thirty miles away from the
rest. In that country grew a fruit-bearing tree called Bojabi,
but none of the beasts knew its name, nor whether its fruit
could be eaten. Then came a year of famine, when, searching
everywhere for food, they noticed this tree, but no one dared
to touch the fruit, as they did not know whether it was fit for
food. At last they decided to send and consult Mbama.
They chose the Rat as their messenger, telling him that he must
go by sea and not along the beach (this to prevent his loitering
by the way) and carry with him one of the fruits in order to
make certain of the identification. He accomplished the trip
safely, appeared before Mbama, and heard from him that the
tree was called Bojabi and its fruit was edible. Next morning
he started homeward, paddled energetically, and arrived in the
afternoon, but the operation of beaching his canoe so absorbed
his intellectual faculties that by no effort of memory could
he recall the name. He had to confess his failure and was
soundly beaten by the disappointed animals, who next dis-
patched the Porcupine. He too succeeded in his errand, but
forgot the name just as he was entering the village on his
return. Then the Antelope went, and he too learnt the name;
but just as he was about to land, a wave upset his canoe, and
the name went clean out of his head. One after another, all
the beasts tried and failed, with the exception of Kudu, the

Tortoise. He at last volunteered but the rest jeered at him for his presumption and even began to beat him. But the Gazelle interposed saying: " Let him go on his errand. We all have failed, and it is well that he should fail too! "

But the Tortoise wisely went to consult his mother before setting out. She warned him neither to eat nor drink while on the sea, or, in fact, before reaching his destination. " It was through neglecting this precaution that the others forgot the name." The Tortoise attended to her instructions, reached Mbama, received his message, and next day started on the return journey. To keep the name in mind, he sang, as he paddled:

" Elephant! eat the Bojabi fruit! Straight! straight! straight!
    Bojabi!
    Buffalo! eat the Bojabi fruit! Straight! straight! straight!
    Bojabi! "

And so on, varying the song by beginning each line with the name of a different animal. In this way he nerved himself to keep straight on.

He had gone some distance when his canoe was capsized by a large wave, but he clung to it and was carried ashore, still repeating: " Bojabi! Bojabi! " The canoe was somewhat damaged, and he had to repair it, but kept on singing his song, and once more started on his journey. Just as he was approaching the landing-place where all the beasts were gathered to await his coming, a great wave caught the canoe, and his friends ran into the surf, seized it and him and carried them in triumph up the beach, he still shouting: " Bojabi! " But they did not understand what he meant, and, when they begged him to tell the name of the tree, he said he would only do so when they had reached the town. They carried him up, and he then made the further stipulation that, before he delivered the message, he should be allowed to carry his share of the fruit into the house. This he did and then revealed the name, after which there was such a rush to gather the fruit as to justify the Tortoise's foresight in making provision for his mother, whose advice had brought him success.[20]

A Tortoise story collected in Nyasaland (1894)[21] exhibits the hero in anything but an amiable light: he has been robbed by the Iguana and is as vindictive and relentless as Shylock in exacting his pound of flesh — quite literally, for the unfortunate Iguana is cut in two, and the creditor carries off the tail and two hind legs rejoicing. I prefer to give a pleasanter episode, related to me by a stray Kavirondo[22] — not, I fear, a model character — who had somehow or other found his way to the Mission at Ngao and was supposed to be working about the place, but preferred telling me tales and helping me to shepherd my own tortoise — a pet whose sad history cannot be related here.

A Lion had assumed the shape of a man and came to court a girl at a certain village. Having obtained her own and her parents' consent, he took her home, her sisters and some girl-friends accompanying her. At nightfall he became a Lion again and, leaving the girls in his hut, went to summon the other lions. He thought the girls were all asleep, but one of them had seen the transformation and, as soon as all was quiet, she called her companions, and they made their escape. They had walked a long way when, tired out and frightened, they met with a Tortoise who, on hearing of their plight, came to the rescue by swallowing them all. He then ate a quantity of grass and leaves and kept on his way. Presently the Lion, who had for some time been on the track of the girls, came up with the Tortoise and asked if he had seen them, which the Tortoise denied. The Lion, however, was suspicious, and, noticing that the Tortoise's body seemed greatly distended, asked him what he had been eating. The Tortoise answered: "Only grass," and, when the Lion was still incredulous, coughed up a quantity to convince him. This seemed to be proof positive, and the Lion took himself off, while the Tortoise travelled on till he reached the girls' village, and there, before the eyes of their astonished parents, brought them up safe and sound.

This unpleasant mode of rescue is also practised by the Tortoise in a Benga tale,[23] where, having won a wife who is coveted by the Leopard, he swallows her, with her servants and all their goods. When questioned by the Leopard, he declares that he has eaten large quantities of mushrooms — which is, in fact, the case. But the Leopard, less easily satisfied than the Kavirondo lion, insists that he shall " go on vomiting," till furniture, goats, slaves, and at last the wife, are produced. " Tortoise thought to himself: ' I have no strength for war.' So, though anger was in his heart, he showed no displeasure in his face." But nevertheless, he enjoyed a very complete revenge when his time came.

This aspect of the Tortoise recalls the " Great Tortoise " of the Zulus,[24] who, in his turn, appears to be related to Usilosimapundu and Isiququmadevu. But usually, in the tales, he is not conceived as gigantic — merely as our familiar little friend of the forest and veld.

CHAPTER XIII
SPIDER STORIES

THE SPIDER of West Africa, Anansi,[1] is a very different being from the Spider whom we occasionally find in the Bantu area associated with creation, or acting as intermediary between heaven and earth. So in the Angola story [2] of the son of Kimanawezi who married the daughter of the Sun and Moon, we find that the Sun's handmaidens, when they come down to earth to draw water, ascend and descend by means of a spider's thread. Similarly, the Lower Congo people relate that the Spider brought down fire from heaven.[3] The Duala represent the other animals as consulting the oracle of the Spider, in the story of " The Animals and the Tiger-Cat " [4] (*Mbanga-njo*). They had clubbed together to clear a site for a village, but had no axes; the only one who possessed any was Mbanga-njo. He, when applied to, refused to lend an axe unless they could tell his name, which had hitherto been a family secret. The little *Iseru* Antelope (probably identical with " Cunnie Rabbit ") was deputed to ask advice of the Spider, who told him to go into the forest and, when he came to a trap with a bird in it, to take the bird out and go on till he came to a fish-trap. He must take out the fish he would find in it and put in the bird, and return to the first trap and leave the fish in it, and then hide and await the result. Presently the two sons of the Tiger-Cat came along to look at their traps, and each of them exclaimed in astonishment: " Oh! my father Mbanga-njo! — who ever saw the like? " When they had gone on their way, Iseru returned to his village, called all the animals together by means of the signal-drum, and said: " Now let us fetch the axes from the home of him whose name we do not know." So they went to Tiger-cat's house and made their request. " Tell me my name." " Your name is Sango Mbanga-njo." As much surprised as Tom-tit-tot and others in like circumstances, he handed over the axes, and Iseru was lauded by all the animals for his good sense.

Schön [5] records a story in which the Spider ascends to heaven by his thread, in order to attend a wedding-feast; but his conduct when he gets there is quite in accordance with the general West African estimate of his character. He is ungrateful to the Cobweb which enabled him to reach the sky (and which is spoken of as if endowed with a separate personality); the Cobweb is offended and refuses to take him back to earth; the Dove offers to do so for a consideration, but, on arriving, instead of giving her the promised gold, he roasts and eats her. There was some justification for the poor Dove's remark when hesitating over the bargain: " With you people of the earth, if a man makes it day for you, you make it night for him."

Ellis [6] says that the Gold Coast tribes hold the human race to be descended from the Spider — which probably means that he was once a totem, or one of the animal deliverers and Demiurges (like Yehl and Ioskeha) who may or may not — this is not a point I feel competent to discuss — be glorified totems. In any case, his character has suffered considerably since his descent from mythology into folklore.

The usual Spider or " Anansi " story of West Africa is of a type which falls into line with the Hare, Jackal and Tortoise stories of other regions. He is a less pleasing personality than these, and one is inclined to deny him a single redeeming feature; but the Hausa, at least, do not appear to take so harsh a view. Mr. Rattray [7] says: " The Hyena is . . . the personification in Hausa folklore of all that is

PLATE XXXIV

View on the Calabar River, Southern Nigeria. After a photograph by P. Amaury Talbot.

greedy and treacherous. Quite a different character from that ascribed to the *gizo-gizo* (spider), for instance, whose cunning and plausibility are rather admired than otherwise." This cannot be said of the Temne, who, while duly impressed by Mr. Spider's cleverness, draw a very clear distinction between it and the more endearing wiles of Cunnie Rabbit.

We find him not only astute and resourceful, but mean, greedy and cruel, and his treatment of his own family is a scandal to any decent African. It is curious that his son (sometimes called Kweku Anansi and, in the West Indies, Tacoma) usually appears in a much more favourable light. Whether this son is supposed to be a spider pure and simple is not clear: the Bushongo cosmogony and various facts in Bushman mythology prepare one for the weirdest relationships between animals; and the Temne, it appears, say that the Spider's wife is *Koki*, the "Praying Mantis."

Sometimes we are told — and the statement probably marks a late stage of myth-development — that the Spider was formerly a man. One Hausa story [8] says that he was a smith who played a remarkably low-down trick on the Lion and was by him torn to pieces and trampled in the dust. The pieces joined together became the Spider. The Temne [9] say he was once "round lek pusson" and acquired his present more or less flattened shape through being stuck to, and forcibly detached from, the Wax Girl — the local equivalent for the Tar-Baby. The explanation of his small waist given by the same people [10] is this: Hearing that feasts were to be held in the surrounding villages, the Spider determined to secure a supply of meat from all. He therefore took up his position in a central spot and gave each of his children a rope, of which he had tied the other end round his waist. He then instructed each of them to pull his end of the rope when the feasting was about to begin at the village which he had reached, so that their father might lose no time in repairing thither.

Unluckily for him, all the dinners began at the same time, so that he was pulled simultaneously in several directions, and his figure shows the results to this day.

A peculiarity everywhere attributed to the Spider is his inability to pronounce words in the ordinary way. In Hausa he speaks with a lisp and says *shaki* for *sarkin* (" chief "), *doyina* for *droina* (" hippopotamus "), etc. The Gold Coast people describe him as talking through his nose. Even in the West Indies his queer speech is invariably emphasised.[11]

Typical Spider stories are found among Tŵi, Hausa, Vai and Temne, to name no more. They are markedly absent from the folklore of Calabar, Ikom, and Yoruba,[12] where the Tortoise figures most prominently, and from that of Senegambia and French Guinea, so far as I have been able to examine it, which favours the Hare — or whatever animal whose name the French authorities have translated " *lièvre*." This is the case in the Tug-of-War story already mentioned.

The Spider, for all his cunning and resourcefulness, is not invariably successful; — witness the following tale, told by the Hausa and, in a somewhat different form, by the Anyi of the Gold Coast.[13]

The Spider's wife owned a cow, which the Spider — always described as afflicted with an insatiable appetite — desired to eat. He could not touch it (this is a point of African custom too often overlooked) without his wife's permission, which she was not likely to give. So he feigned sickness and desired her to consult a certain one-eyed wizard, to be found at a place which he indicated to her. He then tied a patch over one eye, took a short cut through the bush, and reached the spot before she could get there. Not recognising him, she paid the fee and said she had come to ask his advice about her husband, who was very ill. He told her it was impossible that the patient could recover, " if you do not give him this cow of yours, that he may go to the bush with it, to some

place where there is no one, not even a fly, and there kill it."
(The stipulation for the absence of flies is felt by the narrator
to be the acme of meanness: the Spider does not intend to
lose even the smallest particle of the meat.) The wife went
home and found her husband groaning in bed. He was, as
might be expected, eager to try the remedy, and insisted, in
spite of his wife's remonstrances, that he could crawl, if he
could not walk. In fact, he already felt so much better that
he got out of bed and caught the cow. They set out, accompanied by their son, but had to travel a long way through the
bush before they could find a suitable place and, even then,
there was one fly there. However, the Spider concluded
that this was negligible, so he killed the beast, skinned it,
and then, thinking that the red of the sunset, seen through
the trees, was a distant fire, sent off the boy to fetch a brand,
that they might roast the meat. While he was on the way,
the sun went down, but he could still see a red spot, which he
took to be a fire, though it was in fact the open mouth of the
bush-demon known as the Dodo. The boy tried to light
a bit of dry grass at the supposed fire, when he was startled
by a voice saying: " Who are you? " In his fright, he could
only answer: " My father says you are to come," and the
Dodo rose up and followed him. When they reached the place,
the Dodo said: " Here I am," and the Spider retorted. " Who
called you? " " The Dodo said: ' Your son called me.' And
the Spider was about to strike the boy, but the Dodo said: ' You
must not beat him.' So he refrained and cut off one lump of
meat and gave it to the Dodo. And the Dodo said: ' For the
sake of a little thing like this does a friend summon a friend?
Add to it, increase it.' And so on, and so on, until the Dodo
had taken all the Spider's meat from him."

But, even so, Dodo was not satisfied, but, on the Spider's
pointing out that there was no meat left, said: " Even if you
give me yourself, I shall not refuse." The Spider, ignoring

this broad hint, handed over, first his son and then his wife, whom the Dodo stowed away in the elephant-skin sack where he had already secured the meat. As he was still unsatisfied, the Spider began to pick young pumpkins which were growing close by, but though he cleared the whole garden, he could not fill the bag and found himself at the end of his resources. " So the Dodo opened the mouth of the bag and said: ' Come here, get in.' And the Spider entered by compulsion, not of his own wish." [14]

Then Dodo tied up his bag, shouldered it and went on through the forest, looking for a convenient place to roast his prey. Presently the Camel came along, like a chief, with a long trail of followers singing his praises. He took no notice of the Dodo and passed on. Soon after, the Dodo met the he-Goat, with a similar procession; he too passed on, saying nothing. Then came the Rat and was about to pass likewise, when his " tail " drew his attention to the fact that Dodo was carrying something. The Rat, no doubt made suspicious by past experience, stopped and questioned Dodo; but the latter lost his temper and swallowed him — to little purpose, however; for the Rat, three times over, emerged unhurt from various parts of his person.[15] " Then the Dodo fell down and died." The Rat had the bag opened, and out came the Spider with his wife and son. On hearing his story, the Rat said: " Worthless one, take your meat and get off home. Allah has been good to you this day," and so departed; while the Spider, not much disturbed by this candid address, gathered up the meat of which he had so nearly been deprived, went home with his family, and sent his slaves to cut up the Dodo, who was apparently considered edible.[16]

We have already seen that the Spider sometimes figures instead of the Tortoise in the Tug-of-War story.[17] The Hausa version of this presents some novel features and an interesting sequel.[18] He is not concerned with asserting his dignity against the Elephant and the Hippopotamus — only with obtaining a supply of food which, to do him justice, he this time intends to share with his family. He brings the Elephant a message, as from the Hippopotamus, asking for a hundred baskets of grain and promising to send a horse in return, at harvest-time. He makes the same promise to the Hippopotamus in consideration of a hundred baskets of fish. When the time comes to redeem his promise, he hands each creditor the end of a rope, telling him that the horse is at the other end, but is very wild and vicious. Both pull with all their might, unconsciously move along the rope and at last, meeting face to face in the forest, discover the trick. Naturally, their first thought is to discover the Spider and pay him out; but he is quite ready for them. He finds the skin of a dead antelope, gets inside it and wanders about — presenting, of course, a lamentable appearance. He meets the Elephant who inquires what has reduced him to this condition. " I was unfortunate enough to quarrel with the Spider, and he pointed his hand at me. Those at whom he points his hand waste away as I have done." The Elephant believed him, for (like the Lion in a similar predicament) [19] " he was a fool," and at once gave up the search, and — the Hippopotamus meeting with a similar experience — the Spider escaped.

We may now relate an Ewe tale [20] which in some respects resembles the one given in Chapter V, though it makes no allusion to the spirit-world. The Spider had a friend named Detsyovi, who, during a time of famine, happened to be strolling through the Bush, when he saw a millstone grinding by itself and a stream of honey flowing beside it. Detsyovi ate as much honey as he wanted and then took some, with a supply of flour, for his wife and children at home. This he did from time to time, and so they were enabled to live and grow fat. One day the Spider (*Yiyi*) came to see Detsyovi and

asked him where he got the food on which the family appeared
to be thriving. Detsyovi refused to tell him, on the ground
that he was too talkative. Yiyi, however, left him no peace
till he consented, but said they would wait till the next morning, when the women went to fetch water. The Spider was
too impatient to wait for daylight, but came along while it
was yet dark, with a water-jar on his head, rattling the gourd-
dipper inside it, and called out that the women were already
on their way to the well.[21] Detsyovi, looking out, saw that it
was still too early, and told him to wait till the women swept
out the courtyard. Yiyi at once took up a broom and began
sweeping, as noisily as he could, and then hurried to his friend,
telling him that it was time. But Detsyovi, seeing no sign of
daylight, said that he would go with him when the sun rose.
Then the Spider went a little way off and set fire to some
bundles of sticks, hoping that the glare would deceive Detsyovi; but the latter refused to come out, and both went to sleep
again till morning.

When, at last, it was really daylight, they went into the
forest together, and Detsyovi led the Spider to the place where
the millstone was grinding and the honey flowing. Yiyi
shouted aloud: "Why! there's food here, and we have to
go hungry!" Detsyovi said: "Don't make such a noise!"
They both stooped down and drank some honey, and then the
Spider hoisted up the millstone on to his head. The stone
began to sing, telling him to carry it back and put it down;
but he would not listen. He went round with it to all the
people in the neighbourhood, who paid him cowries for various
quantities of flour, till his bag was full of money. But when
he grew tired and wanted to carry the stone back to its place,
he found that it had stuck to his head, and he could not lift it
off. The weight crushed him into small pieces, which were
completely covered by the stone. "That is why we often
find tiny spiders gathered together under large stones." [22]

If the Spider had not carried off the millstone from its place in the forest people could have gone there to this day, in times of scarcity, and got food.

Among the Ewe the Spider has, on the whole, the character which we have already indicated, though there are one or two curious traces of his figuring as a benefactor. Spieth says: [23] " The Spider surpasses all the beasts of the field in courage and cunning." (His courage is not, as a rule, conspicuous elsewhere.) " He gets the better of the Leopard . . . and also of the Elephant . . . he borrows money from a chief and refuses, even after numerous reminders, to repay it. By his magic power, he delivers the whole population of a town from the destructive ' sword-bird.' Yet, on the other hand, it was the Spider who brought sores, and even death, into the world."

The stories given as evidence of the last two statements are not very clear, and are probably remnants of some older tradition. Anansi has so few redeeming points in his character that it will be well to give the first of them,[24] with all its obscurities.

Once, in time of famine, the children of God (Mawu) came down to earth, and the Spider (Yiyi) asked them if his daughter Yiyisa was there (in heaven, presumably). He requested that, when they returned, they would take her a small parcel which they were to fetch from his house. If he were not at home when they called, they would find it lying on the hearth and were to carry it away without further ceremony. This was because he intended to get himself tied up in the parcel; and, for the same reason, he bade them tell his daughter not to open it until she was in the inner compartment of the house. His daughter was, naturally, much surprised at seeing him, but received him cordially and did all she could to make him comfortable, only informing him that he would have to go elsewhere for the night, as no one else slept in that town.[25] The Spider asked the reason, adding that nothing would induce him to leave the place. Yiyisa answered: " There is a bird here with a beak as long as from Ho to Tsibu; and, if we stay, he will come and eat us." The Spider replied, boasting of himself by his laudatory names [26]: " The bird will have no desire to eat me — me, the Little Gun! — me, the Little Gourd! — I will stay here! " Accordingly, he remained, and set about sharpening his knife to such an edge that " if a fly settled on it, it became as water." During the night, the bird set out, singing:

" We birds, we birds, we eat human flesh!
　We birds of Akem, we birds of the free-born, we eat human flesh!
　When we cry aloud, no other bird cries!
　When we cry aloud, the grass dies in the bush! "

The Spider sat in the inner room, keeping up his courage by the repetition of his praise-names, till at last the tip of the bird's beak — which preceded him by several hours — reached the town. The Spider hacked it off with his knife and continued to cut off fresh pieces, till he killed the bird. Then he struck up his war-song:

" We Spiders, we Spiders, we live in the wall!
　We Spiders of Akem, we Spiders of the free-born —"

and so on, adapting the bird's slogan to his own use.

The people, when they came back and heard this, rejoiced greatly, but told him there was yet another plague for him to get rid of — a man covered with sores, who would not permit them to sleep in their town. He desired them not to leave the place, and, in the night, he heard this pestilent person approach, singing:

" Ado says, ' The angry man shall kill me! ' "

The Spider began to dance and went on till morning, when he told the man to come again and sing to him. The people

PLATE XXXV

Women of the Bankutu tribe, showing cicatrised patterns on the body.

assembled; the man sang, and the Spider danced with great vigour, till at last he became infected with the man's sores.

Nothing I have been able to discover throws any light on this mysterious statement. It is not even clear whether the sores were transferred from the man to the Spider, thus freeing the former, or whether the latter merely caught the infection. The narrator goes on to say:

" At first Mawu had not made any sores in the world "— perhaps there is an idea of Pandora's box here — " but when the Spider had got them, they spread among men. Formerly they were only with Mawu, but now they are spread abroad through the world, because of what the Spider did."

It is thus evident that he was a very partial benefactor; and in the next story,[27] though it appears that his intentions were to some extent good, he only succeeds in causing disaster. The tale, as we have it, cannot be very near its primitive form, whatever that may have been; but its importance is attested by the existence of two West Indian versions,[28] in one of which (very obscure) Annancy marries his daughter to Death, while in the other he sends her to Death's house as a servant.

This, too, begins with the statement that " there was a famine in the land." Death, whose habitat is not clearly indicated (he is taken for granted as dwelling within easy reach of, but not among, mankind) kept himself alive by snaring game. To do this more efficiently, he hoed a broad road about six miles long and set his traps in it. The Spider, finding that there was plenty of meat in Death's house, came cadging there with a huge basket; and, in order to have an excuse for repeating his visits indefinitely, he finally gave Death his daughter in marriage.

Death warned his wife not to pass along the broad road when she fetched water from the river; and, for a time, all went well. But one morning, after heavy rain, unwilling to

take the narrow side-path through the wet grass, she went
by the road, stepped into a trap and got killed. Death, when
he found her body, was hampered by no sentimental scruples,
but cut it up and set the joints to dry by the fire. Yiyi,
missing her when he paid his usual call, asked where she
was and was told that he would find her if he removed
some of the meat. Though not in general an affectionate
parent, he was so far roused as to say: " I am now going
home, but I will come again; and I am not going to take you
by surprise — I shall make open war on you." He went
away, sharpened his knife to such a point that it would split
a fly, flung the weapon at Death and fled. Death discharged
an arrow, which set the Bush on fire but did not hit the Spider
— he being by this time safe in his house. Death lay in wait
for him outside the village and, in the meantime, amused
himself by shooting at the women who passed through the
gardens with their water-jars, on their way to the river. After
a while, he went to look, found that he had killed several,
and exclaimed in delight: " Why, this is game! I need never
go and set traps in the Bush any more! " In this way, Death
came into the world. The narrator seems to mean by this the
world of men — the animals having experienced Death's
power for some time previous to the Spider's unlucky
intervention.

Nothing more is said about the Spider himself — but it
is to be presumed that he escaped — at any rate for the time
being. In both the Jamaica versions, he is represented as
outwitting Death. He climbs the rafters, with his wife and
children, while Death waits below. One by one, they are
forced by exhaustion to let go and are seized and put aside
for future consumption. Annancy tells Death he is so fat
that he will " pop " if he falls on the ground, and so, " if you
no want me fat fe waste, go an' fetch someting fe catch
me." [29] Death fetches a cask of flour from the next room,

and Annancy, dropping into it, raises such a dust as to blind him for the time being and allow his victims to get out of reach.

It may yet be possible to recover a more satisfactory version of the Ewe legend, which may make these fragmentary tales more intelligible and also throw some light on the Spider's mythological position.

CHAPTER XIV

STORIES OF WITCHCRAFT AND WEREWOLVES

STORIES about witches distinctly characterised as such are not very common in Africa — certainly not among the Bantu. The personage who, in European tales, would figure as the witch more often belongs to the numerous and weird family of ogres or *amazimu*. Bleek's theory[1] that Bantu "ancestor-worship and belief in the supernatural give rise to horrible ghost-stories and tales of witchcraft," while beast-fables are conspicuous by their absence, scarcely needs refuting at this time of day; and Jacottet[2] comments on the comparative rarity of such legends, except among the Herero, a people peculiarly open to non-Bantu influences.

Some interesting particulars as to Hausa witches are given by Tremearne,[3] most of them tending to bear out the above view — viz., that the witch is rather a preternatural or, at any rate, abnormal being than a mere human creature possessed of magical skill. Thus we find that " a witch and Dodo are often interchangeable "; " when a witch is killed, every bit of her must be destroyed, for even a single drop of her blood can kill the victim "— just as the remains of the *zimwi* in the Swahili story give rise to a pumpkin-plant which develops equal powers for mischief. Another unpleasant peculiarity is the following: " All witches have many mouths which they can cause to appear all over their bodies at will, and the owner can turn them back into one by slapping herself." [4] The *rimu* of the Wachaga [5] is, in one case, detected by his possession of a second mouth in the back of his head, and one tribe of ogres, according to the Baronga,[6] have one in the nape of the neck, where it is usually hidden by their long hair.

But witchcraft, though not often mentioned in the tales, occupies (as is only too well known) a prominent place in African folk-belief. The terror which makes small boys — and indeed older people — in Nyasaland reluctant to go out after dark, is not ghosts or bogies, as we understand them, but *afiti*, wizards. In East Africa, I have been assured in all seriousness that wizards (*wanga*) are in the habit of knocking at people's doors by night, and woe to those who open and answer them! They entice you (or perhaps induce you by hypnotic power) to follow them into the forest and there kill you. My informant did not expressly mention for what purpose, but every one knows it; and the theory and practice of *ufiti* seem to be wonderfully uniform, from the Tana to the Cross River, and beyond, for there can be little doubt that it underlies the Obi and "Voodoo" rites reported from the West Indies and the Southern States of America.

A mistake which has sometimes been made with regard to these last is to treat them as normal manifestations of African religion, whereas they represent not merely unauthorized but illicit and positively criminal practices. It should be remembered that most, if not all, of the slaves *voluntarily* sold by their own tribe, in the days when the trade flourished, were either criminals or debtors. Similarly, we find some writers even now confusing witches and witch-doctors [7] — which is much as if one made no distinction between the thief and the policeman.

Witches, in general, do not seem to be credited with such multifarious activities as in Europe. Though one does hear of their causing injury or death through spite and revenge, their principal *raison d'être* as a society (in parts of East Africa, at any rate, they appear to form an organized guild) is to feed on the bodies of those recently dead — doubtless in order to secure a cumulative supply of strength, wit, courage and other desirable qualities. To this end, when deaths from natural causes occur too infrequently, or the " subjects " are unsuitable, they cause people to die by means more or less occult. It is generally believed, and probably with reason, by those in a position to know, that they possess an extensive knowledge of poisons; and it also seems likely that they often kill by suggestion.[8]

The Nyasaland natives believe that it is not through poison that the victims are killed, but (as our authority not very clearly puts it) " by supposed power against them through medicine." [9] Witches can make themselves invisible, dance in the air, and move from place to place regardless of the ordinary laws of matter; and the dread of them explains many funeral customs — e.g., the drumming and dancing kept up night and day till the corpse is buried, the abandonment of the deceased's house, which is shut up and left to decay, the fact that no one will sleep in it while the burial rites are going on, etc., etc. They make their fire on a recent grave, and it can be seen for miles — hence any light of unknown origin is regarded with suspicion. (It is not an actual fire, but the grave itself becomes luminous, "shining with an uncaused light.") I remember being assured that some flames of unusual height and brilliancy, observed during the grass-burning season on Nyambadwe hill, near Blantyre, were caused by *afiti*. So, too, the Baziba [10] never venture near a fire seen in the distance at night, believing that it marks the place where the witches are seated in council, deliberating who shall next be killed.

Witches have power over certain animals, whom they employ as their messengers or familiars.[11] Such are the owl, the hyena, the leopard, sometimes the lion, a kind of jackal, snakes, etc. The Zulus believe that the baboon is sent out by *abatagati* (wizards) on " villainous errands," as is also the wildcat. These errands are of various kinds. "The leopards will go to any house and carry off fowls or goats just as they are ordered. The snakes, too, will hurt any victim chosen by the wizard." [12] Or, as the Zulus say, the wildcat may be sent to suck other people's cows, or to collect *izidwedwe*, i.e., old rags which have been in close contact with people's bodies and which may be supposed to absorb some of their personality and, therefore, can be used for bewitching them.

When it has been decided to hold a cannibal feast, these messengers, especially "the owl who sits on the head of the chief" (presumably the arch-sorcerer) are sent out to summon the witches to the grave where the unholy fire has been kindled. The grave is opened (the well-known habits of hyenas may explain this point), the dead man brought out, restored to life, killed again, cut to pieces and eaten — sometimes on the spot; but sometimes the "meat" is carried home and hidden, after being divided among the participants.[13]

Every member of the witches' corporation takes it in turn to provide a victim, and no one is allowed to evade the obligation, even if it entails the sacrifice of his or her nearest relation. A popular song recorded from Pemba [14] (by no means contemptible as poetry) gives expression to this idea, being the lament of a mother who has sacrificed her daughter and — so to speak — sold her soul for nothing, since she has not obtained what she was led to expect in return.

In the cases referred to above, the victim is consumed *after* death and burial (whether always revivified and killed again, as in Nyasaland and Zanzibar, does not seem clear); but with some West African tribes (e.g., the Mpongwe), the procedure is different. Here, if accounts are to be trusted,[15] hypnotism appears to be at work. The witches remain, to all appearance, asleep in their huts; but "their real selves," or, as theosophists would say, their astral bodies, go out into the forest to hold their nocturnal orgies, while, by the same, or some analogous process, they bring out the " self " of the destined victim, extract his " heart's life " and consume it. The person thus treated dies, if the whole of his life is eaten; if it is not eaten all at once he suffers from a lingering illness, but will recover, if even a part of it is restored.

Corpses are sometimes restored to life for other purposes than that of being eaten. Zulu sorcerers are said to dig up a dead person in order to make of him (or her) a familiar, known by the name of *umkovu*. They give certain medicines to bring back the life, then " they run a hot needle up the forehead towards the back part of the head, then slit the tongue " [16] — or, according to another authority, [17] cut off the tip, so that he can only speak " with an inarticulate confused sound." These beings are sent out by night to work charms, or place poison in the kraals. They go about " shrieking, yelling and making night hideous " — though presumably not while engaged on the errands just mentioned — and have the power of compelling the grass to twine round the feet of a belated traveller, so as to hold him till they come up. " If they call a man by his name, and he is green enough to answer to it . . . he is drawn like Sindbad's ships to the loadstone rock . . . they soon finish him, cut his throat, pull out his tongue and enrol him in their . . . corps." [18]

The appearance of an *umkovu* in a kraal is a presage of death, and if any one there happens to be ill at the time, it is certain he cannot recover.

One of the rare Suto tales dealing with witchcraft may be given here, [19] because it illustrates some points in what has already been said, and also because of some remarkable coincidences with one presently to be quoted, from the distant region of Calabar. It is sometimes given as an account of the way in which witchcraft was first introduced among the Basuto: in that case it is not clear whence it was derived.

A young girl, recently married to a man who lived at a

distance from her own home, was called one night by her
mother-in-law and went with her to a ravine, where they
found the people with whom the older woman " used to
practise witchcraft, also ghosts (*dithotsela*) and baboons and
many other animals." The woman had brought with her two
sticks, one black and one brown; and, having ordered the whole
assembly to sit down, she shook the black stick at them, and
they all died. She then waved the brown one towards them,
and they all returned to life. She then handed them to her
daughter-in-law and told her to use them. She waved " the
staff that kills," left the people dead on the ground and returned home to tell her husband. In the morning, the chief of
the village called all the people together and found that there
was some one absent from many of the huts. He then went
with his wife to the place of the meeting and found the people
still stretched on the ground. The woman brandished the
brown stick, and they all returned to life: the ghosts (who had
presumably been embodied for the occasion) vanished away,
but the human participants were all seen to be naked.[20]   On
reaching home, the young wife refused to stay any longer in
such a place, but returned to her parents, to whom she said:
" I have been married among witches; I even know already
how to practise witchcraft; if I had known, I would not
have married there." The mother-in-law was very angry
and, the next night, sent a familiar in the shape of an *obe*
(" a fabulous animal of very large size ") to fetch her. She
tried in vain to awaken her parents and the other people in
the kraal, was carried off and cruelly beaten with sticks by
the assembled witches. The *obe* carried her back, and when
her parents got up in the morning, they found her bruised
and swollen all over. The same thing happened again twice,
but on the fourth occasion the *obe* was killed by armed men
posted in accordance with a witch-doctor's directions. The
witch came next morning and asked for the *obe's* skin, which

was refused, and she was ultimately driven from her village and " went away for good."

The story told by the Ikom of the Cross River (Southern Nigeria) [21] also professes, if not to account for the origin of witchcraft, at least to relate how it became known to that particular tribe.

A chief named Ndabu, who had been childless for many years, consulted a " juju man," or witch-doctor, and was advised by him to put away all his wives except one, from whom, after certain ceremonies had been performed, he might expect a family. On the birth of the eldest child, the witch-doctor prophesied that one of the chief's sons would " some day discover something which the Okuni people had never heard or known of before." One of the Okuni chiefs, Elullo, became jealous of Ndabu's power and influence, and conspired with Elilli, one of the discarded wives, to get rid of him. Both of these people belonged to the witch-society, the existence of which was then unknown to all outside their own circle. They could not directly injure Ndabu and his house, as he kept powerful " medicine " to protect them; but they decided to " put a witch into " the youngest son, Amoru, and so use him for their purposes. Elullo then invited Ndabu, with all his family, to dinner and bewitched the portion of food set aside for Amoru. The effect of this was that, when summoned during the following night by Elullo (who came to the house in the shape of an owl), he was compelled to go; but the influence seems to have been limited, for Amoru retained his own individuality and, when given human flesh to eat at the witches' feast, hid it and only ate the yams provided with it. Every night, for six weeks, he was forced " by the witch inside him " to go and join in their revels, but, instead of eating the meat, he always took his share home and carefully put it by. At last they told him " it was his turn to provide a body for food, but Amoru said he was too young

PLATE XXXVI

Charms to protect a village against witchcraft and other evil influences. Bakongo tribe, on the Loange River, a tributary of the Kasai. After a photograph by E. Torday.

and had no one to give. Then Chief Elullo said: 'You have a father and mother and plenty of brothers and sisters, we shall be pleased to eat any of them.'" The boy entreated them in vain to let him off; but at last they agreed to wait till his turn should come round a second time, when he was to hand over one of his parents. As the time drew near, he became more and more uneasy and at last confided in his eldest brother, showing him the hidden store of meat to prove that his words were true. They then agreed upon a plan for catching the witches.

That night, when Amoru went as usual to the witches' meeting, Elullo reminded him of his obligation, and he replied that he would give his eldest brother, Nkanyan. The chief told some of the people to go and fetch Nkanyan, taking with them the " night-calabash," which was always carried by the witches on such errands, in order magically to prolong the darkness. Amoru, however, insisted that Elullo, being the chief, ought to accompany them, and he consented — Amoru going first to show the way. When they entered the hut, the man carrying the " night-calabash " held it out three times towards Nkanyan; the third time Nkanyan sprang up and smashed it with his matchet. Immediately it was daylight, and the witches began to run out and try to escape. But Nkanyan called the people from the other huts, and, being naked, the miscreants were at once recognised and caught. Ndabu called the other chiefs together; the witches were tried, condemned, and burnt alive, and Elullo put to death with tortures.[22] Amoru was sent for treatment to a noted witch-doctor who " took the witch out of his heart and put it under a rock," after which he was quite cured. " The people then collected all the ashes . . . and threw them into the river, saying they had got rid of all the witches in their town."

An exceedingly curious account of an organization intended to counteract the doings of the witches' guild was obtained some years ago in Nyasaland. Unfortunately, I can only give it from memory as received at second-hand, in the hope that documents relating to this or similar cases may become available at some future time. Societies of this sort are not uncommon — in fact, the " Human Leopards " of Sierra Leone were, in the first instance, a body whose object was to protect the community against witches.

A member of the society was brought to trial for killing a man, which he admitted, but justified, on the plea that the victim was a witch. All the circumstances, and his character, being taken into consideration, he was discharged with a caution. His account of the society, and his connection with it was somewhat as follows:

When he was a young man, a succession of deaths occurred in the village where he lived, so rapid and so unaccountable as to occasion a good deal of talk. He thought over the matter for a long time and finally consulted his father, asking whether he knew of any remedy for this state of things. His father replied that there was one, and had he been younger, he would have tried it himself; that his son could do so, if he felt able, but it was a great undertaking, requiring courage and resolution, as well as physical strength. The son declaring himself willing, the old man told him to repair to a certain doctor, whom he named, at a village some distance away, and put himself under his direction. The doctor kept him under instruction for some time and, when his initiation was complete, sent him home. " On the way," said he, " you will meet a funeral party. One of the bearers will give you his end of the bamboo pole " — to which the corpse, wrapped in mats, is slung — " you must take it and go on."

When the young man had gone some distance, he saw the head of the procession approaching along the narrow path, and seized by a sudden panic, turned aside and hid in the long grass, till he thought they had passed by. He came out again

and went on, but presently saw a second funeral and again
hid himself. The same thing happened again, and gradually
the conviction dawned on him that it was one and the same
procession and that he could not escape. So he went forward
boldly and lifted the pole from the bearer's shoulder to his
own. As it touched him, he felt a kind of explosion in his
head and knew no more. When he regained consciousness,
he was lying on the path alone. He got up and went on his
way without further adventure.

When he next met the doctor — after some time — he
related his experience, expressing some doubt as to whether
what he had seen might not be an illusion. The answer was:
" You are right; there was no funeral, it was I." Probably
the idea was to test his endurance by means of some hypnotic
trick; but in the absence of trustworthy details, it seems idle
to attempt any explanation.

When he reached home, he seems either to have formed a
local branch of the secret society or got into communication
with such members as may have been within reach. Their
procedure was to watch by night near a recent grave and seize
upon any person approaching it, who, by the nature of the case,
it was believed, could only have come on a ghoul's errand.
They killed him by inserting a poisoned splinter of bamboo
into the body, in such a way as to leave no external traces. The
victim would go home and — conscious of guilt, or knowing
that he could prove nothing against appearances — dared not
complain and died in a few days. The last, however, knowing that Europeans took a different view, reported the matter
to the magistrate before his death. Hence the trial.

The belief that sorcerers can change themselves into lions,
leopards, hyenas, or other animals, seems to be found all over
Africa as a matter of actual, living belief. At any rate, it
is no more than thirty years since an old man was tried at
Chiromo (Nyasaland) on a charge of murdering unoffending

travellers — leaping on them out of the long grass, as they passed. He admitted the murders, alleging, in all good faith, that from time to time he turned into a lion; he always " felt it coming on " and was at such times driven by an irresistible instinct to kill some one.[23]

We have seen that such animals are sent by wizards to do their bidding; this is not incompatible with the belief (held concurrently or as a local variation) that the wizards themselves may assume their shapes, and that the hyenas which, unless due precautions are taken, invariably come and scratch the soil from a newly made grave are, in fact, *afiti*. This implies the power of turning back again when desired, and is distinct from the idea of the dead coming back in animal form; yet there is a link beween the two in the notion that people can, by taking certain medicines, ensure that they shall change into certain animals when they die. This is probably, though not in all cases necessarily, for the sake of working mischief, so that such people may be classed as posthumous werewolves.[24]

Sometimes it is believed that people turn into animals while asleep — i.e., the soul leaves its human body and enters for the time being that of an animal. Gaunab, the being in Hottentot mythology who is sometimes described as the " devil," can assume at will any shape, human or animal — the latter, apparently, only by day. These avatars of his, whether buck, jackal, or any other creature, are invulnerable and never fly from the hunter.[25]

When the late Walter Deane, a mighty hunter and much beloved by the Congo natives, was killed by an elephant at Lukolela in 1888, the natives insisted that this was no ordinary elephant, but " bad fetish "— probably the expression used by an interpreter familiar with Europeans.[26] This may have meant one of three things: either (*a*) it was a " were-elephant," the shape temporarily assumed by a hostile sorcerer, or (*b*) it might have been sent by such a sorcerer to kill Deane, or (c) — a case very similar to the last, but yet distinguishable — it might have been the totem-elephant of some enemy. In the absence of fuller information, the question must be left undecided.

In Abyssinia, where (as among the Somali, Masai and others) all workers in iron are a race apart and to some extent outcasts, blacksmiths are supposed to turn into hyenas and commit depredations in that shape, like the wolf in the classical instance recorded by Apuleius.[27] A case is related by a European who "may be said to have been nearly an eye-witness" of the occurrence.[28] Coffin, who lived in Abyssinia for several years during the early part of the last century, had engaged one of these men as a servant. One evening he came and asked for leave of absence till next day. "This request was immediately granted, and the young man took his leave; but scarcely was Mr. Coffin's head turned to his other servants, when some of them called out, pointing in the direction the Buda had taken: 'Look, look, he is turning himself into a hyena!' Mr. Coffin instantly looked round, but though he certainly did not witness the transformation, yet the young man had vanished, and he saw a large hyena running off at about a hundred paces distance. This happened in an open plain, without tree or bush to intercept the view."

Whatever may be thought of the above, it is certainly an item in folk-belief, which is what concerns us here; and the same writer records elsewhere[29] how the people of Adowa asserted that a man once shot at one of six hyenas and hit it in the leg. They all made off, and when the men, who pursued them with spears, came up with them, they saw "five Budas carrying a lame person." The man was found to have a fresh shot-wound in the leg, and the Budas — like the witches in the two stories already given — had no clothes on.

The werewolf idea frequently recurs in folk-tales; but usually in a different form from that hitherto mentioned; instead of a man turning himself into an animal, we have an animal turning himself into a man, for the purpose of securing for his wife a human being whom he intends to kill and eat, though his purpose is in most cases defeated, either by a brother or sister of the wife, by some helpful animal, or otherwise. The most popular beasts in this connection are the leopard and the hyena. But the story occurs in innumerable variations, the suitor being sometimes, not an animal but an ogre — disguised, of course — or even a mere " robber," while in a region long subject to European influence, he is, frankly, " the Devil." It should also be noticed that the Wachaga (whose folklore unites two separate streams of tradition) have an extremely fluctuating conception of their *irimu*. Sometimes he is called a " were-panther " (but even as such his shape seems to differ from that of the ordinary leopard), but sometimes he appears as an ordinary human being, except for a second mouth at the back of his head, and yet again, as a shapeless monster, with bushes growing out of him, like the Zulu *Usilosimapundu*. There is more than one Chaga tale relating the courtship of such a being, and one where a hyena (not called an *irimu*) forces a girl to marry him and keeps her in his den till rescued by an old woman. But this tale, as it stands, seems to be a confusion of two different themes, and it is better to take a fairly typical one from Nyasaland.[30]

A girl refused all suitors who presented themselves (this is the usual opening and serves to point a moral against pride and over-fastidiousness), but was at last attracted by a handsome stranger from a far country, who was, in fact, a transformed hyena. Her parents consented, and the marriage took place. After some days, the husband prepared to take his bride home, and her little brother, who suspected something wrong, begged her to let him come too; but she refused, because he had sore eyes.[31] He waited, however, and then followed them, crouching down and hiding in the grass whenever he was about to come up with them. When he thought he was too far from home to be sent back, he joined them openly, but his new brother-in-law drove him back with threats and blows. So he dropped behind, but still followed them secretly and reached the village, where they so far took pity on him that they allowed him to sleep in the hen-house. Here he stayed awake, and when it was quite dark, he found that many hyenas had assembled (during the day all the people in the village had taken human form). They went round and round the house where the bride was sleeping and sang:

" Let us eat her, our game, but she is not yet fat enough! "

In the morning, he told his sister what he had heard, and she refused to believe him; so, at nightfall, he asked her to tie a string to her toe and pass the end out through the wall of the grass hut, where he could get it. When the hyenas began their dance, he pulled the string, so as to awaken her, and she heard them for herself. Next day, he borrowed his brother-in-law's adze, saying that he wanted to make himself a spinning-top, and constructed a wooden receptacle of some sort, evidently having magical properties, for, not only was he able to get into it with his sister, but, on his singing a certain incantation, it rose into the air with them and carried them safely home, despite the pursuit of the hyenas.

A story very similar to this is told by the Mpongwe,[32] of a leopard who, hearing how a certain girl has announced that she will accept no man as a husband whose skin is not perfectly smooth and flawless, gets himself treated by a medicine-man so as to fulfil the conditions and carries home his wife, who has a narrow escape of being eaten, but is saved by an enchanted horse, thoughtfully provided by her father. This horse, however, introduces an alien element into the conclusion, and will require a passing notice in our last chapter.

CHAPTER XV

RECENT AND IMPORTED MYTHS

IT DOES not come within the scope of these pages to attempt definitions of mythology and folklore, or to say where the line should be drawn between them. But it seems to me that, in an old civilisation, though folk-belief may still be a living thing, it does not as a rule throw up new shoots of myth. Not that the mythopoeic faculty is by any means dead, even in these islands, as witness the legends of the Mons angels and the Russian army at Aberdeen. But there is a difference — better felt than expressed — between such fictitious narratives as these, disseminated (no doubt in all good faith) usually through the medium of the newspapers, and the equally fictitious narratives related and believed as sober fact, in Africa. I should not include among the latter such rumours as that of the miraculous fish caught at Zanzibar and bearing texts from the Koran on his sides — an anecdote whose proper home would seem to be the columns of *Tit Bits* or the *Daily Mail*. But any day in casual conversation, one may hear of occurrences which might have been taken direct from some mediaeval chronicle. One was informed, for instance, how the women of Mambrui, during a long drought, went on pilgrimage to a ruined mosque in the woods, and there, in the pauses of their prayers, heard the spirits of "the old Sheikhs" chanting, within the walls, "*Amin*" and "*La illah ill'Allah.*" And the rain came down in torrents before they reached home. Or how a godless soldier of the Seyyid's guards — "one of those Hadhrâmis, you know, who have no respect for anything" — shot down the glittering

PLATE XXXVII

1. Ancient Pillar at Mambrui, from which the urn is said to have been shot down.

2. Ruined house at Lamu. Note the rows of niches along the wall which are used as shelves. They were often filled with valuable china by rich Arabs.

bowl which used to finish off the top of the great pillar just outside the town, and fell down dead before the fragments reached the ground. Or how my informant's grandfather was cured of his blindness through remedies revealed to him in a dream by " our lord Hamza." [1]

A remarkable example of these modern myths is the following, sent me in MS. by the Rev. K. Becker, formerly of the Neukirchen Mission, at Kulesa on the Tana. His account is translated from the notes of one of his native teachers, who got the narrative at first hand from an aged woman at Mwanathamba — a village not far from Ngao. I may mention that I had heard of the story before receiving Mr. Becker's MS. and had twice walked over to Mwanathamba in order to secure an interview with Hadulu — said to be the heroine of the tale — but without success.

This woman belonged to the Buu tribe,[2] who now occupy the country round Ngao, about thirty miles from the sea. According to the narrator, at the time when these events took place — which we may put at from fifty to seventy years ago — they were sunk in degradation and wickedness, chiefly owing to their drinking habits. They used to make intoxicating liquor from the juice of a species of Borassus palm (*muhafa*), which produces edible fruit; and besides the other evils arising directly from drunkenness, they killed so many palms by persistent tapping, that the food supply was sensibly affected.

Now a certain man named Mpembe, living at Sambae, was one day visited by a white man, dressed in a long white garment; his hair, also, was long, like that of a European woman. He told Mpembe, who was a man of influence and standing, being a member of the witch-doctors' guild, that he should exhort his countrymen to leave off their sinful practices. Mpembe obeyed, and with some apparent result, as the people, though inclined to scoff at first, became frightened and effected an ostensible reformation, though many of them continued in secret to act as they had done heretofore. The stranger thereupon visited Mpembe a second time and sharply rebuked him, in so much that he nearly died of fright.

One day, about this time, three young girls were out watching the rice-fields, to drive away the birds from the ripening crops. One of them belonged to the Buu tribe, and her companions to the neighbouring tribes of Ngatana and Kalindi. One day, when the birds were less troublesome than usual, they left their posts to pick up firewood in the forest and saw the white-clad stranger — his figure surrounded by a mysterious radiance — standing among the trees. They were terrified and ran back to the rice-field, crouching down to hide themselves in the standing grain. But, when they ventured to look again, they saw him coming nearer — the nimbus which surrounded him growing brighter all the time — till he stood under a *muhafa* palm, when he bowed himself to the ground, and they heard him say: " Amen! amen! the people cry, ' Hunger! hunger! hunger! ' Yet I have given you the fruit of the *mukindu* and of the *muhafa* and of the *mukoma*, to eat thereof, but ye have wasted and destroyed them through your sin." He had a long staff in his hand with which he struck the trunk of the palm again and again, and at every blow some of the leaves fell, till at last it was quite bare. Except for the word " Amen," which, of course, was unknown to the girls, he spoke in their own language. He then addressed them as follows: " I have done this that you may tell your people of it and warn them that, if they go on spoiling the trees and refuse to give up their other sins, I shall do terrible things among them! At such and such a place I saw a drunkard who had climbed a palm; I said to him: ' Come down! ' but he only mocked at me. I touched him with my staff, and he fell dead. Tell your people to go and fetch his body, and let this evil-doing cease out of the land! "

Presently there arose a terrible tempest: the wind beat down the rice in which the girls had hidden themselves and even threw them to the ground, and they saw the stranger rise into the air and disappear among the clouds.

At the same time, Mpembe, at home in his village, received some supernatural intimation which caused him to tell the people that the stranger of whom he had spoken to them had appeared to three girls in the rice-field, and that their friends ought to go and look for them, as they would be helpless with terror. They went and found that it was as he had said, and heard the whole story from the girls.

However, the warning had no lasting effect. The Wabuu failed to mend their ways, and the stranger's words were fulfilled, for some time after this, the Tana changed its course (as it seems to have done several times previously) and the Buu tribe were forced to leave the fertile bottom-lands, which ceased to be productive when no longer periodically flooded by the river. Then, too, the *muhafa* palms died throughout their country, and they were not only deprived of the intoxicating drink in which they were wont to indulge, but of the fruit which they might legitimately have used. The narrator then goes on to describe the present distribution of the tribes represented by the three maidens and the first introduction of Christianity.

It is possible — as suggested by the missionaries at Ngao — that some wandering friar, of whom all record is lost, may have penetrated the Tana forests about the middle of last century. But an examination of the story makes it more probable that we have here a product of the myth-making fancy, under the influence of Christian teaching, projected backwards to a period long before the establishment of the Neukirchen mission in 1887.

It is interesting to compare with this a Chaga tradition (unfortunately somewhat vague and scanty) reported by Gutmann.³ At a not very distant period — "the first Europeans had already come to us" — was seen the apparition of a light-complexioned man floating through the air at high noon. He had a bell in either hand and cried aloud:

> "Pay every debt thou owest to thy brother!
> If thou hast an ox of his, restore it.
> If thou hast a goat of his, restore it.
>   The King commands it!
> Let every stranger in the land return to his home.
> Every child kept in pawn ye shall set free.
> Cease from deeds of violence, break the spear!
>   The King commands it!"

At sunset he appeared again and was seen in different places, but never touched the earth. The Chief of Moshi heard of him and ordered his men to keep on the lookout. But, though they sat gazing at the sky till driven indoors by the chill of the evening, they never saw him again.

Another example of a recent — or at all events highly modernised — story from the same region is that of the fight with the pool already mentioned in Chapter IV.⁴

Turning from indigenous myths of recent origin to those which can be set down with tolerable certainty as introduced from without, we are confronted by some very interesting problems of diffusion. Where Arab influence has extended, we may expect to find Moslem traditions; and such legends may be found more or less naturalised in the folk-lore of the Swahili, the Hausa, and various peoples in the Eastern and Western Sudan.⁵ The tales of the *Arabian Nights*, too, are widely current in East Africa, whether originally imported in a literary form, or by purely oral transmission, it is hard to say, but I am inclined to the latter supposition, judging from the number of stories one hears (casually told by caravan porters and other quite illiterate people) which, though of the same general character, are not to be found in that collection and no doubt belong to the great mass of floating tradition of which only a small part has been reduced to literary form in the *Nights*.

India, too, has contributed, directly and indirectly, to the folklore of East Africa. The story of the " The Washerman's Donkey " [6] has been traced to the *Sumsumara Jataka* and that of " The Heaps of Gold " to the *Vedabbha Jataka*, though it has been derived through a Persian channel. [7] A version of the " Merchant of Venice " was related to me in Swahili by a Pokomo, as told to him by an Indian at Kipini who, he supposed, had " got it out of some book of his own." [8]

The stories of Abu Nuwâs have already been referred to as, in some cases, mixed up with those of the Hare. They are not to be found in the *Arabian Nights*, but seem to be a common property of Arabic-speaking story-tellers and are contained in a chap-book circulating in Syria. [9] Some of his adventures are identical with those of Khoja Nasreddin, the famous Turkish jester, but not necessarily derived from them. There are also points of contact with the Arab and Berber *Si Joha (Jeha)*. Abu Nuwâs was a real person, a poet and humorist who lived (A.D. 762–815) at the court of Harun-al-Rashid and — like Theodore Hook and others — gained such a reputation for wit and whimsicality as to attract to himself all the anonymous good things of his own day, as well as those current before and since. Some of his repartees are really humourous, but his specialty lies in practical jokes, and, according to the legend, he became such a nuisance that Harun-al-Rashid and Jaafar resorted to every possible stratagem to get rid of him. These stratagems and the expedients whereby he defeats them sometimes, in Africa, coincide more or less with the more primitive Hubeane and Kalikalanje cycles; and we have seen how his name, Banawasi, has become a common noun, denoting a clever, resourceful person, or even an epithet for the Hare. Harun becomes, vaguely, " the Sultan," or " the

Chief " — though in some Swahili versions his name and that
of Jaafar are preserved, — and at Delagoa Bay, he is even
localised into the Portuguese Governor of Mozambique.[10]   A
favourite incident is that of his being ordered, by the Caliph
or the Governor, to build a house in the air. He sends up a
large kite with bells attached to it and, calling attention to the
sound which, he says, is that of the workmen's hammers, he asks
for stones and lime to be sent up. This being declared impossible, he is absolved from his share of the contract.

Again, when the Sultan has ordered his house to be burnt
down, he appears resigned to his fate and only begs leave to
take away the ashes in a sack. These he sells to the Portuguese
(a people, in the narrator's view, very easily gulled) for
their weight in silver, making them believe that the sack contains valuable presents which he is taking to their king. Coming back with the price, he reports that there is a wonderful
market for ashes in the Portuguese possessions; consequently
the Sultan and all the townspeople burn their houses down and
load seven ships with the result. These fall in with a Portuguese squadron on its way to avenge the trick; the ships are
sunk and only a few of those on board escape by swimming.
The Sultan seeks for Abu Nuwâs, to have him killed, but he is
nowhere to be found.[11]

Yet in spite of this, he shortly afterwards cheats a different set of Portuguese and induces the Sultan to kill all his
cattle in order to sell the hides and bones at fabulous prices.
He is then thrown into a lion's den, but tells the lion that the
Sultan has sent him to scratch him whenever his hide feels
uneasy. The beast is so pleased with this delicate attention
that he does Abu Nuwâs no harm.

One of the jests common to Si Joha,[12] Nasreddin and Abu
Nuwâs is that of the borrowed saucepan, returned with a
small one, because it has produced a young one in the interval.
On the next occasion, the lender is more than willing, hoping

to get his own back with interest a second time — but the saucepan never returns, the borrower explaining that it is dead.[13]

Anecdotes of Joha were told me at Lamu: they were chiefly of the Eulenspiegel kind and evidently derived from Arab sources. The one I remember best tells how when his mother desires him to " mind the door," he takes it off the hinges and carries it on his back.[14] Other jests of a somewhat similar nature are related at Lamu as taking place at the neighbouring town of Shela, the local equivalent of Abdera, Gotham, the German Schilda or the French Saint-Maixent. In one of these, a hunter, having taken a bush-buck out of a trap and being in too great a hurry to slaughter it ritually, lets it go, charging it with a message to his wife. The Berbers tell a somewhat similar story of Si Jeha,[15] but give it quite a different turn. Si Jeha had caught three hares and, one day, when expecting some visitors, gave two to his mother, telling her to kill and cook one and keep the other in a corner of the house. The third he took with him to the fields. When the guests, directed by his mother, joined him there, he let the hare go, bidding it go and tell the mistress that it was to be killed for breakfast. Seeing the men's astonishment, he told them that he had two wonderful hares, of which one always returned to life when the other was killed; and, in proof of this, when they reached home he showed them the live hare in the corner. The distribution of these drolleries, and their relation to the native African tales of Hubeane, etc., might well form the subject of a separate volume.

At Mambrui, in 1912, an old lady named Mwana Mbeu binti Sadiki, a native of Shela and said to be aged 116 (though this I doubt), told me the following story. Unfortunately, I could not take it down word for word in the original Swahili, but I wrote out the substance of it soon afterwards:

A childless couple consulted a soothsayer, who told them

that they would have a son if they followed his directions (not recorded); but he would turn out a spendthrift. The son was born in due course, and they gave him a good education, but by the time he had completed his university career their whole property was consumed. Having absolutely nothing left, they proposed to sell him, but he (taking the same line as Admetus with his parents) pointed out that it would be more to the point for him to sell them. More submissive than the Greek couple, they agreed, and he disposed of them in return for clothes, a sword, a dagger, and a horse, and rode off. On the way he fell in with a man carrying to the Sultan of the next town a letter containing orders to kill the bearer on arrival. (The reason of this was not made clear: the man was described as a *fisadi* — a waster, or general bad character.) The messenger handed over this letter to the young man, who agreed to deliver it and put it into his turban for safety. Proceeding on his journey, he found himself crossing a waterless desert and was nearly dead with hunger and thirst when at last he came to a well near which lay a dead ewe. There was neither rope nor vessel of any kind at the well, but he unwound his turban, forgetting all about the letter fastened into its folds, lowered it into the well and sucked the water from it after drawing it up. Finding the letter soaked, he spread it out to dry, became acquainted with its contents, and destroyed it. He cut open the carcase of the ewe, found that the lamb to which she had been about to give birth was alive, killed, roasted, and ate it. Then he journeyed on and at length reached a country where the Sultan's daughter had announced that she would only consent to marry the man who could beat her at chess — unsuccessful competitors to lose their heads. The youth presented himself, played and won. He was then required to enter on a further contest and to guess riddles proposed by the princess. (The game of chess may be due to confusion with another story, as there is no previous

PLATE XXXVIII

BANTU TYPES, BASUTO

1. Woman grinding.
2. A family stripping maize.

hint of *two* contests.)   He guesses all hers and then defeats her by asking: "Who is it who wore his father, rode his mother, ate the food of the dead" (it should rather be "ate of that which was never born") "and drank the water of death?"   Here the story, as told to me, ended with the marriage of the youth and the princess.

Parts of it struck me at the time as vaguely familiar, yet I could not place it, nor could I, for some years after, discover anything analogous to it, till I happened to re-read Hindes Groome's *Gypsy Folk Lore* [16] and found that Mwana Mbeu's tale is substantially identical with the Turkish Gypsy story of "The Riddle," though the conclusion of the latter — in which the princess gets at the story by unfair means — is wanting.   The editor says: "When I translated this story I deemed it unique, though the Bellerophon letter is a familiar feature in Indian and European folk-tales, and so too is the princess who guesses or propounds riddles. . . . Now, . . . I find it is largely identical with Campbell's West Highland tale, 'The Knight of Riddles,' No. 22 (ii, p. 36), with which cf. Grimm's 'The Riddle,' No. 22." [17]   But in both these, as well as in the further variants cited by Köhler and others, the riddle is different, whereas the Turkish Gypsy version is very nearly the same as Mwana Mbeu's; it also occurs in a Russian tale.   Otherwise the European versions differ greatly from it and sometimes from each other; but an Arab enigma runs as follows: "Who is he who rode on his mother, armed with his father, and drank water neither of the earth nor the sky, while he carried death on his head?" [18]

On the whole, it seems most likely that the original home of the tale, in this form, is Arabia, whence the Gypsies carried it to Europe.

From the point of view of the diffusion of folk-tales, five stories grouped by Junod as "Contes Etrangers" [19] are extremely interesting.   One of these, "Bonaouaci" (= Abu

Nuwâs) has already been noticed. The adventures of Djiwao (João) are a mixture of exotic and native elements. The former are to be sought rather in the East than in the West, though there may be some European touches. We are reminded of three different tales to be found in Swahili: Sultan Darai (the episode of the enchanted castle and the serpent — here replaced by Sakatabela, a white woman with seven heads), Sultan Majnun (the "Nunda, eater of people"), and Kibaraka (the magic horse which delivers the hero).[19a] The end of the tale brings in the old trick of Hlakanyana boiling the mother of the cannibals; but the victim in this case is Gwanazi, chief of Maputa — who, by the bye, was still living when the story was taken down.

Only one of these tales seems to be distinctly European, "La fille du roi," which, the narrator said, her informants had heard in Portuguese from some of the Europeans for whom they worked at Lourenço Marques. It is Grimm's "The Shoes that were Danced to Pieces," of which at least one Portuguese version has been recorded.[20] A few Portuguese stories have found their way to Angola [21] — if anything, it is rather surprising that there are no more.

But one of the most remarkable instances of diffusion is the story given by Junod under the title "Les Trois Vaisseaux." A "white man"[22] has three sons, all of whom, unknown to their father and to each other, are in love with the same girl. Each asks his father for a ship and all three set out on a trading voyage — so thoroughly has the tale been localised that we are told the names of the three districts near Delagoa Bay where each of them landed in order to sell his goods. An old woman persuades the eldest to buy an old, broken basket, which has the properties of the magic carpet; while she sells to the second a magic mirror, and to the third a powder which will restore the dead to life. They see in the mirror that the girl with whom they are in love is dead and being laid out; the eldest brother transports all three back in a twinkling by means of the basket, and the third resuscitates the maiden. The question now is who had the greatest share in saving her life, and consequently who shall marry her — and, in this version, it is left undecided.

A Yao version, " The Story of a Chief," obtained in Nyasaland some twenty years ago,[23] is altered almost beyond recognition and has lost much of its exotic character; moreover, the point is somewhat obscured by the statement that it is a man who has been brought back to life and whom, consequently, each of the brothers claims as his slave.[24]

I cannot help thinking that this belongs to the class of legal problem stories, where the audience is sometimes expected to supply the conclusion,[25] and that in the genuine form no decision is reached. It is found (with an unsatisfactory decision) on the Kru coast,[26] and bears a certain resemblance to the Congo " How the Wives Restored their Husband to Life ",[27] which may, however, be quite independent. Here, the women agree to settle the matter in this way: " Let us each cook a pot of food, and take it to him as soon as he can eat; and let him decide out of which pot he will take his first meal! " He decided in favor of the one who actually revived him, " and the majority of the people said he was right in his judgment; but the women round about said he should have put the food out of the three pots into one pot, and have eaten the food thus mixed."

The foregoing is only a hasty survey of a few outstanding points in what might well be a separate field of investigation. It is subsidiary to the main purpose of this book, but some notice of it is necessary in a comprehensive view of the subject.

APPENDIX

ARMENIAN

I. VAHAGN (See Chap. V, p. 42).

THE conclusion that Vahagn was Agni, i.e., a fire-god in its different aspects, is difficult to escape. But what does his name mean? Windischmann, followed by Lagarde and Hübschmann, identified him with the Iranian Verethraghna, a genius of victory, on the basis of the slight resemblance between the two names and of the fact that Vahagn grants courage to his worshippers. Moreover, both Vahagn and Verethraghna were identified by ancient Hellenizers with Herakles.

Windischmann's view is untenable, not only because Verethraghna is represented in Armenia by other more unmistakable names, but also because the Vahagn myths have nothing in common with the Avestic Verethraghna, although as we have seen, both gods were identical in pre-Vedic and pre-Avestic times. Windischmann's view on this matter has so completely dominated Western scholars that no one has bestowed any thought on the Vahagn myths which we have just examined. It is true that the Avestic Verethraghna was also born in an ocean. But he does not fight against dragons nor is he closely associated with fire. (The dragon fighters of Iran are Atar, the fire, Tishtrya, the rain-star which conquers Apaosha, the Iranian genius of drought, Thrætona, and Keresāspa.) Although, as has been noticed by Avestic scholars like Lehmann, Jackson, and Carnoy, the only tangible traits of Verethraghna remind us of Indra, the individuality of his figure and of his activities is not so sharply defined as those of Vahagn or of Indra.

Moreover, it is very difficult to derive the name of Vahagn from Verethraghna. How did the strong " r's " of " Verethra " become entirely lost in a language that revels in r's, while the very weak *aghn* survived? Granting even that this is what happened, what is the place of Vahagn among such forms of Verethraghna's name as *Vrtan* (perhaps also *Vardan*), *Vahram*, and *Vram*, which occur in Armenia?

For these reasons, as well as his manifest connection with the fire, it seems best to consider Vahagn's name as a compound of *Vah* and *Agni*. By some Sanscrit scholars this has been interpreted as Fire-bringer. The sacrificial Agni is called in the Vedas *havya-vah* or *havya-vāhana* (Macdonell, p. 97). But *Vah* must have meant something else than " a bringer " to the old Armenians. It is interesting to note that all the names and adjectives derived from Vahagn use only the first syllable as if it were a divine name by itself. His temple was called the Vahevahyan temple. His priests were known as Vahunis or Vahnunis. Men claiming descent from Vahagn were often called Vahe, Vahan, and Van — a corruption of Vahan. Wackernagel (quoted by Gelzer) suggests that at his rites or mysteries, the enthused worshipper must have shouted " Vahe'vah," as at weddings Greeks shouted ὑμενήιος ! for ὑμήν. The resemblance would perhaps have been more striking if he had cited the case of σαβοί for σαβάζιος in the Dionysia.

If there is anything in the classical testimonies bearing upon the kinship of the Armenians with the Thracian races, and in particular with the Phrygians, one might set the ancient Phrygian satyr or rather god Hyagnis beside Vahagn. (See on Hyagnis, *La Grande Encyclopédie* and *Pauly-Wissowa*, *s.v.*) At first glance the similarity between the two names is just as striking as that between the Vedic and Avestic Indra, or the Vedic Nâsatya and the Avestic Nâonhaithya. What is more, just as " Vahagn," " Hyagnis " (the supposed father and perhaps the duplicate of Marsyas) also is a compound word, for both Agnis and ὔης occur alone. Agnis stands for Hyagnis in the Mosaic of Monnus (*Pauly-Wissowa*, *loc. cit.*) and ὔης or ὔας is confessedly a Phrygian god. Both Aristophanes and the Assyrians knew him as such. It would seem that at the stage of development in which we meet with Hyagnis and Marsyas in Phrygian mythology, they had become divested of their original character in favor of the all-victorious Sabazios or Dionysos, becoming mere flute-players and musical inventors who adorned his procession. But the original relation of Hyagnis to the fire can be legitimately inferred from his transparent name, and Marsyas' interest in the fertilizing rivers is a commonplace of classical mythology and geography. It is not unlikely that some representation of Hyagnis with reeds as his symbol gave rise to the misapprehension that he was an inventor of the flute and other allied musical instruments. For the Greek the flute was Phrygian and every reed suggested a flute. The *Vah* of Vahagn and the ὔης of Hyagnis are identical with ὔης used as a name or title of Dionysos. When we consider the fact that the Greek *v* was bilabial, then we can easily see how a *v* could change into a *ὐ*. But we may observe the same phenomenon between other cognate languages; for example, the Greek ἑσπέρα appears as *vespera* in Latin. One may even say that between the different members of the Thracian family *h* and *v* interchanged freely. So the Phrygian word for bread given by

Herodotus as βεκος is *hatz* in Armenian. The Greeks usually, and not without some foundation, associated this word ὗης, "Hyas," with their ὕειν, "to rain." In fact *Vah* and *Hyas* must be brought together with Vayu, the air and weather god of the Vedas (and of the Avesta) and the other self of Indra. According to Darmesteter, the Avestic Vayu fights on the side of Mithra against the Devas by means of the tempest. We may even compare the Zoroastrian Vae i vah ("the good Vayu") with the Armenian Vahevah mentioned above, and conclude that the resemblance is not fortuitous. On the other hand the Armenian word *aud*, "air," "weather," adequately represents the Vedic and Avestic *Vata*, which, according to Macdonell, is Vayu in its physical aspect.

The inevitable inference is that Vahagn-Hyagnis was originally a lightning god with special reference to weather and to rain, very much like the water-born Agni or the Apam Napat as well as the Lithuanian Sventa Ugnele (Holy Fire) who bears the title of *Visiya*, "the fruit bringer" or "increase giver" (*ARW* i. 368), which is a clear reference to his relation to the rain.

A. von Gutschmid finds that the Armenian legend about St. Athenogene, who took the place of Vahagn in Ashtishat, has a peculiar relation to game and hunting. From this he has inferred that among other things Vahagn was the patron of game and hunting. This theory finds a partial confirmation in Adiabene, southeast of Armenia, where Herakles was adored and invoked as the god of the hunters. (Gutschmid, iii. 414.) This Herakles may be Vahagn, but more probably it is Verethraghna, whose worship also has spread westward.

Moses tells us that Vahagn was worshipped in Iberia also and sacrifices were offered before his large statue. (i. 31.) A euhemerized but very interesting form of the Agni myth is found in the Heimskringla, or chronicles of the kings of Norway, by Snorro Sturleson (see English translation by Sam. Laing, London, 1844, i. 33 f.). Agne (fire) is the son of King Dag (day), who was slain in his ship *in the evening*. Agne overcomes the Finnish chief *Froste* (cold) in a battle and captures his son Loge (Luke, Lewk?) and his daughter Skialf ("shivering"). The latter, whom Agne had married, contrived to avenge the death of her father in the following manner: Agne, on her own instance, gave a burial feast in honor of her father, and having drunk copiously, fell asleep. Thereupon she attached a noose to the *golden* ornament about his neck, the tent was pulled down, and Agne was dragged out, hauled up, and hanged close to the branches of a tree. He was buried in Agnefit.

According to this naturalistic myth, fire is related to the day and therefore to the sun. It conquers the cold and is conquered in turn by it, and being extinguished, it returns to the tree (its mother?). This is another echo of the ancient fire-myths.

II. WITCHCRAFT AND MAGIC (See CHAP. VI, p. 48).

The ancient Armenians were much given to witchcraft and divination. John Mantaguni (5th century) mentions no less than twenty-five forms of magical practices. Eznik's short notices on bringing down the moon remind us of the same practice among the Thessalians, so often spoken of by Latin writers, such as Apuleius, Horace, Petronius, etc. Horace says:

> Non defuisse masculae libidinis
> Ariminensem Foliam
> Et otiosa credidit Neapolis
> Et omne vicinum oppidum
> Quae sidera excantata voce Thessala
> Lunamque coelo deripit.

This was a most difficult feat performed by the witch, either as an expression of anger or as an exhibition of great skill.

Bringing down the moon is found in Chinese encyclopedias as a favorite trick of Taoist doctors. The following quotations were furnished by Prof. Hodous of the Kennedy School of Missions, Hartford, Conn.:

According to the *Hsüan Shih Chi*, written during the T'ang dynasty, " In the T'ang dynasty in the reign of T'ai Ho (827–836 A.D.) a certain scholar named Chow possessed a Taoist trick. At the mid-autumn festival he met with his guests. At the time the moon was very bright. He said to his guests when they were seated, ' I am able to cut off the moon and place it into my sleeve.' In order to do this he commanded them to empty the room. He took several hundred chopsticks, tied them with a string, and mounted them saying, ' I am about to climb up and take the moon.' Suddenly they noticed that heaven and earth were darkened. Then he opened the room and said, ' The moon is in the dress of Mr. N. N.' Then with his hand he raised the dress. Out of a fold of the dress there came out a moon over an inch in diameter. Suddenly the whole house was very bright and the cold penetrated the muscles and bones."

The *Yu Yang Tsa Tsu*, written towards the end of the eighth century, records another instance: " In the beginning of the reign of

Ch'ang K'ing (821–825 A.D.) a hermit called Yang was in Tch'eu Chow (Hunan). It was his custom to seek out those who were searching after the Tao. There was a local scholar called T'ang. The natives called him a man a hundred years old. Yang went to him and he persuaded him to stop a night. When night came he called a girl saying: ' Bring the last quarter of the moon.' The girl pasted a piece of paper like the moon on the wall. T'ang arose and bowed to it saying: ' Tonight there is a guest here, you should give him light.' When he finished speaking the whole house was as bright as if he had hung up candles."

It is suggested that the magicians performed this wonder by means of mirrors.

Armenian magical texts of a later date tell us that the sorcerers climbed up a ladder of hair to tie the moon to the mountain top and the sun to its mother!

III. ADDITIONAL NOTE ON SEMIRAMIS. By W. J. Chapman

(See Chap. X, p. 68).

In the Nöldeke Festschrift, Lehmann-Haupt has shown that the Assyrian queen Sammuramat (fl.c. 800 B.C.), probably a Babylonian by birth, is the historical figure about whom the legendary story of Semiramis has gathered. But this does not account for the fact that the Semiramis of legend has characteristics which unmistakably belong to the goddess Ištar, and that in the story, as Ctesias tells it, she is connected with north Syria, the seat, in Graeco-Roman times, of the worship of the Syrian (= Assyrian) goddess. Yet a third factor in the legend (cf. A. Ungnad, *OLZ* [1911], 388), seems to be a reminiscence of the very ancient Babylonian queen Azag-Bau, who is said to have founded the dynasty of Kiš.

The Semiramis of Herodotus (i. 184) is clearly the historical Sammuramat; in Ctesias, the supernatural birth of the great queen and her disappearance from the earth in the form of a dove (Assyr. *šummu*) is just as unmistakably mythological; yet a third version of the story, that of Deinon (Aelian, vii. 1, i), according to which Semiramis is a *hetaera*, who having won the affections of King Ninus, asks leave to rule for five days, and when once she is in possession of the government puts the king to death, is pure folklore. Yet Deinon's account reminds us of Azag-Bau, for Babylonian tradition made the latter " a female liquor-seller " — in so far corresponding to the Greek *hetaera*, and in the omen-tablets we read: " When a child is bisexual, that is an omen of Azag-Bau, who ruled over the land."

This idea underlies the version adopted by Ctesias: " Ein Mannweib, die Semiramis, hatte das Reich gegrundet; ein weibischer Mann (the legendary Sardanapalus) brachte es ins Verderben " (Duncker, *Gesch. des Altertums*, iii. p. 353).

The mutual relationship of the three chief variants of the story would be explained, if we suppose that Sammuramat was originally an epithet of the goddess Ištar, or possibly of the primeval queen Azag-Bau; compare the Gilgamesh Epic, vi. 13, where Ištar says to the hero: " Thou shalt enter into our dwelling amid the sweet odors (sammati) of cedar-wood." Semiramis would then mean " fond of sweet odors." There is, however, another etymology, which is also of ancient date, *summu râmat*, " fond of the dove," the dove being the sacred bird of Ishtar (Diodorus, ii. 4). See Alfred Jeremias, *Izdubar-Nimrod*, pp. 68–70.

W. J. CHAPMAN

The Armenians ascribed the Urartian works in Van, especially a mighty dam, to Semiramis' building activities. She is supposed to have chosen that city as her summer residence. The saga reported that she died in Armenia. As she was pursued by her armed enemies, she fled afoot, but being exceedingly thirsty she stooped to drink water (from a source) when she was overtaken by her enemies. How she died is not clear, but the sagas spoke of the enchanting of the sea, and of the beads (?) of Shamiram in the sea. There was also a stone called Shamiram, which, according to Moses, was prior to the rock of the weeping Niobe. Those who are acquainted with the classical form of the Semiramis legend will easily perceive how the Armenians have appropriated the details about her building palaces and water-canals in Media and her death in India.

See also on Semiramis, Lenormant, *La Légende de Semiramis*, Brussels [1873]; Sayce, "The Legend of Semiramis," *Hist. Rev.*, 1888; Art. "Semiramis" in *EBr* 9th and 11th ed; Frazer, GB², iii, 161 ff.; Uhlrich Wilcken, *Hermes*, xxviii [1893], 161 ff., 187 ff.; F. Hommel, *Gesch. Bab. u. Assyr.*, Berlin [1885], pp. 630–632; C. F. Lehmann-Haupt in Nöldeke *Festschrift*. For the Assyrian text see Walter Andrae, *Die Stehlenreihen in Assur*, Leipzig [1913], p. 11, and compare Lehmann-Haupt, *Die historische Semiramis und ihre Zeit*, Tübingen [1910].

IV. THE CYCLOPS (See Chap. XI, p. 85).

The Cyclops, and especially Polyphemos, are to be found every-where in Europe and Asia (see e.g. W. C. Grimm, "Die Sage von Polyphem," *ABAW*, 1857, p. 1 ff.; J. and W. Grimm, *Kinder und Hausmärchen*, No. 130; W. R. S. Ralston, *Russian Folk Tales*, London, 1873, ch. iii; Herodotus, on the Arimaspians, iv. 27; G. Krek, *Einleitung in die Slavische Litteraturgeschichte*[2]; Graz, 1887, pp. 665–759; G. Polivka, "Nachtrage zur Polyphem-sage," *ARW* i. [1898] 305 f.). The black giant whom Sinbad the Sailor, Odysseus-like, blinded on his third voyage, is well known to readers of the *Arabian Nights*. Polyphemos appears also in Russian folk-lore, with the name of Licko, with the sheep under which his tormentor escapes, and with his cry, "No man has done it," while he is bewailing his lost eye. It is perfectly evident that certain im-portant details, such as the one single round eye and the burning of it, have disappeared from the rationalizing and short Armenian ac-count. The modern descendants of the Cyclops in Armenia are one-eyed beings, who are either gigantic devils or a monstrous race living in caves. Each individual weighs a hundred times more than a human being. In the day-time they sit on their roofs in wait for travellers, animals, birds, jinn, monsters, whom they may devour. When nothing comes they procure a whole village for their dinner. For other versions of the Cyclops story, see J. A. MacCulloch, *The Childhood of Fiction*, London, 1905, Chap. 10.

V. THE AL (See Chap. XI, p. 88).

A magical text of uncertain date says: "St. Peter, St. Paul and Silas while they were travelling, saw on the roadside a man sitting on the sand. His hair was like snakes, his eyebrows were of brass, his eyes were of glass, his face was as white as snow, his teeth were of iron, and he had a tusk like a wild boar. They asked him: 'What art thou, impure, accursed and awful beast, etc.? . . .' He answered: 'I am the wicked *Al.* I sit upon the child-bearing mother, I scorch her ears and pull out her liver (?) and I strangle both mother and child. Our food is the flesh of little children and the liver (?) of mothers with child. We steal the unborn infants of eight months from the mother and we carry them, deaf and dumb, to our King. The abyss, the corners of the houses and of stables are our habitation.'"

Another magical text says: St. Sisi (Sisoe) and St Sisiane (Sisinnios), St. Noviel and the angel St. Padsiel had gone a-hunting with the permission of Christ. They heard the cry of an infant and going in its direction, they surprised the *Al* in its evil work. They caught him and bound him to the Al-stone. Thereupon came the mother of the *Al* and they said: "What does it mean that you enter the womb of mothers, eat the flesh and drink the blood of infants and change the light of their eyes into darkness, etc."

Mher

Mher was the son of the Hero David. While avenging his father, he sees before him an open door which he enters with his fiery horse and the door closes behind him. Ever since that day Mher lives in that cave. The underground river Gail (Lukos) flows under the cave with a terrible rumbling. Once a year (either on the festival of Roses, originally a fire and water festival, or in the night of the ascension identified with the night of destinies) Mher's door is opened. Anyone near-by enters and is led by Mher to his great treasures, where the poor man forgetting himself allows the door to be closed upon him. Some day Mher will come out of the cave, mounted on his fiery horse, to punish the enemies of his people. That will be the *dies irae* for which the Armenians of the Van region wait with impatience.

VI. THE FINGER-CUTTERS OF ALBANIA

Moses of Kalankata, in his history of Albania (in Armenian, pp. 39–42), describes a sect of "finger-cutters" which has unmistakable affinities with devil-worship and witchcraft. Vatchakan, the King of Albania in the last quarter of the 5th Century, was a zealous persecutor of all heresies and of heathen practices. He was especially endeavoring to uproot the "finger-cutters," when a boy came to him with the report that while he was crossing the pinewoods on the bank of the River Cyr, he saw that a multitude of people had stretched a boy on the ground, and having bound him to four pegs by his thumbs and large toes, they flayed him alive. As they descried the stranger, they pursued him in order to use him also as a victim; but he fled from them, and leaping into the river swam to an islet where he climbed a tree, and, unseen by his pursuers, he observed the whole procedure, but more particularly those who participated in this bloody rite. These he denounced to the King by name. They were arrested by his command and put to torture, but no confession could be extorted from them. As they were all being led to the place of execution, the King singled out a young man among them, and through the promise of life and freedom, finally induced him to confess what took place at the secret gatherings.

The following is the testimony given by this young man: " The devil comes in the form of a man and commands the people to stand in three groups. One of these (?) must hold the victim without wounding or slaying him. The whole skin is taken off along with the thumb of the right hand and carried over across the chest to the little finger of the left hand, which is also cut off and taken along. The same process is repeated on the feet, while the victim is alive. Thereupon he is put to death; the skin is freed from the body, prepared and laid in a basket. When the time of the evil worship arrives, they make (set up?) a folding chair of iron (sic!) with feet which closely resemble the feet of that man (or the feet of man?). They place a precious garment on the chair. The devil comes, puts on this garment and sits on the chair and having taken the skin of the human sacrifice along with the fingers, he is seen (becomes visible?). If they are unable to bring him the customary tribute [of a human skin], he commands them to peel off the bark of a tree. They also sacrifice before him cattle and sheep, of whose flesh he partakes in the company of his wicked ministers. [Further] they saddle a horse which they keep ready for him. This he rides and gallops off until the horse comes to a stop. There the devil vanishes. This he does once a year."

The King commanded the young man to repeat this ghastly ceremony on the prisoners themselves before the royal army. Many of them were thus flayed and murdered in the presence of their own families. There were slain on that day many *poisoners*. For it was a practice of the members of that sect that each (?) one should, on the devil's command, poison some one [during the year?]. If he was unable to find a victim, the devil harassed him so persistently that he finally gave the poison to a member of his own family. Those that were slothful in these religious duties or denounced any one [of the devil worshippers to the authorities] were visited by the devil with blindness and leprosy.

AFRICAN

ADDITIONAL MYTHS SUPPLIED BY CAPTAIN J. E. PHILIPPS OF THE UGANDA PROTECTORATE

RUANDA (East Central AFRICA)

(*Ex-German, Congolese and British*)

Principal Authorities:

1. The Muniginya Mututsi NIRIMBILIMA, first cousin of the Sultan YUHI MUSINGA, reigning Umwami of Ruanda.
2. The Mwega Mututsi woman KANTARAMA of INDUGA County (Ruanda Proper).
3. The Muhutu ARCADI NDERESE of Bugoie County (N. W. Ruanda).
4. The Muhutu RWAKAZINA of Bufumbira (Brit. Ruanda).
5. The Mututsi KABANGO of the Rutshuru (Congolese Ruanda), and others.

I

THE COMING OF MAN (Ba-tutsi)

The Mututsi KIGWA, a Muniginya, came down to INDUGA from the heavens with his wife, a Mwega, and his two sons named KATUTSI and KAHUTU. He found on earth the aboriginal clans of BAGESSERA, BAZIGABE and BASINGA, all BA-HŬTU. All were equal. There was no King. They attacked the family with stones. They knew no other weapons.

On his deathbed KIGWA instructed his sons to teach the aborigines the arts of civilization, which they did. The smelting of iron, and the manufacture of spears and knives resulted.

KATUTSI had a daughter. He told KAHUTU to go to another hill across the river and marry her.

He wished to establish a separate branch of the family to avoid too close intermarriage.

KAHUTU at first refused as the relationship was too close, but *faute de mieux* consented so that the race should neither lose its purity nor die out.

PLATE XXXIX

Bantu Types
People of the Safwa tribe (north of Lake Nyasa).
(See page 372.)

KAHUTU's wife (and her offspring) were thenceforward called the "ABEGA ba Kulya," "The nether Princess(es)." Cf. Luganda: Mu-MBEGA, or Mu-MBEDJA = a princess.

It was stated by KATUTSI that "The Banya-GINYA shall bear kings." To which KAHUTU replied: "And the Ab-EGA the mothers of Kings."

The word "RUANDA" = "the Kingdom," in the Kinya-RUANDA tongue.

The story is taken down verbatim from (1), but varies considerably in detail as told by other informants, usually as to whether they are Ba-tutsi or Ba-hŭtu. The inhabitants of the INDUGA County alone consider themselves to be of the true Ruanda stock.

II

THE COMING OF CATTLE (THE COW).

By the Banya-RUANDA Cattle are considered second only to man in the world-creation.

Umwami NDORI (NDAHIRO) had a daughter, NYIRARUCHABA, who was driven out from their home (ULUGO) by him.

She went into the wilderness of KANAGGE above MSAHO (Lake KIVU). Her father thought her dead.

NYIRARUCHABA saw two strange animals in a rocky forest glade. One was a cow and the other its (bull) calf. The cow appeared to be rubbing itself in the mouth of a small rocky depression. When it moved into the forest, she went and examined the place and found a white liquid in a pool. This she tasted and found good.

Every morning she watched the cow: first it suckled the calf and then descended into the hollow to try and relieve the pressure of milk in its udders, by rubbing against a mound in the cave mouth, as the calf could not drink enough.

While in the forest shortly afterwards she met an exiled Muhutu who possessed nothing, and they lived together. NYIRARUCHABA had been drinking regularly of the milk to sustain her and wanted someone to help her to keep and tame the cow for herself. She suggested first catching the calf. But the Muhutu was afraid and said: "If we catch the calf, the mother will go away and not give us more milk." But she caught the calf herself, without help, and put it in their hut of leaves. Next day she went, taking the calf as a protection against an attack by the mother's horns. She let the calf suck and then went and drank from the udders herself. Daily she did this till the cow became accustomed to her and it was no longer necessary to conceal herself with the calf to do so. Eventually she learnt to milk into a primitive vessel. Her man told her to do this daily. Both drank. One day at the edge of the wilderness she met a strange man who said: " I seem to know you." She said: " Perhaps." He said: " We are all in distress. The King is ill of a mortal disease." She gave him a clay vessel of milk to take to the King as medicine. She placed a reed-" straw " in it and told the man to take it to the King, but that the effectiveness of the medicine would be spoilt if it was told that the donor was a woman. She feared her father might suspect sorcery from a woman. NDAHIRO consented to try it, after the bearer had tasted it, and in two days he recovered after years of sickness. After pressure, it was revealed that it came from a girl in the wilderness. Eventually NYIRARUCHABA was sent for and found: the cow and calf followed her to the King. He was overjoyed to see her. She said the milk was the sap of trees, fearing harm to the cow, of which she was fond.

One day, however, the King came upon her milking the cow, naked.

He discovered the secret, but was angry to find his daughter naked, against taboo.

The cow had calves by the bull calf, and the King had great power and honour as their possessor.

He ordered his daughter to teach the herdsmen to milk, and that women were never again to milk cows. Some years after the " Abapfumu " (priests) of BUKARA predicted the appearance of large herds of cattle from the caves near Lake RUHONDO (Mulera) and that there would be no more peasantry or poverty. All would own cattle and all be equal as at first.

The King, apprehensive for the government of the Ruanda (realm), decreed that all cattle were a royal appurtenance, as they are in Ruanda to this day. The cattle appeared in the reign of CIHANGA and he apportioned them to his people as his herdsmen.

And thus it is in Ruanda to this day.

Taken down verbatim from (2). Variations in detail in other narratives is inconsiderable.

III

THE COMING OF MAN (Ba-Hŭtu)

(*British* RUANDA: *Bufumbira*)

(*a*) LUGANZU is in Ruanda (Bufumbira) tradition the first man on earth. He is believed to have descended from the heavens and first set foot on earth at this spot (Plate XII). The footprints of a cow, calf, and dog are clearly visible, as also marks representing that of a bow and arrow.

The footprints of LUGANZU and the kneeprints of his wife are also shown. These had to be cleared of moss before photographing. The Muhutu Chief MUZERERO of NYARUSIZA (Bufumbira) is here seen in the traditional position and attitude of LUGANZU. A passing Munya-RUANDA woman is posed in the knee marks of LUGANZU's wife.

The place is a mile north of the foothills of MT. SABINYO (BIRUNGA Range). The Anglo-Belgian (Congo) frontier runs upon the slight rise seen in the near background.

(*b*) LUGANZU's cattle trough (Plate XIII). Curious rock formation. The troughs contain no water except occasional rain pools and are not now used to water stock. Twenty yards from the site shown in Plate XII.

A young Mu-TUTSI is seen seated. The peculiar Ruanda hair pattern (UMUSUNZU) is very visible. The Ba-TUTSI maintain it longer and more carefully than the other two Banya-RUANDA races, viz, the Ba-HŬTU and the Ba-TWA.

NOTES

ARMENIAN

The complete titles and descriptions of the works cited in the Notes will be found in the Bibliography.

INTRODUCTION

1. Herodotus, vii, 73. This view is confirmed by other evidence. The Armenian language, like Thracian, is a Satem language. The old Armenians were addicted to beer-drinking just like their Western brothers. The old Armenian ideal of human beauty was the large proportioned, bright (blue?) eyed, fair complexioned man. We shall later see that the Armenian religion also bears some important testimony to their original identity with the Thracians.

CHAPTER. I

1. It is barely possible that, as Jensen maintained in his *Hittiter und Armenier*, the Armenian word *shand*, " lightning," is a reminiscence of the Cicilian or Hittite *sanda*, *sandan* (see Frazer, GB³, part 4, *Adonis, Attis, and Osiris*, i. 124 f.). Sanda, who was identified with Hercules, was a god of fertility, and may well have been a tribal variety of Tushup, the Hittite weather god.

2. We have now very clear evidence of the presence of Indo-Iranians among the Kassus of the lower part of the Zagros range, the Mittanis of Northern Mesopotamia, and the Hittites of Asia Minor, before and after the 15th century B.C.

3. *ERE* ix, 900.

4. American Indians had a similar rite according to Longfellow's *Hiawatha*, XIII. In the spring naked women rose on a certain night and walked around the fields, to make them fertile. The same thing is reported of some parts of Germany (Frazer, i. 138–139).

5. See L. R. Farnell, *The Cults of the Greek States*, Oxford, 1896–1909, vol. 5; artts. " Dionysos " and " Sabazios " in Roscher, Pauly-Wissowa, and Daremberg-Saglio; G. Davis, *The Asiatic Dionysus*, London, 1914.

6. The most unmistakable one of these is Hyagnis (see Chap. V and Appendix I). Hyas seems to be identical with Hayk, and

Marsyas-Masses with the name of the sacred mountain Massis (Ararat). The *Dio* of Dionysus is often explained as " god," and may be found in the Armenian word *Di-kh*, " gods."

7. Codex La Cava calls *Istvo*, "Ostius," "Hostius." See A. V. Rydberg, *Teutonic Mythology*, tr. R. B. Anderson, London, 1889. As for *Astvads*, Agathangelos (5th cent.) defines it as "one who brings about," an explanation which seems to have struck the philosophical fancy of the ancient Armenian Fathers. Others have related it to *Hastvads*, " creature " or " creation," from the Persian *hast*, " exists." Another old writer saw in it the Cimmerian word for " unction." The Persian *yazd*, the Avestic *astvat*, " incarnate," the Hindu *Asdvada* (Brahma?), the Celtic *Duez*, and the Teutonic *Tiwaz* (Ziu) (both of which are in reality cognates of the Greek Zeus), were drawn into the task of shedding light on the mysterious *Astvads*. Patrubani, a Hungarian Armenian who teaches in the University of Budapest, undertakes to explain it from the Vedic *vaŕtu*, " habitation," Gk. ἄστυ, " city," which by the addition of " ç," Indo-Germanic " ig " (to honor), would mean " that which the city worships." Prof. Nar of Moscow identifies *Astvads* with *Sabazios*, a view which the present writer held for a while independently of Nar.

8. The loss of an initial *p* before *r* or *l* is not an uncommon phenomenon in Armenian (see C. Brugmann and D. Delbrück, *Grundriss der vergleichenden Grammatik der Indogerman. Sprachen*,[2] Strassburg, 1886–1900, i. 503, and A. Meillet, *Grammaire arménienne*. The intervening *e* presents no difficulty. The Latin *periculum* is probably represented in Armenian by *erkiuλ*, " fear."

9. The Slavic character of things Thraco-Phrygian has lately been attracting some attention (see G. Calderon, "Slavonic Elements in Greek Religion," *Classical Review* [1913]. The Letto-Slavic character of the Armenian language has been known for the last four decades through the researches of Hübschmann. Here it may be noted that something of this had already been observed in the folklore of the Armenians (see Chalatianz, *Intro.*).

10. *Die alten Thraker*, Vienna, 1893–4 (*SWAW*), ii. 60.

11. Gladys M. N. Davis, in a recent work called *The Asiatic Dionysos*, London, 1914, has revived an older theory that would identify Dionysos with the Vedic *Soma*. This book has been very severely criticised, but its main contention is worthy of further investigation.

12. See also A. Meillet, " Sur les termes religieux iraniens en Arménien," in *Revue des études arméniennes*, i, fasc. 3, 1921; M. H. Ananikian, " Armenia," in *ERE*.

Chapter II

1. Eλishe (5th cent.), speaking of the Sassanian Mihr, reports that the Persians considered him as the helper of "the seven gods," which means Auramazda with the six Amesha Spentas. Dolens and Khatch (pp. 201–203) maintain this view, and also aptly point to the Phoenician pantheon with seven Cabirs, and Eshmun the *eighth*. Even in India Aditi had seven, then with the addition of the sun, eight children.

2. Farther west, especially in Persianized Lydia, Anahita was represented with a crescent on her head.

3. Agathangelos, p. 34.

4. See detailed description in Sandalgian's *Histoire documentaire*, p. 794.

5. A thorough comparative study of the Armenian church rites is still a desideratum. When we have eliminated what is Byzantine or Syrian, we may safely assume that the rest is native and may have preserved bits of the pagan worship. Among these rites may be mentioned the abjuration of the devil in Lent, the Easter celebrations, the Transfiguration roses and rose-water, the blessing of the grapes at the Assumption of the Virgin, the blessing of the four corners of the earth, etc.

Chapter III

1. Agathangelos, p. 590.

2. Seeing that Anahit was in later times identified with Artemis and Nane, with Athene and Mihr and with Hephaistos, one may well ask whether this fathering of Aramazd upon them was not a bit of Hellenizing. Yet the Avesta does not leave us without a parallel in this matter.

3. Agathangelos, pp. 52, 61.

4. *Ibid.*, pp. 52, 61, 106.

5. *Ibid.*, p. 623.

6. It is noteworthy that his Christian successor is a hurler of the lightning.

7. See artts. "Calendar (Armenian)" and "Calendar (Persian)" in *ERE* iii. 70 f., 128 f.

8. Al-Bīrūni, *Chron.*, pp. 202–203.

9. This is an important instance of the Adonis gardens in the East, overlooked by Frazer. Readers of his *Adonis, Attis, and Osiris* know how widely the custom had spread in the West.

10. See Chap. 8.

11. Gregory the Illuminator substituted the festival of St. John Baptist for that of the Navasard, but as that festival did not attain more than a local popularity (in Tarauntis) the later Fathers seem to have united it with the great festival of the Assumption of the Virgin, at which the blessing of the grapes takes place. These Christian associations gradually cost the old festival many of its original traits.

12. Al-Bīrūni, *Chron.*, p. 199.

13. Moses, ii. 66; Agathangelos, p. 623. Gelzer and others have made of his title of *Vanatur*, "hospitable," a separate deity. However corrupt the text of Agathangelos may be, it certainly does not justify this inference. Further, *Vanatur* is used in the Book of Maccabees to translate Zeus Xenios. For a fuller discussion of this subject see art. "Armenia (Zoroastrian)" in *ERE* i. 795.

14. Al-Bīrūni, *Chron.*, p. 200.

15. Quoted by Alishan, p. 260. It is perhaps on this basis that Gelzer gives her the title of "mother of gods." This title finds no support in ancient records.

16. Agathangelos, p. 590. This cannot be Zoroastrian.

17. Moses, ii. 12.

18. *Ibid.*, ii. 53.

19. Agathangelos, p. 612.

20. Moses, i. 31.

21. *Kund* in Persian may mean "brave." But the word does not occur in Armenian in this sense.

22. The Iberians also had a chief deity called Azmaz (a corruption of Aramazd), whose statue, described as "the thunderer" or "a hurler of lightning," was set up outside of their capital, Mdskhit. A mighty river flowed between the temple and the city. As the statue was visible from all parts of the city, in the morning everyone stood on his house-roof to worship it. But those who wished to sacrifice, had to cross the river in order to do so at the temple. (Alishan, p. 314.)

23. Whenever she may have come to Persia, her patronage over the rivers and springs need not be regarded as a purely Iranian addition to her attributes. The original Ishtar is a water goddess, and therefore a goddesss of vegetation, as well as a goddess of love and maternity. Water and vegetation underlie and symbolize all life whether animal or human. Cf. *Mythology of all Races*, Boston, 1917, vi. 278 f.

24. Agathangelos, p. 52.

25. Dio. Cass., 36, 48; Pliny, *HN* v. 83.

26. Strabo, xi. 532C. Cumont thinks that this was a modification of ancient exogamy (see art. "Anahita" in *ERE* i. 414, and his *Les*

religions orientales dans le paganisme romain, Paris, 1907, p. 287). Yet it is difficult to see wherein this sacred prostitution differs from the usual worship paid to Ishtar and Ma. As Ramsay explains it in his art. "Phrygians" (*ERE* ix. 900 f.) this is an act which is supposed to have a magical influence on the fertility of the land and perhaps also on the fecundity of these young women. Cf. arts. "Ashtart" (*ERE* ii. 115f.) and "Hierodouloi (Semitic and Egyptian)" (*ERE* vi. 672 f.).

27. Faustus, iii. 13.

28. Alishan, p. 263.

29. Moses, p. 294.

30. Justina was a Christian virgin of Antioch whom a certain magician called Cyprian tried to corrupt by magical arts, first in favor of a friend, then for himself. His utter failure led to his conversion, and both he and Justina were martyred together.

31. We have already seen (p. 11) that Ishtar as Sharis had secured a place in the Urartian pantheon.

32. Agathangelos, pp. 51, 61.

33. Moses, ii. 60.

34. *Ibid*, ii. 12.

35. Faustus, v. 25.

36. Agathangelos, p. 591.

37. Cicero, *De imperio Pompæii*, p. 23.

38. Agathangelos, p. 59; Weber, p. 31.

39. Farther west Anahit required bulls, and was called Taurobolos.

40. *HN* xxxiii. 4; see Gelzer, p. 46.

41. Pliny, *loc. cit.*

42. Moses, ii. 16.

43. *Eraz*, "dream," is identical with the Persian word *raz*, "secret," "occult," and perhaps also with the Slavic *raj*, "the other world," or "paradise." *Muyn* is now unintelligible and the μούσος of the Greek is evidently a mere reproduction of the cryptic *muyn*.

44. Moses, ii. 12.

45. Tiur's name occurs also as Tre in the list of the Armenian months. In compound names and words it assumes the Persian form of Tir. We find a "Ti" in the old exclamation "(By) Ti or Tir, forward!" and it may be also in such compound forms as *Ti-air, Ti-mann*, a "lord," and *Ti-kin*, "a Ti-woman," i.e., "lady," "queen." Ti-air may be compared with Tirair, a proper name of uncertain derivation. However, owing to the absence of the "r" in Ti, one may well connect it with the older Tiv, a cognate of Indo-European Dyaus, Zeus, Tiwaz, etc., or one may consider it as a dialectical variety of the Armenian *di*, "god." See also p. 13.

46. Eznik, pp. 150, 153, etc. Synonymous or parallel with this, we find also the word *bakht*, " fortuna."

47. Pshrank, p. 271. See for a fuller account Abeghian, p. 61f.

48. Perhaps because, like the temple of Nabu in Borsippa, it contained a place symbolizing the heavenly archive in which the divine decrees were deposited.

49. Agathangelos.

50. " The Writer " was confused with the angel of death in Christian times. He is now called " the little brother of death." It is curious to note that the Teutonic Wotan, usually identified with Mercury, was also the conductor of souls to Hades.

51. Nabu, the city-god of Borsippa, once had precedence over Marduk himself in the Babylonian Pantheon. But when Marduk, the city god of Babylon, rose in importance with the political rise of his city, Nabu became the scribe of the gods and their messenger, as well as the patron of the priests. On the Babylonian New Year's Day (in the spring) he wrote on tablets, the destiny of men, when this was decided on the world mountain.

52. *Farvardin Yasht,* xxvii. 126.

53. Moulton, p. 435. Even the Arabs knew this deity under the name of ᵉUᴛārid, which also means Mercury, and has the epithet of " writer."

54. There lies before us no witness to the fact that the Armenians ever called the planet Mercury, Tiur, but it is probable. The Persians themselves say that Mercury was called *Tir,* " arrow," on account of its swiftness.

55. See G. Rawlinson's *Herodotus,* app. Bk. i, under Nebo.

56. Jensen derives Tir from the Babylonian Dpir = Dipsar, " scribe." However, he overlooks the fact that the East has known and used the word Dpir in an uncorrupted form to this day. Tir may even be regarded as one element in the mysterious Hermes Tresmegisthos, which is usually translated as " Thrice greatest." It seems to be much more natural to say: Hermes, the greatest Tir. However, we have here against us the great army of classical scholars and a hoary tradition.

57. Eznik, pp. 122, 138; also Eλishe, ii. 44. F. Cumont, in his *Mysteries of Mithra,* wrongly ascribes these myths to the Armenians themselves, whereas the Armenian authors are only reporting Zrvantian ideas.

58. Greek Agathangelos; Moses, ii. 18.

59. Agathangelos, p. 593. One of the gates of the city of Van is to this day called by Mihr's name (Meher).

60. These human sacrifices may also be explained by Mihr's prob-

able relation to Vahagn. Vahagn is the fierce storm god, who, as in Vedic and Teutonic religions, had supplanted the god of the bright heaven. Vahagn may have once required human sacrifices in Armenia, as his Teutonic brother Wotan did.

61. Eznik, pp. 15, 16.

CHAPTER IV

1. Moses, ii. 14.
2. *Ibid.*, ii. 14.
3. *Ibid.*, i. 14.
4. Anania of Shirag, ed. St. Petersburg, p. 48.
5. *Ibid.*, ii. 14; Greek Agathangelos. Josephus calls the Nana of Elam, Artemis.
6. Moses, ii. 14; Greek Agathangelos.
7. Apollodorus, iii. 14, 3.

CHAPTER V

1. *Ibid.*, i. 31: Agathangelos, pp. 106, 607.
2. Agathangelos, p. 106.
3. *Ibid.*, p. 606.
4. The Armenian word for "reed" is eλeg. The Phrygian cognate of eλeg is probably at the root of the Greek ἐλεγεῖον, "elegy," which originally had nothing to do with elegiac poetry, but meant a doleful melody accompanied by the flute. The relation of the reed to the flute is well known to those who are familiar with the Greek myths of Pan. Armenian also possesses the word eλer in the sense of "dirge" (see F. B. Jevons, *History of Greek Literature*, New York, 1886, p. 111), but eλer has nothing to do with "elegy."
5. Alishan, p. 87.
6. The district of Goλthn seems to have clung to the old paganism more tenaciously than any other in Armenia.
7. All these facts are recognized and clearly expressed by Oldenberg, p. 105 f.; Lehmann, in P. D. Chantepie de la Saussaye, *Lehrbuch* ii. 27; Macdonell, § 35; Moore, i. 254 f.
8. There is a great temptation to connect Aravan, the son of Vahagn (Moses, i, 31), with this Vedic priest, as some have already connected the Bhṛgu of the Vedas with Brig = Phrygians. Atharvan could easily pass to Aravan through Ahrvan. However, the name is also Avestic.
9. Chalatianz, p. xiii. Even in Egyptian mythology the Sun-god is sometimes born out of an egg, but he is born also out of the lotus-stalk, for he is said to have spent his childhood in the lotus flower. Cf. *Mythology of All Races*, Boston, 1918, xii. 25, 50.

10. Macdonell, pp. 89, 98.

11. Abeghian, p. 83 f. It is a very strange and significant coincidence that in the Veda also the sea-born Agni is related to the lightning (*Rig-veda-Sanhita: a collection of ancient Hindu Hymns*, tr. H. H. Wilson, London, 1850–88, vi. 119, note), and that Agni gives rain (*Ibid.*, p. 387). Cf. also Oldenberg, p. 167 f.; Macdonell, § 35, where the sea is identified with the heavenly sea.

12. Oldenberg, p. 120.

13. We would suggest that this is the origin of the use of *baresman* both in India and in Iran at the worship of the fire and of the baresman at the Magian worship of the sun. The grass or stalk cushion upon which the sacrifice is laid and the bunch of green stalks or twigs held before the face were perhaps supposed to be an effective charm, meant to work favorably upon the sun and the fire.

14. Sandalgian's theory that Vahagn came to Armenia straight from Vedic India has no sound foundation.

15. See Appendix, I, Vahagn.

CHAPTER VI

1. Moses, ii. 19.

2. *Ibid.*, ii. 77. The modern Armenian use of the word " sun " in the sense of " life," is due perhaps to the fact that the sun brings the day, and days make up the sum of human life.

3. Abeghian, p. 41.

4. Agathangelos, p. 125.

5. Xenophon, *Anab.*, iv. 5. 35.

6. *Discourses*, Venice, 1860, p. 198–9.

7. Ed. Patkanean, p. 66.

8. *Yasht*, vii. 4; Al-Bīrūni, *Chron.*, p. 219.

9. Eznik, p. 180.

10. Abeghian, p. 49.

11. *Dâdistân-î Dînik*, lxix. 2; *Sikand-Gûmânik Vijâr*, iv. 46.

12. Eznik, p. 217. See also Appendix II, Witchcraft and Magic.

13. Abeghian, pp. 41–49; Tchéraz, in *TICO* ii. 823 f.

14. Alishan, in one of his popular poems, calls the Milky Way the manger from which the dragon may break loose. This is the echo of some myth which we have not been able to locate. A modern Armenian legend says that the Milky Way was formed by two brothers who worked together in the fields and then divided the crop on the threshing-floor. One of them was married and the other single. In the night the married one would rise and carry sheaves from his stack to his brother's, saying, " My brother is single and needs some con-

solation." The other would do the same, saying, " My brother is married and needs help." Thus going to and fro they scattered the straw.

15. Abeghian, pp. 41–45.
16. Pshrank, p. 198.
17. Alishan, p. 89.
18. Abeghian, p. 45; Pshrank, p. 198.
19. Quoted by Alishan, p. 98.
20. It is well known how later Zoroastrianism degraded the genii of all the planets in demoniac powers.
21. Eznik, p. 153 f.
22. Al-Bīrūni, *Chron.*, p. 211.

Chapter VII

1. Here it is worth while to notice how Kuhn in his exhaustive study of fire-myths, called *Die Herabkunft des Feuers*,[2] Gutersloh 1886, summarizes his conclusion. He says (p. 35): " The myths which have just been compared show the same belief among the Indians, Greeks, and Italians in regard to the fact that the earthly fire has been brought to mankind as a heavenly spark in (the form of) the lightning by a semi-divine being who was originally (and) generally imagined as a winged being, as a bird. The people must have thought that the spark is produced in the clouds by twirling, just in the same manner as they saw the fire gotten out of the primeval instrument, through a circling friction."

2. Possibly the fear with which iron is supposed to inspire evil spirits is also due to the fact of its containing and producing sparks like the flint. A curious passage of the 1st Book of Jalal ad-Dinar-Rumi's *Mathnavi* makes much of the fire which iron and stone contain, and which may not be extinguished by water.

3. Aspirated " p " became " h " in Armenian, as " pater," Armen. *hayr*. The Phrygian word for fire is said by Plato to have resembled the Greek πῦρ

4. In many places these ancestral spirits have become just spirits, undefined and general.

5. There were in Armenia at least three towns of the gods: Baga-yarij in Derzanes, Bagavan in Bagrevand, and Bagaron on the river Akhurean. See H. Hübschmann, *Die Altarmen. Ortsnamen*, pp. 410–11.

6. Alishan, *Hayapatum*, p. 79.

7. " Story of the Picture of the Holy Virgin," in Moses of Chorene.

8. Lazare of Pharpe (5th cent.), p. 203.

9. *ARW* xvii. [1914] 479. Similar customs are reported also of the Belgians. See Frazer, *GB*³, part 7, *Balder the Beautiful,* London, i. 194 f.

10. Many of the German sacred fire-festivals were also taken under the patronage of the church and started from a candle (Kuhn, *Die Herabkunft des Feuers*², p. 41 f.).

11. See Frazer, *GB*³, pt. 7, *Balder the Beautiful,* i. 131, for a very interesting and fuller account of the Armenian New Fires at Candlemas. In fact the whole Chapter V constitutes the richest material on new fires and the best treatment of this subject. Notice that securing fruitfulness, for the fields, trees, animals, etc., is the chief motive of the fires, but next comes the desire to prevent disease. These fires were intended to exert some favorable influence on the fire-god in general and on the lightning (rain) god in particular. The February fires in England, which were kindled on Candlemas, if productive of bad weather, heralded thereby the coming of the rainy season, i.e. the spring. For in this sense alone it is possible to understand the old English verses:

> " If Candlemas be dry and fair
> The half o' winter's to come and mair;
> If Candlemas be wet and foul
> The half o' winter's gane at Yule."

See also artt. " Feu " in *La Grande Encyclopédie;* " Fire " *in EB*⁹; " Candlemas " in *ERE* iii. 189 f.

CHAPTER VIII

1. *Annals,* vi. 37.

2. Lehmann, " Religionsgesch. aus Kaukasien und Armenien," in *ARW*, iii. [1900] 4 f.

3. There are those who have explained Vartavar from the Sanscrit as meaning " sprinkling with water," and it can possibly mean also " increasing the waters." However befitting, this Sanscrit etymology is far-fetched.

4. For the numerous references on this subject, see the General Index of Frazer's *Golden Bough,* under " Fire," " Water," etc. It would be worth while to inquire also whether the Roman Rosalia (*Rosales esces*) and the Slavic and Macedonian Rousalia are in any way related to the Armenian Vartavar. See G. F. Abbott, *Macedonian Folk-lore,* Cambridge, 1903, pp. 40 ff. These western festivals, however, come much earlier.

5. Al-Bīrūni, *Chron.,* pp. 199, 203.

6. The Armenians had other methods of fire-making.

CHAPTER IX

1. Abeghian, p. 59 f.; Lehmann, "Religionsgeschichte aus Kaukasien und Armenien," in *ARW*, iii. [1900] 10 f.

2. The name Massis for this snow-capped giant of Armenia seems to have been unknown to the old Urartians. It may be an Armenian importation, if not a later Northern echo of the Massios, which was in Assyrian times the name of the great mountain in the plain of Diarbekir. According to Nicholas of Damascus (see Josephus, *Ant. Jud.*, I. iii. 6) this mountain was known also by the name of *Baris*, which Sandalgian compares with the Sacred mountain *Hara-berezaiti* of the Avesta.

CHAPTER X

1. Here, of course, the valuable tale of the epics has vanished before the Biblical conception of the spread of mankind, but a dim memory of the events that led to the separation of the Armenians from their mighty brethren of Thrace or Phrygia, as well as something of the story of the conquest of Urartu by the Armenians, seems to be reflected in the biblicised form of the legend.

2. Moses, i. 10, 11.

3. Alishan, p. 126.

4. Dr. Chapman calls my attention to the passages in Sayce's and Sandalgian's works on the Urartian inscriptions, where they find the name Huas or °Uas. Sandalgian also explains it as Hayk. (*Inscriptions Cunéiformes Urartiques*, 1900, p. 437.) See also the appendix on Vahagn in this work.

5. A. H. Sayce, *The Cuneiform Inscriptions of Van*, p. 719.

6. This is the prevailing view among modern scholars. The word that was current in this sense in historical times was *azat* (from *yazata?*), "venerable." Patrubani sees in Hayk the Sanskrit *pana* and the Vedic *payn*, "keeper"; Armen. *hay-im*, "I look."

7. Republic, x. 134.

8. Patrubani explains *Armenus* as *Arya-Manah*, "Aryan (noble?)-minded." The Vedic Aryaman seems to mean "friend," "comrade."

9. This is not impossible in itself as we find a host of Arabic words and even broken plurals in pre-Muhammedan Armenian.

10. Nychar is perhaps the Assyrian Nakru, "enemy" or a thinned-down and very corrupt echo of the name of Hanaçiruka of Mata, mentioned in an inscription of Shamshi-Rammon of Assyria, 825–812 B.C. (Harper, *Ass. and Bab. Liter.*, p. 48).

11. Moses, i. 15. See also additional note on Semiramis, Appendix III.

12. *Republic*, x. 134.

13. Pamphylians were dressed up like the Phrygians, but they were a mixed race.

14. See art. " Gilgamesh " in *EBr* [11]; also F. Jeremiah's account of the myth in Chantepie de la Saussaye, *Lehrbuch* [3], i. 331f. Frazer in *GB*[3] part iv, *Adonis, Attis, and Osiris*, ch. 5, gives an interesting account of kings, who, through self-cremation on a funeral pyre, sought to become deified. He tells also of a person who, having died, was brought back to life through the plant of life shown by a serpent (as in the well-known myth of Polyidus and Glaucus, cf. Hyginus, *Fab.* 136, and for Folk-tale parallels, J. Bolte and G. Polivka, *Anmerkungen zu den Kinder- und Haus-Märchen der Brüder Grimm*, Leipzig, 1913, i. 126 f.). Further, we learn through Herodotus (iv. 95.) that Zalmoxis, the Sabazios of the Getae in Thrace, taught about the life beyond the grave, and demonstrated his teaching by disappearing and appearing again.

15. Sayce, *Cuneiform Inscriptions of Van*, p. 566. We may also point to the verbal resemblance between Er-Ara and the Bavarian Er, which seems to have been either a title of Tiu = Dyaus, or the name of an ancient god corresponding to Tiu.

16. For the real Tigranes of this time we may refer the reader to Xenophon, *Cyropaedia*, iii. 1. Aždahak of Media is known to Greek authors as Astyages, the maternal grandfather of Cyrus the Great.

17. According to classical authors the historical Astyages was not killed by Tigranes, but dethroned and taken captive by Cyrus.

18. According to Herodotus (i. 74) the name of the first queen of Astyages was Aryenis. *Anush* is a Persian word which may be interpreted as " pleasant." But it may also be a shortened form from *anushiya*, " devoted." This latter sense is supported by such compound names in Armenian as connect *anush* with names of gods, e.g. Hayka-nush, Hranush, Vartanush, etc.

Chapter XI

1. See art. " Fairy " in *ERE* v. 678 f. See also Kirk, *Secret Commonwealth of Elves*, etc. Its analysis largely supports ours which was made independently on the basis of more extensive material.

2. Herodotus, iv. 9. The Greek view of the origin of the Scythians was that they were born from the union of Herakles with a woman who was human above the waist and serpent below.

3. Goldziher, " Wasser als Dämonenabruhrendes Mittel," in *ARW*, xiii. [1910] 274 f. This may have reference to water in its relation to the birth of fire or to the lightning.

4. Agathangelos, p. 57. Cf. the cross of the archangel Michael in graveyards of Roman Catholic churches, e.g., French.

5. *Prolegomena to the Study of Greek Religion*, Cambridge, 1903, p. 540.

6. This description is based on the account given by Alishan and in Pshrank. Some confusion has arisen in regard to the true nature of this old rite, owing to the fact that Shvod was thought to be *Shubat*, the Syriac name of a month corresponding to February. But it is certain that originally Shvod was the name of a class of spirits.

7. For a comparative study of serpent-worship and serpent-lore see art. "Serpent" in *ERE* xi.

8. According to Frazer, *GB*³, part 7, *Balder the Beautiful*, London, 1913, ix. 15, the serpent's stone is identical with the serpent's egg. This, however, is not quite certain. Nor should this egg be confused with that in which a fairy's or dragon's external soul is often hidden (*ibid.*, ii. 106f.).

9. Later magical texts use the word "dragon" in the sense of evil spirit.

10. For parallels see J. A. MacCulloch, *The Childhood of Fiction: A Study of Folk-Tales and Primitive Thought*, London, 1905, chap. 14, "The Dragon Sacrifice," and E. S. Hartland, *The Legend of Perseus*, London, 1894–96.

11. Chalatianz (p. 12) speaking of modern Armenian folk-tales about the dragons' reciprocated love for highborn matrons and maids, mentions also the fact that there are many parallels in Slav, Rumanian, and Wallachian folk-tales, and that it is the sons or brothers of these infatuated women who persecute the monster, often against the enamoured woman's will.

12. See art. "Changeling" in *ERE* iii. 358f.

13. We know that the Persian Aži Dahaka, a corporeal creature and helper of Ahriman, had a human representative or could personify himself as a man.

14. Quoted by Alishan, p. 194.

15. This pulling up of the dragon out of a lake by means of oxen appears also in Celtic (Welsh) folklore.

16. In England the Lambton Worm required nine cows' milk daily. Luther, in his *Table-Talk*, describes a diabolical child — a "Killcrop," which exhausted six nurses. The house-serpent also is often fed on milk, while in other instances the serpent is said to be disinclined to milk.

17. House-fairies (the Brownie of Scottish folk-lore) thrash as much grain in a night as twenty men can do. See Kirk, *Secret Commonwealth*, Introd. by A. Lang, p. 24.

18. There is a contradiction here. In the original Persian story the world-destroyer is the dragon himself, chained by the hero Thraetona.

19. These rocks were exposed in the morning to his eyes in order to neutralize their baleful influence during the day. The evil eye is blue. Before it, mountains, even the whole world may flame up. (Pshrank, p. 180.)

20. For whirlwinds in connection with jinn, fairies, demons, and witches see " Fairy " in *ERE* v. 688*a*.

21. Alishan, p. 66. In more recent collections of folklore, God, angels, and even the prophet Elijah, have taken the place of the ancient weather god and his helpers. The usual weapons are iron chains and the lightning. Sometimes it is a cloud-monster that is being driven hard and smitten with the lightning so that he shrieks. At other times it is the dragon hung in suspense in the sky that is trying to break his chains in order to reach and destroy the world. Angels pull him up and fasten his chains. The thunder-roll is the noise of the chains and of the affray in general. According to another and probably older account, the dragon that lives in the sea or on land, must not live beyond a thousand years. For then he would grow out of all proportion and swallow up everything. Therefore, just before he has reached that age, angels hasten to pull him up into the sky. There he is often represented as being consumed by the sun, while his tail drops down on earth to give birth to other dragons. A magical text of more recent date speaks of the Serpent who remains in hiding for one hundred years, then is taken into the skies, like a dragon, where he acquires twelve heads and four bridles (Lkam, Arabic). The lightning is often a sword, arrow or fiery whip which the Lord is hurling at the devil, who is fleeing, and who naturally and gradually has taken the place of the ancient dragon, as the Muhammedan Shaytan crowded out the eclipse dragon.

22. Abeghian, p. 78.

23. Here, however, the meteorological dragon seems to have become fused with the eschatological dragon. Whether these two were originally identical or can be traced to different sources is an important question which need not be discussed here. See Frazer, *GB*[3] part 7, *Balder the Beautiful*, London, 1913, i. 105 f.

24. Abbott in his *Macedonian Folk-lore* (chap. xiv.) gives a very interesting account of the dragon beliefs there, which have a close affinity both with the Indian Vṛtra and the Armenian Vishap. The Macedonian dragon is a giant and a monster, terrible, voracious and somewhat stupid, but not altogether detestable. He is invariably driven away by a bride who boldly asserts herself to be " the Light-

ning's child, the Thunder's grandchild and a hurler of thunderbolts!"
Here Indra and Vṛtra are unmistakable.

25. The relation of such doctrines to the faith of the Yezidis is
unmistakable (J. Ménant, *Les Yezidis*, p. 83; Parry, *Six Months in
a Syrian Monastery*, p. 358 f.

26. In Greek and Latin mythology the powers of Hades accept
only black gifts and sacrifices, such as black sheep, heifers, beans, etc.

27. Among other things this would recall the arrows of Herakles
which had been dipped in the bile of the Lernean Hydra.

28. Alishan, p. 191; Abeghian, p. 104f.

29. Vahram Vartabed, quoted in Alishan, p. 194.

30. Perhaps the fairies' dart, which killed people and cattle in
Scotland and elsewhere, is a dim reminiscence of this hunting habit
of the fairies.

31. Modern Armenian folk-lore also knows of witches with a tail
who fly to foreign lands astride upon such jars.

32. Cf. the Muslim "Brides of the Treasuries," fairy guardians
of hidden treasure. Western fairies also are often imagined as
mortal and as seeking to attain immortality through intermarriage
with human beings. However in other instances it is they who try to
free human children "from dying flesh and dull mortality" by im-
mersing them in fairy wells. In Pshrank (p. 194), a man stumbles
into a wedding of these fairies, near *the ruins of a water-mill*. After
an oath upon the Holy Eucharist, he is allowed to taste of their wine
of immortality and to take a wife from their number.

33. I owe this identification to Dr. J. W. Chapman. For the
Telchins, see Blinkenberg, "Rhodische Urvölker," in *Hermes*, 1
[1915] pt. 2, pp. 271 ff. and the authors named by him. In an article
in the *Hushartzan* (Memorial Volume) of the Mechitarists of Vienna,
Nicolaos Adontz finds in Torch the Hittite god Tarqu.

34. Moses of Choren makes Torch the head of the noble house
called "Angeλ Tun," interpreting the word *Angeλ* as "ugly." The
expression means rather "The Vulture's House," and Torch's connection with that house is an unfounded conjecture of Moses' own or of
his legendary sources.

35. See Appendix IV, The Cyclops.

36. Eznik, p. 191, Eλishe, p. 65.

37. An 11th cent. writer reports that a woman died leaving a husband and some children. While the man was perplexed as to how to
take care of the orphans, a very beautiful woman appeared unexpectedly and lived with him, taking good care of him and the children.
But after a while for some reason she disappeared. She was recognized as a female Dev. Modern Armenians are still catching

mermaids by sticking a needle into their clothes. These can be married or held in servitude and they will stay as long as the needle remains.

38. Eznik, p. 178.

39. Faustus, v. 2.

40. Moses, iii. 55.

41. Eznik, p. 178 f.

42. *Vendidad*, xviii. 45–52.

43. Under the influence of later Persian romantic conceptions of the Peris or Houris, the modern Armenian Parik has also become a most charming fairy.

44. Eznik, p. 97 f.

45. See on the modern Armenian Devs, Chalatianz, p. xiii f.; Lalayantz, "Traditions et superstitions de l'Armenie," *Revue des traditions populaires*, x. [1895] 193f; F. Macler, art. "Armenia (Christian)," in *ERE* i. 802; Pshrank, p. 170. Macler's is a good summary of the two preceding studies. The present-day Armenian Dev is a very large being with an immense head on his shoulders, and with eyes as large as earthen bowls. Some of them have only one eye (Pshrank, p. 170).

46. Goldziher, *ARW* x. [1907] 44.

47. This "mother of the Als" resembles the Teutonic devil's grandmother.

48. Quoted by Alishan, p. 222.

49. To steal unborn children is a trait of the nocturnal demon Kikimora of the Slavs also, but rather a rare notion among other peoples. The tribute mentioned in the text resembles the Scottish tradition of the similar tribute paid by the fairies to the devil, usually a human victim (see J. A. MacCulloch, artt. "Changeling," "Fairy," in *ERE* iii. 360, v. 678).

50. Modern Parsis burn a fire or light in the room, probably for the same purpose. (See J. J. Modi, art. "Birth (Parsi)" in *ERE* ii. 661, though the writer fails to give the reason underlying this practice.)

51. The spirits of Wednesday, Friday, and Sunday eve, of which Abeghian (p. 120 f.) and, following him, Lalayantz (*Revue des traditions populaires*, x. [1895] 3), speak, are Christian inventions. Wednesday and Friday, as fast days, and Sunday as a holy day, are supposed to avenge themselves on those who do not respect their sanctity.

52. The *Als* are known also to modern Armenian folklore (Abeghian, p. 108 f.). But sometimes the Devs assume their functions (see Pshrank, p. 170), and they not only steal the mother's liver, but

also bring the child, probably born, to their chief, substituting for him a changeling. See also Appendix V, The *Al*.

53. As this seems to be a self-contradiction, it is perhaps better to take it as a refutation by Eznik of those who said that the Nhang was a personal being.

54. In a similar manner the Teutonic Nixies showed themselves in the form of bulls and horses, and lured men maliciously into the abyss. (S. Reinach, *Orpheus*, Eng. trans., London, 1909, p. 133).

55. Alishan, p. 62 f.

56. Faustus, v. 36.

57. See p. 68.

58. Eznik, p. 98 f. It is difficult to tell whether these beneficent spirits belonged to the original stock of Armenian beliefs or whether they were a survival of the Urartian or even Babylonian spirit world. Plato does not mention them in his brief and philosophical " Er " myth, although how the dead hero's body was taken up whole (intact), without some process of healing, is hard to see. The myth about a slain hero's return to life is, however, rather foreign to Greek thought, and this trait may not have reached him at all. G. H. Basmajian, an Armenian Assyriologist, in his short *Comparative Study of our Aralez and the Babylonian Marduk* (Venice, 1898), points out that Marduk had four dogs, Ukkumu, " the snatcher," Akkulu, " the eater," Ikšuda, " the snatcher," and Iltepu, " the satisfier," and that he himself is said in a cuneiform fragment from Koyunjuk, now in the British Museum (K. 8961), " to recall the dead to life," and (line 10) " to give life to the dead bodies." Yet this view, which had already been held by Émine and V. Langlois (*Collection des historiens anciens et modernes de l' Arménie*, Paris, 1867–9, i. 26, note 1), cannot be said to be the last word on this interesting but obscure point. Marduk's dogs do not lick wounds, nor is Marduk himself specially famous for restoring dead heroes to life. Licking wounds to heal them is the most important feature of these gods or dog spirits. (For a parallel see p. 204 of the African section of this volume.) Prof. Sayce saw some connexion between the Arall mountain and the Armenian Aralez, while another scholar has suggested Aralu or Hades as a possible explanation. Basmajian comes perhaps nearer to the solution. Sandalgian (*Histoire documentaire de l'Arménie*, ii. 599) quotes the letter of Sargon speaking of golden keys found in the temple of Khaldis in Mutzatzir, in the form of goddesses wearing the tiara, carrying the dented harp and the circle and treading upon dogs which made faces. But the same author (pp. 754–759) says that *arales* meant for the ancient Armenians inhabitants of Arali (Summerian Hades), but later generations, having forgotten

the original sense of the word, developed the myth of the Aralezes, from the last syllable which conveyed to them the meaning of lapping.

59. Alishan, p. 177 f.

60. See also Isaiah, xxxiv. 13, Jeremiah, l. 39, in the old Armenian version.

61. Alishan, p. 185.

62. The sea-bull resembles the Celtic Water-bull, the *Tarbh Uisge* of the West Highlands, which had no ears and could assume other shapes. It dwelt in lochs and was friendly to man, occasionally emerging to mate with ordinary cows. The similar *Tarroo Ushtey* of the Isle of Man begets monsters. Both have a curious resemblance to the *Bunyip*, a mythical water monster of the Australian blacks. See J. A. MacCulloch, *The Religion of the Ancient Celts*, Edinburgh, 1911, p. 189; *Mythology of All Races*, Boston, 1916, ix. 280.

63. Besides many of the above mentioned spirits, modern Armenians know at least two others, the Hotots and the Old Hags of the Swamps. The Hotots are like devils, but they are not devils. In the winter and in the spring they live in rivers and swamps. When they appear they are all covered with mire. They do not deceive men as the devils do, but they allure them by all sorts of dances, jests, and grimaces. When the unsuspecting victim follows them for the sake of being amused, — and who can resist the temptation? — they pull and push him into their miry abode. The Old Hags of the marshes also live in pools and swamps. They are terrible to see. They are enormous, thick, and naked, with heads as big as bath-house domes, with breasts as large as lambs hanging down. Horses, oxen, buffaloes, men, children and other living beings are drawn into their watery abode and drowned by them. (Pshrank, pp. 171–172.) See also Appendix VI, "The Finger Cutters of Albania."

CHAPTER XII

1. See E. W. Lane, *Arabian Nights*, i., notes on the first chapter, or his *Arabian Society in the Middle Ages*, ed. by S. Lane-Poole, London, 1883, p. 106 f.; also the extravagant cosmogony in the first chapter of ath-Tha'labî's *Qisas al-'anbiyâ*.

2. See chap. iii., part 3, on Tyr; also Abeghian, p. 16 f., and Pshrank, p. 168.

3. Herodotus (iv. 127) tells us that the Scythians challenged Darius who was invading their country and anxiously seeking an encounter

with the retreating barbarians, to violate the graves of their kings, if he wished to force them to fight.

4. The temptation is very great to read in this light the well-known report of Herodotus (v. 4) that the Thracians mourned at a birth but were very joyful at a death. The father of historians and folk-lorists, whose bias to see in everything Thracian some sign of belief in immortality was strong, may be describing a Thracian funeral only imperfectly, i.e., through the very noisy funeral-feast. The funeral-feast is and was a widely spread custom. See artt. " Death and Disposal of the Dead," *ERE*, iv. 411 ff., " Feasting," *ib.*, v. 801 ff.; and W. Caland, *Die vorchristlichen baltischen Totengebräuche, ARW* iii.

5. For more details on burial customs among the Armenians, see Abeghian, p. 16f; Pshrank, p. 256, and " Funeral Rites " in *EBr* [11], xi. 329.

6. A. V. W. Jackson, *Die Iranische Religion,* in Geiger and Kuhn, *Grundriss,* ii. 685.

7. *Vendidad,* iii. 35. Darkness was also the distinguishing feature of the house of Lie.

8. Pshrank, p. 198.

9. For the more Avestic form of this myth, see A. V. W. Jackson, *Die Iranische Religion,* in Geiger and Kuhn, *Grundriss,* ii. 663f. See also *Mythology of All Races,* Boston, 1917, vi. 320. That a dread, alarming dragon, who flies above the entire realm of air, and terrifies Jove and the other gods, as well as the powers of Hades, will bring the world to an end, is known also to Apuleius. (Bk. iv. 33, 35.)

10. Pshrank, p. 234; Abeghian, p. 20.

11. J. A. Stewart, *The Myths of Plato,* London, 1905 (the myth of Er, *Repub.,* 613E to 621D, with parallel trans., pp. 134–151; observations on the myth of Er, pp. 152–172).

AFRICAN

Citation by author's name refers to the same in the Bibliography. Where an author has written several works they are distinguished as [a], [b], [c], etc.

INTRODUCTION

1. The *type* is what strikes the newcomer among any people, just as a stranger will often perceive the family resemblance between brothers and sisters who are considered most unlike by their own relatives. A Welsh schoolfellow once told me that " all English people looked alike " to her, when she first came out of Wales into England.

2. Chatelain, pp. 16,17.

3. *Ibid.*, p. 22. Chatelain, after stating what I believe to be perfectly true, that " the myths and tales of the negroes in North, Central and South America are all derived from African prototypes," goes on to say: " Through the medium of the American negro, African folk-lore has exercised a deep and wide influence over the folk-lore of the American Indian." This I take leave to doubt. It will scarcely apply, one would think, to remote tribes in the Amazon basin; and, since I have found how closely the adventures of the Mouse-deer in the Malay Peninsula correspond to those of Brer Rabbit (see *Mythology of All Races*, Boston, 1916, ix. 203), and have been told of parallels in Gaelic folk-lore (unpublished as far as I know), I incline more and more to the view that the same or similar incidents may occur to people independently all over the world, and receive in each case the appropriate local setting. Of course this is not to deny the possibility of derivation in other cases.

4. The " semi-Bantu " or " Bantoid " languages, which are discussed and illustrated in Sir. H. H. Johnston's *Comparative Study of the Bantu and Semi-Bantu Languages*, may prove to be a series of connecting links which will leave the linguistic dividing-line less clear than we had supposed. Meinhof and Westermann's theory as to the origin of the Bantu languages would, if substantiated, tend in the same direction.

5. Colenso, s. v. *inkata*.

6. Roscoe, [a], p. 369.

7. D. A. Talbot, p. 157. See also two interesting letters on

this subject by Mr. James Stuart (a magistrate of many years'
experience among the Zulus) and Mr. N. W. Thomas in the
Athenæum for May 29, 1915.

8. This word is not, in South Africa, applied to unmixed " natives," such as Zulus or Basuto. Most Cape Hottentots are of
mixed blood, as a result of slavery in the past.

9. *JAS*, xii. [1913], 74.

10. Hollis, [a], p. 330. The smiths are spoken of by Hollis as
though they were Masai, but it is probable that they were originally
a distinct tribe.

11. *E. g.*, Nyanja, *mi-zimu;* Chwana, *ba-dimo;* Chaga, *wa-rimu;*
Duala, *be-dimo;* Swahili, *wa-zimu.* It is worth noting that the
same root, with a different prefix, is used to denote the monstrous
cannibals or ogres who figure in so many Bantu fairy-tales — *amazimu, madimo, mazimwi, marimu, etc.* Duala, exceptionally, uses
the same word for both.

12. Tylor, i. 328–41, where these stories are explained as nature-
myths.

13. Meinhof, [c], p. 110.

14. This, as we have seen, must not be taken too absolutely, but
it would be interesting to ascertain if, and how far, legends of the
" dreadfulness " of the Abatwa exist in parts where the earlier
population has been peaceably absorbed.

15. Ellis, [a], p. 208.

CHAPTER I

1. Ellis, [a], p. 28.
2. Rattray, [c], pp. 10, 11.
3. Taylor, [b], p. 47.
4. Irle, pp. 72, 73.
5. Dennett, [b], p. 167.
6. Rattray, [c], pp. 20, 21. Ellis spells *Nyankupon*, Rattray
Onyankopong. The diacritic marks used by the latter have not been
reproduced.
7. Torday and Joyce, pp. 20, 24, 38, 41, 120. " Bumba " is
evidently from the verb *bumba* (*umba*) used in many Bantu languages for " make," in the sense of shaping, moulding, as clay, etc.
Lubumba is the name of the Creator among the Baila and other
people living east of the Bushongo.
8. Irle, p. 73.
9. Chatelain, p. 10.
10. Dennett, [a], p. 2.

11. *Ibid.*, p. 133.

12. Smith, p. 300.

13. Macdonald, i. 59–75, esp. pp. 66–7.

14. Hetherwick, *JRAI* xxxii. [1902], 89–95.

15. Bleek, *Comparative Grammar*, § 390.

16. *Ibid.*, [a], p. 112.

17. Junod, [c], ii. 405.

18. *Ibid.*, ii. 281.

19. *Ibid.*, ii. 390.

20. *Ibid.*, ii. 392.

21. *Ibid.*, ii. 327–8.

22. Dundas, *JRAI* xliii [1913], 31.

23. Callaway, [b], pp. 7, 16, 19, etc. As to Unkulunkulu, there has never been any doubt that this means " the great, great one," being a reduplication of the root -*kulu*, " great." But why is it not " Umkulumkulu," as one would expect, for a noun of the person-class? Perhaps *inkosi* was originally understood, — *inkosi-enkulunkulu* would be " the great, great chief "; and to make this adjective into a proper name, the initial vowel alone, not the whole prefix, would be dropped and *u* substituted.

24. Literally " reed." The connection between reeds and human origins will be considered in the next chapter.

25. Van der Burgt, p. 214.

26. Roscoe, [a], p. 290f.

27. Ibid., p. 312f. That is, officially recognized under the old *régime,* prior to the introduction of Mohammedanism and Christianity.

28. Ibid., pp. 146, 313.

29. Junod, [c], ii. 281.

30. Chatelain, p. 10.

31. Torday and Joyce, p. 20.

32. Jacottet, [b], iii. 118.

33. Ibid., ii. 102.

34. Fülleborn, p. 316.

35. Jacottet, [b], iii. 118.

36. Macdonald, i. 295.

37. Orpen, quoted by A. Lang, *Myth, Ritual, and Religion,*[2] London, 1906, ii. 35f.

38. Dennett, [a], p. 74. In an Angola story (Chatelain, No. xiii) " the Sun's people " descended to earth by a spider's thread, to fetch water. Can there be a hint here of the sun's rays drawing up moisture? English country people speak of " the sun drawing water," when the rays become visible as pencils of slanting light in a cloudy sky.

39. Callaway, [a], p. 152 (*ubani ongapot 'igodi lokukupuka aye*

ezulwini?); [b], p. 56. The spider's thread or a rope or a vine as a means of ascent occurs in Polynesia, Melanesia, and Indonesia (see *Mythology of All Races*, Boston, 1916, ix. 66). Descent or ascent by a basket or cord or spider's thread occurs among American tribes, north and south (*ibid.*, x. 290; W. H. Brett, *Legends and Myths of the Aboriginal Tribes of British Guiana*, London, 1880, p. 29.)

40. Junod, [c], ii. 410; [a], p. 237, note 2.
41. *Ibid.*, [a], p. 237.
42. Callaway, [a], p. 147, and see note at end of the story.
43. Gutmann, [a], pp. 5, 6.
44. *Ibid.*, [b], p. 153. The word translated "kraal" is *itimba* in Ovir's version, which means the little pen in which lambs and kids are placed for safety during the daytime, while the flocks are grazing. Raum has *tembo*, as to the translation of which he seems doubtful. Gutmann renders it by "Hof des Mondes."
45. See *Mythology of All Races*, Boston, 1916, ix. 72, 78.
46. Gutmann, [b], p. 152.
47. *Ibid.*, pp. 149, 150.
48. See note 41, *supra*.
49. Fülleborn, p. 335.
50. Macdonald, i. 298.
51. Gutmann, [a], p. 34.
52. Cronise and Ward, p. 265.
53. Tremearne (No. 84), p. 401.
54. *Ibid.* (No. 93), p. 424.
55. Gutmann, [b], p. 132.

CHAPTER II

1. Junod, [c], ii. 280.
2. Macdonald, i. 74.
3. *Ibid.*, i. 284.
4. Torday and Joyce, p. 20.
5. *Ibid.*, p. 39.
6. Information obtained from Bwana Amiu, an old Somali trader living at Mambrui, who had had dealings with the Wasanye and knew them well. He said the tree was that called Mkupa by the Swahili and Garse (*a* pronounced almost like *u* in "but," though the Wasanye give it the broad sound of *a* in "father") by the Galla, and that it played an important part in marriage and funeral ceremonies. This last statement was confirmed by the Wasanye at Magarini.

7. Callaway, [b], pp. 9, 15, 31ff., 41.

8. *Ibid.*, pp. 15, 42.

9. Colenso, p. 213, last note, under *Hlanga* (*U*); cf. the Chwana use of the corresponding form, *lo-tlhaka*, which clearly means "a reed."

10. Callaway, [b], p. 42.

11. Casalis, [b], p. 254.

12. Junod, [c], ii. 326.

13. *SAFJ* ii. [1880], 92f.; also Irle, pp. 28, 75.

14. Casalis, [b], p. 54.

15. Quoted in Werner, p. 71; for *Kapirimtiya* see Scott, p. 215, and Macdonald, i. 279. Cf. Moffat, p. 263.

16. Stow, pp. 37, 47.

17. *Ibid.*, p. 3.

18. Hollis, [a], p. 226.

19. Irle, p. 75.

20. Hollis, [a], p. 266.

21. Stannus, *JRAI*, xliii. [1913] 121f.

22. Roscoe, [a], p. 214. Here it is only said that Kintu was "supposed" to be descended from the gods. The Galla (with whom the royal house of the Baganda is believed to have affinities) distinctly state that the progenitor of the Uta Laficho (their principal clan) came down from the sky.

23. *Manuel*, p. 149; Roscoe, [a], p. 460.

24. *Emiumbo* — i.e., bundles of plantains tied up in leaves for cooking.

25. The list includes maize and sweet potatoes, which, as they were introduced into Africa by the Portuguese only in the 16th century, must have been inserted in modern recensions of the legend.

26. Roscoe, [a], pp. 136, 214.

27. Stanley, pp. 218–220.

28. *JAS* xii. [1912–13], 363–4.

29. Hollis, [a], p. 153.

30. *Ibid.*, [b], p. 98.

31. Melland and Cholmeley, p. 21. See also the Nyanja tale of "Kachirambe" in Rattray [a] p. 133.

32. Hahn, pp. 37, 38, 48, etc.

33. *Ibid.*, p. 61; Moffat, p. 258.

34. *Ibid.*, p. 122ff.

35. Kroenlein, p. 329.

36. Schultze, p. 447.

37. Hahn, p. 61; see also pp. 65–74, 86–89, 92, and Schultze p. 448.

38. Kerr Cross in *Nyasa News*, No. 6 (Nov. 1894), p. 189; also Fülleborn, p. 316; Merensky, pp. 112, 212.

39. Melland and Cholmeley, 20.

Chapter III

1. Callaway, [b], p. 3.
2. Scott, p. 419.
3. Fülleborn, p. 15.
4. Junod, [c], ii. 328.
5. *Occasional Paper for Nyasaland*, No. 2 [1893], p. 36.
6. Taylor, [b], p. 136.
7. Macdonald, i. 288.
8. Jacottet, [b], ii. 111.
9. *Ibid.*, [b], iii. 116.
10. *Ibid.*, [b], ii. 109 (a different story from that referred to in note 8).
11. Kropf, [a], p. 156.
12. Krapf, [b], s. v. *mjisikafiri* (sic), p. 230, and *gisikafiri* (sic), p. 83.
13. Duala stories given in *MSOS* iv. [1901], 223 (*Afrikanische Studien*), cf. also, p. 181.
14. Christaller, in Büttner [a], i. 53ff.
15. *Globus*, Sept. 23, 1909, p. 174.
16. Meinhof, [b], p. 19.
17. Wundt, cited by Meinhof, [b], p. 18.
18. Meinhof, [c], p. 38. cf. *MSOS* iv. 183.
19. Bleek, [b], pp. 69–73.
20. See Schultze, pp. 147–8.
21. Lloyd, [b], p. 37.
22. Hollis, [b], p. 98.
23. For an illustration of this tube see Hollis, [b], p. 26. More ornamental ones are made by the Baganda.
24. See *Man*, xiii. [1913], 90.
25. Abarea did not say, but on reflection I think that he must have meant, that the bird was afterwards deprived of his topknot, as having proved a faithless messenger. The species of hornbill with which I am tempted to identify him, has no crest.
26. Gutmann, [a], p. 124; [b], pp. 119, 156.
27. A Masai and Nandi "burial" custom, borrowed by the Kikuyu and others. The ceremonies connected with this exposure (see Hollis, [a], p. 304, [b], p. 70). show that it is not a case of callous indifference.

28. Gutmann, [a], p. 125.

29. *Ibid.*, [a], p. 125, [b], p. 40.

30. Gutmann, [a], pp. 124–5; [b], p. 65.

31. This suggests the practice of witches (see *infra.* ch. xiv). But there is a close connection between hyenas and witches.

32. In this case it was not the woman who was to blame.

33. Roscoe, [a], p. 315 and, for Mpobe, p. 465; *Manuel*, pp. 161, 179.

34. Seidel [b], iii. (1897), p. 363: "Mugosha, bana bamwe babili ne Lirufu." With this notion of *Lirufu*, cf. M. Kingsley, p. 117: "One side of him" — a spirit supposed to haunt the Bush in Calabar, Cameroons and the Ogowe region — "is rotten and putrefying, the other sound and healthy, and it all depends on which side of him you touch whether you see the dawn again or no."

35. Chatelain, pp. 95, 225, 274 (note 251), 304, 308.

36. *Ibid.*, p. 249, cf. also p. 223, story of "King Kitamba kia Xiba."

37. *Ibid.*, pp. 11, 274 (note 245), 283–4.

38. Thomann, pp. 134, 138, 143.

39. "Tom Tit Tot," "Rumpelstilzchen," etc. The motive occurs in a Jamaica story given by Jekyll, p. 11 (cf. also "Mr. Titman" in Smith, p. 20), but this is probably of European origin.

Chapter IV

1. See Kingsley, especially chapters 5 to 9; Spieth and Ellis, *passim*.

2. Raum, pp. 334 ff. Cf. Gutmann, [a], pp. 142–7.

3. Gutmann, [b], p. 152.

4. *Mzimu* or *mu-zimu* as a locative appears to be used in Swahili for a place in which offerings are made to the spirits (see Krapf, s. v.). *Zimwi* (originally *li-zimwi*, and therefore cognate with Zulu *i-zimu*, Sutu *le-dimo*) means a kind of ogre or demon, like the *irimu* of the Wachaga, Wakikuyu, etc. The word is more or less obsolete in ordinary Swahili, having been replaced by the imported *shetani* or *jini*.

5. See Callaway, [b], p. 148, note. Perhaps the meaning may be "people of our stock" ("seed"), see *i-dlozi* in Kropf's *Kaffir Dictionary*.

6. In Swahili, the names of animals, whatever their grammatical form — they usually have the ninth prefix or its equivalent — are given the concords of the person-class. In some languages, while

retaining their own class in the singular, they are given a special plural prefix.

7. Werner, p. 46.

8. Callaway, [b], p. 144.

9. Raum, p. 338.

10. Gutmann, [a], p. 129.

11. *Ibid.*, [b], pp. 104, 131–2.

12. *Ibid.*, [a], p. 130.

13. Casalis, [b], p. 261.

14. Callaway, [a], p. 318.

15. *Ibid.*, p. 317.

16. Obst, in *Mitteilungen aus den deutschen Schutzgebieten*, ii [1900], 130.

17. Melland, p. 24.

18. Gutmann, [b], p. 105, etc.

19. Raum, p. 336.

20. Gutmann, [b], p. 107.

21. *Ibid.*, [a], pp. 169ff.

22. Raum, p. 336.

23. *Ibid.*, *loc. cit.*

24. Gutmann, [b], p. 109.

25. *Ibid.*, p. 106.

26. *Ibid.*, *loc. cit.*

27. Velten, [c], p. 180.

28. Scott, p. 416.

29. Junod, [b], p. 387.

30. *Ibid.*, [c], ii. 350.

31. *Ibid.*, ii. 379.

32. *Ibid.*, ii. 356, 358.

33. Scott, *s.v. nkalango*, p. 450.

34. *Strychnos sp.*

35. Junod, [b], p. 305.

36. *Ibid.*, pp. 385, 388.

37. Rehse, p. 388.

38. Junod, [c], ii. 359.

39. See Meinhof, [b], p. 18.

40. Callaway, [b], p. 142.

41. *Ibid.*, p. 198.

42. Macdonald, i. 62.

43. Callaway, [b], p. 199.

44. Junod, [c], ii. 312, 358.

45. Callaway, [b], p. 215.

CHAPTER V

1. Gutmann, [b], p. 104.

2. Some of these stories, relating rather to an upper than an under world, have already been mentioned in Chap. 1.

3. Junod, [a], p. 264; but see his note on this story.

4. Callaway, [a], p. 331.

5. Tylor, i. 338.

6. Callaway, [a], p. 296.

7. As we shall see in Chapter XIV, certain animals (or familiar spirits in their shape?) are employed as messengers by witches. The leopard is certainly counted as one of these in Nyasaland — though not so prominent as the owl and the hyena; and this is given as a reason why the Zulus never mention his proper name, *ingwe*, in ordinary conversation — calling him *isilo* "(*the*) wild beast," *par excellence*. At the same time, *Isilo* was a title of the Zulu kings and (as in Uganda) no one outside the royal house might wear or use a leopard-skin. See also (for the Lower Congo), Dennett [a], p. 69. Is there any connection between these two ideas? or do they belong to entirely separate streams of tradition?

8. A legend attached to a ruined site, near Kipini, called *Kwa Waanawali Sabaa*, relates how seven little maids, pursued by Galla raiders, called to God for help, when the earth opened and swallowed them up. (Information obtained on the spot in 1912.)

9. This "False Bride" motive recurs in various African stories; a good example (combined with the "Holle" motive) is the tale of the Kirondovo in Gutmann, [a], pp. 34–6.

10. Grimm, *Kinder- und Hausmärchen*, No. 24, with some (not all) of the variants enumerated in Bolte and Polívka, i. 207ff; Hausa, "The Ill-Treated Maiden," Tremearne, p. 426; Temne, "The Devil's Magic Eggs," Cronise and Ward, p. 265.

11. J. Grimm, *Deutsche Mythologie*, Göttingen, 1835, p. 164, etc. English variants of the Holle story in Halliwell-Phillips, p. 39, J. Jacobs, *English Fairy Tales*, London, 1890, No. 43, *More English Fairy Tales*, *Ib.*, No. 64; West India, in Smith, p. 31, "Mother Calbee."

12. Gutmann, [b], p. 117, Nos. 63, 68; Junod, [a], p. 237.

13. Co-wives, in "Three Women," p. 110; in Chaga tale, Gutmann, [a], pp. 34–6; Duala, in Lederbogen, *MSOS* vi. [1904], 82; Konde, a tale mentioned by Fülleborn, p. 335.

14. Tremearne, p. 401.

15. "Kgolodikane," *SAFJ* i. [1879], 110.

16. Notes 9 and 13, *supra*.

17. Gutmann, [b], p. 118.
18. See Note 16, to Chapter IV.
19. Gutmann, [b], p. 110, cf. also [a], p. 36.
20. Probably a tabu affecting one returned from the spirit-world.
21. Zimmermann, i. 163, cf. "Candoo" in Smith, p. 28.
22. This no doubt refers to the retribution which was to follow disobedience. But it is not clear why, after coming to pieces and being restored to life, Anansi should be let off with a beating after his second transgression. Perhaps the incident is intended to account for the spider's patched and mottled appearance.
23. *SAFJ*, i. [1879], 75.
24. Wolff, p. 135.
25. Chatelain, p. 127.

Chapter VI

1. Cf. *Mythology of All Races*, Boston, 1916, x. 255, 298.
2. Junod, [c], ii. 327–8, see also pp. 279–80; Merensky, in *Mitteilungen der geogr. Gesellschaft zu Jena*, vi. [1888], 111–4; Meinhof, [b], p. 33; [c], p. 117.
3. Callaway, [a], pp. 3–40.
4. Macdonald, i. 297.
5. Chatelain, p. 131, "The Son of Kimanaueze," especially pp. 133, 141.
6. Dennett, [a], pp. 7, 74. For Duala, see Lederbogen in *MSOS* iv. [1902], pt. 3, *passim*.
7. Rehse, pp. 134, 371. Ryang'ombe, the "Eater of Cattle," seems to be known also among the Bahima (Roscoe, [b], p. 134, speaks of "the fetish Lyagombe"), the Warundi (Van der Burgt, p. 216), and the Wanyaruanda (*idem.*, and P. Loupias in *Anthropos*, iii. [1908], 6). Van der Burgt explains his name as meaning possibly "celui qui coupe les cordes du prisonnier"; he is the chief of departed spirits (so also Rehse, p. 134), and was once a man, but after his death took up his abode in the Kirunga volcano. As the word *ng'ombe* is still used for "cattle" in Kiziba, where also the legend of his ox-eating exploits (on the day of his birth!) is current, but not among the other peoples named, it is possible that his name and cult were adopted by the latter, while the meaning of the name and perhaps of the legend was forgotten. It is remarkable that, while Rehse says his cult in Kiziba is confined to the Bahima (the Hamitic ruling race who came in from the north), in Ruanda, according to P. Loupias, the royal family (with one exception expressly mentioned) and high chiefs are never initiated into his mysteries,

which belong to the Bahutu, the Bantu people previously in occupation.

8. Dempwolff in Ehrenreich, iv. 249, Rattray, [a], p. 133; Macdonald, ii. 336.

9. A hyena in two cases, which is no doubt the earlier form of the incident. In the Nyanja version (Rattray, [a], pp. 54, 133) there is an unexplained peculiarity; a girl finds a hyena's egg and carries it home to her mother, who puts it into the fire. The Hyena comes to demand the egg and has to be appeased with the promise of the unborn child. I have come across no other reference to the eggs of the hyena, though there seems to be a widespread idea that its reproductive organs are abnormal.

10. Hahn, p. 134; Schultze, p. 447.

11. Hahn, pp. 65–7; Bleek, [b], pp. 77, 78–9; Meinhof, [a], pp. 172–7; Schultze, p. 447.

12. Meinhof, [a], p. 177.

13. Hahn, p. 66; Bleek, [b], p. 77; Schultze, pp. 448, 450.

14. Bleek, [b], p. 78.

15. Hahn, pp. 85, 86, 92.

16. Schultze, p. 450.

17. Meinhof, [a], p. 172.

18. Probably it is a hole dug in a sandy river-bed during the dry season, when the water trickles out so slowly that it takes a long time to secure a supply.

19. Hahn, pp. 42, 43, 45, etc., and references there given to Kolbe and others.

20. Bleek, [b], p. 80; Meinhof, [a], p. 174. The berries called "wild raisins" are the fruits of a shrub called by the Herero *omuvapu*.

21. Properly ! Uriseb (with cerebral click and high tone on first syllable), also spelled Urisib and Urisip. It is symptomatic of the chaotic state into which Hottentot traditions have fallen, that Schultze's informants make Uriseb the son of Gã-gorib, the "Thruster-down," whom, as a matter of fact, they only mention as "Uriseb's father" (p. 448). There is also considerable confusion between Tsui-Goab and Haitsi-aibeb, if the two are not identical, as Hahn thinks.

22. Junod, [c], ii. 327–8.

23. Merensky, "Till Eulenspiegel in Afrika," in *Mitteilungen der geogr. Gesellschaft zu Jena*, vi. [1888], 111f.

24. Callaway, [a], p. 3.

25. *Ibid.*, pp. 37–40. This story is elsewhere given to the hare (for variants see *FL* xv. [1909], 344; *African Monthly*, vii. [1910] 247). Since writing the article in the latter I have discovered several

other versions, notably a Hottentot one (Schultze, p. 415), and " The
Hare's Hoe," to which Junod ([c], ii. 223) says he knows of no
African parallel.   The existence of well-marked Berber and South
European variants seems to point to its having come into Africa from
the Mediterranean region, and to have been adapted by the natives
in some cases (not in all) to the myth of their favourite animal.
Thus the Hottentot, the European, and the Berber versions make
the protagonist a human being or the jackal; the Bantu usually tell it
of the hare, though sometimes of a boy (Luyi), a girl (Herero), an
old woman (Bena-Kanioka), or a man (Nyasaland, Elmslie, *FL* iii.
[1892], 92), and West Africans of the spider, cf. Tremearne, pp.
237, 367, 380, and reff. there given; Schultze, p. 415.

26. Rehse, p. 155.

27. Baumann, [b], p. 186.

28. Tylor, ii. 335f.

29. See Breysig, pp. 10, 17, etc.

30. Jacottet,[c], p. 70, another version, p. 76; see also [a], p. 204,
and Casalis, [a], p. 97.

31. Cf. Khwai-hemm of the Bushmen (*infra*, p. 289); Isiququmadevu und Usilosimapundu of the Zulus (Callaway [a], pp. 34,
86, 184); Seedimwe of the Subiya (Jacottet, [b], ii. 54, 61, 67), etc.
In Kikuyu (Routledge, p. 309) the Swallower is the Rainbow.

32. Junod, [a], p. 201; cf. also Kachirambe (Rattray, [a],
p. 133).

33. Breysig, p. 12.

34. Thomann, p. 145.

35. A *pumpkin* of similar character is found in a Shambala tale
(Seidel, [b], p. 174), in Swahili (*Kibaraka*, p. 25), and in Hausa
(Rattray, [b], pp. 300, etc.).

36. Similarly, Kalikalanje (Macdonald, ii. 339) kills his mother,
after destroying the demon Namzimu.

CHAPTER VII

1. Schultze, p. 387.

2. Breysig, pp. 18f., 39; for Marduk, pp. 105, 108,

3. Meinhof, [b], p. 20, see also p. 17.

4. Spieth, in *Abhandlungen des deutschen Kolonialkongresses,*
for 1905, p. 504.

5. S. Reinisch, *Sitzungsberichte der philos. histor. Klasse der Kais.
Akad. der Wissenchaften in Wein,* cxlviii. [1904], Abh. v. 93, cited
by Meinhof, [b], p. 17.

6. Lloyd, [b], p. 67.

7. *Ibid.*, pp. 38, 53.

8. Bleek, [c], p. 9; Lloyd, [b], pp. 38-9, 51, 53.

9. Lloyd, [b], p. 399.

10. Barnes, p. 111.

11. Taylor, [b], p. 97.

12. Bentley, pp. 161, 381.

13. *Ibid.*, p. 370.

14. Hahn, pp. 23, 43, 74, etc.

15. Plural of *Kimia* = Swahili *Kilimia*, "the hoeing star," from *lima*, "hoe." The name is almost universal among Bantu tribes, from the Tana to the Great Fish River. The Pokomo and the Yaos, and possibly a few others, make the word a plural: the group is generally treated as one body.

16. Lloyd, [b], pp. 85-98. Bleek, [c], p. 11, gives a somewhat different version, quoted in Lloyd, p. 96. The two versions have been combined in the text.

17. Torrend, p. 314; Theal, [a], pp. 56-66, [b], p. 323.

18. Lloyd, [b], pp. 73ff.

19. Gutmann [a], p. 149.

20. Lloyd, [b], pp. 45-55.

21. Hollis, [b], p. 97.

22. Gutmann, [a], p. 178. Ellis ([b], p. 65) records a similar notion of the Ewe, but it is possible that he misunderstood his informants, as nothing is said of it in Spieth's more recent work, based on much fuller material.

23. Gutmann, [a], p. 177. For greeting of new moon, see Taylor, [b], pp. 49, 63. (Giryama); Van der Burgt, p. 235 (Warundi); Dennett, [a], p. 7.

24. Gutmann, [a], p. 180, [b], p. 144.

25. Dennett, [b], pp. 113, 142.

26. Spieth, p. 533; Ellis, [b], pp. 47-9. For a Hausa tradition, see Fletcher, p. 94.

27. Cf. Dahse in *ZE* xliii. [1911], 46-56.

28. Jacottet, [b], ii. 146, cf. also for Luyi, iii. 139.

29. Callaway, [a], pp. 293-5.

30. Gutmann, [b], p. 153, "Der durchhauene Regenbogen."

31. Routledge, p. 308.

32. *Ibid.*, p. 309.

33. Jacottet, [c], p. 56, and note on p. 58.

34. Callaway, [b], p. 383, cf. *Mythology of All Races*, Boston, 1916, x. 287f.

35. Rehse, pp. 129, 146. Kayurankuba is said to be a son of the lake-spirit Mugasha (apparently identical with the Mukasa of the

Baganda). According to some, Kayurankuba causes thunder by striking the rocks (with his spear?). Cf. the legend given by Rehse, p. 329.

36. Hewat, p. 91.

37. Gutmann, [a], p. 178.

38. Dennett, [a], p.7; the story given below is also referred to in [b], p. 119.

39. Gutmann, [b], p. 149, and the curious legend in Rehse, p. 388.

40. Dennett, [b], p. 120.

41. *Ibid.*, [a], pp. 133–4.

42. See pp. 117, 118, 132, *supra*.

43. Hollis [a], pp. xix, 264–5, cf. p. 278. Merker, however, (p. 197), says that the expressions *Ng'ai nanjugi* and *Ng'ai narok* are not to be taken in the sense given in the text, but really mean, "the divine red" and the "divine black" (or "blue"), being applied to the red of sunrise and sunset, and to the cloudless sky. "Tatsächlich sehen die Leute in diesen Erscheinungen keine Götter, auch nichts Gott ähnliches oder gleich ihm zu verehrendes." At the same time he admits that God is often called *Ng'ai narok* in prayers, but the Masai themselves are unable to explain this epithet. Thunder and lightning, according to this authority, are not independent beings, but the phenomena produced by Ng'ai's eldest son, *Ol gurugur*, who thus "verkündet . . . dass Gott den Menschen wegen ihres schlechten Betragens grollt, und ermahnt sie zugleich zur Besserung." Barsai, Ng'ai's eldest daughter, is responsible for the rain, which is a sign that God is well pleased with the state of things on earth. Others have taken Ng'ai as a personification of rain.

44. Lloyd, p. xv.

45. Steere, *SAFJ*, i. [1879], 121.

46. Swahili sea-lore, of course, is largely borrowed from the Arabs and perhaps from Indonesia, whence came the outrigger canoe and, no doubt, the coconut. There are some mysterious beings: Makame, — whose rock is at the back of Mombasa Island, between the Indian burning-ghat and Mzizima — and Sheikh Manamana, to whom boatmen make offerings as they pass, throwing some trifle into the water. I have not been able to discover anything about Makame of Mombasa, but a legend (too vaguely and fragmentarily heard to be recorded) about a similar person near the north point of Zanzibar Island, suggests that he was originally a drowned man. The sea is called Mbu by the Congo Bavili (Dennett, [a], p. 8; [b], pp. 114, 123) and its indwelling spirit (who is also the North Wind) Chikamasi.

47. See pp. 126, 179, *supra*.

CHAPTER VIII

1. Klamroth, " Die religiösen Vorstellungen der Saramo," *ZKS* i. [1910], 37, 118, 189. A most valuable document.

2. Spieth, p. 684.

3. A. Werner, " Pokomo Folk-lore," *FL* xxiv. [1913], 469–72.

4. By a writer in *Blackwood's Magazine*, November, 1917, who, however, calls the creature *ngoloko*. (This name I heard applied, by the Pokomo, to a certain fabulous serpent of gigantic size. See the above-quoted paper in *FL* p. 467.) The writer of the article was shown a curious footprint alleged to be that of the " *ngoloko* "; but I learn from a correspondent that a European who had seen a tracing made from this footprint pronounced it to be that of an ostrich, and this is confirmed from the testimony of another person, who had himself examined the footprint. A Swahili correspondent at Lamu writes: " As to the Ngoloko, it is true: the Lamu people call him by the name of *milhoi*; people sometimes see him, and the man who sees him — if the *milhoi* does not succeed in killing him — loses his senses. The *milhoi* is tall and has one leg like that of an ass." If he meets a man, he begins by asking him the names of all his relations, and then, if he stands still in astonishment, he strikes him with his claw. But if you recognise him in time, you can put him to flight by threatening to strike him with a saw — the only thing he fears. (The reason for this is that he has seen huge trees sawn through in the forest and cannot understand how so small an instrument produces so great an effect — a touch of actuality which must have been introduced in recent times.) The writer goes on to say that he knows an old man at Witu, who has seen and wrestled with the *milhoi* (this, not explicitly stated elsewhere, is a point of contact with *Chiruwi*) and lost his senses in consequence. " And in the books of Islam there is the account of him: they say he originated with the *jinn* who ascended to heaven to listen to the voices of the angels " [the MS. has "of the *jinn*," but I feel sure this is a clerical error], " and were struck down with *zimwondo* " [presently explained to be shooting stars] " by the angels." (See also Steere, 1884, p. 240, s. v. *milhoi*.) Of course this account is coloured by various — no doubt partly literary — influences.

5. Hollis, [a], pp. 127, 265.

6. Schultze, p. 392.

7. *Ibid.*, pp. 404, 448.

8. Taylor, [b], p. 32.

9. *FL* xxiv. 472.

10. Scott, p. 97.

11. Krapf, [b], pp. 162, 387.

12. Colenso, p. 592; Kidd, [a], p. 127.

13. Chatelain, p. 91. For one-legged beings in Celtic folk-lore (the *Fachan*), see J. F. Campbell, *Popular Tales of the West Highlands*, Edinburgh, 1890, iv. 298. For Melanesian one-legged beings see C. E. Fox and F. H. Drew, *JRAI* xlv. [1915], 188.

14. MS. notes.

15. Scott, *ubi supra*; Macdonald, i. 71; Stannus in *Man*, xv. [1915], 132.

16. Smith, pp. 284, 457.

17. Jacottet, [b], ii. 138, cf. p. 122.

18. Junod, [a], p. 197, and [b], pp. 291, 313, 363; also Callaway, [a], p. 199 and note; Tremearne, pp. 123, 212, 401, 454; Chatelain, pp. 32, 254, 279, 334 note; Irle, p. 76; Fülleborn, pp. 55, 335; Cronise and Ward, pp. 21, 179. For Mugasha, the one-legged lake-spirit of the Baziba, see Rehse, pp. 129, 146.

19. Jacottet, [a], p. 246 (and note), [c], p. 160. With this story it is interesting to compare that of "Mbukwana's Wife and Daughter," in Junod, [b], p. 241, and that of "Umxakaza-Wakogingqwayo" in Callaway (where the Half-men are called *Amadhlungundhlebe*).

20. See Jacottet's note on "*Hase fuhlaele fu, ha u na tema fu*," [c], p. 164: He gives up this sentence as unintelligible, but the clue supplied by his rendering of the latter half, together with the hint that "the words are probably meant to be Zulu," suggested the conjectural equivalent given in the text.

21. See Colenso, p. 705, s. v., and Bryant, p. 756 (*uMdava*).

22. P. 118, note 11, and p. 181, note 4, *supra*.

23. Gutmann [b], p. 73, No. 37, "Der wandelnde Dornbusch." The following tales, Nos. 38–45, deal with the Irimu in his various manifestations: in some of them he shows affinity with the Werewolf. One remarkable point (p. 75) is the possession of a second mouth at the back of the head. This feature is known to the Baronga (Junod, [a], p. 257), and something like it is attributed to witches by the Hausa (Tremearne, pp. 154, 425, 433).

24. *Watoto na Zimwi*, in *Kibaraka*, p. 25. Variants: *Tselane*, Jacottet, [a], p. 69, and [c], p. 62; *Usitungu-sobenhle*, Callaway, [a], p. 74; *Demana and Demazana* and "The Cannibal's Wonderful Bird," Theal, [a], pp. 111, 125; "The Child and the Drum" (Gazaland), Kidd, [b], p. 233; *Kgolodikane* (Chwana), *SAFJ* i. [1879], 110; a Herero one recorded by Büttner under the title "Die alte Frau welche die Kinder in den Sack steckt," *ZAS* i. [1887], 189; Duala, Lederbogen in *MSOS* (Afrikanische Studien)

vi. [1903], 78 ("Der Mädchen und der Mann") and numerous others. The Hausa "Mender of Men" (Tremearne, p. 401) resembles these in its opening incident: some girls, picking herbs in the forest, take refuge from a shower in a hollow baobab-tree; the Devil (here called "Iblisi," — an Islamized conception) closes the tree and refuses to let any of them out unless she gives him her cloth and her necklace. All do this, except one, who accordingly remains imprisoned, but is fed through a hole by her mother. Here the tale coincides with "Tselane" (the reason for the girl's being shut up alone is more intelligible than in the latter), and the Hyena who is subsequently introduced behaves exactly like the *Ledimo* cannibal, except that he eats his victim on the spot instead of carrying her round in a bag. The sequel, relating how the mother took her daughter's bones to "the City where Men were Mended," brings the story into the "Holle" group.

25. Cronise and Ward, pp. 172, 178. The first of these introduces the "Debble" as the Swallower (cf. *Kholumodumo*, etc.), with the additional details that he can only be split open by an enchanted thorn, and that an old woman among the people released insisted on going back for her possessions and perished in consequence. The "debble" in three other stories (pp. 152, 160, 167), while less certainly identifiable with the *izimu*, is sufficiently curious; his power of shape-shifting is a conspicuous feature, and in one he assumes the form of a bearded stone which causes every passer-by making audible remarks on its peculiarity, to fall down unconscious.

26. Routledge, pp. 315, 324.

27. Gutmann, [b], p. 73.

28. *Ibid.*, p. 87, No. 44, "Die Frau des Rimu."

29. In the variant given by Raum, the wife accidentally discovers his cannibal propensities, by going into his compartment with a lighted torch. Here the *Irimu* is a hyena, and a genuine *versipellis*, for every night, he says, "Skin, turn inside out!" and becomes a hyena. Every morning, at dawn, he says, "Hair, turn inward!" and becomes a man. The Were-Hyena will reappear in Chapter XIV.

30. No explanation is given of how she escaped: it would seem from what has gone before that a knowledge of the password would not avail to open the rock from the *inside*. Perhaps some detail has been omitted by the narrator. The device by which discovery is delayed (the original crudity has been softened in the text) not infrequently occurs in African tales, and is well known in European folklore. Sometimes, by way of euphemism, the fugitive is made to spit on the threshold, the hearth-stone, etc, with the results indicated above.

31. Gutmann, [b], p. 92.

32. Apparently growing wild — an abnormal occurrence, for though a wild banana-tree is not uncommon in some parts of Africa, it never bears fruit. In Nyasaland it is called *msorokoto* (while the cultivated banana-plant is *mtochi*), and the children collect its black, shining seeds to string into necklaces.

33. *Supra*, p. 250. Cf. also the story of " Sultan Darai " in Steere's *Swahili Tales*, where a pumpkin or cucumber-plant springs up from the dead mother's grave. Here, however, the connection between the plant and the deceased is not immediate.

34. Jacottet, [c], p. 4.

CHAPTER IX

1. Taylor, [b], p. 32.
2. Beech, in *Man* xv. [1915], 40.
3. Krapf, [b], s. v. *Mbilikimo*, p. 214.
4. Taylor, [b], p. 35.
5. Johnston, [a], p. 53.
6. Stannus, in *Man* xv. [1915], 131.
7. Callaway, [a], pp. 352–5. Much the same account was given to Chatelain (pp. 269–70) of the Batwa in Angola. In the text Callaway translates the word given as " arrow " by " bow," but the original is *ngomcibitsholo*. It is worth noting that the bow is an essentially Bushman weapon, and that this word for " arrow," containing a click and having no recognisable Bantu analogue, probably belongs to the Bushman language.
8. F. Boyle, *The Savage Life*, London, 1876, p. 36.
9. Torrend, p. xv.
10. Rosen, pp. 88ff. In the Pokomo language *h* corresponds to the cerebral *t* of Swahili: thus, *-tatu*, " three," becomes *-hahu*. These same people are called *Wat* by the Galla. This word cannot be supposed to have any connection with *Wa-twa*, unless it were the original form and the Bantu had mistaken the initial *Wa* for a prefix. But this is a question of etymology, which has no place here.
11. Van der Burgt, p. 4.
12. Torday and Joyce, pp. 22, 39, 52.
13. Gutmann, [a], p. 6.
14. *Ibid.*, [b], p. 131, No. 81.
15. *Ibid.*, [b], p. 132, No. 83.
16. *Ibid.*, [b], p. 131, No. 82. Neither of these last says anything about the big heads of the dwarfs, who seem to have in all respects the appearance of ordinary children.
17. Junod, [c], ii. 405.

18. Macdonald, i. 291.

19. Jacottet, [b], ii. 141, gives a Subiya account of the Tulala-Madindi, "those who sleep in holes"—a race of pygmies much like those described in the text, but with a physiological peculiarity, not elsewhere mentioned: they live only on the juices of meat, and their digestive arrangements are unlike those of ordinary human beings. In a note to this passage (p. 142), he mentions a Basuto legend of the little men called *Lujara Marete*, who are described as asking the usual question, "Where did you see me first?" Jacottet demurs to Chatelain's account, as the Little People are never cannibals, and the Amazimu never small.

CHAPTER X

1. Frazer, i. 1.

2. See Livingstone, p. 12: "The different Bechuana tribes are named after certain animals. . . . They also use the word 'bina,' to dance, in reference to the custom of thus naming themselves, so that, when you wish to ascertain what tribe you belong to, you say, 'What do you dance?'" He does not further mention the dances, which, no doubt, were intended to influence the totems.

3. Frazer, iv. 4.

4. Roscoe, [a], p. 320.

5. Dundas, *JRAI* xliii. [1913], 66.

6. *Ibid.*, p. 32.

7. Ellis, [b], p. 100, cf. pp. 71, 74.

8. Gutmann, [a], pp. 37–44.

9. MS., written out for me (in the "Nyika" dialect of the Warabai) by a native teacher at Kisulutini. I heard a similar story being related to my porters by an old woman at Fundi Isa, but was not able to take it down. A variant, in which the sexes are reversed, is given by Velten ([b], p. 71) under the title "Geschichte von Sultanssohn der ein Affenkind heiratete." The ape-maiden's tail is taken charge of by her grandmother, who magnanimously says, "I will wear two tails, that she may become a human being and we may be saved." When she becomes proud and refuses to feed or recognise her relations, the grandmother returns at the head of the clan and hands over the tail in the face of the Sultan's family.

10. Gutmann, [a], p. 38.

11. Hollis, [b], p. 6.

12. Junod, [c], i. 336.

13. Junod, "Le chat de Titichane," [a], p. 253, "Le gambadeur de la plaine," [b], p. 353, also [c], i. 338.

14. Frazer, iv. 52–55, see also i. 125, ii. 293, 552, 561, iii. 451.

15. Possibly we are to understand that he was invisible by day, as the husband, when watching the gardens at night, sees and shoots him. It is to be noted that the failure of the wife's incantations is only final when dawn appears before the totem is completely resuscitated.

16. Mansfeld, pp. 220–3.

17. Hollis, [b], p. 8.

18. Where two totems are mentioned, the clan has been sub-divided.

19. Bentley, p. 353, s. v. *mpangu*.

20. Macdonald, ii. 366. The title of this story, " The Girl that refused a Husband," and its opening sentences belong to an entirely different one and have no connection with what follows.

21. Junod, [a], pp. 138–42.

22. Wolff, pp. 120, 132. There is a totemic touch, also, in Uvwikeve (*Ib.*, pp. 112, 132) where directions are given not to kill the lice on an infant's head, on the ground that they are " its soul " (*ntima gwa mwere*). I have not, so far, come across a louse totem.

23. An even better illustration is the story of Unyandemula (Wolff, pp. 123, 145), where the girl, who has run away from home after being punished by her parents, is swept off by a flooded river and discovered in the way mentioned above, when her younger sister comes to fetch water. She is restored to her home through the agency of a witch, who warns the parents that she must on no account be scolded, or she will turn into water — which ultimately happens. This is a link with the European group of " Undine " stories; cf. also the Xosa " Tangalomlibo " (Torrend, p. 314; McCall Theal, p. 56). We are also reminded of the numerous legends in which totem-ancestresses, on being reproached with their origin, resume their former shape and are lost to their husbands. The Twi legend referred to in Chapter I shows quite clearly the totemic character which is quite obscured in the cases given in the text.

24. Weeks, p. 361.

25. Johnston, [c], ii. 921.

26. Chatelain, pp. 157, 183, 197, 209.

27. Jacottet, [c], p. 32, note.

28. Merker, pp. 214–5.

29. Hollis, [a], p. 107.

30. Harris, [a], p. 61.

31. Meinhof, [b], pp. 29, 30.

32. E.g. Cronise and Ward, p. 296.

33. I.e. in the tales, as distinct from his place in the myth already

discussed. He sometimes wins a race by a trick, in a variant of the famous Hare and Tortoise (the European Hare and Hedgehog) story. He is also found in Ronga stories (cf. Junod, [a], pp. 89 117, 136).

34. See Junod, [a], p. 87, and further, "L'Épopée de la Rainette," p. 109. This frog is locally called *chinana*. I have seen it at Blantyre, in the Shire Highlands, where the Anyanja call it *chiswenene* or *kaswenene* (the ordinary frog is *chule*), but never heard of its figuring in folk-tales.

35. The Parrot (Fang), the Crowned Crane (Zambezi), the Honey-guide (Ila), the Dog (Benga and Duala), the Gorilla (Mpongwe), the Zebra, the Swallow, etc.

36. Theal, [b], p. 275.

37. Junod, "Le petit détesté," [a], p. 170.

38. Nassau, "Borrowed Clothes," [b], p. 198.

39. Related in conversation by Dr. Sanderson of Nyasaland.

40. It seems clear, from Stow's account (pp. 32, 33), that the Bushmen had totems. Each tribe had its "emblem" (e.g., the Python, Eland, Rhinoceros, Elephant, Ostrich, etc.), "conspicuously painted in some central part of the great cave of the chief of the clan." Stow does not mention the Mantis among these "emblems" — but he may have outgrown the status of a mere clan totem; and he appears to be represented in some of the cave-paintings.

41. I have heard the same term used for a butterfly — I think at Lamu. The Mantis is also called *vunda-jungu*, "break the pot."

42. Junod, [c], ii. 312.

43. *Ibid.*, p. 358.

44. Hahn, pp. 42, 45, and reff. there given.

45. Kidd, [a], p. 183; [b], p. 210.

46. By the Anyanja, and the Swahili (see above, Note 41). The Giryama call it "break the bow" (*vundza uha*), probably with some similar notion. But the Zulu *isitwalambiza* simply means "the pot-carrier," from the attitude of the forelegs, which are raised as though carrying a burden, or — as the European prefers it — as if praying. (One of my earliest recollections is being told that the people near Trieste used to say the mantis was "praying for rain.")

47. Bleek, [c], pp. 6–9; Lloyd, [a], p. 5; Bleek in his 1873 Report, gives a list of twenty-four texts relating to the Mantis, most of which, unfortunately, are still unpublished. For Orpen's account of the Maluti Bushmen's "Cagn" (not apparently recognised as the Mantis), see his article in *Cape Monthly Magazine*, July, 1874, and Bleek's comments thereon.

48. Lloyd, [b], p. 53.

49. Bleek [c], pp. 6–9.

50. A. Lang "Natural Theology," in *Ballades in Blue China*, London, 1883, p. 108.

51. Lloyd, [b], pp. 3–15.

52. *Ibid.*, pp. 23–33.

53. Lloyd, [a], p. 5.

54. Bleek, [c], p. 9.

CHAPTER XI

1. Lloyd, [b], p. 61.

2. Junod, [b], p. 280.

3. Cf. Junod, [a], pp. 89, 90.

4. Beech, p. 58; cf. Krapf, [b], p. 152. "Kipanawazi(*sic*), a kind of hare. The Kipanawazi is believed by the Mohammedans to ferry souls over a river. It will ask them who has beaten it with a *muiko* [*mwiko*, wooden spoon] . . . and will then say *a-ku-pindusha* [he overturns you]." The above is sufficiently obscure, and I have never come across any other reference to this belief. But *mwiko* also means "a taboo," and possibly the meaning is that the infringement of such would upset the ferryman's boat.

5. E.g., the order to produce eggs; the building of a house in the air, etc.

6. Jacottet, [c], p. 33.

7. Hollis, [a], p. 107.

8. There does not seem to be any rabbit, properly so called, indigenous to Africa, though there are several species of hares, and possibly one or more of these may have intermediate characteristics. It is curious that, in some stories (i.e., a Giryama one printed by Taylor), we hear of the Hare having "a house with several entrances," which can only be a burrow. It is possible that the animal meant in these cases is that known in South Africa as the "Jumping Hare" (*Pedetes caffer: Springhaas* of the Boers), which is not really a hare at all, and "constructs complex burrows in which several families live together" (Lydekker). The "Steppenhase" (Gutmann), *Kilyo-dang'a* of the Wachaga, who attribute to him most of the usual hare stories, may be an East African species of *Pedetes*.

9. Madan, p. 57.

10. Campbell, ii. App. viii. p. 365. The seven "Bootchuana" tales here given are described as "absurd and ridiculous fictions, presented to the notice of the reader only because they exhibit, in a striking manner, the puerile and degraded state of intellect among the natives of South Africa." The source of the tales is not indicated, and it is clear from the style that they are not exact translations of

native texts.   Those which are versions of well-known tales have
some interesting variations, suggesting that some features of older
tales have been preserved.

11. Junod, [a], pp. 90–109.

12. So Hlakanyana makes a whistle out of the Hare's bones; and
the Hare, in one Suto version (see Jacottet, [c], p. 16 note), from
those of the " Rabbit " (*hlolo*).   In Jacottet's version of the latter,
the Hare steals a flute belonging to a frog.   There seems to be a
reminiscence of this in the " quills " which Brer Tarrypin made out
of " de big een er Brer Buzzard's wing-fedders " (Harris, [b], No.
14, end), and on which he played a triumphant air.   Cf. also the
following story (No. 15), " Brother Fox Covets the Quills."

13. So, with the Baganda (*Manuel*, p. 279), the Hare induces the
Elephant to let him cut slices of flesh from his thighs, so that he can
dance more easily.

14. It is a common trick of the Hare to raise the alarm of war and
then rob the gardens; cf. Macdonald, ii. 332 (Yao), and a Makua
version (MS.) obtained from Archdeacon Woodward.

15. The Tar-Baby incident occurs in other connections, but this
is the most frequent.

16. Cf. Jacottet, [c], p. 26, and the references there given; also
Harris, [b], No. 20, p. 102, " Brother Rabbit takes some Exercise."
This theme occurs in European folk-lore as " Chicken-Licken "
(Halliwell-Phillips, p. 29; R. Chambers, *Popular Rhymes of
Scotland*, Edinburgh, 1847, p. 211).

17. See Harris, [a], No. 17, " Mr. Rabbit Nibbles Up the Butter."

18. *Ibid.*, No. 12, " Mr. Fox Tackles Old Man Tarrypin."

19. The Baronga — at least the men of full age — wear head-
rings like those of the Zulus, but brightly polished, whereas the Zulus
consider a dull lustre the correct thing.   The material is either beeswax
or a kind of gum found on mimosa trees, which is plastered over a
ring made of plaited grass or bullock's sinews.   Similar naïve attempts
at disguise (invariably successful) are removing the skin (frequent in
Nyanja stories), cutting off the ears, plastering with mud, etc.   Brer
Rabbit, when he victimises Miss Cow (*Uncle Remus*, IX), adopts no
disguise, but is not recognised when he puts his head out of the brier-
patch, because " his eyes look big as Miss Sally's chany sassers."   So
in the Angola " Jackal and Hare " (Chatelain, p. 209), Hare is
unrecognisable because he " opens big eyes in the hole."   The disguise
in " Brother Rabbit Frightens His Neighbors " (*Nights*, XXII),
is probably a recent touch.   " Dey aint seed no man w'at
look like Brer Rabbit do, wid de coffee-pot on he head, an de cups
a-rattlin' on he gallus, en de platters a-wavin' en a-shinin' in de a'r.

. . . ' I'm ole man Spewter-Splutter, wid long claws en scales on
my back! '."

20. The famous Tar-Baby episode occurs in this story, and elsewhere in numerous variants, ranging from Mozambique (Makua) to
Cameroons (Duala), and even beyond the Bantu area. Weeks suggests
(p. 367) that " the Tar-Baby is the fetish called Nkondi, but in the
story as we have it, a concession is made to civilization . . . in what
I believe to be the original story, the Nkondi image causes the victim
to stick by its own inherent fetish power. . . . It is apparent that
the narrators have lost faith in the magical powers of their fetish and
have introduced the wax and the tar to render their stories a little more
reasonable to themselves." This explanation seems to be supported by
the independent testimony of a Duala native, who told Prof. Meinhof
that figures covered with pitch are set up in forest clearings as a protection against demons (*Spukdämonen*). The figure holds a bowl of porridge in its hand as a bait: the demons demand some, and, getting no
answer, strike it and stick fast ([c], p. 119). Among the mischievous
tricks of these spirits is mentioned that of their setting up again the trees
which have been felled. A similar incident (grass and weeds coming
up again after hoeing) occurs in the Xosa story of " The Bird that
made Milk " (Torrend, p. 296), where it is the bird that works the
magic. In the Kongo and Mbundu versions, it is the Leopard who is
caught by the Tar-Baby, with the Temne, Vai, etc., the Spider (Cronise and Ward, p. 96, Johnston, [b], p. 1087). Ellis ([b], p. 275),
gives an Ĕwe variant, where the adventure is ascribed to the Hare and
forms part of the tale to be given presently in the text.

21. Junod, who had not a complete version before him, fails to
recognise the importance of this incident and doubts ([a], p. 86)
whether it really belongs to the same Hare and should not rather be
attributed to some other species, not distinguished for intelligence.
As told e.g. by the Giryama, the episode appears in its true light.

22. The Ĕwe have the curious variation that the animals decided
to cut off the tips of their ears and extract the fat from them, which
was to be " collected and sold, and with the money they would get
for the fat, they would buy a hoe and dig a well." Most versions
agree in representing the Hare as fraudulently profiting by the work
of the other animals, which he has refused to share; but the Winamwanga (Dewar, p. 11) describe the animals as trying to procure water
by stamping on the ground. (This is not stated to be a magical
operation, but a Swahili parallel where they are described as *singing*,
makes it probable that it was.) All fail except the Hare, who is
ungratefully driven away and prevented from drinking by the rest.
He revenges himself in much the same way as described in the text

and is eventually caught by the Tortoise. The Winamwanga live to the northwest of Lake Nyasa. A similar Nyanja story in Rattray, [a], p. 139.

23. This is told by the Baganda in a different connection, but in the Sumbwa version it follows on the Tar-Baby episode. Cf. Brer Rabbit's stratagem to get rid of Brer Buzzard, when the latter was watching the hollow tree in which he was hidden (*Nights*, p. 229). " ' I got de 'vantage on you, Brer Buzzard . . . kaze I kin see you en you can't see me! ' Wid dat Brer Buzzard stuck he head in de hole en look up, en no sooner is he do dis dan Brer Rabbit fill he eyes full er san'." . . . I have been obliged to follow a somewhat eclectic method in the text, as it is impossible to give in full, or even to summarise, all the various Hare stories.

24. This story is related in Büttner [a], p. 95, of the Hare and the Mongoose and explains why the former has long and the latter has short ears: the adventure ended in a fight, in which the Hare tore off his opponent's ears and appropriated them.

25. For this incident in another connection, see *supra*, p. 215. It is so widely distributed that one is inclined to think it one of the primitive elements in the Hare legend; perhaps it has some ultimate mythological significance, though hardly, I think, that attributed to it by Prof. Meinhof. In a MS. Giryama version, which I owe to the kindness of Mr. Hollis, the mothers are not to be killed but sold to the Coast-men for bags of grain — cf. Monteil, p. 135, "Le Lièvre, la Hyène et l'Autruche." The Hottentots tell this story of the Jackal.

26. The story was related to me with this finale by an old Swahili named Mwenye Ombwe, at Maunguja, near Mombasa. The episode which follows is given mainly from a version taken down in Pokomo, at Ngao in 1912. (See *FL* xxiv. [1913], 475.) It occurs, in a different connection, in Taylor, [b], p. 126, as the conclusion of a tale, the earlier part of which is identical with "The Hare and the Lion," in Steere.

27. Bleek [b], pp. 8–10.

28. Taylor [b], p. 130. I have a MS. version dictated in Giryama by Aaron Mwabaya at Kaloleni; but it wants the opening incident given by Taylor, which supplies the motive for the sequel. Other variants: Chinamwanga, Dewar, p. 129; Ronga (or rather Makua), Junod, [a], pp. 131, 135; and in America, "Compair Lapin et Michié Dinde," in Fortier, p. 24, as well as a version published in an American magazine by the late J. Chandler Harris. In Nyasaland, the tale is told of the Cock and the Swallow, or of a bird called *ntengu* and the wild cat; and elsewhere we find further variations.

29. Part of this story occurs as " The Hare and the Elephant," in Hollis, [a], p. 107, with some additional touches. The Hare, after finishing the honey, asks the Elephant to hand him up some stones for throwing at the birds. He then puts them into the honey-bag that the loss of weight may not be noticed, and asks to be set down. On finding out his loss, the elephant pursues him, and he takes refuge in a hole; the elephant, inserting his trunk catches him by the leg, and the Hare calls out that he has got hold of a root. The Elephant lets go and lays hold of what is in fact a root; the Hare groans and cries, " You are pulling me to pieces! " and finally makes his escape. He takes refuge with the Baboons, who, on being questioned by the Elephant, agree to betray him in return for a cup of the Elephant's blood. He allows them to shoot an arrow into his neck (as the Masai do to their cattle) and bleed him into a small cup which — unknown to him — has a hole in it: the cup is never filled, and the Elephant bleeds to death.

30. Schultze, p. 451.

31. *Ibid.*, p. 496.

32. Bleek, [a], p. 67; Metelerkamp, p. 78. The story of the Animals and the Well is told of the jackal by the Hottentots: see, *inter alia*, " The Story of a Dam," in *SAFJ* i. [1879], 69, and " The Animals' Dam," in Metelerkamp, p. 88. There is a noteworthy detail which affords a point of contact with the Tar-Baby story: the Tortoise covers his shell with some sticky substance, in order to catch the Jackal.

33. A Khassonke (French Sudan) version, however, attributes it to the Hare (Monteil, p. 29, " Le Lièvre et l'hyène à la pêche des mares de Doro "). He induces the Hyena to let him mount by telling him that no one is allowed to come to the fishing except on horseback, and that all the horses will be fed on dried fish. The greedy Hyena falls into the trap at once, but gets no fish and is driven away by the information that, as the catch has been so good, it has been decided to sacrifice a horse to the water-spirit. The Hyena is still running, adds the narrator.

34. Schultze, p. 461.

35. Gordon, p. 61.

CHAPTER XII

1. Cf. *inter alia*, Jacottet, [c], p. 32, " The Jackal."
2. Harris, [a], p. 89, No. 18, and p. 130, No. 26.
3. Junod, [a], pp. 87, 109, 127, 149.
4. Cronise and Ward, p. 70.

5. Hobley, p. 114.

6. Some variants: Bakwiri (Schuler in *MSOS* xi. [1908], 201); Duala (Lederbogen, *Ibid.*, iii. [1901], 204); Subiya (Jacottet, [b], ii. 40); Ila (Smith, p. 116).

7. Bleek, [b], p. 32; see also "The Ostrich Hunt" in Metelerkamp.

8. *Ibid.*, p. 27; see also Introduction, p. xxvii. Bleek thinks this story is "probably of Hottentot origin." Whether he had any evidence for this beyond its "striking resemblance" to the undoubtedly Hottentot tale of "The Giraffe and the Tortoise," and his own assumption that Bantu tribes have no animal stories, does not appear. (In the latter the Tortoise chokes the Giraffe which has swallowed it.) It seems to me that its mention of the Rain as a person suggests derivation from the Bushmen, to whom Hottentot folklore doubtless owes a great deal, while the Herero and some other Bantu tribes have also been directly in contact with them.

9. *Supra*, note 22 to p. 297.

10. In "The Girl who Ate Pork" (Kibaraka, p. 91), a story of non-African provenance, though no doubt embodying some African touches, the serpent to whom the woman has promised her first-born child, on finding that she is prepared to keep her word restores the infant to her, after twice "putting it into his mouth and taking it out at his nose"—a performance of which I find no other cases recorded.

11. Monteil, p. 45.

12. Ellis, [c], p. 258.

13. E.g. Cronise and Ward, p. 231, "Mr. Spider pulls a supply of beef."

14. This feat is given by the Mandingo (Monteil, p. 49) and by the Bemba (*JAS* ii. [1902–03], 63) to the Hare; by the Temne (Cronise and Ward, p. 117) to the Spider. But I think that it properly belongs to the Tortoise.

15. Nassau, [a], p. 37. Variants: Duala (*MSOS* iii. [1901], 170); Yabakalaki-Bakoko of the Cameroons (Seidel, [a], iii. 275). This version also adds that the two beasts subsequently discovered the trick, and the Tortoise has been hiding from them ever since.

16. Jacottet, [b] ii. 38 note. The various versions of this story are as follows: Basuto (Jacottet, [a], p. 42, and see notes in Junod, [a], p. 100); Bena Kanioka Kassai region (*Anthropos*, iv. [1909] 449); Subiya (Hare, Jacottet, [b] ii. 38); Benga (Nassau [b], p. 129, No. 14. No. 16, p. 140, is to some extent a variant of this); Xosa (Theal, [a], p. 115. In this case the Monkey is sent, and forgets the name on the way back. No other messengers are mentioned, nor is

it said that Hlakanyana succeeds in learning the name; but he proceeds to plunder the tree and inculpate the Monkey). Other variants mentioned by Jacottet and Junod have nothing to do with the name part of the story. These are: Ronga (Junod, [a], pp. 98ff., the story of the Hare already alluded to in Chap. XI); North Transvaal (*Revue des traditions populaires*, x. [1895], 383); Lower Ogowe (Mizon in *Ibid.*, iv. [1889], 648 — a variant of Nassau's No. 16, "Tortoise, Dog, Leopard, and the Bojabi Fruit"). Jacottet also refers to an Ewe story recorded by G. Härtler (in Seidel, [a], vi. [1901], 127); but this is a version of "Chicken-Licken," "Henny-Penny," etc., so close to our own and told in a way so unlike the genuine African story that I cannot help suspecting it to be a recent importation from Europe.

17. This does not apply to the Benga story given in the text, which seems to me in several respects less primitive than Jacottet's Suto version.

18. Junod, [a], pp. 98 *et seq.*

19. Jacottet, [a], p. 43: "Motlatladiane motlatla ne signifie rien, ce sont de simples assonances." The Subiya call it *bundelemoo*, the Bena Kanioka *muchiabanza* — words of which no one seems to know the meaning. Whether *bojabi* is the recognised name of a tree in Benga at the present day, Nassau does not explain.

20. Nassau, [b], p. 129. In the Suto version the Lion, as chief of the animals, sends off a succession of messengers (not particularised by name) to Koko (the first ancestress of the tribe?) to ask the name of the tree. They chant it on the way back, but all stumble against an ant-heap and forget it. At last the Lion goes himself, but fails likewise. The Tortoise then goes and stumbles like the rest, but contrives to keep his wits and remember the name. The Lion, angry that so insignificant a creature should be more successful than himself orders him to be buried. All the animals then went to eat the fruit of the tree, carefully leaving that on the topmost branch untouched. (No order to this effect has previously been mentioned but it is clearly implied in what follows — cf. Junod, [a], p. 102 "la branche du chef.") During the night, the Tortoise comes out of his hole, eats the fruit on the top branch and buries himself again. "Le lendemain le propriétaire de l'arbre leur demanda: 'Pourquoi avez-vous si mal agi, de manger les fruits que je vous avez dit de ne pas toucher?' Les animaux lui répondirent: 'Ce n'est pas nous qui y avons touché, nous ne savons qui a pu les manger.' On déterra la tortue, et on lui demanda ce qui en était: elle répondit: 'Comment avais-je pu les manger, puisque vous m'aviez si bien enterrée?'"

The Subiya version, which, as already said, makes the Hare the hero, names an Antelope (*unsa*) and the Chameleon as messengers, and adds that, on the arrival of the second, Leza told him that, if he forgot the name this time, the next who came to ask for it should die. The Hare, however, found grace in his sight and was spared. In the Bena Kanioka version, the only messenger sent prior to the Tortoise is the *ngulungu*, Antelope. Maweza, when telling the Tortoise the name gives him a little bell which, he says, will recall it to him if he forgets it. The animals show themselves ungrateful and refuse the Tortoise a share of the fruit; after they have eaten of it themselves, they kill him (probably, though this is not said, battering his shell to pieces). But the little ants knead clay, make him a new body (stick his shell together?) and restore him to life. The animals kill him once more, and again the ants restore him. This time he uproots the tree, and all the beasts perish. So far as I know, this conclusion stands alone. The story has points of contact with the numerous ones which try to account for the laminae of the Tortoise's shell.

21. Seidel, [a], iv. [1898], 137.

22. These people, whose proper name is Luo (Jaluo), live near the northeastern corner of the Victoria Nyanza. I regret to say that I did not succeed in taking down a complete version of this tale, and have had to trust largely to memory; but it strangely resembles " L'homme au grand coutelas " (Junod, [a], p. 144), except that the Tortoise is substituted for the Frog.

23. Nassau, [b], pp. 33, 34.

24. Callaway, [a], p. 339.

Chapter XIII

1. *Anansi* is the Twi name of the Spider. Rattray, [b], ii. 294, says: " The Ashanti name for a story, even when the Spider does not appear in the narrative at all, is *anansesem*, literally ' words about a spider.' " Hence the well-known expression " Annancy " (or " Nancy ") stories in the West Indies. Cf. Tremearne, pp. 31–33.

2. Chatelain, pp. 133, 135.

3. Dennett, [a], p. 74, [b], p. 31.

4. Lederbogen, *MSOS* (*Afrikanische Studien*), iv. [1901], 180.

5. Schön, p. 200.

6. Ellis, [a], p. 339, [c], p. 259.

7. Rattray, [b], i. 108.

8. *Ibid.*, i. 128.

9. Cronise and Ward, p. 109.

10. *Ibid.*, p. 279.

11. Rattray, [b], ii. 90, 92, 124, 306, 307; Jekyll, pp. 4, 9.

On the Gold Coast he is said to talk through his nose. It may be remembered that the Bushmen have a special dialect (with peculiar clicks) for each of the animals figuring in their tales. Cf. also M. Kingsley, p. 140, and Zimmermann, ii. 17.

12. Ellis, [c], p. 258.

13. Rattray, [b], ii. 106; Delafosse, p. 170. The latter has an additional incident at the beginning; the Spider marries " Heaven's daughter," who had been promised to whatever suitor should succeed in breaking up a plot of ground without scratching himself while the work was going on. The Elephant and all the other animals fail to pass the test; the Spider succeeds by a trick. " Dodo " is called " La Mort " by the French writer, and the story ends with his swallowing all the beef and leaving the Spider none. Concerning Dodo, whose characteristics are somewhat variable, but who certainly belongs to the tribes of Ogres, *Mazimwi*, etc., see Tremearne, pp. 124–6 and tales Nos. 14, 32, 73, etc. Of these, No. 32, " How Dodo frightened the Greedy Man," is virtually identical (except that a man takes the place of the Spider) with the one in the text, though shorter. Rattray's version is literally translated from a complete Hausa text and contains some crudities, necessarily softened down in our abstract.

14. Rattray, [b], ii. p. 114. The bag looks like a more civilized substitute for the actual swallowing of the older and cruder story. The same may be the case in such stories as that of " Tselane," " The Child in the Drum," etc., where, too, it may be meant to make the rescue more plausible.

15. Cf. the curious incident of the Elephant and the Tortoise referred to on p. 313.

16. In Tremearne, the conclusion is different: the son, left by Dodo to watch the bag, lets his father out, and they make their escape.

17. *Supra*, note 14 to p. 314.

18. Rattray, [b], ii. 124.

19. *Ibid.*, ii. 81, where this incident forms the conclusion of " The Spider and the Lion." Cf. also Thomas, p. 63.

20. Spieth, p. 573.

21. Similar tricks occur in " The Spider and the Crows " (Rattray, [b], ii. No. 28), where he (*a*), lights a fire to make them think day is breaking, (*b*) beats the fowls to make them raise an outcry, (*c*) gives the Moslem call to prayer.

22. Barker, p. 84.

23. Spieth, p. 34*. (Starred references to this work denote pages in the Introduction.)

24. Spieth, p. 584.

25. A Hausa tale given by Tremearne (p. 397) mentions a town where no one is allowed to sleep. No explanation is given.

26. Literally " drink-names." Eẅe chiefs and warriors, at drink-ing-bouts, take " great names, greater than themselves," which they shout on these festive occasions, and also in battle, in order to keep up their courage and terrify their enemies. See Spieth, p. 622.

27. Spieth, p. 590.

28. Smith, p. 69; Jekyll, p. 31.

29. Jekyll, p. 33. This version differs from Miss Smith's in mak-ing the barrel full of quicklime, instead of flour.

CHAPTER XIV

1. Bleek, [b], p. 25.

2. Jacottet, [c], p. 266.

3. Tremearne, pp. 153–156.

4. *Ibid.*, p. 154.

5. Gutmann, [b], p. 75; Tremearne, p. 397.

6. Junod, [a], p. 247.

7. E.g. Craster, pp. 302, 311, 317. On this, see M. Kingsley, pp. 163, 168, 211, etc.

8. See M. Kingsley, p. 162.

9. Scott, p. 345.

10. Rehse, p. 131.

11. Scott, p. 312 (*manchichi*), 451 (*nkandwe*), 345, 648; Miss D. M. Abdy in *JAS* xvi. [1917], 237. The Leopard's employment in this capacity may be distinct from the quasi-sacred character which attaches to him all over Africa (a subject not yet fully worked out), marked, e.g., by the skin being reserved for chiefs, in some cases for the Supreme Chief only. Among the Zulus of Natal, the proper name of the leopard, *ingwe*, is tabu: the reason given being his con-nection with wizards. But it is curious that another of these " famil-iars," the hyena, should, in East Africa (where, however, as far as I know, he is not associated with witchcraft), be regarded as more or less sacred. Cf. *inter alia*, Krapf, [b], p. 68, s. v. *fisi*, and Hollis, [b], pp. 7, 11.

12. Miss Abdy, *JAS*, xvi. [1917], 237.

13. For details, see Scott, pp. 345, 648; Miss Abdy, *op. cit.*, p. 235; and cf. Craster, pp. 254, 299. Nassau, [a], p. 123, says that when the " witchcraft company hold their meetings, an imitation of the hoot of the owl, which is their sacred bird, is the signal call."

14. Craster, p. 300.

15. Nassau, [a], p. 123, [c], pp. 150–168.

16. Colenso, p. 282.

17. Bryant, p. 322.

18. *Natal Colonist*, Dec. 27, 1873. I remember being told by a native in Nyasaland that, if addressed by a *mfiti* at night, one must on no account answer him; however, testimony was by no means uniform on this point, some saying that the right course was to defy him and threaten him with the *mwavi* ordeal. Baboons are said in Natal to be witches' familiars, and a solitary " rogue," turned out of the troop when old and vicious, might have given rise to some of the stories about *imikovu*, but they are not nocturnal in their habits.

19. Jacottet, [c], p. 266, and Casalis, [b], p. 289.

20. This seems to be a common condition of witch-revels. It is sometimes mentioned as a means of recognising witches when surprised by night. See Abdy, *loc. cit.*, p. 234; Krapf, [b], p. 260.

21. Dayrell, p. 32.

22. Such touches are not common in African folk-tales, not so much so as in Grimm. But a study of these Ikom stories reveals a crudity and ferocity which are not typically African. One may perhaps conjecture that Calabar, being one of the principal *foci* of the slave-trade, attracted to itself, in the course of three centuries, the worst elements in two continents.

23. Johnston, [a], p. 439.

24. Scott, p. 562 (Anyanja); *JAS* v. [1906], 267.

25. Schultze, p. 450 (Nama). See also Nassau, [a], pp. 201–3; Du Chaillu, pp. 52–3.

26. J. R. Werner, pp. 277, 320.

27. See refs. in J. G. Frazer, *The Golden Bough*,[3] x. 308–14, especially p. 313. It seems scarcely possible to maintain in Africa the distinction drawn by this eminent authority between werewolves and witches.

28. Pearce, i. 287–8, note.

29. *Ibid.*, ii. 340–1.

30. MS. notes.

31. In the variants, the child who effects the rescue usually suffers from some skin disease or other disability, which is given as a reason for not desiring his or her presence.

32. Nassau, [b], p. 68, " Leopard of the Fine Skin."

Chapter XV

1. For these and similar stories, see *FL* xxv. [1915], 457f.

2. The four Pokomo tribes of the Lower Tana are Ngatana, Dzunza, Buu, and Kalindi: the second being comparatively unimportant. See *FL* xxiv. [1913], 456–7. The Tana has repeatedly changed its course during its annual inundations; the last important

occasion of its doing so seems to have been about sixty years ago, when (as related in the sequel to the legend), the Buu tribe had to shift to their present abode in the neighbourhood of Ngao.

3. Gutmann, [b], p. 151, "Der Glockenbote."

4. *Ibid.*, p. 109, see *supra*, p. 188. As to the bringing up to date and imparting local colour to either imported or native stories see Junod, [a], pp. 274-6, 284 (note 1), 291 (note).

5. See Monteil, pp. 166–202. The legends there given do not include those of Moses and the beggar whom God refused to help (*Kibaraka*, p. 38), and of David and the old woman who laid a complaint against the wind for carrying off her flour (*ib.*, p. 130). I have been unable to get any information about the originals of these.

6. Steere, p. 3. See *FLJ* iii. [1885], 128, 130.

7. *Notes and Queries*, Ser. xi. iv. [1911], 82.

8. *FL* xxvi. [1915], 63.

9. M. Pickthall, *Oriental Encounters*, London, 1918, p. 275. Mr. Pickthall informs me, in a private letter, that most of the Abu Nuwwâs stories referred to in the text "in Syria and Egypt are ascribed to Joḥha (or Hâjj Joḥha). Abu Nuwwâs was always the court jester in the stories that I used to read and hear. The greatest yarn of all — nearly interminable — is of how he extracted money out of Haroun-er-rashîd by the news of his own death and escaped the proper punishment of such a fraud. How far these stories correspond to the actual history of Abu Nuwwâs . . . I do not know; but all the stories I have heard concerning him had something of the colour of history." Some of the genuine Abu Nuwwâs stories are certainly current in Swahili.

10. Junod, [a], p. 292. Some Abu Nuwwâs stories in Beech, [b], pp. 58–85.

11. See A. Campbell, *Santal Folk-Tales*, p. 25, quoted by Hindes-Groome, p. 263.

12. See Mouliéras, ii. 4, 12, 13. The Berber stories published by Mouliéras seem to be derived from a very old Arabic collection. It is interesting to observe that those stories have spread into Sicily and Italy, where the name Joha has become Giufà or Giuccà. But the latter seems more of a simpleton than Joha, who is a mixture of cunning and imbecility, the latter no doubt assumed in many cases. "Les anecdotes où il figure sont en effet de deux sortes: dans les unes, il cache sous une sottise apparente un esprit caustique et narquois; dans les autres, il nous apparaît comme le niais le plus ridicule" (Basset, in Mouliéras, ii. 6).

13. Mouliéras, ii. 89.

14. *Ibid.*, ii. 18. It is a favourite incident in Italy.

15. *Ibid.*, ii. 143.

16. Groome, p. 9.

17. *Ibid.*, p. 12.

18. Bolte and Polívka, i. 188–202.

19. Junod, [a], pp. 274–322. The stories are: " Les aventures de Djiwao," p. 276; " Bonaouaci," p. 291; " Les trois vaisseaux," p. 304; " Le jeune garçon et le grand serpent," p. 314, and " La fille du roi."

19a. An enchanted horse figures in a Mpongwe tale (see p. 347 *supra*), showing that, in this form, it must be of fairly recent origin.

20. Bolte and Polívka, iii. 80; cf. also " The Three Girls," in Groome, p. 141.

21. Chatelain, pp. 43, 53.

22. Evidently an Indian, as appears later on.

23. A. Werner, pp. 247–9.

24. There may, however, have been some misapprehension on the translator's part: *mundu* (= *homo*, not *vir*) may equally well mean a man or a woman, and if the intention of marriage was not explicitly stated, the mistake might easily arise.

25. Dennett, [a], pp. x-xii.

26. Thomann, p. 136. Here the conclusion is sufficiently repugnant to the moral sense: " Mais le père dit à son tour: ' Tous trois vous avez le même mérite et il n'est impossible de donner trois maris à ma fille. Je ne peux donc que vous autoriser à être ses amants." It is only fair to say that this conclusion would not be generally accepted by Africans. In the only other case where a decision is stated the girl is compelled to remain single (I have unfortunately lost the reference).

27. Dennett, [a], p. 32.

BIBLIOGRAPHY

ARMENIAN

I. ABBREVIATIONS

ABAW . . . Abhandlungen Königlich-Preussische Akademie der Wissenschaften zu Berlin.

ARW . . . . Archiv für Religionswissenschaft.

EBr[11] . . . . Encyclopedia Britannica, 11th ed.

ERE . . . . Encyclopedia of Religion and Ethics.

OLZ . . . . Orientalische Litteraturzeitung.

SBE . . . . . Sacred Books of the East.

SWAW . . . Sitzungsberichte der Wiener Akademie der Wissenschaften.

TICO . . . . Transactions of the International Congress of Orientalists, London, 1893.

VKR . . . . Verhandlungen des zweiten internat. Kongresses für allgemein. Religionsgeschichte, Basel, 1905

II. ENCYCLOPEDIAS

DAREMBERG, V., and SAGLIO, E., *Dictionnaire des antiquités grecques et romaines*, Paris, 1887ff.

ENCYCLOPEDIA BRITANNICA, Cambridge, 11th ed., 1910–11.

ENCYCLOPEDIA OF RELIGION AND ETHICS, ed. J. Hastings, Edinburgh, 1908ff.

ERSCH, J. S. and J. G. GRÜBER, *Allgemeine Encyklopädie der Wissenschaften und Künste*, Leipzig, 1818–50.

GRANDE ENCYCLOPÉDIE, LA, Paris, 1885–1901.

PAULY, A. F. VON, *Realencyclopädie der classischen Altertumswissenschaft*, New ed. by G. Wissowa, Stuttgart, 1904ff.

RÖSCHER, W. H., *Ausführliches Lexicon der griechische und römische Mythologie*, Leipzig, 1884–1902.

III. SOURCES

For the Indo-European period down to Christian times the most important native sources are:

AGATHANGELOS, 5th cent., ed. Venice, 1865.

ANANIA OF SHIRAG, 7th cent., ed. Patkanean, Petrograd, 1877.

EZNIK, 5th cent., ed. Venice, 1826.

EXISHE (ELISÆUS), 5th cent., ed. Venice.

FAUSTUS OF BYZANTIUM, 5th cent., ed. Venice, 1869, also in V. Langlois, *Collection des historiens anciens et modernes de l'Arménie*, Paris, 1857–9.

MOSES OF CHOREN, 5th cent., *History and Geography of Armenia*, ed. Venice, 1865.

OHAN MANTAGUNI, 5th cent., ed. Venice.

The ancient Armenian version of the Old Testament is useful for names. We also gather short but valuable notices from Xenophon's *Anabasis*, Strabo's *Geography*, and the works of Dio Cassius, Pliny, and Tacitus. Alishan has gathered in his *Ancient Faith of Armenia* (in Armen.), Venice, 1895, a good deal of very valuable material from edited and unedited works of the mediæval writers. The Armenian language itself is one of the richest sources of information, along with the church ritual and scientifically collected folk-lore. Among the latter we may name Abeghian, *Armenischer Volksglaube*, Pshrank, *Crumbs from the Granaries of Shirak*, and parts of Srvantzdian's *Manana* (see under IV. Literature).

IV. LITERATURE

Besides many articles in *ARW*, *EBr*[11], *ERE*, Daremberg et Saglio, Pauly-Wissowa, Röscher, and *La Grande Encyclopédie*, the following works may be noted.

ABEGHIAN, M., *Armenischer Volksglaube*, Leipzig, 1899.

AHARONIAN, A., *Les croyances des anciens Arméniens*, Geneva, 1912.

ALISHAN, L. *Ancient Faith of the Armenians* (Armen.), Venice, 1895.

ARAKELIAN, H., *La religion ancienne des Arméniens* in *VKR*, p. 291f.

ASLAN, K., *Etudes historiques sur le peuple arménien*, Paris, 1909.

BALASSANIAN, S., *History of Armenia*[2] (Armen.), Tiflis, 1896.

BASMAJIAN, G., *Critical Study of our Aralez and the Babylonian Marduk*, Venice, 1898.

——*True History of Armenia*, Constantinople, 1914.

CARRIÈRE, A., *Les huit sanctuaires de l'Arménie payenne*, Paris, 1899.

CASSEL, P., *Drachenkämpfe*, Berlin, 1868.

CHALATIANZ, G., *Märchen und Sagen*, Leipzig, 1887.

CHANTEPIE DE LA SAUSSAYE, P. D., *Lehrbuch der Religionsgeschichte*[3], Tübingen, 1905.

CUMONT, F., *Die Mysterien des Mithra*, Leipzig, 1903.

——*Texts et monuments figurés relatifs aux mystères de Mithra*, Brussels, 1896–9.

DAGHAVARIAN, N., *Ancient Religions of the Armenians* (Armen.), in *Banassēr*, 1903.

DAVIS, GLADYS M. N., *The Asiatic Dionysos*, London, 1914.

DER-MESROBIAN, S., *Critical History of Armenia*, Venice, 1914.

DOLENS, N., and KHATCH, A., *Histoire des anciens Arméniens*, Geneva, 1907.

EMIN, M., *Recherche sur le paganisme arménien, in Revue de l'Orient*, N.S. v. 18.

——*Moses of Khoren and the Old Epics of the Armenians*, Tiflis, 1886.

ERMAN, A., *Handbook of Egyptian Religion*, tr. A. S. Griffith, London, 1907.

FARNELL, L. R., *The Cults of the Greek States*, Oxford, 1896–1909.

FRAZER, J. G., *The Golden Bough*,[3] London, 1907–15.

GEIGER, W., and KUHN, E., *Grundriss der iranische Philologie*, Strassburg, 1895–1904.

GELZER, H., *Zur armenische Götterlehre, in Berichte der Koniglich-Sächsischen Gesellschaft der Wissenchaften, phil. hist. Classe.*, 1895, pp. 99–148.

GUTSCHMID, A. VON, *Kleine Schriften*, Leipzig, 1889–94.

HOMMELL, F., *Grundriss der Geographie und Geschichte des alten Orients*, Munich, 1904.

HÜBSCHMANN, H., *Armenische Grammatik*, Leipzig, 1897.

Hushartzan (A collection of essays by various scholars), Vienna, 1911.

INJIJIAN, L., *Armenian Archaeology*, Venice, 1835.

JACKSON, A. V. W., *Iranische Religion*, in Geiger-Kuhn, *Grundriss d. iran. Philologie*, Vol. ii.

JASTROW, M., *Die Religion Babyloniens und Assyriens*, Giessen, 1905–12.

JENSEN, P., *Hittiter und Armenier*, Strassburg, 1898.

KARAKASHIAN, A., *Critical History of Armenia* (Armen.) Tiflis, 1895.

LAGARDE, P., *Armenische Studien*, Göttingen, 1887.

——*Purim*, Göttingen, 1887.

LANGLOIS, V., *Collections des historiens anciens et modernes de l'Arménie*, Paris, 1867–69.

MACDONELL, A. A., *Vedic Mythology*, Stuttgart, 1897.

MAEHLY, J., *Die Schlange in Mythus und Kultus*, Basel, 1867.

MEYER, E., *Geschichte des Alterthums*,[2] Berlin, 1909.

MOORE, G. F., *History of Religions*, vol. i, Edinburgh, 1914.

Moulton, J. H., *Early Zoroastrianism*, London, 1913.

Nazaretian, *Armenians and Armenian Mythology* (Armen.), in Bazmawep, 1893–4.

Oldenberg, H., *Die Religion des Veda*, Berlin, 1894.

Paton, L. B., *Spiritism and the Cult of the Dead in Antiquity*, New York, 1921.

Patrubani, *Beiträge zur Armenischen Etymologie*, Budapest, 1897.

Pshrank, *Crumbs from the Granaries of Shirak*, a collection of eastern Armenian folk-lore.

Sahag-Mesrob, *Urartu*, Constantinople, 1909.

Sandalgian, J., *Histoire documentaire de l'Armenie*, Paris, 1917.

Sarkissian, B., *Agathangelos and his Many-centuried Mystery* (Armen.), Venice, 1892.

Schrader, O., *Arische Religion*, Leipzig, 1914.

Seropian, Bshp. M., *Armenia and Hayastan*, n. d.

Siecke, E., *Drachenkämpfe*, Leipzig, 1907.

Srvantzdian, *Manana*.

Stockelberg, " Iranian Influence on the Religious Beliefs of the Ancient Armenians," in *Report of the Imperial Archaeological Society of Moscow, Oriental Comm.* (Russian), ii. pt. 2, Moscow, 1901.

Tchéraz, M., *Notes sur la mythologie arménienne*, in *TICO, ii.*, London, 1893.

Tisdall, W. St. Clair, *The Conversion of Armenia to the Christian Faith*, Oxford, 1897.

Unguad, A., *Das Gilgamesch-Epos*, Göttingen, 1911.

Weber, S., *Die Katholische Kirche in Armenien*, Freiberg, 1903.

Windischmann, F., *Die persische Anâhita oder Anaitis*, in *Abhandlungen der König. Bayr. Akadamie der Wissenchaften*, i. *Classe, viii.* pt. 1, Munich, 1856.

V

A large number of works on Folk-lore have been used, among which the following may be named.

Abbott, G. F., *Macedonian Folk-Lore*, Cambridge, 1907.

Conway, M. D., *Demonology and Devil Lore*, New York, 1879.

Crooke, W., *The Popular Religion and Folklore of Northern India*, London, 1897.

Hartland, E. Sydney, *The Legend of Perseus*, London, 1896.

Kirk, Rev. R., *The Secret Commonwealth of Elves, Fauns, and Fairies*, ed. A Lang, London, 1893.

LANE, E. W., *An Account of the Manners and Customs of the Modern Egyptians.*

——*Arabian Society in the Middle Ages,* ed. S. Lane Poole, London, 1883.

RALSTON, W. R. S., *Russian Folk-tales,* London, 1873.

RHYS, SIR JOHN, *Celtic Folk-lore,* Oxford, 1891.

WENTZ, W. Y. E., *The Fairy Faith in Celtic Countries,* Oxford, 1911.

WUNDT, W. M., *Elemente der Völkerpsychologie,*[2] Leipzig, 1913.

Also the following articles:

" Dragon," in *Daremberg-Saglio.*

" Phrygians," in *ERE* ix.

" Serpent," in *New Schaff-Herzog Encyclopedia of Religious Knowledge.*

" Serpent Worship," in *EBr*[11].

VI. PRINCIPAL ARTICLES CONNECTED WITH ARMENIAN MYTHOLOGY IN THE ENCYCLOPEDIA OF RELIGION AND ETHICS (VOLS. I–XII)

ANANIKIAN, M., " Armenia (Zoroastrian)," i. 794–802.

CARNOY, A. J., " Magic (Iranian)," viii. 293–6.

CASARTELLI, L. C., " Charms and Amulets (Iranian)," iii. 448.

——" Dualism (Iranian)," v. 111–2.

CRAWLEY, A. E., " Fire and Fire-Gods," vi. 26–30.

CUMONT, F., " Anāhita," i. 414–5.

——" Art (Mithraic)," i. 872–4.

——" Architecture (Mithraic)," i. 744–5.

EDWARDS, E., " Altar (Persian)," i. 346–8.

——" God (Iranian)," vi. 290–4.

——" Priest, Priesthood(Iranian)," x. 319–22.

GRAY, L. H., " Achaemenians," i. 69–73.

——" Barsom," ii. 424–5.

——" Blest, Abode of the (Persian)," ii. 702–4.

——" Cosmogony and Cosmology (Iranian)," iv. 161–2.

——" Fate (Iranian)," v. 792–3.

——" Festivals and Fasts (Iranian)," v. 872–5.

——" Fortune (Iranian)," vi. 96.

——" Heroes and Hero-Gods (Iranian)," vi. 661–2.

——" Life and Death (Iranian)," viii. 37.

——" Light and Darkness (Iranian)," viii. 61–2.

JACKSON, A. V. W., " Ahriman," i. 237–8.
——" Amesha Spentas," i. 384–5.
——" Architecture (Persian)," i. 760–4.
——" Art (Persian)," i. 881–4.
——" Ashmounds," ii. 114–5.
——" Avesta," ii. 266–72.
——" Demons and Spirits (Persian)," iv. 619–20.
JONES, H. S., " Mithraism," viii. 752–9.
LEHMANN, E., " Ancestor Worship and Cult of the Dead (Iranian),"
    i. 454–5.
MacCULLOCH, J. A., " Branches and Twigs," ii. 831–3.
——" Changeling," iii. 358–63.
——" Fairy," v. 678–89.
——" Serpent," xi. 399–411.
MACLER, F., " Armenia (Christian)," i. 802–7.
——" Calendar (Armenian)," iii. 70–3.
MILLS L. H., " Ahuna-Vairya," i. 238–9.
——" Barsom," ii. 424–5.
——" Behistūn," ii. 450–4.
MODI, J. J., " Birth (Parsi)," ii. 660–2.
MOULTON, J. H., " Iranians," vii. 418–20.
PATON, L. B., " Ashtart," ii. 115–8.
——" Ishtar," vii. 428-34.
RAMSAY, W. M., " Phrygians," ix. 900–11.
SAYCE, A. H., " Armenia (Vannic)," i. 793–4.
——" Median Religion," viii. 514-5.
SODERBLÖM, N., " Ages of the World (Zoroastrian)," i. 205–10.

AFRICAN

I. ABBREVIATIONS

FL . . . . . Folk-Lore.
FLJ . . . . . Folk-Lore Journal.
JAS . . . . . Journal of the African Society.
JRAI . . . . Journal of the Royal Anthropological Institute.
MSOS . . . . Mitteilungen des Seminars für orientalische Sprachen.
SAFJ . . . . South African Folk-Lore Society's Journal.
ZAS . . . . . Zeitschrift für Afrikanische Sprachen.
ZE . . . . . Zeitschrift für Ethnologie.
ZKS . . . . . Zeitschrift für Kolonialsprachen.

II. BIBLIOGRAPHY

BARKER, W. H., and SINCLAIR, C., *West African Folk-Tales*, London, 1910.

BARNES, REV. H. B., *A Nyanja-English Vocabulary*, London, 1902.

BAUMANN, S. O., [a], *Durch Massailand zur Nilquelle, Reisen und Forschungen der Massai-Expedition*, 1891–93, Berlin, 1894.

——[b], *Usambara und seine Nachbargebiete*, Berlin, 1891.

BEECH, MERVYN W. H., [a], *The Suk, Their Language and Folk-Lore*, Oxford, 1911.

——[b], *Aids to the Study of Kiswahili*, London, [1917?].

BENTLEY, W. HOLMAN, *Dictionary and Grammar of the Congo Language as Spoken at Saõ Salvador*, London, 1887.

BLEEK, W. H. I., [a], *The Languages of Mozambique*, London, 1856.

——[b], *Reynard the Fox in South Africa*, London, 1864.

——[c], *A Brief Account of Bushman Folk-Lore and other Texts.* . . . *Second Report concerning Bushman Researches presented to both Houses of Parliament of the Cape of Good Hope*, Cape Town, 1875.

See also LLOYD, MISS C. L.

BOLTE, J., and POLÍVKA, G., *Anmerkungen zu den Kinder — und Hausmärchen der Brüder Grimm*, 3 vols., Leipzig, 1913–18.

BREYSIG, K., *Die Enstehung des Gottesgedankens und der Heilbringer*, Berlin, 1905.

BRINCKER, H., *Wörterbuch und Kurzgefasste Grammatik des Otjiherero.* Herausgegeben von C. G. Büttner, Leipzig, 1886.

BRYANT, A. T., *Zulu-English Dictionary*, Pietermaritzburg, 1905.

BÜTTNER, C. G., [a], *Zeitschrift für Afrikanische Sprachen*, Berlin, 1887–90.

——[b], *Anthologie aus der Suahili-Litteratur*, Berlin, 1894.

CALLAWAY, HENRY (late Bishop of St. John's), [a], *Nursery Tales and Traditions of the Zulus*, London, 1868.

——[b], *Religious System of the Amazulu*, London, 1870.

CAMPBELL, J., *Travels in S. Africa* (Second Journey), 2 vols., London, 1822.

CASALIS, EUGÈNE, [a], *Etudes sur la langue séchuana*, Paris, 1841.

——[b], *Les Bassoutos*, Paris, 1859.

CHATELAIN, H., *Folk-Tales of Angola.* (*Memoirs of the American Folk-Lore Society*), Boston and New York, 1894.

COLENSO, J. W., DD., LL.D., Late Bishop of Natal, *Zulu-English Dictionary*, Pietermaritzburg, 1905.

CRASTER, CAPTAIN J. E. E., R. E., *Pemba, the Spice Island of Zanzibar*, London, 1913.

CRONISE, FLORENCE M., and WARD, HENRY W., *Cunnie Rabbit, Mr. Spider, and the other Beef. West African Folk-Tales*, London and New York, 1903.

DAYRELL, E., *Ikom Folk Stories from Southern Nigeria*, London (Royal Anthropological Institute Occasional Papers), 1913.

DELAFOSSE, MAURICE, *Essai de Manuel de la langue agni*, Paris, 1901.

DENNETT, R. E., [a], *Notes on the Folk-Lore of the Fjort (French Congo). With an Introduction by Mary H. Kingsley*, London, 1898.

——[b], *At the Back of the Black Man's Mind, or Notes on the Kingly Office in West Africa*, London, 1906.

——[c], *Nigerian Studies, or the Religious and Political System of the Yoruba*, London, 1910.

DEWAR, EMMELINE H., *Chinamwanga Stories (Iviri vya Chinamwanga)*, Livingstonia, 1900.

DU CHAILLU, PAUL B., *Journey to Ashango-Land*, London, 1867.

EHRENREICH, P., *Baessler-Archiv. Beiträge zur Volkskunde* (edited by Ehrenreich), Leipzig and Berlin. In progress since 1910.

ELLIS, A. B., [a], *The Tshi-speaking Peoples of the Gold Coast of West Africa*, London, 1887.

——[b], *The Ewe-speaking Peoples of the Slave Coast of West Africa*, London, 1890.

——[c], *The Yoruba-speaking Peoples of the Slave Coast of West Africa*, London, 1894.

FLETCHER, R. S., *Hausa Sayings and Folk-Lore*, London, 1912 [1911].

FORTIER, ALCÉE, *Louisiana Folk-Tales*, Boston, 1895.

FRAZER, SIR J. G., *Totemism and Exogamy*, 4 vols. London, 1910.

FÜLLEBORN, DR. FRIEDRICH, *Das deutsche Njassa und Ruwumage-biet, Land und Leute (Deutsch Ost-Afrika*, Bd. 9), Berlin, 1906.

GORDON, E. M., *Indian Folk-Tales*, London, 1909.

GROOME, FRANCIS HINDES, *Gypsy Folk-Tales*, London, 1899.

GUTMANN, BRUNO, [a], *Dichten und Denken der Dschagganeger*, Leipzig, 1909.

——[b], *Volksbuch der Wadschagga*, Leipzig, 1914.

HAHN, THEOPHILUS, PH. D., *Tsuni-||Goam, the Supreme Being of the Khoi-Khoi*, London, 1881.

HALLIWELL-PHILLIPS, J. O., *Popular Rhymes and Nursery Tales*, London, 1849.

HARRIS, JOEL CHANDLER, [a], *Uncle Remus, or Mr. Fox, Mr. Rabbit, and Mr. Terrapin*, London, n. d.

——[b], *Nights with Uncle Remus*, London, n. d.

HEWAT, M. L., *Bantu Folk-Lore, Medical and General*, Cape Town, 1906.

HOBLEY, C. W., C. M. G., *Ethnology of the A-Kamba and other East African Tribes*, Cambridge, 1910.

HOLLIS, A. C., [a], *The Masai, Their Language and Folk-Lore*, Oxford, 1905.

——[b], *The Nandi, Their Language and Folk-Lore*, Oxford, 1909.

IRLÉ, J., *Die Herero: ein Beitrag zur Landes-, Volks-, und Missions-kunde*, Gütersloh, 1906.

JACOTTET, ÉMILE, [a], *Contes populaires des Bassoutos* (vol. xx of *Collection de contes et chansons populaires*), Paris, 1895.

——[b], *Études sur les langues du Haut-Zambèse. I. Grammaire Soubiya et Louyi*, 1896. *II. Textes Soubiya*, 1899. *III. Textes Louyi*, 1901. (*Publications de l'école supérieure des lettres d'Alger, tome* xvi), Paris.

——[c], *The Treasury of Basuto-Lore*, vol. i. (no more published), London, 1908.

JEKYLL, WALTER, *Jamaican Song and Story*, London, 1907.

JOHNSTON, SIR H. H., [a], *British Central Africa*, London, 1896.

——[b], *Liberia*, 2 vols. London, 1906.

——[c], *George Grenfell and the Congo*, 2 vols. London, 1908.

JUNOD, H. A., [a], *Chants et contes des Baronga*, Lausanne, 1897.

——[b], *Les Baronga*, Neuchâtel, 1898.

——[c], *The Life of a South African Tribe*, London, 1913.

Kibaraka, Swahili Stories (revised ed.), Zanzibar, 1896.

KIDD, DUDLEY, [a], *The Essential Kaffir*, London, 1904.

——[b], *Savage Childhood*, London, 1906.

——[c], *The Bull of the Kraal and the Heavenly Maidens*, London, 1908.

KINGSLEY, MARY H., *West African Studies*, London, 1899.

KRAPF, J. L., [a], *Reisen in Ost-Afrika, ausgeführt in der Jahren, 1837–55*. Kornthal and Stuttgart, 1858.

——[b], *A Dictionary of the Swahili Language*, London, 1882.

KROENLEIN, J. G., *Wortschatz der Khoi-Khoin (Namaqua-Hottentotten)*, Berlin, 1889.

KROPF, A., D. THEOL., [a], *Das Volk der Xosa-Kaffern im östlichen Südafrika*, Berlin, 1889.

——[b], *A Kaffir-English Dictionary*, Lovedale Mission Press, 1899.

LIVINGSTONE, DAVID, *Missionary Travels and Researches in South Africa*, London, 1857.

LLOYD, MISS C. L., [a], *A Short Account of Further Bushman Material Collected (Third Report concerning Bushman Researches, presented to both Houses of Parliament of the Cape of Good Hope)*, London, 1889.

——[b], *Specimens of Bushman Folk-Lore*, Collected by the late W. H. I. Bleek, Ph. D., and L. C. Lloyd, and edited by the latter. With introduction by George McCall Theal, D. Litt., London, 1911.

MACDONALD, REV. DUFF, *Africana, or the Heart of Heathen Africa*, 2 vols., London, 1882.

MADAN, A. C., *Lala-Lamba Handbook*, Oxford, 1908.

MANSFELD, DR. ALFRED, *Urwald-Dokumente: Vier Jahre unter den Crossflussnegern Kameruns*, Berlin, 1908.

Manuel de langue Luganda, par L. L. et C. D. des Péres Blancs. Einsiedeln, 1894. (Cited as *Manuel*.)

MEINHOF, C., [a], *Lehrbuch der Namasprache*, Berlin, 1909. (Band xxiii of Lehrbücher des Seminars für orientalische Sprachen).

——[b], *Die Dichtung der Afrikaner*, Berlin, 1911.

——[c], *Afrikanische Religion*, Berlin, 1912.

MELLAND, FRANK H., and CHOLMELEY, EDWARD H., *Through the Heart of Africa*, London, 1912.

MERENSKY, A., *Deutsche Arbeit am Nyassa, Deutsch-Ostafrika*. Berlin, 1894.

MERKER, M., *Die Masai: Ethnographische Monographie eines ostafrikanischen Semitenvolkes*, Berlin, 1910.

METELERKAMP, S., *Outa Karel's Stories*, London, 1914.

MILNE-HOME, MARY PAMELA, *Mamma's Black Nurse Stories*, Edinburgh and London, 1890.

MOFFAT, ROBERT, *Missionary Labours and Scenes in Southern Africa*, London, 1842.

MONTEIL, C., *Contes soudanais* (with preface by René Basset), Paris, 1905.

MOULIÉRAS, A., *Les fourberies de Si Djeh'a: contes kabyles . . . avec une étude sur Si Djeh'a et les anecdotes qui lui sont attribués, par M. René Basset*, 2 vols. Paris, 1892.

NASSAU, R. H., M. D., [a], *Fetichism in West Africa*, London, 1904.

——[b], *Where Animals Talk: West African Folk-Tales*, Boston, 1912.

——[c], *The Elephant Corral and other Tales of West African Experience*, New York, 1912.

PEARCE, NATHANIEL, *Life and Adventures . . . during a Residence in Abyssinia from the Years* 1810 *to* 1819. Ed. by J. J. Halls, 2 vols. London, 1831.

RATTRAY, R. SUTHERLAND, [a], *Some Folk-Lore Stories and Songs in Chinyanja, with English Translation and Notes*, London, 1897.

——[b], *Hausa Folk-Lore, Customs, Proverbs, etc.* With preface by R. R. Marett, 2 vols., Oxford, 1913.

——[c], *Ashanti Proverbs*, Oxford, 1913.

RAUM, J., *Versuch einer Grammatik der Dschaggasprache*, Berlin, 1909.

REHSE, HERMANN, *Kiziba, Land und Leute*, Stuttgart, 1910.

ROSCOE, REV. JOHN, [a], *The Baganda*, London, 1911.

——[b], *The Northern Bantu*, Cambridge, 1915.

ROSEN, ERIC VON, *Träskfolket:Svenska Rhodesia-Kongo-Expeditionens Etnografiska Forskningsresultat*, Stockholm, n. d. [1917?].

ROUTLEDGE, W. S., and K., *With a Prehistoric People: The Akikuyu of British East Africa*, London, 1910.

SCHÖN, J. F., *Magana Hausa*, London, 1885. (The reissue of 1906 omits the English translation.)

SCHLENKER, C. F., *A Collection of Temne Traditions, Fables, and Proverbs, with an English translation*, London, 1861.

SCHULTZE, LEONHARD SIGMUND, *Aus Namaland und Kalahari*, Jena, 1907.

SCOTT, D. C., *A Cyclopedic Dictionary of the Mang'anja Language spoken in British Central Africa*, Edinburgh, 1892.

SEIDEL, A. [a], *Zeitschrift für afrikanische und ozeanische Sprachen*, Berlin, 1895–1903.

——[b], *Geschichten und Lieder der Afrikaner*, Berlin, 1896.

SMITH, PAMELA COLMAN, *Annancy Stories*, New York, 1899.

SPIETH, JAKOB, *Die Ewestämme, Material zur Kunde des Ewe-Volkes in Deutsch-Togo*, Berlin, 1906.

STANLEY, H. M., *Through the Dark Continent*,[7] London, 1889.

STOW, G. W., *The Native Races of South Africa*, London, 1905.

TALBOT, MRS. D. AMAURY, *Women's Mysteries of a Primitive People*, London, 1915.

TALBOT, P. AMAURY, *In the Shadow of the Bush*, London, 1912.

TAYLOR, REV. W. E., [a], *African Aphorisms, or Saws from Swahililand*, London, 1891.

——[b], *Giryama Vocabulary and Collections*, London, 1891.

THEAL, GEORGE McCALL, [a], *Kaffir Folk-Lore*, London, 1882 (2d ed., 1886).

——[b], *The Yellow and Dark-Skinned Peoples of Africa South of the Zambesi*, London, 1910.

THOMANN, GEORGES, *Essai de Manuel de la langue néoulé*, Paris, 1905.

THOMAS, NORTHCOTE W., *Anthropological Report on Sierra Leone, Part III., Timne Grammar and Stories*, London, 1916.

TÖNJES, HERMANN, *Ovamboland: Land, Leute, Mission*, Berlin, 1911.

TORDAY, E., *Camp and Tramp in African Wilds*, London, 1913.

TORDAY, E., and JOYCE, T. A., *Les Bushongo*, Brussels, 1910.

TORREND, JULIUS, S. J., *A Comparative Grammar of the South African Bantu Languages*, London, 1891. (Contains in appendix, pp. 283–321, some interesting Tonga and Xosa texts — the latter consisting of four tales.)

TREMEARNE, A. J. N., *Hausa Superstitions and Customs*, London, 1913.

TREMEARNE, A. J. N., and MARY, *Fables and Fairy Tales for Little Folk, or Uncle Remus in Hausaland*, Cambridge and London, 1910.

TYLOR, SIR E. B., *Primitive Culture*,[4] London, 1903.

VAN DER BURGT, R. P., J. J. M. (of the " White Fathers "), *Dictionaire français — kirundi . . . augmenté d'une introduction et de 196 articles ethnographiques sur l'Urundi et les Warundi*, Bois-le-Duc, 1903.

VELTEN, C., [a], *Swahili Märchen* (vol. xviii of *Lehrbücher des Seminars für Orient. Sprachen zu Berlin*), Berlin, 1898.

——[b], *Prosa und Poesie der Swahili*, Berlin, 1897.

——[c], *Safari za Waswahili*, Göttingen, 1901.

WEEKS, REV. J. H., *Congo Life and Folk-Lore*, London, 1911.

WERNER, MISS ALICE, *The Native Races of British Central Africa*, London, 1906.

WERNER, J. R., *A Visit to Stanley's Rearguard*, Edinburgh and London, 1889.

WOLFF, R., *Grammatik der Kinga-Sprache*, Berlin, 1905. (*Archiv für das Studium deutscher Kolonialsprachen*, vol. ii.)

ZIMMERMANN, REV. J., *A Grammatical Sketch of the Akra or Gã Language*, 2 vols. Stuttgart, 1858.

III. PRINCIPAL ARTICLES ON AFRICAN RELIGION AND MYTHOLOGY IN THE ENCYCLOPEDIA OF RELIGION AND ETHICS (VOLS. I–XII)

BASSET, R., " Berbers and N. Africa," ii. 506–9.

CARVER, W. O., " Negroes (United States)," ix. 312–18.

CRAWLEY, A. E., " Hearth and Hearth Gods," vi. 559–62.

——" Human Sacrifice," vi. 840–5.

CROOKE, W., " Ancestor Worship and Cult of the Dead," i. 425–32.

DORNAN, S. S., " Tati Bushmen," xii. 205–8.

FALLAIZE, E. N., " Pastoral Peoples," ix. 661–7.

——" Prayer (Introductory and Primitive)," x. 154–8.

GRANDIDIER, G., " Madagascar," viii. 230–2.

GRAY, L. H., " Calendar (African)," iii. 64–5.

——" Circumcision (Introductory)," iii. 659–70.

——" Demons and Spirits (African and Oceanic)," iv. 565–8.

HADDON, A. C., " Negrillos and Negritos," ix. 271–4.

HARTLAND, E. S., " Bantu and S. Africa," ii. 350–67.

——" Death and Disposal of the Dead," iv. 411–44.

——" Hottentots," vi. 820–3.

HETHERWICK, A., " Nyanjas," ix. 419–22.

JOHNSTON, H. H., " Masai," viii. 480–3.

KEANE, A. H., " Africa," i. 160–5.

——" Ethnology," v. 522–32.

LANDTMANN, G., " Priest, Priesthood (Primitive)," x. 278–84.

LITTMANN, E., " Abyssinia," i. 55–9.

MACCULLOCH, J. A., " Agaos," i. 165–6.

——" Baptism (Ethnic)," ii. 367–75.

——" Cannibalism," iii. 194–209.

——" Lycanthropy," viii. 206–20.

MACRITCHIE, D., " Dwarfs and Pigmies," v. 122–6.

MARGOLIOUTH, D. S., " Muhammadanism (in Central Africa)," viii. 880.

——" Muhammadanism (in N. Africa)," viii. 880–3.

MOCKLER-FERRYMAN, A. F., " Negroes and West Africa," ix. 274–92.

OWEN, M. A., " Voodoo," xii. 640–1.

ROSSINI, C. C., " Hamites and E. Africa," vi. 486–92.

SELIGMANN, C. G., " Dinka," iv. 204–13.

THOMAS, N. W., "Secret Societies (African)," xi. 287–303.

WERNER, MISS A., " Nama," ix. 127–9.

——" Nyika," ix. 424–7.

——" Pokomo," x. 88–91.

——" Zanzibar and the Swahili People," xii. 846–9.

END

Date Due